# BIG-TIME SPORTS IN AMERICAN UNIVERSITIES

For almost a century, big-time college sports has been a wildly popular but consistently problematic part of American higher education. The challenges it poses to traditional academic values have been recognized from the start, but they have grown more ominous in recent decades, as cable television has become ubiquitous, commercial opportunities have proliferated, and athletic budgets have ballooned. Drawing on new research findings, this book takes a fresh look at the role of commercial sports in American universities. It shows that, rather than being the inconsequential student activity that universities often imply that it is, big-time sports has become a core function of the universities that engage in it. For this reason, the book takes this function seriously and presents evidence necessary for a constructive perspective on its value. Although big-time sports surely creates worrisome conflicts in values, it also brings with it some surprising positive consequences.

Charles T. Clotfelter is Z. Smith Reynolds Professor of Public Policy and Professor of Economics and Law at Duke University and a research associate in the National Bureau of Economic Research. His research has covered the economics of education, public finance, and state lotteries; tax policy and charitable behavior; and policies related to the nonprofit sector. His previous books on higher education are *Buying the Best: Cost Escalation in Elite Higher Education* (1996) and (with Ronald Ehrenberg, Malcolm Getz, and John Siegfried) *Economic Challenges in Higher Education* (1991). His most recent book is *After Brown: The Rise and Retreat of School Desegregation* (2004), and he is the editor of the volumes *American Universities in a Global Market* (2010) and (with Michael Rothschild) *Studies of Supply and Demand in Higher Education* (1993). He is also the author of *Federal Tax Policy and Charitable Giving* (1985) and (with Philip Cook) *Selling Hope: State Lotteries in America* (1989). Professor Clotfelter has taught at the University of Maryland and spent one year at the U.S. Treasury's Office of Tax Analysis. At Duke he has been a faculty member in the Institute of Policy Sciences and Public Affairs, now the Sanford School of Public Policy; the economics department; and the law school. He has served as Vice Provost for Academic Policy and Planning, Vice Chancellor, and Vice Provost for Academic Programs.

# Big-Time Sports in American Universities

**CHARLES T. CLOTFELTER**

Duke University

CAMBRIDGE UNIVERSITY PRESS

CAMBRIDGE UNIVERSITY PRESS
Cambridge, New York, Melbourne, Madrid, Cape Town,
Singapore, São Paulo, Delhi, Tokyo, Mexico City

Cambridge University Press
32 Avenue of the Americas, New York, NY 10013-2473, USA

www.cambridge.org
Information on this title: www.cambridge.org/9781107004344

First published 2011

Printed in the United States of America

*A catalog record for this publication is available from the British Library.*

*Library of Congress Cataloging in Publication data*
Clotfelter, Charles T.
Big-time sports in American universities / Charles T. Clotfelter.
p.  cm.
Includes bibliographical references and index.
ISBN 978-1-107-00434-4 (hardback)
1. College sports – United States.  I. Title.
GV351.C56  2011
796.04'30973–dc22      2010050331

ISBN 978-1-107-00434-4 Hardback

*For J.H.C., the Varsity, and Grant Field*

# Contents

# Figures

# Tables

# Preface

Several hundred of the largest American universities do something not seen in universities anywhere else in the world. They sponsor athletic programs whose revenues, media coverage, and notoriety give them a striking resemblance to professional sports franchises. This fact is as unremarkable to most adults who were raised in this country as it must surely be strange to a first-time visitor from abroad. As an American who grew up following football and basketball as a fan and high school sports editor, I accepted as part of the natural order of things that athletic teams sponsored by universities like Georgia Tech and Penn State would compete in highly publicized games and that people like me might become emotionally invested in the outcomes. Even during my college years, when I had a very brief stint as a sports writer, I found nothing out of the ordinary about either the size of the college sports enterprise or the widespread interest in it.

It was not until I became a faculty member that I began to think there might be anything remarkable about the phenomenon of big-time college sports. As I began a career working alongside scholars at two research universities that also operate prominent commercial sports programs, Maryland and Duke, I was surprised at each place not by the attention that the campus and city newspapers devoted to college sports, but by how many faculty and staff members also took a keen interest in the university's teams. The same faculty colleagues who discussed a recent research paper one day might chat about the basketball team's upcoming game the next. And in the first of several brief tours of duty I spent in Duke's academic administration, I was more than a little surprised to discover how thoroughly the offices of the university's top administrators emptied out on the Friday of the first round of the Atlantic Coast Conference basketball tournament. Nor could I fail to notice the perpetual need to consult the basketball team's schedule before setting up a meeting of any significance.

Meanwhile, my administrative service stimulated my own interest in doing research on the economics of higher education. Yet my reading of scholarly research in this area revealed a strange disconnect. Despite what I saw as abundant evidence of the larger-than-life presence of big-time college sports, serious academic research about universities rarely deals with the subject at all. For almost 20 years I was the convener of a working group on higher education at the National Bureau of Economic Research. In the 30 meetings of that group that occurred over this period, scholars presented 176 research papers on topics ranging from financial aid, rising costs, and preferential admissions to faculty retirement, doctoral training, and sponsored research. But only one paper during this entire period had to do with big-time college sports. References to athletics are similarly missing from most official mission statements crafted by universities. Solely on the basis of what is written by those who lead or study these institutions, one could easily conclude that college athletics is little more than a minor extracurricular activity, something that could be added or dropped with no real impact on the university's real work.

Yet my own observations contradicted this official view, suggesting instead that big-time college sports plays quite a big role in the everyday life of universities and the communities and states around them. Indeed, in some regions of the country, and for some Americans across the country, following a favorite college team is a life's passion. The depth of this passion and the bizarre forms it can sometimes take set the commercial sports enterprise apart from all the other activities that universities routinely pursue. Tailgating rituals, painted faces, and screaming fans are part of American higher education as surely as physics labs and seminars on Milton. And this activity is nothing if not prominent, with some college teams playing virtually every one of its games in front of television cameras. In all its colorful manifestations, this enterprise has become by far the most visible feature of many American universities. It was the disparity between this reality and the virtual silence on the subject from scholars and institutions themselves that first motivated me to write this book.

I became increasingly curious not only about the prominent role played by commercial college sports, but also about its remarkable staying power. Despite a steady cavalcade of news stories detailing unsavory aspects of big-time college sports, otherwise reputable and rational universities have continued to operate their programs, striving for athletic success at the same time they pursue excellence in research, teaching, and public service. In the academic spirit of studying "ever-present but overlooked" aspects of everyday life, I decided to employ my skills as a social scientist to ask the same elementary question about big-time college sports that might be posed by a first-time visitor to this country. In fact, I came to find out that this was precisely the same question posed in a major national study published in 1929. If this basic question was being raised eight decades ago, one might think, surely by now we would know the answer. Indeed, if you put this question to the president or a trustee of one of the universities with a big-time sports program, you will get answers. The reasons they are apt to give for competing in big-time athletics might include the life lessons that athletes glean through competition, the donations generated from loyal alumni, the boost in student applications that comes from winning championships, or the school spirit that is created by intercollegiate competition. If you were to ask fans or others outside of universities, you might hear that a main reason for operating these kinds of athletic programs is the money they bring in. But my own experience inside universities made me suspect there was more to it than any of these ready explanations would suggest.

This is a book chiefly about higher education, not sports. In it, I address two questions about universities that operate big-time sports programs. First, why do they do it? What explains the survival and apparent vigor of highly visible and commercialized university-sponsored athletic enterprises? And second, what are the consequences for the universities that operate these enterprises? I believe answering the first question will not only help to temper our expectations regarding the possibility of reform, but also serve as a prism for gaining a better understanding of the ultimate purpose of universities. Answering the second question will be a necessary part of any full consideration of the future of American higher education, particularly as it relates to America's declining global rank in educational attainment and the returns we should expect from our enormous investment in public and private universities.

The phenomenon I focus on is not college athletics in general, but merely the most famous manifestation, "big-time" college sports. I define big-time sports as the highly commercialized and widely followed competition in football and basketball that is undertaken by several hundred American universities. Featuring sizable revenues generated by ticket sales and television, this boils down to football in the NCAA's Football Bowl Subdivision (FBS, formerly Division I-A) and basketball in Division I. I devote little attention to the remaining sports or the less competitive levels of college competition because, although their effects are certainly worthy of attention, they generate neither the revenue nor the outsized problems that the revenue sports do. Nor do I deal with such important issues as gender equity or the general effects of students' participation in athletics.

In assessing the consequences for universities of operating commercial sports enterprises, I present all the relevant factual material I could locate or generate. I draw on previous studies by others and on my own new research using a variety of sources of data. For example, to illustrate the prominence and reach of big-time college sports, I examined and counted newspaper articles about major American universities. For those with commercial sports programs, articles about athletics vastly outnumbered those about any other aspects of these institutions. In the book, I also compare the number of Google hits for university presidents and their football and basketball coaches. I document the breathtaking growth in TV coverage for the two major college sports, to the point that the average basketball team in one of the major conferences now appears on television 27 times a season. Thanks to larger stadiums and longer seasons, attendance at games has grown as well, rising over the past three decades at an average rate of 14% a decade in football and 20% in basketball, compared with just 10% a decade for the U.S. population.[1] I also document the growth in spending on athletics, caused in part by a spectacular escalation in coaches' salaries. For example, the average pay for head football coaches at 18 universities with big-time programs, expressed in constant 2009 dollars, increased from $377,000 in 1981 to more than $2.4 million in 2009.[2]

Drawing on detailed information of different kinds, I examine the business of running a big-time athletic department. I show that, despite the growth in TV revenues, the top programs rely heavily on the strong demand for tickets to games, as well as the willingness of affluent boosters to make tax-deductible gifts to secure the best seats and special perks. An annual donation of several thousand dollars a year can easily be required to obtain the privilege of buying season tickets for some of the most popular college football and basketball teams. At the comparatively impoverished end of the big-time college sports pecking order are universities with shorter histories, smaller crowds, and less expensive coaches. They must rely on mandatory student fees and institutional subsidies to pay the bills, in some cases using those sources to cover 70% or more of the athletic budget. For the universities whose teams seldom contend for championships but are lucky enough to be members of established conferences, the sports enterprise is sustained thanks to revenue shared by more successful conference members. Much of this shared revenue comes by way of television and advertising. I show that televised college games are saturated with advertising. Not only are commercials shown during time-outs, pitches for consumer products appear throughout game broadcasts as well.

I also collected new evidence on the connection between big-time sports enterprises and the academic work of the universities that house them. I utilize computerized records from digital archives used by students and other researchers to show how the pace of academic work responds to the schedule of games in the NCAA's annual basketball tournament, and specifically how work is affected at a university whose team wins or loses in the tournament. Students who enroll in universities with big-time sports programs are more affluent and politically conservative than those who go to other universities. And once they are there, they tend to spend less time studying and more time in organized activities, and they are more likely to engage in binge drinking. To see if big-time sports hurts a university's overall quality, I examine changes over time in indicators of quality that are used in *U.S. News* rankings.

The staying power of big-time college sports, and the fact that universities continue to come forward to start new programs of their own or move to a more competitive level, whetted my curiosity about how athletics might be used to bolster the political and financial support that universities constantly seek. To gain insight into this use of college sports, I present new evidence on the political affiliations of athletic boosters compared with other university stakeholders. I also make use of detailed information I gathered through open-records requests to various public universities for the lists of guests invited to sit in presidential boxes at football games, to see what they imply about the institutional uses of big-time football.

I do not neglect the much-debated topics of values and reform. Some of the most serious costs associated with big-time college sports arise when the values of commercial sports come into conflict with time-honored values of universities. Although these costs cannot be quantified, they are an indispensable part of any university's full accounting of the pros and cons of running a commercial sports enterprise. I find, however, that there are some surprising positive entries as well in this value assessment. The book concludes by noting the prospects for reform without delving into the many detailed proposals that have been put forward. Although there is every reason to be skeptical about these prospects, I note several intriguing possibilities, including a change in federal tax policy and a proposal to spin off college teams as separate entities.

Because the research for this book required collecting and analyzing many different kinds of data over the course of several years, I relied on the able assistance of a large number of bright, energetic, and well-trained students, most of whom were students at Duke. They included Rene Alarcon,

Janeil Belle, Laura Brookhiser, Saidi Chen, Celeste Clipp, Ryan Fleenor, Alexis Kirk, Sam Lim, Robert Malme, Ryan Miller, Sara Pilzer, Holly Presley, James Riddlesperger, Jaime Rooke, Cullen Sinclair, Kevin Wang, Garth Weintraub, and Lila Zhao. I received invaluable assistance in gaining access to data sets and other information from a number of people: Mark Alesia, Anthony Broh, Molly Brownfield, Maureen Devlin, Joline Ezzell, Anne Fletcher, Tara Hofher, Deborah Jakubs, Han Kim, Amy Perko, Jill Riepenhoff, Amy Taylor, and Mark Thomas. I obtained restricted-use data from UCLA's Higher Education Research Institute, the National Survey of Student Engagement, the Consortium for Financing Higher Education, and JSTOR. I also used data collected and made available by *USA Today* and the *Indianapolis Star*. Financial support was provided by a grant from the Spencer Foundation.

For their comments, criticisms, suggestions, and helpful discussions, I am grateful to the following people: John Aldrich, Norm Arkans, John Blackburn, Doug Breckel, Christine Brennan, Keith Brodie, Ford Burkhart, John Burness, Hodding Carter, John Colombo, Paul Courant, Michael Cragg, John Drescher, James Duderstadt, William Friday, Dan Fulks, Malcolm Getz, Michael Gillespie, Craufurd Goodwin, Deirdre Gordon, Kristin Goss, Christoph Gutentag, Paul Haagen, James Hearn, Sherman James, Jim Johnson, Nan Keohane, Peter Lange, Keith Lawrence, Todd Mesibov, Carol Meyers, Robert Mosteller, B. J. Naedele, Roger Noll, Scott Parris, David Pervin, Joseph Quinn, Peter Rossky, Richard Schmalbeck, Michael Schoenfeld, James Shulman, John Siegfried, Orin Starn, Welch Suggs, Tim Sullivan, Bob Sweeney, Douglas Toma, Tallman Trask, Sue Wasiolek, Clifton Wharton, Bonna and Richard Whitten-Stovall, Steve Wieberg, Scott Yakola, and Andrew Zimbalist. For his wise words about one sport and for the phrase "ever-present but overlooked," which he used in a faculty newsletter, I acknowledge my late Duke colleague Irving Alexander. Finally, for her innumerable suggestions and unfailing encouragement, I thank my wife and expert editor, Theresa Newman.

# Glossary of Abbreviations and Terms

| | |
|---|---|
| AAU | Amateur Athletic Union |
| ACC | Atlantic Coast Conference |
| ACE | American Council on Education |
| BCS | Bowl Championship Series |
| Division I | NCAA division incorporating about 300 universities that play basketball at the most competitive level |
| Division I-A | term for Football Bowl Subdivision before 2006, the most competitive NCAA subdivision |
| Division III | the least competitive NCAA division; no athletic scholarships are offered |
| FBS | Football Bowl Subdivision, the NCAA subdivision adopted in 2006 incorporating about 120 universities that play football at the most competitive level, previously called Division I-A |
| IPEDS | Integrated Postsecondary Education Data System; data collected by the U.S. Department of Education, National Center for Education Statistics (NCES) |
| JSTOR | Web-based digital archive of academic journals |
| LSU | Louisiana State University |
| Pac-10 | Pacific 10 Conference |
| NCAA | National Collegiate Athletic Association |
| NC State | North Carolina State University |
| NSSE | National Survey of Student Engagement |
| SEC | Southeastern Conference |
| SMU | Southern Methodist University |
| SUNY | State University of New York |
| Title IX | provision of the Education Amendments of 1972 requiring gender equity in college sports |

| | |
|---|---|
| UBIT | Unrelated Business Income Tax |
| UC | University of California |
| UCLA | University of California, Los Angeles |
| UNC | University of North Carolina |
| USC | University of Southern California |
| UT | Most commonly, University of Texas; alternatively, University of Tennessee |
| UW | University of Washington; alternatively, University of Wisconsin |

# PART ONE

# COMMERCIAL SPORTS AS A UNIVERSITY FUNCTION

ONE

# Strange Bedfellows

Two starkly different worlds coexist today within American higher education. One is the traditional academic world that conforms to the succinct statement offered by economists Claudia Goldin and Lawrence Katz: "The business of colleges and universities is the creation and diffusion of knowledge."[1] Because American research universities have excelled in these functions, today they enjoy global preeminence. Yet there is another world within American universities, just as firmly rooted, that bears no obvious relation to the first. It is the world of big-time college sports, a form of entertainment that has over the course of a century enmeshed itself in the American higher-education scene, becoming part of the popular conception of the "collegiate" experience.

To appreciate the gulf that divides these two worlds, it is instructive to visit the campus of a university that has a big-time sports program. Let us take a quick virtual tour of one of these – the sprawling campus of the University of Texas in Austin. It will be sufficient for our purposes to visit just two buildings on that campus.

The first stop on our tour is a five-story building that is home to the Center for Nano- and Molecular Science and Technology. This brick and concrete building houses offices, equipment, and laboratories used by scientists and engineers. The professors affiliated with this center come from departments like chemistry and biochemistry, physics, biomedical engineering, chemical engineering, electrical and computer engineering, and mechanical engineering. Some of these departments rank among the country's highest rated in their respective disciplines.[2] Together with post-doctoral fellows, graduate students, and other technical staff, some of whom have come to the United States from other countries, these faculty members carry out research projects related to fields like nanoelectronics, nanobiology and nanomedicine, nanoparticle synthesis, and nanomechanics. Their

3

research articles appear in such scholarly publications as *Biochemistry and Bioengineering, Inorganic Chemistry, Journal of Physical Chemistry, Nature, Polymer,* and *Science.* This research has the potential to contribute to such practical advances as better fuel cells and improved therapies for combating human neurodegenerative diseases.

The highly technical research and advanced training that take place in this building exemplify the essential work of research universities – the creation and diffusion of knowledge. Indeed, the center's activities seem to embody perfectly the university's published mission statement:

The mission of The University of Texas at Austin is to achieve excellence in the interrelated areas of undergraduate education, graduate education, research and public service. The university provides superior and comprehensive educational opportunities at the baccalaureate through doctoral and special professional educational levels.

The university contributes to the advancement of society through research, creative activity, scholarly inquiry and the development of new knowledge. The university preserves and promotes the arts, benefits the state's economy, serves the citizens through public programs and provides other public service.[3]

The University of Texas is by no means unique in its devotion to research and teaching. American research universities like it are magnets for the world's best graduate students because they are home to a large share of the world's leading research faculty and doctoral programs. American universities occupy an enviable position of preeminence among the world's research universities, a fact confirmed by global rankings. For example, according to the ranking produced by the *Times* of London, a third of the world's top 100 universities are in the United States. The ranking produced by Shanghai's Jiao Tong University, a ranking heavily weighted toward scientific research output, indicates that more than half of the top 100 are American.[4] In short, the Center for Nano- and Molecular Science and Technology at Texas admirably symbolizes the academic purpose of American universities.

The second stop on our virtual tour of the University of Texas, just a 10-minute walk away, takes us to a realm that is strikingly different from the world of research and teaching. This stop is the university's football stadium, named the Darrell K. Royal-Texas Memorial Stadium. This structure, featuring double decks on one side, can accommodate more than 100,000 spectators, and it was filled to capacity at every one of the seven home games during the 2009 season. At two ends of the stadium are towers, eight- and nine-stories high, respectively, that house luxury suites outfitted with theater-style seats, televisions, kitchenettes, and bars, and are available for lease at rates up to $88,000 a year. The university's football team, which

has played in postseason bowls in each of the past five years, rides to practice every day during the season aboard chartered buses and dresses out in a
locker room equipped with five flat-screen TVs and adorned with a 20-foot
ceiling light in the shape of a longhorn. A professor in the business school
characterized the university's sports facilities as "beyond opulence."[5] The
team's coach, whose salary in 2007 was more than four times that of the university's president and whose name elicited more than 12 times the number
of Google hits, has his own weekly television show, broadcast on 14 local
stations and one regional network each week during the season. Those who
count themselves Texas football fans are legion. They are spread throughout
the state and beyond, and they are by no means restricted to those with a
college education.

The worlds represented by these two buildings at the University of Texas
are astonishingly different. Not surprisingly, they occupy different parts of
the university's organizational chart. One of them is under the jurisdiction
of the university's academic enterprise, and the other is under the control of
the athletic enterprise. The nanoscience center, on the academic side
of the university, exemplifies the rarefied, rational realm that has traditionally been associated with the academic world. Although this academic realm
is by no means innocent of the commercial world, it is largely divorced from
calculations of profit and loss. Facts, reason, and beauty are its raw materi-
als; analysis, study, and free expression are its modes of operation.

By contrast, the stadium and those who work there represent a world that
is unashamedly commercial and thoroughly popular, even populist. This
part of the university is quite literally a part of the country's entertainment
industry. It sells its brand of performance in the commercial marketplace,
depending for revenue on both paying customers and media. Perhaps
its most obvious distinguishing feature is that its normal operations – as
a matter of course – are visible to an extent unmatched by anything that
happens on the academic side. The team's games are carried live on radio,
from Abilene to Wichita Falls, on 40 different radio stations.[6] All 12 of
its games during the 2008 season were televised, and so was its appearance in the Fiesta Bowl the following January.[7] Even ignoring the television cameras, just the gathering of 100,000 individuals in one location is
enough to mark an event as out of the ordinary. It has been said that many
American universities are best known across the country, if at all, not for
their academic programs, but for their football teams, and this remark is as
true today as it was when it was written, more than 80 years ago.[8]

But even setting national recognition aside for the moment and viewing the big-time sports enterprise merely as one organizational unit inside

a university, it still stands apart. On any campus with a big-time athletics program, the football and basketball schedules quite simply rule the university's calendar of events. What other department or school in the university holds the power, merely through its regular operation, to bring the rest of the institution to a halt? What other unit's scheduled activities are so influential that every other department, all the way up to the president's office, makes sure not to schedule any important meeting or event that would conflict with one of those scheduled activities? To anyone who grew up in the United States or who has spent much time around a university with a big-time sports program, none of this will come as a surprise. Both the coexistence of these two disparate realms and the sway of athletics are such familiar traits of the American higher-education scene that they are simply taken for granted.[9] Were it not so familiar, the contrast between these two worlds would surely be cause for wonder.

Here is an authentic case of American exceptionalism: in no other large country in the world is commercialized athletic competition so closely tied to institutions of higher education. To be sure, universities in Europe, Asia, Canada, and elsewhere frequently sponsor "club" teams that compete against each other in a variety of sports, ranging from squash and ice hockey to basketball and badminton. The oldest organized intercollegiate competition still going is the annual Boat Race, which has for more than 150 years pitted against each other crews from the two great British universities, Oxford and Cambridge. But none of these forms of university-affiliated athletic competition generates the revenue or rises to the level of commercial sophistication of American intercollegiate athletics. Only in the United States has there grown up such an elaborate system of publicized and commercialized sports contests involving university-sponsored teams. Although most of the teams sponsored by the 4,000 colleges and universities in the United States are no more famous or commercial than university teams in other countries, the football and basketball teams representing several hundred universities achieve such high levels of revenue and visibility that their universities in effect become part of the American entertainment industry. This is big-time college sports.

## THE EUROPEAN VISITOR'S NAIVE QUESTION

Although this peculiarly American activity may be second nature to most Americans, and thus considered unremarkable, one can only imagine how odd it must appear to a visitor from abroad, whose experience with universities has never included an entertainment spectacle of this order that is put on by universities themselves. This is precisely the hypothetical situation imagined back in 1929 by Henry Pritchett, then president of the Carnegie Foundation for the Advancement of Teaching, when he included the following in his preface to the foundation's lengthy study of college athletics:

Nothing in the educational regime of our higher institutions perplexes the European visitor so much as the role that organized athletics play. On a crisp November afternoon he finds many thousands of men and women, gathered in a great amphitheater, wildly cheering a group of athletes who are described to him as playing a game of football....

When the visitor from the European university has pondered the matter, he comes to his American university colleagues with two questions:

"What relation has this astonishing athletic display to the work of an intellectual agency like a university?"

"How do students, devoted to study, find either the time or the money to stage so costly a performance?"[10]

Pritchett's imagined visitor can easily discover the answer to the second question: it is the university, not the students, that stages the performance. It is the first of these questions, concerning the fundamental purpose of the athletic enterprise, that is the truly perplexing one. And it is as deserving today of careful consideration as it was eight decades ago. Why do universities engage in this activity? This gaudy, wildly popular form of entertainment has no obvious connection to the intellectual work of universities other than the name on the uniforms. Yet big-time college athletics has over the course of a century become woven into the fabric of many American universities. So the visitor's question remains both pertinent and challenging, and it inspires other ones. Why is the enterprise of big-time sports a part of the operation of contemporary American universities? What are the consequences for the universities that undertake it? What, if anything, needs to be done about it? These are the questions that motivate this book.

To explain the existence of big-time college sports, university leaders and outside observers usually offer one of several justifications. First among them is the educational argument: beginning with the ancient Greeks, athletic pursuits have been recognized as a valuable component of a complete education. Through both training and competition, the athlete learns life lessons taught nowhere better than on the field of play. As Harvard president Charles Eliot argued before the 20th century, athletic participation develops such "qualities as courage, fortitude, and presence of mind in emergencies and under difficulties" as well as cooperation and, for some, the "habit of command."[11] While this explanation continues to have real force when applied to students' participation in the variety of sports offered on college campuses, it does little to justify the big-time athletic operation, since college students participate in big-time college sports primarily as spectators. Relatively few of them enjoy the moral and physical benefits of participating in these sports. And for those who do play one of the revenue sports, as we will see, participation often takes on the quality of employment more than that of recreation. Despite their official amateur status, their role begins to morph into one that has many of the markings of a professional player, though certainly without the professional's monetary compensation.

A second common justification for big-time athletic operations is the one that might be the first to occur to many outside observers: money. At least in the public perception, the highly visible football and basketball programs run by universities would appear to be a ready source of income, given the large figures commonly reported for such items as football bowl receipts and coaches' salaries. Indeed, the head basketball coach for the University of Connecticut defended his $1.6 million salary at a time when the Connecticut state government was running a large deficit, telling a reporter that his basketball program brought in $12 million a year.[12] Although some big-time basketball, and football, programs might well turn a profit if run by themselves, universities typically consolidate all their intercollegiate sports under one department, with one budget. And most of these departments lose money, including the one operated by the University of Connecticut. As we will see, however, calculating profit or loss for these departments is not without its complexities and ambiguities.

A third argument that universities sometimes use to justify their investment in commercialized spectator sports is that athletic acclaim begets public attention for the university's academic mission, which in turn pays off in quite tangible ways. Chief among the benefits thought to result from heightened visibility is a boost in applications for admission. Whether it is a Cinderella team's surprising success in the NCAA basketball tournament or the widespread recognition that comes from being a perennial football powerhouse, admissions directors believe that athletic prominence generates student applications. But the hoped-for benefits go beyond generating a stronger pool of applicants. Athletic success, and the notoriety it brings, is believed also to generate more donations, as already noted, and stronger support from state and local governments. Buoyed by the apparent success of newly ascendant big-time football programs at institutions like the University of Connecticut, Rutgers, the University of South Florida, and Boise State, other universities, among them Georgia State and the

University of North Carolina at Charlotte, have announced in recent years their intention to launch football programs of their own.[13]

One more standard justification for big-time athletics is the idea that mass allegiance can help to build the bonds of community on a campus. Having a team to root for has a feel-good effect on students that can build valuable social capital while they attend and continue into later years as alumni. One administrator wrote, "Sports teams can foster a deep sense of community and social solidarity, even when those teams lose more often than they win."[14] Since the vast majority of students become involved in big-time sports, if at all, as spectators rather than as players, this justification also invites careful consideration.

These four justifications make up the conventional answer to the foreign visitor's question. Together they say that America's unique form of university-sponsored commercial sports bolsters the academic mission of the universities that have chosen to engage in this enterprise. Some historians have argued that American colleges latched onto sports in the first place as a way to garner the attention and resources they needed to survive in the country's decentralized, competitive marketplace, and these justifications are consistent with that argument. Is it a coincidence that the country whose universities are recognized as global leaders is the only country whose universities sponsor commercial sports on a grand scale?

## THE CASE AGAINST BIG-TIME COLLEGE ATHLETICS

Despite these purported benefits, the college sports enterprise has long been a target of vigorous criticism. From the earliest days of intercollegiate competition in rugby, boat racing, baseball, and football, beginning well before 1900, college sports competition generated not only throngs of spectators and widespread newspaper coverage, but also episodes of shocking misbehavior and intense controversy. And well before the era of television and multimillion-dollar pay packages, university leaders were worried about the insinuation of commercial motives into college athletics. As a result, "What is to be done about college athletics?" has been a question of vigorous debate for well over a century. The longevity of this debate alone suggests that the problems associated with big-time athletics are not easily eliminated.

As far back as the 19th century, when the ivy-covered universities were the epicenter of football prowess, Harvard president Charles Eliot warned of "great evil" in the commercialization and overemphasis of college sports, particularly the highly popular competition in boat racing, baseball, and football. He declared in his 1893 annual report, "With athletics considered as an end in themselves, pursued either for pecuniary profit or popular applause, a college or university has nothing to do. Neither is it an appropriate function for a college or university to provide periodical entertainment during term-time for multitudes of people who are not students."[15] In 1905, following a frightening number of injuries and deaths in college football contests, President Theodore Roosevelt called representatives from Harvard, Yale, and Princeton on the White House carpet to demand that they reform football's rules. This famous meeting resulted in a set of standardized rules and the creation of an organization of universities that would eventually become the National Collegiate Athletic Association (NCAA).[16] The rules that came out of this new association successfully addressed the plague of football injuries, so this persistent problem was more or less laid to rest.

Not so with the other problems of big-time college sports. In particular, complaints about excessive emphasis on sports continued to bubble up during the 1920s. To address such criticism with research, the Carnegie Commission for the Advancement of Teaching undertook a three-year study of numerous aspects of college athletics. Drawing on site visits to more than 100 colleges and universities, it addressed such issues as the administrative control of athletics inside the university, the consequences of participation, the status of college coaches, recruiting, press coverage of college sports, and amateur status. It documented abuses in recruiting, the undue influence of alumni boosters, slush funds, widespread subsidies to players, high salaries of coaches, and a "distorted scheme of values." As the cause of these defects, the report blamed "commercialism, and a negligent attitude toward the educational opportunities for which the college exists."[17]

In the eight decades since the Carnegie report of 1929, remarkably little has changed in the case against big-time athletics. The reform-minded Knight Commission on Intercollegiate Athletics decried the increasing time demands of televised games, other compromises of academic standards, the high salaries of coaches, abuses in recruiting, and under-the-table payments to athletes. It asserted that big-time athletics had taken on "all the trappings of a major entertainment enterprise."[18] It listed as causes many of the same factors named in the 1929 Carnegie report: the push for revenue, the involvement of media, and the influence of boosters outside the university. Citing practices that threatened academic standards in the pursuit of more revenue, the commission argued that universities were guilty of a "great reversal of ends and means" and, as a consequence, had jeopardized the moral high ground that had traditionally been theirs.[19] In a follow-up report, it stated, "Sports as big business for colleges and universities … is in direct conflict with nearly every value that should matter for higher education."[20]Newspaper columns with titles like "Serfs of the Turf" and "If Games Are a Business, Colleges Invite Problems" criticized aspects of commercial college sports such as the ban on pay to players and universities' dependence upon television and donations from boosters.[21] Books like *College Sports, Inc.: The Athletic Department vs. the University*, *Beer and Circus: How Big-Time College Sports Is Crippling Undergraduate Education*, and *Varsity Green: A Behind the Scenes Look at Culture and Corruption in College Athletics* provided muckraking condemnations of spending excesses, compromised academic standards, and recruiting scandals. The last of these concludes with this denunciation: "The NCAA system of college athletics is broken. It is financially and academically corrupt, and morally bankrupt."[22]

## WHY *DO* THEY DO IT, REALLY?

This listing of justifications on the one side and criticisms on the other does not seem to help very much in answering our imaginary visitor's naive question: What role *does* this brand of commercial entertainment play in a university, such as the University of Texas, that says it is dedicated to research, teaching, and service? It seems reasonable to assume that a university, being a rational and deliberative organization, would not decide to do something on so grand a scale unless it judged that the benefits derived from it would exceed the costs. In light of the problems highlighted by the critics of big-time college athletics, we could probably expect to find that some universities had decided that the benefits to be gained from commercial sports were not worth the costs. Others might decide the opposite. But for at least some universities this would have to be a difficult decision. So we could reasonably expect to observe more than a few universities, having made the decision to participate in big-time sports, changing their minds and dropping out or reentering the fray.

But this is not what we observe. Although there are some universities that have never participated and some that always have, we almost never observe them changing their minds. Instead, the history of big-time sports in American universities presents us with three broad facts. The first is that not all American universities engage in big-time sports competition, though many do, including some of the best universities in the country. Of the 20 highest-ranking American universities on Shanghai Jiao Tong

University's 2008 world ranking, 8 have big-time programs.[23] Second, there continue to exist a few universities that aspire to enter the ranks of big-time sports universities. But the really striking fact is the third one: once a university adopts big-time sports, it almost never goes back. Of the 72 colleges and universities that were ranked in the top 100 by football success in 1920 and have remained national universities, all but 9 were still competing at the highest level in intercollegiate football (FBS) in 2009.[24] The University of Texas, for example, began intercollegiate football in 1902, and since that year it has played football at the highest competitive level every year.[25] Texas has had, in effect, 107 annual opportunities to stop doing it, but it has consistently chosen to stay in this game.

Every university that runs a commercial sports operation, or is considering it, makes such a calculation on a regular basis, or should be doing so. And the fact is that hundreds of American universities operate big-time sports programs, and have been doing so for a long time. Although their decision making may be more complex and decentralized than that of comparably sized corporations, those who administer contemporary universities are not stupid. Their decisions are usually made soberly and in consultation with competent and experienced analysts, and they rarely make the same mistake over and over. So when we observe so many intelligently run institutions doing something again and again, it should be an indication that the benefits – at least as they perceive them – exceed the costs. But that does not answer the question of why. What role does commercial sports play that makes it so valuable that many American universities keep doing it, year after year?

One logical way of finding the answer to this question would be to consult those who ought to know best: universities themselves and scholars who specialize in studying universities. Surprisingly, neither of these seemingly definitive sources provide much help in answering the question. Those who lead and think deeply about universities rarely acknowledge that athletics has any significant part in the purpose or operation of these great institutions, let alone describe athletic competition as a central function. In formal mission statements laying out their institutional aims and aspirations, universities rarely mention athletics at all. In this regard, the mission statement of the University of Texas quoted earlier is typical. Despite the larger-than-life, actual prominence of athletics at universities like Texas, their leaders typically ignore that activity altogether when putting together a formal statement listing their institution's essential functions and objectives.

A similar lack of attention to the role of intercollegiate athletics characterizes most of the scholarly research about universities. Like other levels of education, higher education has long been a subject of sustained and serious scholarly study. But to read most scholarly research about American higher education, one would conclude that commercial college sports did not exist at all. Studies such as these devote their attention instead to topics like research, university governance, teaching, faculty time and recruitment, admissions, and financial aid.[26] Nor is there a mention of big-time sports in the National Survey of Student Engagement (NSSE), one of the student surveys most widely used to assess the quality of the undergraduate college experience. This survey asks about participation in recreation and sports, but not about being a fan or spectator at college games.

This inattention to athletics – by those who should know higher education best – presents a striking paradox. In light of the obvious prominence of big-time college athletics, why do those who should know the most about universities so often act as if it did not exist at all? Ask a handful of people on the street what they know about the University of X, and likely as not they will say that what they know best is its football or basketball team. Its famous coaches or players will be known by vastly more people than its president or most prominent faculty members. Can college sports truly be so marginal to the real business of universities to be worthy of so little attention? Surely the operation of big-time sports programs, on the basis of their fame alone, justifies more attention than that. Indeed, how can an activity so prominent not be a "core mission" of universities? More to the point, what explains the reluctance of universities to acknowledge the prominent role of big-time sports in the daily operation of their institutions? Do academic leaders view big-time sports as an embarrassment, like the dissolute, ne'er-do-well cousin consigned to the corner when society calls?

This question of purpose is not merely a subject for scholarly seminars. It has been raised on Capitol Hill by those who question whether big-time athletics is in fact an activity related, in a legal sense, to the exempt, educational purpose on which the favorable tax treatment of universities is based. Currently, contributions made to university athletic departments are tax deductible, just like contributions that fund academic programs. Representative Bill Thomas, chair of the House Ways and Means Committee, implicitly questioned the legitimacy of this treatment in 2006 in a public letter to then-president of the NCAA, Myles Brand. He asked "whether major intercollegiate athletics further the exempt purpose of the NCAA and, more generally, educational institutions." The numerous questions Rep. Thomas asked in his seven-page letter contained several not so veiled criticisms, among them: "Corporate sponsorships, multimillion dollar television deals, highly paid coaches with no academic duties, and the dedication of inordinate amounts of time by athletes to training lead many to believe that major college football and men's basketball more closely resemble professional sports than amateur sports." The letter also noted "escalating coaches' salaries, costly chartered travel, and state-of-the-art athletic facilities," as well as "commercialized entertainment."[27] As we will see, contributions have become a major source of revenue for big-time sports programs, so any serious proposal to alter their tax treatment would surely strike fear in the hearts of athletics directors.

Whether or not universities like to admit it, big-time athletics must be counted as one of their significant activities. The facts I document in this book make it impossible to avoid this conclusion. Just how big a part of their total activity it constitutes remains an issue that can be put aside for the moment. But I believe the evidence will show that big-time athletics is too important to be relegated entirely to the sports pages. There is too much at stake for American universities to do so. Since World War II, American research universities have been the envy of the world, as illustrated by their dominance in lists of top universities in the world. Today they represent a prime export industry in a country plagued by chronic trade deficits. At issue is whether the university entertainment enterprise is a threat to American higher education or instead is one of its reasons for success. Big-time athletics brings with it the promise of attention and commercial gain, but also the necessity of compromise and the threat of unsavory publicity, all of which creates perennial tensions over the proper role of this enterprise. These tensions appear to be intensifying, as a result of the growing commercial value of college football and basketball. How these tensions are resolved not only will have a direct effect on the quality of universities, but will also say a great deal about universities' actual objectives.

To answer the basic questions about the role and effect of this peculiarly American activity, we must go beyond the ongoing shrill debate over big-time college sports, finding a path between the moralistic denunciations on the one side and the moralistic justifications on the other. This will require looking at universities as they are, not simply as one might wish them to be. It will also require shaking off the silence that has characterized so much of the scholarly research about universities. Rather than treating athletics as if it did not exist or as some minor extracurricular activity, researchers need to acknowledge the significance of commercial college sports. If this activity is important enough to command the popular attention, media coverage, and rancorous debate that it does, it is worth being taken seriously.

## THIS BOOK

The first order of business is to understand why so many American universities embrace big-time athletics and what the real consequences are of doing so. Taking the university itself as the primary object of interest, this book asks two main questions: First, what purpose does this particular activity serve in universities? Second, what are its effects on the functioning of universities? The study will look at the financial and nonfinancial costs and benefits for institutions and higher education more broadly associated with this activity. Third, as discussed in the concluding chapter, what implications flow from the answers to the first two questions?

My aim in writing this book is to describe the phenomenon of big-time college sports as it is, trying to make sense of why so many smart institutions have decided it is a worthwhile enterprise to be part of. I begin by looking at the striking disconnect between what universities *say* about the importance they attach to athletics (practically nothing) and the reality of a spectacularly visible college sports industry. Using some sources of data never before employed for the purpose, I document the tremendous power of big-time college sports and, by implication, the significant role that universities have taken on in the country's entertainment industry.

To understand big-time college sports, it is illuminating to examine the four main roles it plays in American universities. First, it is a consumer good, and it has a market that is worthy of study, in part for its size and in part for its peculiarities. Demand in this market takes on spectacularly unconventional forms, with some customers acting like zealots or crazed lunatics, while market supply is controlled by one of America's most effective cartels. Second, big-time college sports is a business enterprise, operated by universities that follow a business model whose logic leads to some unavoidable conflicts with deep-seated academic traditions. I look into the details of the business operation, including the frequently asked question of whether these athletic enterprises make money or lose money. Third, big-time sports is an instrument universities can employ to build and sustain the support of powerful constituencies. By examining the VIP guest lists at football games, it is possible to gain a new perspective on universities' strategies for institutional advancement. I also review what statistical research can tell us about the beneficial advertising effect that is often claimed for big-time college sports. Fourth, big-time sports has an educational role. Using surveys of student time use and attitudes, I investigate the claims that big-time sports strengthens the sense of community on a campus and look as well at differences across campuses in such activities as studying and binge drinking.

Not all the important consequences of running a big-time sports program can be measured. But no analysis of those effects can be complete without a consideration of the intangible costs incurred when actions taken on behalf of the athletic enterprise end up clashing with cherished academic principles. Such conflicts do take place. They are, in fact, a cost of being in the big-time college sports business. To the likely surprise of at least some readers, I will argue that some values are actually served, not undercut, in ways not often recognized. Because some of the intangible benefits I identify extend beyond campus boundaries, universities themselves cannot necessarily be counted on to weigh costs and benefits in the same way society might.

This book has the least to say about the topics that take up most of the ongoing debate about college sports: NCAA regulations and how they ought to be revised. Instead, it steps back to ask how we got to where we are and what forces sustain this remarkable enterprise. I do take up the question of policy, but that question is preceded by the economist's concern with incentives and self-interest. Is there any reason to believe that the decisions made by intelligently run institutions like universities result in a situation that is not in their best interest, or in society's? Such an unhappy outcome would not be without precedent, as studies of pollution, overfishing, and arms races illustrate. In any case, readers who anticipate a list of reforms that promise to solve the problems of big-time college sports will surely be disappointed.

As I use the familiar term, "big-time" college sports is synonymous with *commercial* college sports. In practice this boils down to university athletic departments with large budgets, because along with large budgets come the characteristics that make these programs so lovable and so problematic. In addition to big budgets, these programs usually enjoy high levels of attendance and extensive media coverage, including at least some TV coverage. They actively recruit athletes and award scholarships based on athletic ability, and they employ professional and highly compensated coaches. All of the universities in this group have a men's basketball team that plays at the highest level of competition (NCAA Division I), and most of them also field a football team in the most competitive group (Football Bowl Subdivision, or FBS). These athletic departments are generally characterized by sophisticated business planning, a keen awareness of marketing and media, and serious fund-raising, as well as highly paid professional coaching staffs in the two major revenue sports. Their teams are widely known, thanks to heavy attendance at games, frequent television appearances, other media coverage, and a history of competition.

This book focuses almost entirely on the sports of football and men's basketball, although for a few universities a sport such as women's basketball, hockey, or baseball may take on some of the characteristics of the two major revenue sports. It therefore devotes little attention to the athletic programs of liberal arts colleges, nor does it include the contemporary Ivy League, whose stated policy precludes offering athletic scholarships. The teams and the universities that sponsor them attract the bulk of attention in American intercollegiate athletics. Hundreds of thousands of spectators attend their games in person and millions more watch them on television. Their players, coaches, and contests are covered widely by sports reporters in every conceivable form of media. Their stadiums and arenas are the largest, their budgets are the biggest, their recruits are the most talented, their coaches are the highest paid, and their teams are the most competitive.

Beyond several dozen universities with the very largest programs, there is no obvious line to draw between universities that do or do not qualify for the "big-time" designation. Ranked simply by their athletic expenditures in 2009, the universities with the 100 largest athletic programs, listed in Table 1.1, constitute a group of institutions that would probably qualify no matter what criteria one used. Annual expenditures for these programs ranged from $112.9 million (Texas) to $20.0 million (Marshall), and together those 100 accounted for more than a third of all the expenditures on athletics made by the roughly 2,000 colleges and universities that reported data to the U.S. Department of Education. By way of comparison, the average Broadway show in 2008–2009 grossed about $22 million.[28] A majority of the universities in this list belong to one of six major conferences and have widely recognized names.[29] Most play football at the highest level (FBS). It is universities from this list that year after year dominate the final rankings in college football and, to a lesser extent, men's basketball. The list includes all of the top 25 highest-ranked football teams in 2009 and 18 of the top 25 teams in basketball in 2009–2010.[30]

Although all have well-known athletic teams, these universities can by no means be lumped together as "jock schools." In fact, some of them are among the best universities in the world. More than half of the 100 universities with big-time programs are recognized for their strong academic programs: 53 of them were ranked among either the top research universities in the Shanghai Jiao Tong University ranking or the top national universities as determined by *U.S. News*.[31] In other words, the University of

Table 1.1. *Top 100 universities by expenditures on athletics,*
*in millions of dollars, fiscal year 2009*

| Rank | University | Expenses ($ M) |
|---|---|---|
| 1 | University of Texas at Austin | 112.9 |
| 2 | Ohio State University | 102.1 |
| 3 | University of Florida | 101.5 |
| 4 | Louisiana State University | 94.0 |
| 5 | University of Tennessee | 92.5 |
| 6 | University of Wisconsin – Madison | 87.7 |
| 7 | Auburn University | 85.5 |
| 8 | University of Alabama | 81.8 |
| 9 | University of Oklahoma | 81.4 |
| 10 | University of Southern California | 80.2 |
| 11 | University of Michigan – Ann Arbor | 79.2 |
| 12 | University of Georgia | 76.5 |
| 13 | Pennsylvania State University | 76.5 |
| 14 | University of South Carolina | 75.6 |
| 15 | Stanford University | 74.7 |
| 16 | University of California – Berkeley | 73.4 |
| 17 | Florida State University | 73.1 |
| 18 | Duke University | 71.1 |
| 19 | University of Iowa | 70.7 |
| 20 | University of Minnesota | 70.3 |
| 21 | University of North Carolina at Chapel Hill | 70.0 |
| 22 | Texas A&M University | 70.0 |
| 23 | Oklahoma State University | 68.8 |
| 24 | University of California – Los Angeles | 66.2 |
| 25 | University of Kentucky | 65.9 |
| 26 | University of Kansas | 65.8 |
| 27 | University of Notre Dame | 64.7 |
| 28 | University of Virginia | 63.7 |
| 29 | University of Arkansas | 62.9 |
| 30 | Boston College | 62.9 |
| 31 | University of Nebraska | 62.8 |
| 32 | Michigan State University | 60.9 |
| 33 | University of Washington | 60.6 |
| 34 | University of Oregon | 60.2 |
| 35 | University of Maryland – College Park | 59.7 |
| 36 | University of Connecticut | 58.5 |
| 37 | Purdue University | 57.5 |
| 38 | Clemson University | 56.2 |
| 39 | University of Missouri | 55.6 |
| 40 | Indiana University | 55.1 |
| 41 | University of Miami | 54.5 |
| 42 | University of Louisville | 54.4 |

| Rank | University | Expenses ($ M) |
|------|------------|----------------|
| 43 | Rutgers University | 54.1 |
| 44 | University of Illinois at Urbana-Champaign | 53.7 |
| 45 | West Virginia University | 53.4 |
| 46 | Arizona State University | 53.3 |
| 47 | Syracuse University | 52.1 |
| 48 | University of Arizona | 51.6 |
| 49 | Virginia Tech | 50.9 |
| 50 | Oregon State University | 50.2 |
| 51 | Northwestern University | 48.6 |
| 52 | Baylor University | 48.5 |
| 53 | University of Colorado at Boulder | 48.2 |
| 54 | Georgia Tech | 48.1 |
| 55 | Texas Christian University | 46.5 |
| 56 | Kansas State University | 46.1 |
| 57 | University of Pittsburgh | 45.8 |
| 58 | North Carolina State University | 45.8 |
| 59 | Iowa State University | 45.8 |
| 60 | Vanderbilt University | 44.1 |
| 61 | Wake Forest University | 43.9 |
| 62 | Texas Tech University | 42.3 |
| 63 | University of Mississippi | 41.3 |
| 64 | Mississippi State University | 36.5 |
| 65 | Washington State University | 35.9 |
| 66 | Brigham Young University | 35.6 |
| 67 | Southern Methodist University | 35.4 |
| 68 | University of South Florida | 35.1 |
| 69 | University of Cincinnati | 35.0 |
| 70 | San Diego State University | 34.5 |
| 71 | University of Memphis | 33.5 |
| 72 | University of New Mexico | 32.0 |
| 73 | University of Nevada – Las Vegas | 31.9 |
| 74 | University of Utah | 31.0 |
| 75 | Rice University | 30.7 |
| 76 | University of Hawaii at Manoa | 30.5 |
| 77 | University of Central Florida | 30.0 |
| 78 | University of Houston | 29.6 |
| 79 | Georgetown University | 29.0 |
| 80 | East Carolina University | 28.4 |
| 81 | University of Tulsa | 27.1 |
| 82 | Temple University | 26.9 |
| 83 | California State University – Fresno | 26.7 |
| 84 | New Mexico State University | 25.6 |
| 85 | Miami University – Oxford | 24.7 |

*(continued)*

Table 1.1. *(continued)*

| Rank | University | Expenses ($ M) |
|------|------------|----------------|
| 86 | University of Wyoming | 24.7 |
| 87 | University at Buffalo | 23.4 |
| 88 | University of Texas at El Paso | 22.9 |
| 89 | Central Michigan University | 22.5 |
| 90 | University of Alabama at Birmingham | 22.4 |
| 91 | Eastern Michigan University | 22.0 |
| 92 | Ohio University | 21.9 |
| 93 | Colorado State University | 21.7 |
| 94 | Western Michigan University | 21.7 |
| 95 | University of Nevada – Reno | 21.4 |
| 96 | Florida International University | 21.3 |
| 97 | Western Kentucky University | 21.0 |
| 98 | Tulane University of Louisiana | 20.8 |
| 99 | Boise State University | 20.5 |
| 100 | Marshall University | 20.0 |
| | | $5,045.2 |

*Source*: U.S. Department of Education,
http://www.ope.ed.gov/athletics/GetDownloadFile.aspx, 5/11/10.

Texas has a lot of company. Dozens of American universities house these two strikingly different enterprises, the academic one devoted to the traditional activities of research and teaching and the athletic one engaged in supplying a wildly popular form of commercial entertainment.

## A PREVIEW

Although they rarely acknowledge it, the American universities that operate big-time commercial sports enterprises are in the entertainment business. University leaders often justify these enterprises on instrumental grounds, for their supposed ability to boost student applications and alumni donations, for example. But a more reliable explanation for their existence is that university stakeholders simply desire them because they want to have competitive teams. To be successful in this business, a university must maintain an enterprise that is quite different from the other, academic entity that controls the traditional functions of teaching, research, and service. Thus two dissimilar enterprises have come to coexist within these universities in a reluctant but necessary symbiotic embrace, each one needing something only the other can provide, but each one wary of the other. The educational side of the university desires athletic success because its stakeholders demand it, though it is reluctant to use educational funds to subsidize it. The entertainment side – composed largely of the athletic department – needs the academic imprimatur that only the educational side can provide. Owing to the education side's reluctance to provide subsidies to it, the athletic side is driven to exploit the commercial value of its product. But the uneasy marriage between these two entities is constantly threatened by two imperatives: the desire to win and the need to raise revenue to make that possible.

Because of the popularity of intercollegiate athletics, these universities have become major players in the nation's entertainment industry, and their social significance exists to a large extent in the world of popular, or populist, culture. Not only do these universities compete with one another for research grants or faculty, they also compete with *American Idol* and professional sports for the attention of the average citizen. Contrary to the impression that universities give in their official statements, therefore, entertainment has in fact become a significant function of these American universities. Recognizing this entertainment function and the conflicts that come with it helps to explain some otherwise curious aspects of American higher education. Not only does it explain the outsized attention given to sports in big-time sports universities, the high salaries paid to coaches, and the rampant commercialism, it also helps to explain the value of the NCAA cartel and the reluctance of universities to acknowledge the importance of athletics to their overall missions.

It should come as no surprise that the pursuit of athletic success can lead to some inherent problems. In the winner-take-all environment of athletic competition, in which success is defined only in relation to the competition, there is no natural stopping point to spending. There will always be ways to spend more money that will increase the chance of coming out ahead. Central to the ability to win is recruiting high-value athletes. In carrying out this all-important function, the imperative to win makes it logical to push to the limit whatever rules exist. This imperative also heightens the importance of getting the best coach and having the best facilities. Thus being competitive implies constant pressure on both budgets and recruiting rules. One implication is that the kinds of problems associated with big-time college sports are not amenable to an easy structural fix, because they are a direct consequence of deliberate and clear-eyed decisions. Hence there is a fundamental tension in these universities between the academic and entertainment functions. It is not easily resolved.

Despite its well-documented problems, the entertainment function in America's big-time sports universities is not an altogether bad thing. Not only are students and alumni provided with games to attend, teams to follow, and communities to be a part of, the inhabitants of surrounding cities and states get something to cheer for and be proud of. Often, the teams that are the objects of this attention and devotion are also models of interracial tolerance and cooperation, and they offer examples of high achievement among those with humble origins. Perhaps these benefits could be derived in other ways or at less cost. But regardless of one's ultimate calculation of the benefits and costs of big-time sports, viewing these universities through the prism of their athletic operations leaves little alternative but to revise our view of their basic aims. Just as surely as they perform the traditional functions of teaching, research, and service, these universities are also in the entertainment business.

# TWO

# Priorities

The fall of 2009 witnessed noteworthy decisions about athletics at two flagship American universities – the University of California at Berkeley and the University of Alabama at Tuscaloosa. At Berkeley, the faculty senate voted on a resolution regarding subsidies to the university's athletic department. In the wake of stunning rates of unemployment and home foreclosures in California, a state budget crisis marked by furloughs for state employees, a proposed 32% increase in tuition, a projected university deficit of $150 million, and student protests over planned cuts, the issue of athletic subsidies rose to unaccustomed prominence.[1] The precipitating factor was information revealing not only that the athletic department was regularly subsidized by the university, but also that the department had run additional deficits. What raised the ire of critics was the revelation that the central administration had, two years before, forgiven an accumulation of past department overruns amounting to more than $30 million.[2] At a tense faculty senate meeting where administrators sought to defend the subsidies, the debate on the floor ultimately came down to university priorities. A world of limited resources had become one of shrinking resources. Was athletics worth $7 million a year, or more?

The faculty senate declared it was not. By a vote of 91 to 68, the faculty body decided to ask the chancellor to put an end to annual subsidies and to require the repayment of the previous year's unbudgeted deficit. One faculty supporter of the resolution told the student newspaper, "The resolution is about priorities.... Will our world-class public university put entertainment ahead of education?"[3] The vote itself was not binding, of course, because the Berkeley faculty, like that in most universities, has little more than symbolic influence in shaping university decisions. With the approval of the university's regents the following spring, the university pressed on with plans to finance upgrades to its football stadium by borrowing money and charging fans $2,700 and up for "seat licenses" giving purchasers the rights to buy season tickets for the new stadium's best seats.[4]

The second decision was announced without debate by the administration at the University of Alabama that December. As its football team prepared for the upcoming national championship game, scheduled shortly after New Year's Day in Pasadena, the Alabama central administration announced it would cancel three days of classes that January so that students, faculty, and staff could attend the game.[5] Although this decision was perhaps merely a pragmatic response to an unspoken reality, it was criticized as an example of misplaced priorities. Indeed, it was an action that could not easily be reconciled with the university's mission statement, which appears on the university's Web site:[6]

Our Mission

To advance the intellectual and social condition of the people of the State through quality programs of teaching, research, and service.

Although this decision by the University of Alabama was unusually stark in exposing the conflict between academic and athletic priorities, it was by no means unique among the many choices routinely made by many American universities. Earlier that season, for example, the University of North Carolina had instructed the 12,000 university and hospital employees at its Chapel Hill campus to leave work at 3 PM, without pay, on a weekday in order to clear the parking lots and ease the traffic jams expected for the nationally televised football game scheduled for that evening.[7] Some university presidents make it their business to meet personally with prized high school recruits during their campus visits.[8] Much more common are the everyday policies that accommodate academic practices to the demands of big-time athletics, such as relaxed admissions standards and special dormitories.

The canceling of classes to accommodate a football game would surely have puzzled the foreign visitor imagined by Henry Pritchett in 1929, who naively asked what commercial sports had to do with the operation of a university. But this is precisely the question with which any serious study of the role of big-time sports in American universities must begin. To make sense of the decisions and policies of the American universities that operate these big-time programs, it is necessary to be equally naive and pose the fundamental question "What is the university's purpose?" To most outsiders, this simple question will no doubt seem rather straightforward, one that should be easy to answer. But to those who work inside universities, the reality is apt to look a lot more complicated, more nuanced. A skeptic might even wonder whether the university *has* a purpose, or can have one. Scholars of higher education have pondered this question, and their analyses turn out to depend on considerations of organization and internal decision making. If we want to explain why universities engage in commercial sports entertainment, therefore, we must address these issues of organization, decision making, and collective purpose.

Before expending much effort in trying to answer the visitor's question concerning the role of and justification for commercial athletics in American universities, we might want to ask whether this function is really important enough to warrant serious attention in the first place. If big-time sports is merely an incidental, optional, and insignificant activity, unrelated to the real business of a university, why bother worrying about it? If, like the human appendix, this department has no important function in the larger enterprise, except perhaps when things go badly, it should ultimately be of little consequence for the institution. As we will see in the next chapter, a uniquely American set of historical circumstances led to the insinuation and growth of athletic competition sponsored by universities in this country. If, as seems likely, the original reasons for this growth are long gone, it is quite possible that today's giant college sports enterprises are in fact of little practical consequence for the main work of the universities. And if that is the case, one could justify viewing big-time athletic departments as separate from the goals and functions of the university to which they are attached, being there only by virtue of historical accident. No one taking a serious look at universities would need to pay too much attention, even if spectators and the media do. So it will be important to ask, Is big-time sports important for the work of universities?

Evidence presented in the next chapter will establish, I think, that commercial sports is indeed a significant function in universities where it exists and therefore a worthy subject for serious study. But as we will see, there is a striking tendency among those who should know the most about the question to ignore big-time college sports altogether, either as a significant part of the university's structure or as a serious subject within the larger study of higher education. This lack of attention is difficult to reconcile not only with the manifest evidence of popular attention to college athletics but also with the harsh criticism leveled against the role of college sports by some leaders in American higher education.

This chapter addresses two interrelated questions. First, how does commercial sports fit into the larger aim of universities, if at all? This is the foreign visitor's naive question. To answer it, the first part of the chapter examines what those who should know say the purpose of universities is.

The authorities I turn to are universities themselves and scholars of higher education. Are their statements consistent with the reality we observe? As we will see, some prominent university leaders over the years have argued that commercial sports is not consistent with the aims of universities. But if that is the case, why do universities continue to engage in it? This question leads to the second issue this chapter deals with – decision making – which leads in turn to a consideration of the university as an organization. This seemingly esoteric topic turns out to have real significance for how decisions are made, because universities lack the clear chain of command found in armies, corporations, and most bureaucracies. In the end, therefore, it is impossible to divorce the discussion of purpose from that of power.

## COMMERCIAL SPORTS AND THE UNIVERSITY'S MISSION

It is surely no secret that big-time sports has occasionally been criticized as being at odds with the proper aims of universities. Among the critics have been leading figures in American higher education. Consider the pronouncements of six university presidents:

There's too much identification of a university with non-academic aspects, distracting from values of higher education and from desirable values in society. (Unidentified president of a Football Bowl Subdivision university, Knight Commission Study, 2009)[9]

Educational institutions have absolutely no business operating farm systems for the benefit of the National Football League and the National Basketball Association. (Derek Bok, former president, Harvard University, 2003)[10]

Big-time college athletics has little to do with the nature or objectives of the contemporary university. Instead, it is a commercial venture, aimed primarily at providing public entertainment for those beyond the campus and at generating rewards for those who stage it. (James Duderstadt, former president, University of Michigan, 2000)[11]

In truth, why should an institution whose primary devotion [is] to education and scholarship devote so much effort to competitive athletics? (Harold Shapiro, former president, University of Michigan and Princeton, 2005)[12]

The emphasis on athletics and social life that infects all colleges and universities has done more than most things to confuse these institutions and to debase the higher learning in America. (Robert Hutchins, president of the University of Chicago, 1936)[13]

The side shows are so numerous, so diverting, – so important, if you will – that they have swallowed up the circus, and those who perform in the main tent must often whistle for their audiences, discouraged and humiliated. (Woodrow Wilson, president of Princeton University, 1909)[14]

Is big-time sports really inconsistent with the aims of universities? To answer this question, one obvious approach is to find out just what universities themselves say about what their aims are. Fortunately, universities make it easy to do this, because most of them formulate and publicize formal statements of their corporate objectives. Another approach one might take is to consult experts on higher education to see what they perceive to be the role of commercial athletics in the overall operation of universities. After examining a collection of published mission statements, therefore, I turn next to academic studies of higher education in order to discern what importance scholars attach to commercial college sports.

## What Universities Say Their Missions Are

Most universities publish formal summaries of their corporate objectives in the form of mission statements. These statements are readily available for public inspection on universities' Web pages. Most of these pronouncements are brief, running no more than a handful of paragraphs and a few hundred words. Some of them mention their histories or regional ties. Some list honored values and traditional objectives. Some list specific schools or other administrative units, while others stick to generalities. Whatever the length or format, however, almost all of them are sure to mention the three functions traditionally cited by those who speak for universities: teaching, research, and service. This trinity permeates the language of contemporary American universities, from evaluations of faculty performance to speeches by presidents, so it should be no surprise that these three elements consistently show up in university mission statements.

Of the two universities mentioned at the beginning of this chapter, only one, Alabama, has a published mission statement that applies to its main campus. Quoted in its entirety earlier, its 21 words unmistakably feature this academic trinity. UC Berkeley has no published mission statement, but the larger University of California does, running some 400 words in length. And that statement begins by emphasizing the same three activities common to research universities: "The University's fundamental missions are teaching, research and public service." It goes on to elaborate upon these functions, naming areas of instruction, fields of research, and types of public service. It mentions four organizational entities specifically: the extension service, medical centers, libraries, and museums. Indeed, the variety of activities under the umbrella of the modern university inspired former chancellor Clark Kerr to coin the term "multiversity."[15]

Neither of these mission statements, however, mentions athletic competition or entertainment as a function it performs or values. Although both universities receive more national attention for their successful athletic programs than for all other activities put together (a fact that is documented in the next chapter), both mission statements are mute on the subject of athletics. In this omission, these two universities are typical of most other universities that operate big-time sports programs. Although such universities always mention research and teaching as core functions and most also mention service, only a few of them include athletics.

One possible explanation for this omission is that such general statements of purpose simply leave no room for a listing of particular functions beyond broad categories like research, teaching, and service, especially in a statement as brief as the University of Alabama's. But the University of California's statement shows this is not always the case, because it specifically mentions such administrative units as agricultural extension, museums, and libraries. Indeed, this explanation does not hold up, because many mission statements do in fact mention particular activities beyond the big three functions.

To take a closer look at what universities actually say about their objectives, I searched the Web for the mission statements of 58 universities with big-time sports programs. These were the members of the five biggest football conferences plus Notre Dame.[16] Of these universities, only 6, including UC Berkeley, did not have published mission statements in 2008.[17] I analyzed the text of those 52 statements, looking first for references to the big three functions – teaching, research, and service. All of the mission statements cited teaching and research, and all but one cited service. Despite the fact that all of the universities in the sample operated big-time sports enterprises, athletics was mentioned by only five universities, less than a tenth of them.[18]

In fairness, some mission statements are very general, like the one for the University of Alabama already quoted. Statements in this category are written in deliberately broad terms and, as a result, include no references to particular units. Thus it seems unfair to expect that statements of this sort would mention athletics. Therefore, I also counted the number of references to schools and other administrative units, such as a law school. I then compared the number of specific references with the number of universities that actually housed such a unit. In this way I could compare the chance that a university would mention its law school, for example, with the chance that it would mention its athletic program. So how did this 10% chance compare with the likelihood that mission statements would mention other units?

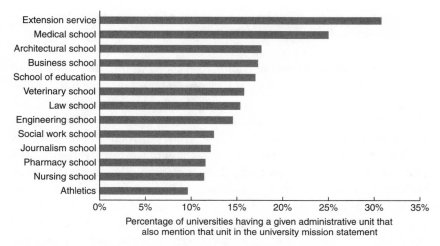

Figure 2.1. Administrative units mentioned in university mission statements. *Source*: Mission statements posted on the Web, May 2008, for 52 universities with big-time sports.

The resulting list of tabulated functions is presented in Figure 2.1. As the figure plainly shows, this 10% rate was low, ranking below the chance that these universities would mention their journalism, pharmacy, or nursing schools. In their mission statements, they were much more likely to mention their extension service, medical school, or school of architecture than they were to mention their athletic program.[19] It is natural to wonder what the source of this reluctance might be. I return to consider this question later in the chapter.

## Athletics as Seen by Scholars of Higher Education

In 2002 Stanford University Press published a collection of essays edited by a prominent scholar of American higher education and written by what one reviewer called "a star cast of authors," whose aim was to consider the future of American research universities.[20] Entitled *The Future of the City of Intellect: The Changing American University*, it dealt with a broad array of topics. It covered issues of long-standing significance, such as the expansion of knowledge, changes in the curriculum, research in the life sciences, interdisciplinary research, faculty recruitment, tenure, unionization, rising tuition, university organization, and student services. It also discussed new trends and challenges, including corporate sponsorship, university–industry research collaborations, the incorporation of new technologies, new revenue streams, demographic changes, and the use of the Internet in teaching. But nowhere in the book's 353 pages is there a single mention of athletics, commercial or otherwise.

The neglect of the subject of commercial sports in this 2002 book is not unusual. It is typical of serious scholarly research on American universities. As far back as 1976 James Michener noted in his book *Sports in America*, "It is easier to find a good study on the effect of the Flemish language on the children of Antwerp than to discover from articles in learned journals what really goes on in the sports department of the university in which the scholars reside."[21] This is not to say that scholars have ignored commercial athletics as a topic of research, only that college sports has been a topic studied on its own, not in relation to "higher education." Most of what is written and published by experts on higher education, like the essays in that 2002 volume, resemble university mission statements in hardly mentioning athletics at all. Books about universities with such titles as *The University in a Corporate Culture* (2003), *Shakespeare, Einstein, and the Bottom Line: The Marketing of Higher Education* (2004), *Higher Education for the Public Good: Emerging Voices from a National Movement* (2005), *American Higher Education in the Twenty-First Century: Social, Political, and Economic Challenges* (2005), and *American Universities in a Global Market* (2010) manage to present general analyses of higher education in the United States without ever mentioning athletics.[22] The same is true for entire volumes of the leading academic journal devoted to higher education, the *Journal of Higher Education*.[23] Commercial athletics is also entirely absent from one of the student surveys most widely used to assess the quality of the under-graduate college experience. The National Survey of Student Engagement (NSSE) asks about participation in recreation and sports, but not about being a fan or spectator at college games.

Were this research about universities in any other part of the world – Europe, the Commonwealth, Asia, Latin America – the failure to take seri-ous note of intercollegiate athletics would not be remarkable. Outside of the United States, intercollegiate athletics is just one of many student activities and has few if any of the commercial attributes of American big-time college sports. But in light of the size and prominence of commercial sports in many American universities, this blind spot in higher-education research is jarring, if not shocking. It is as if scholars of American higher education were living in a parallel universe, completely missing the reality that these universities are in the entertainment business and that this business is the principal thing most people know about their institutions. One reason scholars ignore com-mercial sports as a serious subject might be that they simply do not think it is important enough to worry about. Alternatively, they might believe what the mission statements say, that commercial sports is simply not a proper function of universities. That big-time college sports exists cannot be denied, this view might hold, but it is not worth discussing as part of the "real" work of universities. For scholars taking this view, spectator sports is simply not a higher-education topic. It is a topic for a newspaper's sports section. If big-time college sports belongs to the people's university, these scholars focus only on the scholars' university, the city of the intellect.

When scholars study aspects of big-time sports, and they do, the focus tends to be on sports as a freestanding enterprise, not as a regular function of the universities that sponsor it. In economics, these studies deal with such aspects of university athletics as finances, the effects of athletic success on applications for admission and charitable donations, the economic value of recruiting star players, and how conferences and the NCAA influence competitive balance among teams. Numerous studies examine the cartel-like aspects of the NCAA. In addition, some studies address such topics as the history of college sports, the psychology of fan devotion, and the cultural significance of gender roles and sports pageantry. In this book, I draw heavily from the findings of studies like these. As interesting as they are, however, they do not embody the view that athletics is a central function of universities or that its operation affects these central functions. Their message is that college sports stands on its own as a topic worth studying, but the activity has little to do with the other things universities do.

The gulf that I have sketched between athletics and serious study of higher education is not absolute. A few academic studies do treat athletics as an activity that has the potential to affect the principal work of universities. Two studies, by former Princeton president William Bowen and his coauthors, focus on highly selective institutions and the consequences of having a sizable portion of athletes in the student body. They demonstrate that athletes, who are often given preference in admissions, tend to bring down the academic quality of these elite colleges and universities. These studies focus on the athletes themselves and their effect on the undergraduate experience at their institutions, not on the commercial enterprise and its relationship to the university's main work. To be sure, some studies, including books by Thelin (1994), Zemsky, Wegner, and Massy (2005), and Weisbrod, Ballou, and Asch (2008), do address, or at least note, the topic of corporate mission that I deal with here. Interestingly, some of the books that probe most deeply into the consequences for universities of big-time athletics are those written by former university presidents. Beside Bowen's, these include books by former presidents of Michigan, Harvard, and Princeton.[24]

The spirited criticisms that have been leveled at big-time college sports over the years carry with them the assumption that commercial sports, as practiced by American universities, is at cross-purposes with those institutions' educational objectives. Yet it is difficult to prove that any conflict exists, except in the opinion of these critics. Neither the formal statements made by universities nor the scholarship produced by experts address the role – actual or desired – of commercial sports in universities. In fact, a paradox pervades serious discussions of the role of big-time athletics in American universities. In the popular perception, it is an important part of universities. But in the intellectual world of institutional pronouncements and scholarship, big-time sports is seldom more than a footnote.

### DECISION MAKING AND THE BOOSTER COALITION

When considering how commercial sports fits into the broader aims of universities, it is easy to speak glibly about the university as if it were a monolithic body with a unified purpose. But according to scholars who have studied them as organizations, universities are anything but. Unlike armies and business corporations, which tend to have clear objectives and disciplined hierarchical command structures, universities feature vague missions, decentralized organization charts, and weak presidents. Shortly after he was appointed president of Columbia University in 1948, Dwight D. Eisenhower discovered how much less authority his new position carried than did his previous one, supreme commander of the Allied Forces. Meeting with Nobel Prize–winning physicist I. I. Rabi for the first time, Eisenhower remarked that he was always glad to see employees of Columbia honored. The professor responded, "Mr. President, the faculty are not *employees* of the University – they *are* the University."[25] As a consequence of their limited authority, university CEOs and their lieutenants – provost and deans – regularly suffer the indignity of having their employees refuse their legitimate requests.[26] This is not to suggest that presidents and provosts are without the power to nudge their institutions in one direction or the other. It is simply to say that top-down, disciplined, hierarchical control, a pillar of the modern corporation, has no real parallel in the modern research university.

This absence of chain-of-command discipline reveals itself with particular clarity when it comes to athletics. Athletic department budgets are commonly outside the purview of routine university budget deliberations. At the University of Michigan, for example, the athletics director was the only major university officer who did not make a budget presentation to the provost, the university's chief budget officer.[27] In universities with big-time sports programs, many presidents learn early on that they have little authority over their celebrity coaches, and often less status. One instructive example was Duke's new president, during his first days in office in 2004, publicly pleading with the university's celebrated basketball coach not to take a job in professional basketball. Such "ritual humiliation," as one Duke professor called this episode, is seldom required to clarify the relative positions of power within the university, however.[28] Another illustration of the limits of presidential power is a statement, remarkable for its candor, made by the president of the University of Florida in an interview with a reporter from the *Chronicle of Higher Education* in 2009.[29]

Q. When your athletics department has all this new ESPN money, these riches of NCAA titles, the highest-paid coaches and athletic director around, how do you keep it from spinning beyond your control?

A. I don't, I don't make any pretense about that.

A survey of university presidents conducted by the Knight Commission about the same time showed that this sentiment was widely shared by presidents of universities with big-time sports programs. One unidentified president who responded to the survey stated a common but seldom articulated reality: "In terms of control over big-time college athletics, I don't believe we have control. Show me a president who won't meet the demands of a winning coach who has the chance to walk out the door for a higher salary someplace else."[30]

## A Peculiar Organization

The limited power of president and provost is just one of the organizational peculiarities of American universities. To understand how it is possible for a commercial entertainment enterprise to thrive inside a university, it is necessary to appreciate these peculiarities. Sociologist James Coleman wrote that modern universities differ from corporations in three ways. First, they have no corporate goal. Unlike corporations, whose focus on profits is clear, the objectives of universities are multiple and vague, as we have seen in their published mission statements. Often, the aim is no more specific than "to be the best."[31] Second, their governance is more akin to that of a community where competing interests vie to achieve their various objectives than to the neat hierarchy pictured in the corporate organization chart. Third, those who carry out the main work of the university are not employees in the traditional sense, but rather "semi-independent professionals."[32]

Yet as gratifying as the Columbia professor's statements might be to the ears of faculty members, limited presidential power does not necessarily imply heightened faculty control. Despite its general agreement that it *does* constitute the university's core (and frequent assurances to that effect by top administrators), the faculty in truth has little authority in university decisions beyond the purely academic realm and often quite limited authority within that realm. To be sure, faculty members do sit on university athletic councils and are sent to NCAA conventions to represent, along with athletic directors, their institutions, but these forms of faculty participation in governance of athletics may be more about form than substance. For example, those appointed to oversee athletics may be athletic true believers. Certainly the perks that often accompany an appointment as faculty athletic representative might predispose some faculty members to sympathize with the athletic department. Of the 307 guests who sat in the president's and regents' boxes during the 2008 football season at Texas A&M, only four were listed as attending all seven home games. One of those was the faculty representative to the NCAA, and another was the chair of the university's athletic council. To quote the blunt assessment in the Carnegie Commission's 1929 report, the forms of faculty oversight the study team observed mostly amounted to little more than "pseudo faculty control."[33] A more recent assessment comes to much the same conclusion, calling faculty oversight of athletic programs "ineffective," exemplified by faculty service on athletic councils that merely rubber stamp decisions made by the athletic department.[34] According to a recent survey of administrators and trustees, this lack of faculty authority over athletics is simply a special case of what is true more generally of university governance. Responses in that survey suggested that the vast majority of faculty governing bodies were no more than advisory or "policy influencing." Only 13% of respondents reported that their institution's faculty deliberative body was "policy making."[35]

An episode at the University of Wisconsin's flagship campus at Madison in 2008 serves to illustrate the faculty's limited authority over athletics. The resignation by one of the faculty members of the university's athletic board brought to light several instances in which the board had been entirely bypassed in major decisions concerning the university's athletic department. Although the university's handbook of faculty policies and procedures called for the athletic board to participate actively in searches and screening to hire head coaches and senior athletic department administrators, the board had been given just two hours' notice before the university announced the hiring of a new head football coach. Nor had the board been involved during the university's contract negotiations with the new Big Ten Network or in discussions of how the revenues would be distributed within the university.[36]

The Berkeley faculty's revolt, despite its air of confrontation, also illustrates the faculty's lack of clout. When the Berkeley faculty rose up in 2009, indignant about the size of subsidies going to the university's athletic department, the most severe action the faculty senate could take was to *recommend* that the chancellor begin to reduce those deficits. The faculty, in short, was even less in charge of the athletic enterprise than was the chancellor.[37] It was much the same story a few months later at Ohio University, when its faculty senate passed what amounted to an equally toothless resolution decrying subsidies to its athletic department.[38]

There can be no more blunt an assertion of the autonomy of the athletic enterprise than this one by a famous basketball coach of the 1980s:

We're not even really part of the school anymore, anyway. I work for the N.C. State Athletic Association. That has nothing to do with the university. Our funding is totally independent. You think the chancellor is going to tell me what to do? Who to take into school or not take into school? I doubt it. I'm paid to win games. If I say a kid can help me win, I'll get him. It's the same at 99 percent of the places in the country.[39]

According to Coleman, the university's lack of a corporate goal and decentralized power structure make it "permeable," easily penetrated by activities that were not part of the European universities on which the American ones were modeled. Examples of new activities that he cited in his 1973 essay included linear accelerators, adult education, ROTC, vocational training, community action and urban redevelopment programs, and policy-related research, few of which would raise an eyebrow today.[40] Although Coleman made no reference to intercollegiate sports (adhering to the scholarly tradition of silence on athletics), his argument applies with equal or greater force to an activity like commercial sports. Since the university had no clearly defined purpose, why couldn't that be part of it? Indeed, one scholar has argued that big-time sports became attached to American colleges and universities in the first place because entrepreneurial college presidents desperately needed outside financial support to make a go of it in America's highly decentralized and competitive higher-education market.[41] Compared with European universities, which relied largely on government largess, American colleges and universities were more numerous and less financially secure. This organizational portrait explains both the outward search for recognition and the opportunity inside to establish a network of supporters.

## Boosters

Inside the university, the lack of strong hierarchical control allows for the growth of semiautonomous fiefdoms, a condition to some extent formalized by the popular "every tub on its own bottom" approach to university budgeting. As every university administrator knows, budgetary autonomy often leads to jurisdictional autonomy, adding to the decentralization, or diffusion, of authority under the university umbrella. As one of the operational units inside the university's decentralized confederation, the big-time athletic department has become unusually autonomous. The reluctance of the academic side to subsidize its operation only strengthens that autonomy.

Fortunately for the athletic programs, since the dawn of big-time college sports, groups of enthusiasts have tended to cluster on the university's periphery to lend their support. In his blistering 1922 critique of universities, *The Goose-Step*, Upton Sinclair used the term "rah-rah boys" to refer to unrestrained alumni supporters who backed college athletic programs. They raised money to augment the salaries of coaches or scouted for talented athletes, often paying them under the table after they enrolled.[42] More recently, sociologist James Frey labeled such supporters the "booster coalition." Not simply a handful of sports enthusiasts who show up at games, this coalition represents an entrenched, well-connected axis of power outside the university's formal decision-making structure. Dominated by successful businessmen, this group differs in ideology and temperament from those who run the rest of the university. According to Frey, they "are used to getting what they want." They pressure universities to select athletic directors who are ideologically in tune with their own predilections.[43] Consistent with this portrait is a survey showing that a hugely disproportionate share of CEOs played intercollegiate sports as college students.[44] Owing to their political and financial wherewithal, Frey argues, the members of this coalition are able to exert influence on regents or trustees. Their efforts allow the athletic department to do whatever is necessary to win games and, in so doing, occasionally deviate from traditional university values or even violate rules.[45]

It is not hard to find anecdotal evidence that boosters exist or that their involvement sometimes results in rule violations. Not only did Upton Sinclair complain about them, they were the subject of sustained criticism in the Carnegie Commission's 1929 report. Boosters were implicated in some of the 20th century's most notorious abuses, including the outright payment of football players at SMU.[46] In recent years, boosters – often in their roles as alumni, trustees, or advisory board members – have publicly called upon their universities to fire coaches seen as unsuccessful. For example, an alumnus of the University of Washington offered scholarships of $100,000 each if the president would fire the university's athletic director and head football coach.[47] At Florida State, the chairman of the board of trustees told a reporter it was time for the university to get rid of its venerable football coach, whose success on the field had waned.[48] At Texas Tech, administrators had to soothe the feelings of alumni who objected to the firing of its winning football coach, who had been found to have physically abused players.[49] And at NC State, a new acting provost began his assignment by dealing with a raft of emails from alumni and other fans calling on him to fire an allegedly underperforming athletic director.[50]

If this dark picture of booster influence is accurate, it would explain a lot of the aspects of big-time sports that have drawn criticism over the years, as well as the consistent failure of attempts to reform the system. It would explain, for example, the persistence with which episodes of recruiting violations come to light, often involving attempts by boosters to compensate recruits, players, or their families. It would help to explain the extraordinary success of fund-raising by athletic departments. It would go a long way in explaining the power of big-time athletic departments to chart their own way without undue interference by academic administrators. Finally, it would be helpful in understanding the commercial orientation of big-time athletics itself. If the booster coalition is dominated by those who have been successful in the business world, one would not be surprised to discover among them a willingness to take advantage of opportunities to raise even more money for the athletic enterprise.

Proof that this story is anything more than a conspiracy theory cooked up by faculty members is hard to come by. I adopted the more modest aim to look for evidence that would at least be consistent with the hypothesis. I used publicly available data on political party registration to test two of the theory's implications – first, that boosters are ideologically distinct from others who lead or teach in the university and, second, that they have more in common with members of the athletic department than with others associated with the university. I found evidence to support the first, but not the second.

Drawing on painstaking Web research by a research assistant, I used information on party registration to compare members of booster organizations with coaches and senior administrators in athletic departments, and also with representatives of other groups of actors in the university, including administrators, trustees, and faculty members. I wanted to find out if the patterns of political party registration of boosters are similar to those of the athletic department and different from those of other university stakeholders. And on the assumption that such coalitions ought to be strongest in universities with big-time athletics, I sought to see if any differences were greatest in universities that compete at the highest level. Ideally, one would prefer to compare universities with big-time sports (those in the FBS) with otherwise similar universities not in Division I, but the scarcity of the latter made it necessary to settle for a comparison of the big with the super-big. Selecting pairs of universities by state that were both private or both public and that were as close as possible in size, I compared FBS universities like Syracuse, the University of Connecticut, and Colorado State with non-FBS universities like St. John's, Central Connecticut State, and the University of Northern Colorado.[51]

To represent the university stakeholder groups besides boosters, I chose individuals from four categories: business and finance administrators, trustees, faculty in economics, and coaches and administrators in athletics. Business and finance administrators were chosen because their jobs are similar to those of their counterparts in the athletic department. I chose faculty members in economics because nearly every university has such a department and economics departments tend to be larger than average. Previous research supports the common perception that university faculty members have liberal leanings. While this generalization applies to economics, the leftward leanings of economists tend to be less pronounced than those of faculty members in a number of other disciplines.[52] In any case, the political leanings of economists are not intended to represent those of the entire faculty, but rather to illustrate differences across universities. The broader aim was to see if there were any discernible differences between universities with big-time sports programs and those with more modest programs.

Using university Web sites and other Web-based data sources to identify individuals in the various groups, together with data on party registration available on the Web for a number of states, we tried to identify the party designation for up to 100 individuals associated with each of 30 universities in nine states.[53] For each category of stakeholder and both types of universities, I calculated the percentage of Republicans among those indicating either of the two major parties, statistically controlling for state, university enrollment, and whether the university was public or private. Thus the calculations correct for each state's general political leanings. Of the five groups of employees and stakeholders, economics faculty members were the least likely to be registered Republicans, but they were similarly inclined in both types of universities, with 32% of them registered as Republican in both. In the non-FBS universities, the four remaining stakeholder groups were quite similar in party registration, with average Republican percentages clumped between 51 and 52%. In the FBS universities, however, boosters stood out, with 71% registered Republican, significantly higher than the 51% of boosters in the non-FBS universities so registered. However, coaches and athletic department administrators at the FBS universities did not follow suit: their Republican share was virtually identical to that in non-FBS athletic departments.[54]

This statistical exercise thus offers only partial support for the booster coalition hypothesis. Although boosters and athletic department leaders did not show the similarity suggested by that theory, boosters who were associated with big-time programs did conform in one measurable respect to the theory's stereotype that boosters have experiences and attitudes distinct from those of other university stakeholders. Judging only from their party preferences, the boosters I identified were ideologically distinct from other groups of employees and stakeholders, and they were distinct from boosters associated with less competitive athletic programs. They were, in a word, conservative. These findings seem fully consistent with the conclusion drawn by one reformist observer of college sports in the 1960s:

> The conservatism that engulfs the American sporting scene to this day stems in no small measure from the alumni groups that control intercollegiate athletic programs throughout the country. Not surprisingly, alumni who have the time, finances, and inclination to involve themselves in, and contribute to the financing of, a professionalized athletic program for college students are usually conservative men.[55]

## Two Enterprises

Inside the walls of universities with big-time athletics programs, two distinct administrative structures coexist. Not only do they differ in function – academic and athletic – they also differ in organizational structure and professional culture. As organizations, these big-time athletic departments have little in common with the academic side of the universities that contain them. In clear contrast to the decentralization and personal autonomy of the academic side, athletic departments are organized as strict hierarchies, reflecting traditions both corporate and military. Former Michigan president James Duderstadt notes the differences in cultures and adherence to rules, observing that the athletic department's dictatorial power is "alien to the academy."[56]

This cultural divide is especially apparent in the organization of teams. In sharp contrast to those who played on the student-run teams of the 19th century, the students wearing the football or basketball uniforms of one of today's big-time sports programs participate as soldiers in a tightly controlled platoon, under the strict oversight of a ruling commanding officer and his lieutenants. One ethnographic study of a big-time basketball team documented the dominant and paternal position of the head coach, which allowed him to wield absolute power over the lives of his players. For their part, these players showed loyalty comparable to that of troops in combat or members of religious cults.[57]

To be sure, the business side of the university – the finance, human resources, and service provision functions – bears many similarities to conventional corporations in its hierarchical organization chart, but most of the academic side of the institution does not. On the academic side, successful university leadership becomes an exercise in persuasion rather than in top-down command and control. This communitarian style of decision making also draws nourishment ideologically from the traditional emphasis that faculty members, in their roles as teachers and department members, place on the values of creativity and independence of thought.

A second way in which these athletic departments differ from most other units in their respective universities is their highly developed commercial orientation and businesslike operation. Big-time athletic departments face a market test to a degree few other units at a university do, with the possible exception of university medical centers. Their financial well-being depends upon attracting paying customers. They must take seriously the principles of modern marketing and use its techniques. They must be sophisticated in their interactions with television and other media, both in trumpeting their achievements and in avoiding unfavorable publicity. And like for-profit business enterprises that compete in the marketplace, they must live in an uncertain world where the possibility that expenses will exceed revenues is an ever-present reality. To be sure, the big-time athletic department is not the only merchant doing business within an otherwise sacred temple of learning. As former Harvard president Derek Bok argued in his book *Universities in the Marketplace*, commercialization has also insinuated itself into scientific research and specialized course offerings. And managing the endowment is certainly a highly commercialized function as well, although this function is often farmed out or placed in a separate nonprofit entity. But it seems fair to conclude that no other unit in American universities more closely resembles a private for-profit firm than the big-time athletic department.

Yet the thing that sets apart the commercialism of the big-time athletic department is the particular industry with which it has most in common – the entertainment industry. Were it an independent company and not a unit inside a large university, a big-time athletic department would readily be classified by Commerce Department statisticians as part of the entertainment industry, alongside professional sports teams. The games played by the football and basketball teams of a big-time program are broadcast widely and frequently on television, lifting their notoriety beyond the local and regional to the national. Their star players, some of them still teenagers, are routinely quoted in print media and interviewed on radio and television. Their biggest stars, however, are the head coaches of football and men's basketball, whose prominence easily surpasses that of any other university employee. And like other stars in the entertainment industry, these head coaches enjoy incomes that put them on a level matched by few others in higher education.

## THE ACTUAL BUSINESS OF UNIVERSITIES

Every university with a big-time sports program has an athletic department to operate that program and a group of stakeholders to ensure continued university commitment to its operation. This coalition of stakeholders must include trustees or their equivalent, but at its core are athletic boosters dedicated to the cause of intercollegiate competition. No matter how much these universities emphasize high-quality research or excellence in teaching, they make it an institutional priority to be competitive, at some acceptable level, in intercollegiate athletics. They do this because big-time sports is not just a means to some academic end. For decision makers in these universities, being competitive in intercollegiate football and basketball is an end in itself. No person can survive as president or chancellor at one of these universities who does not accept this imperative. This fact is captured in the quip attributed to the University of California's Clark Kerr, that the job of chancellor "had come to be defined as providing parking for the faculty, sex for the students, and athletics for the alumni."[58] In order to be successful in this athletic/entertainment enterprise, big-time sports universities turn to professionals to run the enterprise. This group of professionals has expertise that is quite distinct from that required to run the academic side of the university. The academic and athletic enterprises also differ in organizational style, one having the decentralized, loosely organized structure inherited from the medieval university, the other having the tightly managed chain of command of the military battalion.

Despite the preponderant share of attention garnered by their big-time sports programs, the universities that run them are reluctant to admit that they play any significant role. Universities with big-time programs are less likely to mention athletics in their formal mission statements than they are to mention any comparably sized subunit, such as professional schools or the extension service, and are much less likely to mention athletics than they are teaching, research, or service. Similarly, scholars of higher education have a blind spot when it comes to the role of commercial athletics. Although big-time sports is studied as an activity on its own terms, it is seldom studied as an issue of higher education.

This blind spot has the appearance of a parallel universe. Those on the academic side of universities seem not to recognize athletics as a significant part of universities, but those outside of universities, as we will see in the next chapter, see athletics as the preponderant manifestation of universities. One explanation for this disconnect is that, for intellectuals, athletics is not part of what is significant about universities, or at least it *should not be*. By the same token, universities, or at least the committees that write mission statements, could believe that athletics really is not part of their university's mission, or not important enough to merit any mention. An alternative, and less flattering, explanation is that university mission statements were never meant to be accurate, that they should be judged by the same standards as commercial advertising, wherein extravagant claims in the category of "puffery" are not required to be literally true. But not only is ignoring athletics as a serious topic of higher education inconsistent with the best traditions of academic inquiry, it is also unhelpful. If athletics is important enough to be a perennial problem in American higher education, it is important enough to receive serious attention.

# THREE

# The Bigness of "Big Time"

The public school district in Clarke County, Georgia, the county containing the University of Georgia, scheduled an unusual holiday in the fall of 2008. It designated Friday, October 31, as an official school holiday. The reason for this holiday was not Halloween, but rather the Georgia–Florida football game, which was scheduled to be played that year on November 1 in Jacksonville, Florida. This annual contest, which has been known for years as "the world's largest outdoor cocktail party," is played every year in 76,877-seat Jacksonville Municipal Stadium, and many Georgia fans make the 700-mile round trip to attend the game. One year earlier, on the Friday before the 2007 Georgia–Florida game, so many of the district's teachers had called in sick that school officials could not find enough substitutes to fill in. Rather than face the prospect of unstaffed classrooms again, the school district decided in 2008 simply to designate that Friday a school holiday. So did the school districts in neighboring Madison and Oglethorpe Counties.

From Athens to South Bend and from Pasadena to Charlottesville, football Saturdays provide a quintessential demonstration of the reach of big-time college sports. These events attract attention so intense, both local and regional, that weekend activities are planned around them and they become as common a subject of everyday conversation as the weather or the day's top news story. Yet the thousands of spectators attending one of these games represent only a part of the influence of these events. Attendance figures are often dwarfed by the size of the audience that tunes in to watch college football and basketball games on TV. Consider the size of the viewing audience for a 2009 midweek regular-season basketball game between traditional in-state rivals, Duke and the University of North Carolina. That game, played on a Wednesday night in February and carried on the cable network ESPN, drew an estimated audience of 2.6 million viewers, not counting the

1.2 million who watched the game on a regional network. Although 2.6 million was only a tenth of the size of the country's top-rated TV show, *American Idol*, it was still huge – about the same as the population of metropolitan Baltimore.[1]

For the universities that operate at the big-time level, the football and basketball teams can easily generate as much attention as all of the other parts of their universities put together. The very magnitude of the attention these teams and games receive is a central fact about big-time college sports. To establish it beyond the level of anecdote, this chapter documents the "big" in big-time athletics. It begins with a brief accounting of how college athletics in America came to be the way it is today.

## THE EMERGENCE OF BIG-TIME COLLEGE SPORTS

Intercollegiate competition in the United States began shortly before the Civil War, and by 1900 all of the major college sports we know today were being played. Boat racing has the distinction of having been the first sport played between American universities, when crews representing Harvard and Yale met in 1852. The three other principal sports, along with the date and institutions that competed in the first contest, were baseball (1859, Amherst–Williams), football (1874, Harvard–McGill), and basketball (1895, Minnesota State School of Agriculture–Hamline).[2] By all indications, the popularity of these and other sports played by colleges went well beyond those who played on teams, with contests sometimes drawing large crowds and results appearing in newspapers. The 1893 Princeton–Yale football game, played in Manhattan, drew 50,000 spectators.[3] All of these college teams started out as student-run organizations. For the most part, students provided not just the players, but also the coaches and the necessary management. Indeed, for the small fraction of young people, mostly men, who attended college, the latter half of the 19th century was a period of student-led organizing that also included the creation of most of today's college social fraternities.

Although begun as student organizations, college teams soon started down a path that would end both their autonomy and their purely amateur status. Not long after that first boat race between Harvard and Yale, the latter, in 1864, became the first college team to hire a paid professional coach.[4] This organizational feature, which is today as common among intercollegiate teams as it is unknown among intramural ones, was a harbinger of things to come. Another development, fueled by the popularity of the sports among the spectating public, was the tendency of teams to schedule more and more contests, thus necessitating trips away from campus and games on days during the school term. In 1870, just five years after its beginning, Harvard's baseball team was playing a 44-game season, with a majority of those games scheduled during the term.[5] To accommodate the demand for games, college contests were often scheduled for "neutral" sites away from both institutions. Such schedules generated both expenses and, thanks to gate receipts, revenues.

But faculty and university leaders grew unhappy with the consequences of what they saw as a clear case of overemphasis. In his annual report of 1893, Harvard's president Charles Eliot complained of the excessive time devoted to crew, baseball, and football and wasteful expenditures of gate receipts.[6] In due course, the faculty and administration of universities, sometimes with the help of alumni, began to exert authority over these activities. By 1900 the teams in the major sports at many of the largest institutions were no longer being run by students, and the takeover by universities was complete by 1920.[7]

The sport whose transformation laid the groundwork for what is now known as big-time college sports was football, and it remains today the biggest source of revenue for college athletics. In this sport, one sees combined all the elements that would drive intercollegiate athletics for the next century: widespread popularity, the desire of universities to exploit athletic success for their institutional goals, and the collective recognition by universities of the need to regulate competition. By the 1890s, the rugby version of football had won out over the soccer version as the game of choice in college competition. Beginning as a game in which two teams pushed each other until the ball emerged from the "scrum," it had been modified through mutual agreement over time, largely by an association of northeastern institutions, so that the two teams were separated on either side of a scrimmage line, with one player, called a center, passing the ball backward to another, the quarterback.

The game routinely featured violent play, epitomized by one rule stating that a player would be expelled from a game only after the third instance of hitting another player with the fist. A further rule, adopted after the 1887 season, allowed tackling between the waist and the knees, to the detriment of open-field running. Teams responded to this rule by developing "mass plays," including the feared flying wedge. Since it was Harvard that first used the flying wedge, in 1892, its president, Charles Eliot, knew of what he wrote when he described football as "a game played by heavy men who collide at speed, [affording] the spectacle of exciting wrestlings, rushings, and collisions in rapid succession, with an inevitable result of bodily injuries in almost every well-contested match."[8]

One result of these injuries was the first of several instances in which a president of the United States took a very public interest in college athletics. After receiving a report at the end of the 1893 season that numerous midshipmen had been rendered unable to perform their duties on account of injuries sustained playing football, President Grover Cleveland ended the annual Army–Navy game. That storied rivalry would not be resumed on the football field again until 1899.[9]

The problem of football injuries came to a head following the 1905 season, one featuring an especially bloody game that took place, ironically, in the Quaker State, between Penn and Swarthmore.[10] In a second and also very public presidential intervention, Theodore Roosevelt called to the White House representatives from three of the collegiate football powerhouses, Harvard, Princeton, and Yale, admonishing them in no uncertain terms to rewrite the rules so these injuries would cease. Whether or not Roosevelt's outrage was heightened by Yale's dominance over the president's own beloved Harvard team, the president's jawboning got almost immediate results.

Within a few months, the Yale-led old guard had compromised with reform-minded institutions to form an association of colleges and universities that would later become the NCAA. Of more immediate importance, that group produced a set of rules that promised to reduce injuries by discouraging mass plays, thereby opening up play and transforming the game into one that would be very familiar to a 21st-century spectator. Among the newly adopted rules were a foot-wide neutral zone between the two teams, a minimum of six offensive players on the line of scrimmage, a prohibition against tackling below the knees, an increase in the number of officials to four, an increase in the number of yards needed for a first down, from 5 to 10, and a modest allowance for the forward pass.[11]

In parallel with these changes in the game of football was a vastly more significant transformation in American higher education. Spurred by the federal government's Morrill Acts of 1862 and 1890, state universities took shape and grew large in the Midwest, South, and West. In addition to the traditional disciplines, these public universities embraced applied fields like agriculture, engineering, and business. And they helped to democratize American higher education, adding service to the traditional aims of research and teaching. In their appeal to a broad citizenry, it seemed natural for them to fold in "public entertainment" in the form of athletics, to quote

Clark Kerr. He added wryly, "Once started, university spectator sports could not be killed even by the worst of teams or the best of de-emphasis; and few universities seriously sought after either."[12]

By the end of the 1920s, American college football had evolved into a form that would continue into the 21st century with remarkably little change. The bulk of today's defining rules had been adopted by 1929, as were the fight songs, school colors, and mascots. Another aspect of college football that had by 1929 become an established emblem of big-time football was large crowds, made possible by big stadiums. The 1920s was a decade of intense stadium construction. All but two of the universities in the Big Ten built stadiums during the decade, including the gargantuan Michigan Stadium in Ann Arbor, completed in 1927 with a seating capacity of 84,400. Of the 57 universities in the five established conferences in 2010, an astonishing 35 built new football stadiums during the decade of the 1920s.[13]

These stadiums brought with them the capacity to generate large amounts of revenue. Gate receipts were virtually the only source of revenue in those days before radio and television. Football, by virtue of its large stadiums, was the sport with the greatest potential for raising it. Illustrating the revenue potential of football, the University of Illinois team played eight games in 1924, averaging almost 29,000 spectators at the six that were played at their home field.[14] By contrast, its basketball team averaged only about 3,800 spectators a game. Despite its larger number of contests, the winter game had considerably less potential to generate revenue. By the university's own reckoning, however, basketball as well as football turned a profit in the 1924–1925 academic year, whereas its seven remaining teams lost money.[15]

In other ways as well, the big-time athletic programs of the 1920s were strikingly similar to those we observe today. Contemporaneous reports and commentary reveal that college athletics was one of the mostly hotly debated higher-education topics of the day and was also an object of vigorous criticism. It was the subject, for example, of one chapter of a sweeping, observational study of American undergraduate education published in 1928 by the Institute of Social and Religious Research entitled *Undergraduates: A Study of Morale in Twenty-Three American Colleges and Universities.*[16] More exhaustive and famous was the Carnegie Foundation for the Advancement of Teaching report of 1929, *American College Athletics*, a study of athletic programs at more than a hundred colleges and universities that received wide newspaper coverage.[17] Common to both studies was concern over three aspects of college sports: commercialization, the lack of faculty control over athletics, and inattention to the academic missions of universities.

The greatest of these was commercialization, made possible by the financial returns available to successful athletic programs. Sounding this theme in his preface to the Carnegie report, the foundation president, Henry Pritchett, wrote that football

is not a student's game, as it once was. It is a highly organized commercial enterprise. The athletes who take part in it have come up through years of training; they are commanded by professional coaches; little if any personal initiative of ordinary play is left to the player. The great matches are highly profitable enterprises. Sometimes the profits go to finance college sports, sometimes to pay the cost of the sports amphitheater, in some cases the college authorities take a slice of the profits for college buildings.[18]

The problem with the professional coach was not so much his existence as his high salary. The Carnegie report included a survey of 58 large institutions undertaken in the late 1920s which revealed that the average football coach's salary of $86,000 (in 2009 dollars) exceeded that of the average highest-paid full professor on campus by 10%.[19] Other consequences of this commercialization decried by Pritchett were the creation of spectators out of students, the use of players to endorse commercial products, unwarranted influence by alumni and others outside of universities, and the sacrifice of academic objectives. Needless to say, complaints such as these bear an uncanny resemblance to debates about college sports in the 21st century.

Already a popular form of entertainment on the eve of the Depression, college football managed to retain a healthy following through the succeeding decades of rising incomes, expanded educational attainment, and new media. One rough indicator of the game's continued vitality is the growth in the number of games played each year. For one thing, the length of the typical season grew over time. Michigan, for example, played 8 games in 1928, 10 in 1968, and 12 in 2008. In addition, more universities fielded teams. As a result, the total number of college football games increased over time. As shown in Figure 3.1, the number of games showed a relentless, if bumpy, ascent from the earliest days of college football to the outbreak of World War II, with a modest upward trend after the war.

Beneath this growth in aggregate numbers was a ratchet-like mechanism working within each participating university, and the result has been a remarkable constancy in the "brands" associated with big-time college sports. From the early decades of the 20th century, entry into big-time athletics has almost always been a one-way street for institutions aspiring to be national universities. It is the exceptional university that has chosen to walk away once it has entered that realm. We can see this tendency of national universities to remain in the big-time sports business, once in, by looking back at the big-time football powers early in the 20th century.

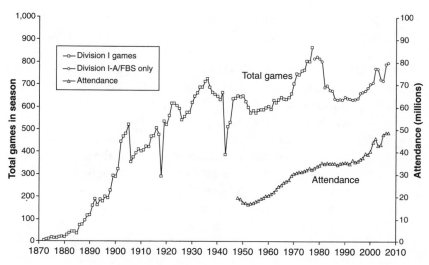

Figure 3.1. The growth of college football: games and attendance.
*Source*: James Howell's College Football Scores, accessed 5/15/09 at http://homepages.
cae.wisc.edu/~dwilson/rsfc/history/howell.

Let us look at the 100 biggest names in college football in 1920 and see what has happened to them since then. How many have continued doing big-time football? To be specific, how many of the top 100 powers of 1920, as measured by their average "power rankings," were also in the top 100 in 2009 as measured by expenditures on athletics?[20] The answer, startling by the standards of consumer products, is the remarkably large number of 60. These are the most familiar names of college football, among them Alabama, Auburn, Florida, Georgia, Georgia Tech, Louisiana State, North Carolina, Southern Methodist, and Virginia in the South; Iowa, Michigan, Nebraska, Notre Dame, Ohio State, Oklahoma, and Wisconsin in the Midwest; and California – Berkeley, Colorado, Oregon, Oregon State, Stanford, Utah, and Washington in the West. One would be hard pressed to find many markets for consumer goods or services in which 60% of today's most successful firms or products had also been among the most successful 90 years before.

Enhancing the fame of these familiar brands are their histories of bat-tle against traditional rivals. Whatever cultural or psychological forces give meaning to being a fan of one of these storied teams, remembered games against bitter rivals must play an important role. How does a Michigan fan describe his or her devotion without eventually uttering the words "Ohio State"? Like the teams themselves, these rivalries have shown remarkable staying power, as illustrated by the stability of football schedules, which for most big-time football programs have changed surprisingly little over the past eight decades. For example, the University of Michigan in 2009 played five of the same teams that were on its schedule in 1929 (fellow Big Ten members Michigan State, Purdue, Iowa, Illinois, and Ohio State). Georgia in 2009 played three teams it had played in 1929, Oklahoma five, and Southern California seven.[21] Similar long-term stability in schedules can be seen in the historical records of most present-day big-time college football programs, and in many cases it extends back to before the late 1920s. Suffice it to say, for most of today's big-time football programs, the patterns of play that had been established by the late 1920s would prove to be very durable.

What of the 40 dropouts from big-time football? Three are, in fact, still in the Football Bowl Subdivision, the most competitive subdivision of the NCAA for football. These include the two oldest service academies, West Point and Annapolis, whose annual football game is one of the storied rivalries in college football, and Utah State. None of these had sufficient athletic expenditures in 2009 to rank among the top 100. Of the remaining 37 institutions that dropped out of the top 100 big-time programs, 28 are private liberal arts colleges or regional universities. All but four continue to field football teams, but at less competitive levels. That leaves only nine national universities that have forsaken big-time football since 1920. These nine constitute the important exceptions to the rule that big-time college football is a one-way street. Seven are elite research universities that joined with Columbia to form the Ivy League in 1954, a conference that decided it would not offer athletic scholarships. Led by Harvard, Yale, and Princeton, these had been among the founding members of big-time college sports in America.

Rather than just scaling back, the other two national universities abandoned big-time football altogether. The University of Chicago dropped football following its 1939 season, and Washington University in St. Louis did so after 1942.[22] The more celebrated of these withdrawals was Chicago's, largely because of the fame of its coach, Alonso Stagg, the success of his teams, and the outspokenness of Chicago's president, Robert Hutchins, in his opposition to football.[23] Even with Hutchins's eloquent attacks on football, however, he did not succeed in getting rid of it until the university's teams had suffered 15 years of mediocre performances, featuring declining attendance, a single winning season, and a disastrous 1939 season, marked by defeats at the hands of Virginia, Harvard, Ohio State, and Michigan by scores of 47–0, 61–0, 61–0, and 85–0, respectively.[24] Chicago's extraordinary president may not have been enough, by himself, to bring an end to football.[25]

Measured in terms of games or attendance, college football grew throughout the 20th century and into the 21st. As a handful of small, regional institutions, and the Ivy League, opted for the less costly levels of competition, the ranks of universities with big-time football were gradually filled by new universities and universities deciding to field teams. Among the prominent additions to the list of big-time football programs after 1920 were those at Duke and the University of Southern California in 1922, UCLA in 1928, Arizona and Arizona State in 1931, Texas Tech in 1932, Miami in 1936, Florida State in 1954, SUNY Buffalo in 1962, Connecticut in 1979, and the University of South Florida in 2000.[26] The steady growth in football attendance occurred in spite of, or perhaps because of, the successive introduction and spread of two new media – radio and television. By 1929, about 10 million American homes had radio sets, and this number doubled by 1934, making it possible for many potential fans to tune into real-time, play-by-play descriptions of games. If some in athletic departments worried that radio might hurt attendance more than it helped, that fear was more pronounced when television came along. The number of TV sets in the country hit the 10 million mark in 1951 and grew rapidly thereafter, adding an average of 5 million sets a year for the next five years.[27] Beginning in 1951 the NCAA strictly controlled the number of televised college football games and signed television contracts giving successive networks the right to broadcast games.

By the middle of the 20th century, big-time college football was firmly established as an iconic feature of popular devotion. This was particularly true for the South and nonmetropolitan Midwest, regions that would not be touched by major league baseball or other professional sports for at least another decade. The popularity of college football in these regions is a legacy of history, geography, and cultural institutions. For a combination of historical reasons, the Northeast never developed the vibrant public universities that dotted the rest of the country. In addition, the concentration of large cities in the Northeast, mid-Atlantic, and upper Midwest made it feasible to have professional football leagues (like professional baseball) in an era of train travel. And the South's allegiance to Jim Crow segregation effectively barred games with the racially integrated rosters that existed in professional football after 1946 and major league baseball after 1947.[28] The 11 states of the former Confederacy, which was home to 23% of the country's population in 1947, had no professional football team. Thus the major potential rival to college football for the attention of football fans, professional football, remained concentrated in the Northeast and Midwest.

The absence of professional teams in the South was amply remedied by college football. The South's devotion to football was so fervent that it even challenged the otherwise unassailable institution of segregation itself. Just a year and a half after the Supreme Court's earth-shaking *Brown v. Board of Education* decision striking down segregated schools, the Georgia Tech football team accepted an invitation to play in the 1956 Sugar Bowl in New Orleans. But the opposing team, Pittsburgh, had a black player. Georgia governor Marvin Griffin, warning that "[t]he South stands at Armageddon," moved to repel this affront to the traditions of segregation by urging the state's board of regents to forbid Georgia Tech from playing the game. But to this, the all-white student body rose up in protest, marching on the governor's mansion and burning Griffin in effigy.[29] The Georgia Tech team played the game. Six years later, when the University of Mississippi erupted in violence over the federal government's effort to enroll James Meredith and Governor Ross Barnett threatened to close the university, football fans were reluctant to pay this price if it meant disrupting the football season. This sentiment was expressed by a white Ole Miss student whose words were captured in the *Eyes on the Prize* documentary about that event:

REPORTER: Do you think if the school had to be closed it would affect the Rebels, the football team?
STUDENT: Yes, that, that's one bad thing about it. Now all the students are really looking forward to all the football games. And if the school is closed, we want the ball games played anyway.[30]

College football grew in popularity in and out of the South. As shown in Figure 3.1, football in the postwar period experienced sustained growth, with total attendance increasing by 50% between 1947 and 1970, and then again by another 50% by 2006. This rate of growth far surpassed that of the population at large. Over the second half of the 20th century, while the American population increased by almost 90%, attendance at college football games more than doubled. Students, whose numbers increased more rapidly than the population as a whole, were no more than a fraction of these paying customers.[31] College football was not primarily an activity for students, nor had it been at any time during the 20th century. It was mass entertainment.

Television, like radio before it, contributed to the renown of college teams, rather than siphoning off potential spectators. It also caused spectacular increases in the commercial value of college sports, as illustrated by the market value of broadcasting the Orange Bowl, all expressed in 2010 dollars. In 1936 the committee that ran the bowl actually had to pay CBS almost $8,000 to broadcast the game on radio. By 1969 NBC was paying the bowl committee for the rights to televise it, some $2.9 million. But by 2011 the price had skyrocketed to $41 million, part of ESPN's $125 million contract to televise three of the top bowl games.[32]

The new medium's potential to create a national market for college football received a tremendous boost in 1984 when the Supreme Court ended the NCAA's control over the broadcasting of college football games. In *National Collegiate Athletic Association v. Board of Regents of the University of Oklahoma*, the Court ruled that the NCAA was engaged in an illegal monopoly.[33] This decision was shortly followed by another momentous development, the advent of cable television. Together, these two forces opened a floodgate of televised college football games. To get a sense of the change in TV coverage, compare the list of games televised in the Chicago TV market on the first weekend in October in the years 1983, 1990, and 2008, as shown in Table 3.1. On that weekend in 1983, only 2 games were televised. Twenty-five years later, 29 games were on TV.

The other major revenue sport, basketball, was slower to develop, but with the help of television and a very different approach by the NCAA, it gained a prominence all its own. Before the Depression, the relatively small arenas for basketball limited the sport's popularity as a form of mass entertainment, although a few regional hotbeds of interest existed in such places as New York City, Indiana, and North Carolina. In 1938 six teams were invited to play in New York's Madison Square Garden for the first National Invitational Tournament, and the next year the NCAA started a tournament of its own.[34]

Invitational tournaments and the annual NCAA championship generated growing fan interest, but also a few high-profile point-shaving scandals. In 1951, a case involving bookies and bribes to college basketball players broke open in New York. Players from City College of New York, Long Island University, Brooklyn College, University of Kentucky, Bradley University, the University of Toledo, and Manhattan College were implicated in game-fixing schemes.[35] Among those implicated in the scandal were two all-Americans from Kentucky and their celebrated coach, Adolph Rupp.[36]

But interest in college basketball grew nonetheless, spurred by television. Data available beginning in 1976 show that attendance grew at an average rate of more than 20% every decade.[37] Because the NCAA had never controlled which games could be televised, many more regular-season basketball games were on TV than was the case in football.[38] But the thing that turned college basketball into a major commercial entertainment success

Table 3.1. *Televised football games, Chicago metropolitan area, first Saturday in October, 1983, 1990, and 2009*

| 1983 – Oct. 8 | | 1990 – Oct. 6 | | 2009 – Oct. 3 | |
|---|---|---|---|---|---|
| Game | Network | Game | Network | Game | Network |
| Alabama–Penn State | CBS | Grambling–Alabama A&M | BET | Michigan–Michigan State | BTN |
| Notre Dame–South Carolina | WGN | Kentucky–Mississippi | TBS | Wisconsin–Minnesota | ESPN |
| | | Eastern Michigan–Toledo | Sports Channel | Arkansas State–Iowa | ESPN2 |
| | | Indiana–Northwestern | Sports Channel | Clemson–Maryland | ESPNU |
| | | LSU–Florida | ESPN | Toledo–Ball State | WPWR |
| | | Washington State–USC | ESPN | East Carolina–Marshall | CBS-CS |
| | | Lafayette–Columbia | ESPN | Pennsylvania–Dartmouth | Versus |
| | | Stanford–Notre Dame | Sports Channel | Sacred Heart–Central Connecticut St. | FCS-Atlantic |
| | | Florida State–Miami | CBS | Iowa State–Kansas State | FCS-Central |
| | | Illinois–Ohio State | ABC | Penn State–Illinois | ABC |
| | | | | Western Michigan–Northern Illinois | CSN |
| | | | | Washington–Notre Dame | NBC |
| | | | | Florida State–Boston College | ESPN |
| | | | | North Carolina State–Wake Forest | ESPNU |
| | | | | LSU–Georgia | CBS |
| | | | | New Mexico–Texas Tech | FCS-Pacific |
| | | | | Air Force–Navy | CBS-CS |
| | | | | William & Mary–Villanova | Versus |
| | | | | South Dakota–North Dakota | FCS-Atlantic |

| | |
|---|---|
| Ohio State–Indiana | BTN |
| Southern Illinois–Western Illinois | FCS-Central |
| Mississippi–Vanderbilt | ESPNU |
| Oregon State–Arizona State | Versus |
| South Carolina State–South Carolina | ESPN Classic |
| Arkansas–Texas A&M | ESPN2 |
| Tulsa–Rice | CBS-CS |
| Auburn–Tennessee | ESPN |
| Oklahoma–Miami | ABC |
| Colorado State–Idaho | ESPNU |

*Note:* Local Chicago TV stations (and their corresponding networks) were WBBM (CBS), WMAQ (NBC), WLS (ABC).

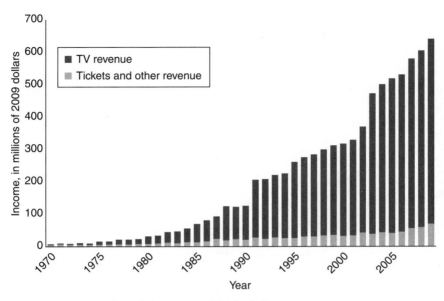

Figure 3.2. Revenue from the NCAA men's basketball tournament, 1970–2010.
*Source*: NCAA, *Official 2010 NCAA Men's Final Four Records Book* (Indianapolis: NCAA,
February 2010), p. 79, http://www.ncaa.org/wps/portal/ncaahome?WCM_GLOBAL_
CONTEXT=/ncaa/ncaa/sports+and+championship/general+information/stats/
m+basketball/final4rbindex.html, 6/15/10.

was the NCAA's decision to stage, and later expand, its own annual men's
championship tournament. Fueled by television, this tournament exploded
in popularity and profitability. Figure 3.2 shows the rapid growth in the
NCAA's income from the tournament and the dominant role of television
in generating that income.

Overseeing the growth of both of these sports was the NCAA, the coalition of universities originally formed following Theodore Roosevelt's
demand that something be done about football injuries. Like the various
athletic conferences, the NCAA's primary objective has been to regulate
competition. Just as competitors in many other realms often seek to reg-
ularize the rules of engagement, colleges from the earliest days of intercollegiate play did the same, initially through conferences and associations
made up of similar institutions. They sought uniform rules of play both
on and off the field, thus making competition more predictable. From the
beginning, institutions worried about who could play on teams and how
those players might be compensated. These concerns remained and led to
the highly detailed body of regulations that govern recruiting and academic
eligibility today. No development was more important than the acceptance,

in 1956, after bitter debate, of the principle that scholarships could be based simply on athletic ability rather than financial need.[39]

As this brief history illustrates, big-time sports, in both size and reputation, grew up firmly attached to American colleges and universities, as they emerged from the 19th century. Some scholars have argued that these institutions were driven by their urgent need to compete for recognition and support, latching onto athletics when they realized it could be one crucial instrument for institutional survival.[40] Whether or not this explanation is exactly right, it is abundantly clear that universities gradually took control over athletic activities that had initially been run by their students. By the beginning of the 20th century, it had become not at all unusual for universities to sponsor athletic teams that took part in contests that attracted large crowds and regular newspaper coverage.

This commercial sports function remained a firmly rooted and remarkably stable aspect of American universities even as those universities grew in size, fueled by the steady rise in the country's population and rate of college attendance. Thanks to generous state support, rising affluence, and the GI Bill, the share of 18- to 24-year-olds with some college education increased from less than 5% in 1920 to more than a third in 2000.[41] This democratization of higher education showed itself in burgeoning enrollments at flagship and other public universities. The University of Michigan, for example, grew from less than 13,000 students in 1925 to 38,000 in 2000.[42] For many of these growing universities, big-time sports became a way to entertain students and appeal to wider constituencies. It remained something of a gift horse inherited from the past. Regardless of the precise genesis of this connection between universities and spectator sports, every university with an established reputation for fielding competitive teams implicitly faced the following prospect on an annual basis: "Among your historical legacies is a tradition of intercollegiate athletic competition. For better or worse, you are in part defined by this tradition. Use it or lose it." Needless to say, most universities that had inherited such legacies chose to stay in the game.

## THE CELEBRITY OF BIG-TIME COLLEGE ATHLETICS

Whether viewed as a commercial product or a cultural phenomenon, college sports has been and continues to be for many Americans one of the best-known aspects of higher education. It is worth spending a few pages backing up such an assertion, if for no other reason than that universities mention athletics so sparingly when describing what they do. To do that,

I have sought out some objective measures of prominence, in the form of newspaper and television coverage and recognition, as measured by Web presence.

## Newspaper Coverage of Universities

As readers of most daily newspapers will know, sports coverage has always been a large part of their content. With the exception of a few national or international dailies that cover business exclusively, the daily newspaper typically has a separate section devoted to sports, a palpable recognition of the widespread interest in sports among readers. Other activities of universities, ranging from gifts for new buildings to student protests, are covered, if at all, in the remaining sections of newspapers. Suppose you picked the nation's most self-consciously authoritative newspaper, the *New York Times*, and examined the coverage given to universities. How would the amount of coverage devoted to sports compare with that given to all other aspects and activities of universities? The answer to this question would provide one ready measure of the comparative prominence of athletics among the various things that go on in universities. Using the *Times*, as opposed to other newspapers, offers the advantages of its national coverage, its unparalleled coverage of serious news, and its availability in a searchable, electronic form.

With the help of student research assistants, I searched the historical records of the *New York Times* to find stories published about each of 74 American universities during the calendar year 2007, classifying each story as either about sports or about any other subject. Among these universities were 58 with big-time football and basketball programs and 16 others with highly ranked academic programs. The first group included all members of the five largest football conferences as they existed in 2010 (Atlantic Coast, Southeastern, Big Ten, Big 12, and Pacific Coast) plus Notre Dame. The second consisted of all remaining universities listed in the *U.S. News and World Report*'s top 26 national universities in 2007, only one of which (Georgetown) had a big-time basketball program.[43] Only stories about university activities or about people currently associated with universities were included in the comparison; stories merely about people who had once attended or been employed by a university that were otherwise not about current university events or organizations were not included. For all but a small handful of these 74 universities, the number of sports stories greatly outnumbered the number of non-sports stories. For the 58 universities with big-time football programs, the *Times* ran a total of 523 sports-related stories in 2007, compared with only 78 stories not related to sports. Non-sports stories thus made up only 13% of the total.[44] By contrast, non-sports stories outnumbered sports stories for our group of 16 universities without a big-time athletic program – a group that included MIT, Cal Tech, Chicago, and all eight Ivy League institutions – by a count of 105 to 65, giving them a 62% share. These simple calculations using articles from a single national newspaper confirm in numbers what casual observation suggested to begin with – that among universities with big-time athletics programs, journalistic attention to universities' athletics programs far exceeds that devoted to all other university functions and events.

Nor is there anything new about this preponderance of attention given to college sports. For the sake of historical perspective, I undertook searches with the same list of universities going back 40 and 80 years, to 1967 and 1927, as shown in Figure 3.3. Although the total number of articles related to these universities differed by year, the percentage breakdowns were remarkably similar. For the 58 current big-time sports universities, non-sports stories made up 15% of all stories in 1967, compared with 39% for the comparison group of 16 universities. In 1927 sports stories exceeded non-sports stories in the *Times* by even more than in the other two sample years. In that year, non-sports stories were only 8% of all stories about the 58 institutions with current big-time programs, compared with 31% for the comparison group.[45]

## Television Exposure

To an extent unimagined in 1927 and certainly unanticipated in 1967, college sports today by way of television receives media exposure that allows games to be witnessed routinely by large portions of the American population. There is no better indicator of the extent of this phenomenon than the extraordinary coverage devoted to any season of big-time men's college basketball. One need only count the number of televised games, which is feasible since almost all big-time programs post this information on the Web. Counting games played in both the regular season and in tournaments, the basketball teams in the five established conferences, plus Notre Dame, appeared on television an astounding 27 times on average during the 2007–2008 year. Of this figure, half consisted of nationally televised games, either on national broadcast networks like CBS and ABC or on national cable networks like ESPN. The other half was made up of regionally televised games. Included in the nationally televised half was the NCAA national championship tournament, broadcast exclusively on

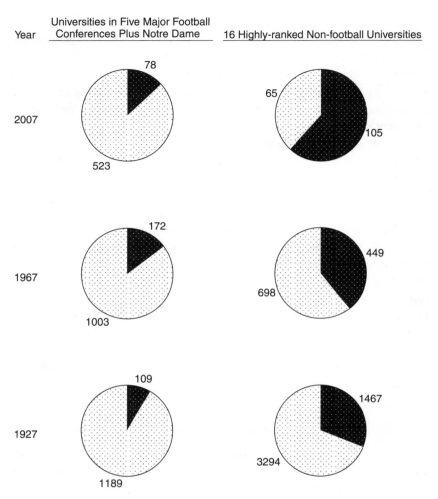

Figure 3.3. Sports and non-sports stories in the *New York Times*, selected universities, 2007, 1967, and 1927 (sports in light; non-sports in dark). See text for list of conferences. Highly ranked universities listed in *US News & World Report* top 26 in 2007.
*Source*: *New York Times*, 2007, 1967, and 1927, accessed via Proquest on 6/9/08.

CBS. A few very visible teams became fixtures on national TV during the winter months. During the 2007–2008 season, for example, North Carolina appeared on national TV 34 times, Duke 31, Kansas 26, and UCLA and Michigan State 21 each. Such extraordinary visibility for college basketball would have been unthinkable without cable TV, which accounted for 87% of the nationally televised games for these teams.[46]

This extraordinary amount of coverage means that many, many viewers can see these games on television. Nielsen ratings provide an estimate of the number of TV viewers. To illustrate, consider the number of estimated viewers for just three basketball games that were shown during the week of January 21–27, 2008: Tennessee–Kentucky (January 22), 1.8 million viewers; Duke–Virginia Tech (January 24), 1.3 million viewers; and Wisconsin–Purdue (January 26), 1.2 million viewers.[47] Although viewership figures such as these are nowhere close to those of the top-rated shows on television, the number of viewers far surpasses the coverage of virtually any university event outside the realm of sports.[48]

To a lesser extent, college football also enjoys extensive television coverage. On a typical midseason weekend, the number of televised football games is comparable to that for basketball, but there are simply more basketball games played, including many on weekday evenings. Television coverage for both sports expanded markedly in the 1980s as a direct consequence of the rise of cable TV, epitomized best by the advent and growth of the cable sports network ESPN in 1979. By one calculation, the total number of hours of nationally televised sports rose from 787 in 1970, when only the three national TV networks offered such coverage, to some 7,300 in 1989, by which time 10 cable channels had begun showing live sporting events.[49]

## Coaches versus University Presidents

While it is impossible to know for certain whether this expanded TV coverage was the cause or the result of the popularity of these college sports, it certainly provided a ready vehicle for that popularity. In the process, it has helped to feed the fame of big-time collegiate coaches. Yet it has long been a fact of U.S. higher education that football and basketball coaches in high-profile athletic programs are often a university's best-known employees. In the opinion of one observer in 1926, the coach had become the "Colossus of the Campus," whose dignity and salary exceeded the university president's.[50] Five decades later, Ohio State president Harold Enarson was said to resent the fact that his football coach, Woody Hayes, routinely garnered greater public acclaim and attracted larger audiences at speaking engagements.[51]

To measure the relative notoriety of coaches and presidents, I sought a contemporary yardstick – the number of hits estimated by Google. Since each hit corresponds to an article, blog, or document naming a person, this can be used as a rough measure of notoriety.[52] The results of this exercise confirmed the suspicion that coaches are usually better known than their university presidents, at least as measured by appearances on the Web. Among the 58 universities with big-time football programs, football coaches recorded more than seven hits for every one recorded by the corresponding university presidents. In only 2 universities out of the 58 did the president have more hits than the football coach, though in basketball, presidents outscored the coach seven times. Basketball coaches weren't as well known as football coaches, but they still easily beat out university presidents as well, racking up more than three and a half hits for every one for the university's president. As one might expect, however, presidents fared much better indeed among the elite institutions without big-time football. In this group, football coaches had fewer than a fifth of the number recorded for presidents, while basketball coaches matched presidents almost exactly.[53] Among the 58 universities with big-time football programs, though, it was the exceptional president who did not share the fate of Harold Enarson, to be overshadowed in popular notoriety by the university's football and basketball coach.

## THE POWER OF "MARCH MADNESS"

There is no better illustration of the popularity of big-time college athletics than the NCAA's annual Division I men's basketball tournament. Known widely by its trademarked name, "March Madness," it is a single-elimination tournament extending over two and a half weeks.[54] Since expanding to its current format in 1985, the tournament has achieved the status of most-discussed topic around office water coolers during the tournament's first week each year. In 2008 it accounted for some 65 hours of broadcast television in most TV markets. In addition, fans across the country took advantage of live video streaming of tournament games provided by CBS, slowing some company computer systems to a crawl. The network reported that 4.8 million unique visitors to its Web page spent a total of 4.3 million hours viewing videos of tournament games.[55]

To see just how large an effect this event really has, I looked for a way to go beyond anecdote and aggregate estimate to measure the effect on actual work. I obtained data on the use of a widely used research tool, JSTOR – a Web-based archive containing digital versions of more than a thousand academic journals from a wide variety of fields. It allows users to view or download pdf copies of journal articles.[56] I obtained permission from 78 research libraries across the country to collect data on the number of articles that users looked at each day using this digital archive. This measure reflects course-related work and other research that is done by students, faculty, research staff, and other library patrons. Of these libraries, 67 were part of universities belonging to the NCAA's Division I, 8 were in universities not in Division I, and 3 were nonuniversity research libraries. For all of these libraries, data were collected on the number of articles viewed each day for the months of February, March, and April in the years 2006, 2007, and 2008.[57] The NCAA basketball tournament occurs during this three-month period.

This tournament, and the media attention accompanying it, could influence the amount and intensity of work in two ways. Let us call these the *media event effect* and the *partisan fan effect*. The media event effect refers to the tournament's influence on workplaces across the country, including universities. This is the phenomenon underlying estimates of time lost by businesses, but to my knowledge it has never been directly measured. What follows is a measure of how big this effect is for the work done in research libraries. Those who work in these libraries are not representative of the American workplace, of course, in part because college students make up a sizable share of the sample being studied. But it is noteworthy that this media event effect is similar between those libraries associated with universities with Division I basketball teams and those libraries with no such connection. The other effect of the tournament, the partisan fan effect, is specific to those universities with a team in the tournament. That effect is discussed in Chapter 7, along with other manifestations of partisan fan behavior.

To see whether the NCAA tournament really does have an effect on work patterns, I examined JSTOR usage in research libraries before, during, and after the tournament. The data used here on the number of articles viewed are ideal for answering this question. In the typical American university, library patrons use the JSTOR site hundreds of times a day, both in library buildings and by remote access from their offices or homes. For the 78 libraries in the sample, the number of articles viewed over the months of February to April averaged 1,037 a day, but for several of the largest university libraries the daily average was more than 2,000. Daily volume tends to vary markedly over the course of a typical week, with Mondays, Tuesdays, and Wednesdays being some 50% higher than the average for the other four days of the week. The lowest rate of use, not surprisingly, usually occurs on Saturdays. Two other regularities are evident at university libraries: a general increase in usage over the course of a semester or quarter and a large dip in volume during spring break or before a quarter break. These breaks are times when undergraduate students are away from campus or taking final exams. Weeks occurring during these breaks were eliminated from the sample. To prevent the largest universities from dominating the findings, daily usage data were converted to comparable units, namely, a ratio to that institution's average number of articles viewed.[58]

The media event effect can be readily discerned by tracing the number of articles viewed over the three-month period surrounding and including the

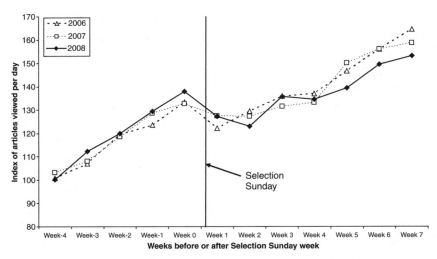

Figure 3.4. The drop in articles viewed in JSTOR after Selection Sunday, 78 research libraries.

tournament. Figure 3.4 does this by showing the average index for Mondays through Wednesdays in each week over the three-month period. Using just these three weekdays makes the general time trends clear, undisturbed by the large variation within each week. In addition, with the exception of each year's championship game, no tournament games were played on these three days of the week.[59]

The day that kicks off this highly orchestrated media event each year is "Selection Sunday," when a committee selects the teams that will be invited and inserts them into the brackets determining where, when, and against whom they will play in that coming week. The publication of these brackets, marked by a flurry of speculation and commentary in the media, has become the occasion for what is popularly believed to be the most intense period of wagering on sporting events in America. The three days between Selection Sunday and the beginning of play on the Thursday of that week are the traditional time for most of this betting, certainly the betting that goes on in the thousands of informal office pools around the country. On the graph, Selection Sunday is indicated by a vertical line. The weeks before and after that day are noted on the horizontal axis with the corresponding negative and positive numbers. Separate lines are shown for each of the three years of data I studied, 2006, 2007, and 2008.

Except for the week immediately following Selection Sunday, the lines for all three years indicate fairly steady increases in JSTOR usage over the three-month period. Excluding that week, average usage increased by an average of 5.4% a week, a secular trend that strongly suggests the effect of looming end-of-semester due dates. But the striking characteristic of both these lines is the dip that occurred in the week immediately following Selection Sunday. This decline averaged 6.7%, and it is all the more striking considering the overall upward trend in usage. Further statistical analysis also indicated an almost 5% reduction in articles viewed during the first two days of the tournament. These declines in research activity are quantitative evidence of the NCAA tournament's media event effect. Similar patterns were evident in libraries attached to universities in Division I and those without this connection.[60]

Unless there existed other, unmeasured factors at work, the record of JSTOR usage shown in Figure 3.4 implies that the NCAA tournament had a measurable influence on the pattern of work in research libraries. This is not to say that the aggregate amount of work was less than it would have been if the tournament did not exist, but only that work patterns have evolved to accommodate the interest in the tournament. Given the copious anecdotal evidence that the tournament attracts widespread attention, especially during the days immediately after the tournament brackets are announced, it would not be surprising to find similar patterns in workplaces outside of universities or research libraries. This is the media event effect, and it reflects the power of the demand for the entertainment provided by this form of big-time college athletics.

## WORTH TAKING SERIOUSLY

This chapter provides hard data to back up one of the central arguments of this book, that entertainment, in the form of big-time college athletics, constitutes a large activity of some American universities. And this has been the case for at least a century. Long before the commercial introduction of the radio, not to mention that of television or the proliferation of cable channels, college football and basketball enjoyed a large following in the United States. This much can be readily surmised from attendance records and the copious coverage of college sports in newspapers. Using measurable dimensions of size and growth to supplement the informal and anecdotal impressions of the widespread popularity of college athletics, the evidence presented here shows that many people attend games and many more watch games on television. In fact, for a university participating in big-time sports, it is likely that more hours are spent by fans attending games or viewing them on TV than are spent by its students, faculty, and staff engaged in the traditional tasks of research, teaching, learning, and service.[61] As Chapter 4 will show, these attendance and viewing figures also embody the potential to generate large revenues. If measured by the dollar value of ticket sales and TV contracts, college basketball and football generate more revenue than major league baseball and about half as much as professional football.

Not only has big-time college sports been hugely popular for at least a century, its commercial footprint appears to be growing. As we have seen in this chapter, attendance at college football games has risen steadily since World War II. Beginning in 1949 at 17.5 million spectators a year, this total attendance grew at an average rate of 1.8% a year, reaching almost 50 million by 2008. Attendance for basketball also grew. Between 1976 and 2009, attendance at Division I games increased at an average rate of 1.7% a year.[62] Boosting the visibility as well as the revenue potential of big-time football and basketball has been television. And rising revenues have been accompanied, not surprisingly, by rising expenditures.

Some commentators have worried aloud about a spending "arms race" in big-time athletics, wherein universities attempt to gain advantage relative to competitors by spending money on facilities, coaches, and recruiting. If all competing universities engage in similar spending, the argument goes, these expenditures will end up accomplishing little except to squander resources that would be better used elsewhere. If there is an "arms race" in spending in big-time college sports, a necessary condition would be that spending for athletics is increasing faster than some comparable metric, such as total spending by the same universities. As explained in Chapter 5, this is the case. Average expenditures for FBS universities between 1989 and 2003, measured in constant FY2006 dollars, rose at an annual rate of 4.5%, compared with just 2.7% for total spending. This comparison suggests that spending on athletics by the top tier of college athletics programs has been rising at a faster rate than both inflation and the growth in total university spending.

Big-time college sports competition looms large in the consciousness of vast swaths of the American public. As a result, many of the nation's largest universities are much better known for their football and basketball programs than for anything else they do. This does not mean that entertainment is more important than the traditional functions of teaching, research, and service. But it does show that athletics is more than a mere footnote in the work of American universities. This actual importance also stands in sharp contrast to the reluctance of universities, in their official statements of purpose, to acknowledge that athletics has any important role in what they do or value.

# PART TWO

# THE USES OF BIG-TIME COLLEGE SPORTS

# FOUR

# Consumer Good, Mass Obsession

Speaking about that other version of football, the one we Americans call soccer, famed Liverpool manager Bill Shankley once remarked, "Football's not a matter of life and death ... it's more important than that." This sentiment will be familiar to many Americans, those who make up the truest of the true fans of American college football and basketball teams. From the Nebraska supporter decked out in red from head to toe on a football Saturday to the East Lansing homeowner whose flagpole flies a green flag emblazoned with a white "S," the most ardent followers of college teams constitute a class of consumers whose devotion to a brand makes them more zealots than mere customers. For them, demand is emphatically brand specific: the commodity is not simply college basketball; it is UCLA basketball, or Tennessee basketball. Like wild blackberries, this institution-specific devotion is out there, firmly rooted, ready for the picking. It was there before the current university leaders arrived, and it will be there after they leave office. It is a hearty perennial, requiring little maintenance. Each university with a history of competitive play can call upon this crop of fan devotion. Without this hearty consumer demand and the commercial value it creates, there would be no big-time college sports.

Not all the spectators and viewers of college games fall into this category of intensity, of course. For some consumers, a college game is merely a game, just one of many possible forms of commercial entertainment that can be enjoyed. Taken together, consumers of various degrees of intensity make up the commercial demand for these college sports. To the TV network that will broadcast it, a college football or basketball game is a marketable commodity. Having purchased the right to broadcast the game, the network hopes to make money by selling time slots to companies that will advertise their own products at various points during the game. There is also money to be made by a university, by selling tickets to spectators, selling the rights to broadcast games, and selling rights to use the university trademarks on a host of consumer items. These sources of revenue, and several others, exist solely because of the strong and widespread demand that exists among Americans for this particular form of entertainment.

Where does this demand come from? Is it "rational"? Does it have social value? Economists will regard the first two of these questions as beside the point, if not unknowable, preferring instead to focus on the act of consuming rather than the motivations that underlie the behavior. Surprisingly, they have something to say about the third question, and I will return to this topic at the end of this chapter. There is no aspect of college athletics more fascinating – or bizarre – than this demand. This chapter looks at big-time college sports as a consumer product, one whose tremendous commercial potential depends on a deep-seated demand that is as colorful as it is hard to explain. To do justice to this topic, it begins by pointing out some of the most unusual aspects of demand. It then describes the demand in more conventional terms, asking who the biggest consumers are. Next it describes the distinctive aspects of the industrial organization of the suppliers in this market, noting in particular the similarities of the NCAA to a textbook monopoly. It then describes how the product's commercial value is exploited through advertising and concludes by reflecting on the social value of the demand for big-time college sports.

## THE KOOKINESS FACTOR

There is a fact about the demand for big-time college athletics that should be acknowledged at the outset, before we undertake any analytical discussion of consumer demand or market structure. The fact: much of what surrounds the demand for college sports is, by any standard, unusual, to say the least. Some of it is larger than life. Some of it is downright weird. And all of it is a by-product of an activity sponsored by universities. The "consumers" of this "product" scream, chant, cry, and paint their faces. Sometimes they do this in stadiums, sometimes in front of television sets. They festoon their cars, trucks, and mailboxes with team emblems. They bedeck themselves in school colors. But what sets this form of consumer demand apart goes beyond such visible markers. Its truly distinctive aspects are its intensity and the degree to which its accustomed behaviors depart from everyday life.

No description of big-time college athletics would be complete without a consideration of the customers' behavior and the larger spectacle that surrounds this unusual form of consumption. In his 1976 book, *Sports in America*, James Michener marveled at the scene he encountered when he attended a Nebraska football game: "[A]n entire state went bananas over football. Ranchers rode in from three hundred miles away, dressed all in red, they and their wives, and they painted the town the same color. At two in the afternoon on a Saturday the stadium was a pulsating red mass."[1] Some fans extended the red theme beyond clothing to include red carpeting and wallpaper at home. In something of an update to Michener, Warren St. John's *Rammer Jammer Yellow Hammer* describes college football mania from the perspective of fans who fill scores of recreational vehicles to follow the University of Alabama's team across the Southeast over the course of a season.[2] Even for those not devoted enough to spend most of each week traveling to the games, the spectacle that is college football goes far beyond the game, or the day of the game.

Two features that seem especially worth noting are the behavior of spectators and the ritualistic aspects of the contests themselves. Behavior that would be judged bizarre at best in the everyday world is accepted at a big-time college sports event without the batting of an eye. For many, standards of polite behavior are checked at the entrance gate to the stadium or arena, just as they are in most spectator sports, amateur or professional, all over the world. It is rare to observe anywhere in daily life adults by the hundreds hurling insults in collective displays of disparagement toward fellow citizens.[3] One scholarly study dryly acknowledged the tacit acceptance of such behavior, noting that fighting and throwing objects onto the court at basketball games was unusual behavior, whereas "'[b]ooing' was not taken into account because it is thought to be a common and socially acceptable form of displaying disapproval, particularly at collegiate or professional basketball games."[4]

But the collegiate version of spectator sports adds to these accepted forms of disparagement an aspect of crowd behavior not common elsewhere: large collections of people chanting and gesturing in unison. When a basketball player for the visiting team misses a shot without touching the rim of the goal, the chant of "air ball" erupts spontaneously in arenas from coast to coast.[5] And supporters of the home team at college games know the team's cheers and do not need the cheerleaders to show them how and when to raise their arms in unison to make the traditional gestures of support. Such crowd behavior at big-time college sporting events is so common that it rarely merits the slightest comment. But it is seen virtually no place else, except in religious observances, military formations, or film clips of totalitarian mass rallies.

The other distinctive but unremarkable aspect of spectator sports that applies fully to big-time college contests is their ritualistic character. Following patterns repeated game after game, season after season, the teams enter the field or court to warm up before the contest. The captains meet for the toss of a coin, or the coaches shake hands in ways that vary only imperceptibly from game to game or year to year. Spectators are directed to stand for the national anthem. The public address system carries standard announcements. Time-outs, penalties, and scores follow predictable patterns, as do post-game actions by players and coaches. And, as already noted, the behavior of fans follows traditions too, such as wearing team colors, standing during all or part of the contest, or making certain arm motions simultaneously at certain points in the game or during the playing of the national anthem.[6]

Some of these fans are most aptly described by the word from which the common term was originally derived: fanatic. In the terminology of economics, these consumers exhibit extreme brand loyalty. Psychologists describe them as heavily identified with a particular team or university and have shown that the self-esteem of these ardent fans can be affected by their team's success in competition. To an extent that goes beyond that of ordinary spectators, these intense fans show high levels of psychological arousal during games.[7] When watching their favorite team play on television, such die-hard fans are more likely than other viewers to feel nervous as the game progresses, shout out during the game in response to the action, and get angry or feel happy according to how well their team plays.[8] In contrast, less invested followers have been observed to "bask in the reflected glory" of their team's success, while shying away when their team loses. In experiments at several universities with big-time football programs, students were more likely after a team victory to wear apparel with the team emblem or use the word "we" when discussing their team than they were after a loss.[9] Such fickleness is not in the nature of die-hard fans, who tend to rise or fall along with their team's fortunes on the playing field, their self-esteem and self-confidence falling when their team loses.[10]

The loyalty these fans exhibit goes well beyond the affection often seen for such iconic brands as Harley-Davidson, John Deere, and Coca-Cola. To an extent rarely observed in most consumer markets, fans of college teams identify closely with an institution, that is, with the firm that produces the particular brand of the commodity they consume. To apply the marketing term "brand" to an esteemed college or university might once have seemed arresting, if not disrespectful, but its application in higher education today has become commonplace in light of its widespread use in many applications.[11] Universities are seen as having particular brand names in the college sports market. Some of the best known, like Notre Dame and the University of Michigan, can be thought of as the Coke and Pepsi, the Colgate and Crest of their markets. As household product brands have trademarks, so too do college sports brands, in their mascots, school colors, and distinctive uniforms (e.g., the gold helmets for Notre Dame and the blue and maize "wing" design for Michigan helmets).[12] Brand loyalty in college sports means that many consumers will follow the teams of exactly one institution, forsaking all others, they will wear clothing bearing the name of their college or university, and some of them will adorn their automobiles and front yards with emblems of that institution. Entire books are written in an attempt to capture this loyalty.[13] What is its source? The most obvious route to affiliation is past attendance, and alumni are indeed the quintessential loyal customers. But for many fans, lifelong bonds of devotion to a team began early in life, often under the influence of a close family member.[14] That loyalties for a college team formed in childhood might endure throughout one's life is consistent with a recent study showing that individuals' preferences for consumer goods are strongly influenced by patterns common to their state of birth and tend to persist through life.[15] A college degree is by no means a requirement for being the fan of a college team. As unremarkable as this fact might seem, it is one major reason it is important not to sweep under the rug the entertainment function of universities that operate big-time sports programs.

No aspect of the mania surrounding college sports provides a better window for observing this demand than the traditional rivalries. In college football, these include such pairings as Michigan–Ohio State, Oklahoma–Texas, Stanford–California, Florida–Georgia, and Auburn–Alabama, to name a few. For example, a *New York Times* reporter described the annual Auburn–Alabama game – dubbed the Iron Bowl – as "a 365-day-a-year topic of heated discussion from Anniston to Zip City, sustaining Alabamans – who have no professional teams to distract them – through swampy springs and stifling summers. The dislike between the two schools defies hyperbole."[16] A book about another football rivalry, between Texas and Oklahoma, describes their annual game in Dallas this way:

Thousands upon thousands of football fans from two states, their brains united into a single altered state, arrive annually at the Cotton Bowl stadium, bellowing exhortations for the spillage of blood. The Texas–Oklahoma game, which now has been conducted one hundred times, and all that surrounds it, has arisen into the manliest of spectacles and is genuinely about as politically incorrect as you can get. You'll find audiences more genteel and reserved at cockfights.[17]

College basketball appears to have fewer of these marquee rivalries than football, but they do exist. A book devoted to one of them, *To Hate Like This Is to Be Happy Forever: A Thoroughly Obsessive, Intermittently Uplifting, and Occasionally Unbiased Account of the Duke–North Carolina Basketball Rivalry*, claims:

The basketball rivalry between Duke and North Carolina has become the greatest rivalry in college athletics, and one of the greatest in all of sports. It is Ali versus Frazier, the Giants versus the Dodgers, the Red Sox versus the Yankees. Hell, it's bigger than that. This is the Democrats versus the Republicans, the Yankees versus the Confederates, Capitalism versus Communism.... This is a rivalry of such intensity, of such hatred, that otherwise reasonable adults attach to it all manner of political-philosophical baggage, some of which might even be true.[18]

This "greatest" claim would no doubt be challenged by many pundits and ordinary fans. Indeed, another distinctive aspect of consumers of college sports is that many of them participate actively in ongoing debates on issues such as which rivalry is the greatest and which is the ascendant team in each. Many college sports fans discuss such topics, along with the outcomes of past games and prospects for upcoming ones, in countless conversations throughout the year. For a portion of these fans, devotion to a team means learning minute details about games, players, coaches, and potential recruits. In the era of AM radio, such devotees often dialed in to ask questions and make comments on evening sports call-in shows. Today they weigh in to the public discourse by posting comments electronically on news and social networking sites like FanNation and on subscription sites like rivals.com, where aficionados can gather detailed intelligence on recruiting prospects for their favorite big-time college program.

Indeed, electronic discussions on popular Web sites provide a vivid picture of the components that make up an ardent fan – devotion to one's team, contempt for its rival, and, often, esoteric knowledge about the history of that rivalry. Here is the modern-day version of college rivalry trash talk, seasoned with the ardent fan's knowledge of arcane trivia. That combination of partisanship and expertise seen in some fans is colorfully illustrated by the back-and-forth postings on a general-interest Web site about the state of Alabama, blog.al.com. Within 24 hours after an article from the *Huntsville Times* was put up on the site in June 2009, more than 100 people had posted a total of 419 messages, many writing late into the night.[19] The article that started the chain of comments expressed the opinion that, despite recently reported "secondary" recruiting violations by Auburn, its football coach should be commended for making the team more competitive. Once begun, the postings ranged far beyond the article's main topic, touching on various aspects of the rivalry, including the Iron Bowl, which for many years was played at Birmingham's Legion Field. A short excerpt from these comments gives a flavor of the conversation.

AU 1 – Questions for bama fans who believe that bama has always gotten the best of AU except for when they were on probation: Was bama on probation during the entire pre-Bryant [Paul "Bear" Bryant, Alabama coach from1958 to 1982] era? Have they been on probation ever since the end of the Bryant era? The reason I ask these questions is that if you will look at the record books, you will see that AU had the advantage during both eras.

AU 2 – I love how 39–33–1 is DOMINATION over 73 games, especially when a vast majority of the games were in Bham [Birmingham] or T-town [Tuscaloosa]. What is the record when we went to a true home and home?

AL 1 – Bham was a neutral field.

AU 3 – the only thing neutral about Legion Field was the 50–50 ticket split. How many "neutral" sites do you know of that has a statue to one of the team's coaches out front? Or that was used as a "home" stadium for most home games except Homecoming, until they finally got their stadium expanded to hold more fans than at Legion Field?

AL 2 – It amazes most intelligent people how these barners [Auburn fans] keep saying Legion Field was a home field for Alabama. The tickets to the game were allocated to both schools equally. So the fans who attended the game (I attended several) were 50–50. There may have been some selling of tickets to make it unequal, but that is the barner's fault. BARNER'S ARE SO STUPID!! Roll Tide!!

AU 4 – I understand that technically Legion Field was a neutral site but by location only. I live in B'ham now and let me tell you, it really is Tuscaloosa east. We are heavily out numbered here.

AL 2 – Lee County [containing Auburn] is a hostile environment for any team but Aubie – it is the same difference. The ticket split is what I am talking about when I say it is neutral. I would sit in the stands and watch half the stadium in orange and blue and the other half in crimson and white. Hostility is a perception anyway.

AU 5 – Guantanamo Bay is a neutral site for terrorists too.

AU 4 – I never attended an IB [Iron Bowl] in the Ham[Birmingham] so I can't really say if the seats were truly split 50–50 or not. Living here I just know how pro Bama this town is and find it hard to believe that it was made fair. But I am not going to argue with someone who said they were at the games. All of that Orange and Blue must have looked so good in that stadium.

AL 2 – I will grant you that Bham is pro Bama (as is most of the state!) ;), and that the mixture of colors for the IB in Bham was great, both schools. I think the main reason for the move away from Bham was the failure of Bham to upgrade Legion Field, the crime rate around the area, and the upgrades that occurred in Tuscaloosa. Bryant Denny [University of Alabama stadium] has an attendance capacity of around 92,000. Legion Field around 80,000 (I think). Financially, it was a good move. ROLL TIDE!!

AU 4 – My wife and I lived in Auburn from 2002 til 2007 and just moved up here to the Ham last year. My wife is from B'ham but you don't realize how sheltered you are when we lived in Auburn during the years preceding last year. After losing, it has been relentless living here in a pro Bama city. And you are right, much of the state is pro Bama much like South Carolina where it is pro Clem"p"son.

AU 3 – "Home field advantage" is more than a ticket split. It's also a state of mind. Remember that for many years LF had artificial turf. Bama had the 'advantage' of practicing and playing on that field many more times per year than Auburn did. That stadium was their second home, they knew the facility as well as they did BDS. Also, the 50/50 ticket split was phased out in the 80's, going to a true "home/away" split in preparation for ending the contract. Part of the reason Legion Field was a "pro Auburn" crowd in the 80's was due to the shift in ticket split, not necessarily to any winning trends on either side. Bo Jackson, a "favorite son" of Birmingham, may have had an impact though. Actually the record for both schools from 1980–89 is almost identical: Bama 85–32–2 (three coaches – Bear, Perkins, Curry) Auburn 86–31–2 (two coaches – Barfield, Dye).

There is no objective measure of intensity when it comes to loyalty of college football fans, of course. But if there were, those who follow Alabama and Auburn would surely rank high. One illustration is the number of fans those teams can attract to their annual spring scrimmage games, practice sessions that have no bearing on any standing. In 2010 Auburn drew an impressive crowd of 63,000 to its scrimmage game. Alabama had an astonishing 91,000. A few fans given to introspection have over the years wondered in print about the origins of their own devotion to a particular team. Two examples of these ruminations have been written by Alabama fans. Warren St. John, whose book followed the RV caravan, recalled his depression, as a college student, after listening to a game in which Auburn defeated his beloved Crimson Tide: "I'd gone off to Columbia to study humanism and the great books – to become a rational being. Crying one's self to sleep over the failure of a group of people you've never met to defeat another group of people against whom you have no legitimate quarrel – in a game you don't play, no less – is *not* rational."[20] *New York Times* editor Howell Raines, like St. John an Alabama native, explored in a 1994 op-ed the depth of his own interest in the Auburn–Alabama rivalry:

I am slam up against my annual realization that I care who wins the Alabama-Auburn football game, and I would like to know why. There are ample reasons not to care. Big-time college football has not been good for higher education, and the sport has too much influence at both of these schools.

At this time of year, I always wonder how many citizens share my secret weakness. Probably we are a vast national tribe: The People Who Ought to Know Better. Yet we drag our solitary sports passions along for years, like dusty baggage from an old love affair.

... Too many athletes are enriching athletic budgets and not getting the education they signed for. That is why it is embarrassing to get caught in the hoopla over this or any big-time game.

That said, I am caught up. Since I do not invest much emotion in professional sports, I am able to study those afflicted with similar passions for, say, the Yankees or the Cowboys with some detachment. The emotional mechanism is the same, no matter whom you pull for. It has to do with childhood imprints. Some people are lucky enough to get imprinted with an interest in the competition between violin soloists or French impressionists.

Others get inculcated with the belief that the annual outcome of an infinitely repeatable recreational game is important. It is part of the conditioning to feel good or bad all year about the outcome of these nonsensical contests. In my case, I think the words 'Crimson Tide' struck my infant ears in a pleasing way. It is all academic now, for the spiny fingers of this silly addiction have long since seized my brain.[21]

One testament to the depth of fan affection is the occasional mention of college teams in published obituaries, such as this example from among the many that appeared in 2010 in the *Birmingham News*: "He was a man of faith who loved his family, his church, his community and the Alabama Crimson Tide."[22]

Although the analysis of individual choices and market demand is the bread and butter of microeconomics, economists normally leave it to others to explain the source of consumers' underlying preferences. There is surely wisdom in this reluctance, but it is hard to resist the temptation at least to make note of a few of the aspects of the demand for college spectator sports that might explain their irresistible hold over many Americans and, by extension, over many American universities.

Everything we know about sports competition suggests that interest in it is global and has been so for much of recorded history. Citing its importance as far back as ancient Greece and Rome, James Michener argued that sports competition fills "a timeless need" in society.[23] To former Yale president A. Bartlett Giamatti, the appeal of sports arises from its similarity to religion, to "the intensity of devotion brought by the true believer, or fan."[24] Although its appeal may be universal, the forms that sports competition has taken over the years have been sharply delineated by country and region. Like preferences for food, the forms that sports have taken have differed markedly by culture, nationality, and period. Thus the particular athletic forms that occupy center stage in competition among institutions of higher education in early-21st-century America – principally, football and basketball – are peculiar to this historical time and this geographic place. One of them, basketball, is played in many countries and even in the Olympics, while the other one is almost wholly unique to the United States. That these

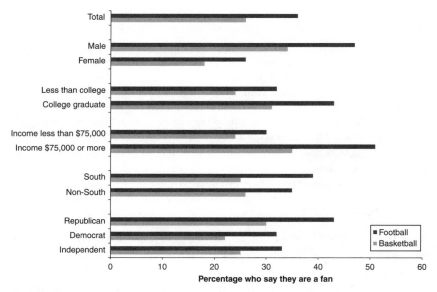

Figure 4.1. Fans of college football and basketball. Percentage of those who say they are a fan.
*Source*: AP/Ipsos Public Affairs Poll, October 16–18, 2007.

sports came to be played in this country by teams associated with colleges and universities is, in Michener's words, simply "a quirk of history," but one whose effect is now unlikely to be undone.[25]

## PATTERNS OF DEMAND FOR COLLEGE SPORTS

Although interest in big-time college athletics is pervasive, it is by no means uniform across the American public. The demographics of demand for college football and basketball show up most clearly along four fault lines: gender, educational attainment, income, and region. Most notably, men make up the majority of college sports fans and the vast majority of the most devoted fans. Typical of the patterns uncovered by national surveys is a 2007 poll that asked adult respondents whether they were fans of college football or basketball. As shown in Figure 4.1, 36% of those polled said they were college football fans, and 26% said so about college basketball.[26] Males were almost twice as likely to be fans as females, a fact that is reflected in the products advertised on televised games. For advertisers, age and gender are often demographic categories that get the greatest attention. For college sports, interest among men is highest on both sides of middle age, among

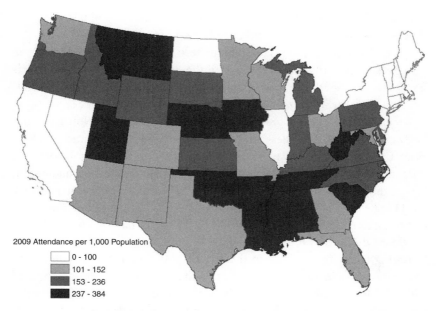

Figure 4.2. Attendance per 1,000 population at NCAA football games, by state, 2009. Omits games at neutral sites.
*Source*: NCAA National College Football Attendance, http://web1.ncaa.org/web_files/ stats/football_records/Attendance/2009.pdf, 8/11/10; U.S. Census Bureau, estimated population, July 1, 2009; http://www.census.gov/popest/states/NST-ann-est.html, 8/11/10.

those 18–34 and those 55 and older.[27] College graduates are more likely to be fans of both sports than are those without degrees, and those near the top of the income scale are more likely to be fans than are the less affluent.

Less obviously, a fourth distinctive demarcation for college spectator sports is region. As explained in the preceding chapter, the South has been a hotbed of enthusiasm for college football, in part because the region lacked professional teams for many years. Much the same can be said about the nonmetropolitan Midwest and West. The resulting regional configuration of demand can be seen in per capita attendance, as shown in the map in Figure 4.2. Six of the 12 states with the highest rates of per capita attendance were in the South. By contrast, states containing many of the nation's biggest urban areas had some of the lowest rates. Although the survey results in Figure 4.1 show a modest 4 percentage point difference between South and non-South, other national polls reveal a larger regional distinction. Especially for football, the South has more than its share of the national demand. A survey taken in 2004 showed that 45% of adults in the South followed college football – this compared with 38% for the Midwest, 28% for the West, and 26% for the Northeast.[28] Another national poll taken in 2009 showed a South/non-South difference of 13 percentage points.[29]

It is easier to describe this regional pattern of demand than to explain it. One possibility is that it has to do with the location of professional sports franchises, though there is admittedly a chicken-and-egg quality to the relationship. The earliest professional football teams, like major league baseball teams, were located predominantly in the urbanized Northeast and Midwest. Not only did these regions contain many of the nation's largest cities, the need to travel by train favored regional concentration. In 1947 the states of the Northeast and Midwest had 54% of the nation's population but 72% of the teams in the two major professional football leagues. In contrast, the 11 states of the former Confederacy, home to 23% of the nation's population, had no professional team (although Miami had one in 1946). But the South did have more than its share of big-time college football teams. Counting teams that ranked in the top 20 of the AP coaches' poll in any year between 1946 and 1948, the South had 38% of these teams, compared with 34% for the Northeast or Midwest.[30] And the Ivy League's departure from big-time athletics probably left behind a pent-up demand for competitive football and basketball that could readily be satisfied by professional teams. Still another factor may have been the South's Jim Crow segregation, which would have been an insurmountable barrier for any racially integrated professional teams.[31]

For college basketball, the demographics of demand are only slightly different, with the regional concentration moving several hundred miles to the north. Based on Nielsen ratings for the 2008 NCAA basketball championship, the five markets having the highest shares of the television viewing audience watching the tournament were, in order, Louisville, Raleigh–Durham, Memphis, Cincinnati, and Columbus, Ohio. The other distinctive feature of the viewing audience for the basketball tournament, according to Nielsen, was its disproportionate share of African Americans.[32]

## SUPPLY AND THE INDUSTRY'S ORGANIZATION

Besides the unusually fierce brand loyalty exhibited by most consumers, noted earlier, three features distinguish the markets for the two college revenue sports. The first is *product differentiation*. In the terminology of antitrust law, the relevant market is "college football," therefore, not simply "football." Although played on nearly identical spaces under nearly identical sets of rules, the college versions of football and basketball are products that are distinct from their professional or high school counterparts. Unlike professional players, college players cannot be paid. Despite the retinue of professional coaches, position coordinators, strength coaches, trainers, team physicians, groundskeepers, videographers, travel coordinators, academic counselors, equipment managers, compliance coordinators, media operatives, fund-raisers, and other business functionaries that surround them, these young men (frequently called "kids" by their coaches) are amateurs. It is not money that motivates them to strive for victory, but presumably something purer. In addition to the youth and amateur status of the players, many sports fans see college competition itself as distinctive from the professional version. Whether this distinctiveness arises from the players' enthusiasm, their life stories, their style of play, or their mistakes, the collegiate versions of football and basketball have retained loyal followings among American sports fans for many decades.

One indication that college and professional sports are viewed as different products is the fact that about as many people are fans of just college or just professional sports as are fans of both versions.[33] In the vernacular of economics, college football and basketball are goods that have close but imperfect substitutes.[34] This trait defines the essence of product differentiation, and the result is that college football and basketball each has its own market, although each is surely affected by the quality of the product offered in the corresponding professional market. Sports commentators have opined that the relative attractiveness of college basketball has been harmed in recent years by the departure of many college stars to the National Basketball Association after playing just one year in college.[35] Still, the college game has managed to retain its own appeal, which is surely dependent on the fact that college players are students – amateurs. To emphasize this all-important difference from the pros, the NCAA has made it a policy to employ the term "student-athlete" for all college athletes, applying the term uniformly and unceasingly to those in revenue and nonrevenue sports alike.[36]

And the market for big-time college sports is large. It accounts for a significant share of the colossal market for spectator sports in the United States. The most popular sport in this country is professional football, with almost a third of all adults who follow any sport naming it as their favorite. Second is baseball, once America's pastime in fact as well as in name, but now with only about half as many naming it their favorite. Third in popularity is college football, with 12% naming it their favorite in 2008. After auto racing (8%) and professional basketball (6%), college basketball was tied with hockey at 5%, and golf ranked eighth.[37] Measured in terms of revenues from ticket sales and television, college football and basketball are together larger than major league baseball, but only about half the size of professional football and somewhat smaller than professional basketball.[38]

The second distinguishing feature of supply in big college sports is that, unlike the competitive market featured in economics textbooks, there exist real *barriers to entry* by other potential suppliers. Nobody outside of higher education can enter this market. Only athletic programs affiliated with a college or university may do so. Although this requirement might seem purely semantic, it constitutes a real barrier that reinforces product differentiation. Adding to this absolute barrier are the more abstract barriers that have grown up over time in the reputations some teams have built up. Like the famous brands of breakfast cereal, the illustrious names of collegiate sports constitute another barrier to entry, simply by virtue of past success, making it hard for otherwise eligible universities to enter the upper echelons of competition. Anyone interested in fielding a team associated with a "storied football rivalry," one steeped in history like that between Auburn and Alabama, not only must have a college or university to sponsor it, but also has to have the requisite history of competition. There are only so many universities with such histories. For those big-time programs, name, mascot, and colors add up to a valuable brand name. Other universities have to use their own bootstraps to make it into the big time. Like a hardwood forest, a big-time college name brand can be developed, but it takes a long time. For an institution with one of these reputations, a decision to stop participating would be tantamount to leaving money on the table. Thus it has been the rare university that has chosen to walk away from big-time athletics. As noted in Chapter 3, of the 72 universities that both ranked among the top 100 college football powers in 1920 and remained national universities, all but 9 have continued competing in big-time football into the 21st century.[39]

Besides product differentiation and barriers to entry, the third noteworthy characteristic of the supply side of intercollegiate athletics is, loosely speaking, *monopoly*. More precisely, the universities engaged in big-time athletics have banded together in two kinds of cartel-like voluntary membership organizations: athletic conferences and the NCAA. Athletic conferences are essentially invitation-only clubs, providing their members with three useful services that most could not achieve on their own. First, they provide their members with playmates, setting up schedules and tournaments. Second, they negotiate TV deals, which can include joining bigger consortiums like the Bowl Championship Series (BCS) or establishing entire cable networks. Third, they allow for member universities to share revenues. Although the membership rolls of the most established conferences have been relatively stable, conference alignments have been subject to periodic upheavals, as with the dissolution of the Southwest Conference in 1996, the expansion of the Atlantic Coast Conferences in 2003, and the periodic additions to the Big Ten and other conferences. In these various realignments, the prospects of TV revenue have trumped both history and geography, as conferences have focused on the number of lucrative TV markets covered by their membership and on whether they have enough members to meet the demands of the BCS.[40]

The other important membership organization is the NCAA, the overarching rule-making behemoth of college sports. Because it controls many vital aspects of the production of college sports, many economists have called it a cartel, a term ordinarily reserved for a group of suppliers who join together to restrict total output and raise prices for the purpose of making more profits, effectively acting as a single monopolist.[41] The NCAA actually exerts control over both its output and one of its major inputs, college athletes.

To understand how the NCAA affects supply in this market, it may be helpful to compare it to an agricultural cooperative, such as one of the numerous milk cooperatives that collect, bottle, and market the milk of many separate dairy farms. (Much of this reasoning applies as well to conferences, but they have become over time less important than the NCAA.) Although substitutes may exist for the product in question (e.g., professional sports), the cooperative controls the supply of the product itself (here, the version of football and basketball produced by colleges and universities). Milk cooperatives typically regulate how the dairy farms operate, so as to ensure both food safety and uniformity of product. In the same way, the NCAA regulates how the universities run their athletic programs, by means of rules covering such important details as how athletes can be recruited, how many players can receive scholarships, and how games must be played.

For individual universities, membership in conferences and the NCAA brings benefits that surely outweigh the costs. By submitting to the authority of the NCAA, a university gives up the freedom to determine the rules of contests, but this sacrifice is surely worth it, because the resulting standardization enhances the commercial value of contests. Without the regulation of playing rules, intercollegiate competition would be chaotic, with rules and criteria for victory always subject to debate (a state of affairs that applies, ironically, to nonathletic competition between universities). But by virtue of the contracts that conferences and the NCAA negotiate with broadcasters, universities are forced to give up the freedom to decide the dates and times of their own teams' games, or indeed the length of a time-out during a televised contest.[42] As a result of these restrictions, the university ceases to be the producer of a consumer product, but becomes merely the supplier of an input into its production. Anyone understands this fact who has attended a college game where players, coaches, officials, and crowd all wait for the signal from the television broadcasters before action can resume. Thanks to TV, college basketball games often begin at 9 p.m. and football games sometimes happen on Thursday evenings. Yet the universities seem perfectly happy to oblige in order to get the TV exposure and income. As Alabama coach Bear Bryant once remarked, "I'll play at midnight if that's what TV wants."[43]

In addition to its role in promulgating and revising the rules of play, the NCAA's major function has been to define and enforce rules applying to recruitment and eligibility. Having reconciled the notions of amateurism with the practice of giving scholarships based on athletic ability alone, the NCAA has become the policeman who enforces a book of regulations whose complexity is a match for any state's income tax law. Key among these regulations is the one that limits the value of an athletic scholarship to little more than tuition, room, and board. By prohibiting college athletes from being paid more than this and enforcing this prohibition across universities, the NCAA acts as a "monopsonistic" cartel, meaning it is the only buyer.[44] The analogy to the milk combine breaks down in only one important regard: whereas milk customers give little thought to which farm produced the milk they buy – since milk is a homogeneous as well as a homogenized product – consumers of college athletics tend to care passionately about who produces the athletic contests they watch or listen to. As we have seen, brand loyalty is a central feature of this market: the version of college football and basketball each producer provides is unique, right down to the mascot and the colors of the uniforms.

Not only do universities join together as buyers to set a low price, they also have combined as sellers to establish a high price, when they offer games to television networks. In their attempts to do this, universities have grouped themselves in different ways. Before the Supreme Court ruled the practice unconstitutional in 1984, the NCAA acted as a monopolist by severely limiting the number of college football games that could be broadcast on national TV networks.[45] Since that decision, conferences have been free to negotiate TV packages for regular-season football as well as basketball games. The NCAA has, however, retained the right to negotiate a TV contract for the season-ending basketball tournaments, the most lucrative of which is the men's Division I tournament. And as groups of conferences, universities have often banded together to enhance their collective earnings from postseason football bowl games. It was such a coalition, the College Football Association, that successfully challenged the NCAA's monopoly over televised football games in 1984. This coalition, made up of some of the strongest conferences, negotiated TV contracts in the years immediately following the 1984 decision.[46] Since the early 1990s, different configurations of conferences have banded together to forge agreements with television networks and the major postseason bowls, with the effect of ensuring an orderly system of choosing teams to play and guaranteeing that a minimum number of the conferences' institutions will be represented in bowls. The most recent version of these agreements is the Bowl Championship Series, which guarantees minimum payments to each of the six largest conferences plus Notre Dame.[47] Much to the consternation of lesser conferences and critics who argued for a basketball-like tournament to select a "national champion," the BCS has decidedly worked to the advantage of the haves of big-time athletics.[48]

## ADVERTISING AND THE COMMERCIAL VALUE OF TELEVISED GAMES

Besides direct ticket sales, the bulk of the commercial value of college football and basketball lies in their attractiveness as vehicles for selling ads on TV. Broadcast and cable networks, working usually through consortiums of universities, such as conferences or the NCAA, pay for the right to telecast college games. These networks make money, in turn, by selling advertising spots to advertisers. From the perspective of television broadcasters and cable companies, college football and basketball games make for attractive programming, for two reasons. First, college contests are comparatively cheap to produce. There are no scripts to write or actors to hire. The players, for the reasons already noted, cost next to nothing. Second, for the host of historical and cultural reasons we have seen, these competitions enjoy wide popularity, as demonstrated by their strong TV viewership. In 2006 sports programs constituted the fifth-largest share of all hours of TV viewing in America, with an average of 4.8 hours a week per household. In average weekly hours of viewing, sports trailed only feature films (9.1 hours), newscasts (8.8), dramatic series (6.7), and sitcoms (6.4).[49]

As previously noted, the two big college spectator sports have had and continue to have a wide following, following only pro football and baseball in popularity among Americans. Not surprisingly, this popularity shows up in TV ratings. During the 2008–2009 viewing season, among the 30 most

frequently viewed individual television programs were four National
Football League games, including the top-ranked Super Bowl, and two
college games, the BCS football championship and the final game of the
NCAA men's basketball tournament. Other programs ranking in the top 30
that year included six installments of *American Idol*, four of *Dancing with
the Stars*, nine episodes of dramatic series, and one major league baseball
game.[50] Among the major televised sports, college football and basketball
appeal to a comparatively well educated audience. Of the eight most popular sports, golf and the two college sports have TV viewing audiences in
which college graduates are most disproportionately represented. This fact
makes the viewers of college sports especially attractive for advertisers trying to reach affluent consumers.[51]

There is no better way to appreciate the commercial value of televised
college games than to take a close look at the advertising that is packaged
into a single bowl game. The Fiesta Bowl has been one of the major postseason football bowls since its inception in 1971. Played in Glendale, Arizona,
it has been one of the five BCS bowls. In 2010 it guaranteed, as did the
other four, a payout of $17 million to both participating teams (an amount
that teams typically share with other institutions in their conferences). As
has become the custom for all of the college bowls, its sponsor was part
of its official name, making it the Tostitos Fiesta Bowl. Scheduled on Fox
for 9 PM on the first Monday night after New Year's Day, with a one-hour
pre-game show immediately preceding, it occupied a time slot designed for
maximum viewing from coast to coast. Its viewership in 2010 might have
been expected to be diminished by its choice of two teams not belonging
to one of the six conferences that made up the BCS, Texas Christian and
Boise State. But the fact that both teams had undefeated seasons – a detail
that bolstered the case of critics advocating a national playoff – promised to
increase interest in the game. Indeed, the Fiesta Bowl became the fourth-
most-watched bowl game of the 2009–2010 season, garnering an audience
of 13.8 million. It also posted that night's biggest audience in each of the
three prime time slots, beating out ABC's premier of *The Bachelor* between
8 and 10 p.m.[52]

Advertising saturated the four hours of the scheduled broadcast. Most
prominent were the 140 commercials aired before the game and during time-outs and halftime. Taking up slightly more than one hour out of
the four devoted to the entire program and averaging a bit less than half a
minute each, they touted the virtues of brands of such products as automobiles, cell phones, candy and snack food, satellite TV, insurance, and
beer. These spots were also used by the network, Fox, to promote upcoming

programs. But these commercials were only the biggest part of the advertising for this game. During the broadcast, usually between plays, products were also mentioned by announcers and displayed on the screen. Twenty "brought to you by" announcements mentioned a total of 17 products. The starting lineups were sponsored: the naming of the players on each team's starting offensive and defensive squads became, four times, the "Merrill Lynch Wealth Management Starting Lineup," each announcement accompanied by the same company logo. Aerial coverage, including a shot of the sunset over Arizona, was sponsored by Bud Light. Other in-game features included "Game Summaries," sponsored by Tostitos and GMC, "Keys to the Game" (Dodge Ram), "First Half Stats" (Ford), "Play of the Game" (Allstate), and a moving camera suspended by wires (DirecTV). The network's cameras also captured advertising signs on the scoreboard and elsewhere in the stadium as well as prominently displayed logos, including several shots of players on the sideline with Gatorade cooler and containers directly in front of the camera. And the image of every player from the front included the Nike swoosh, which appeared on the jerseys of both teams.

But no televised college sports program compares in scale with the annual NCAA men's basketball tournament. Measured in terms of advertising expenditures, this event is larger than the Super Bowl and the World Series put together.[53] In 2008 the tournament brought in some $580 million in advertising.[54] In 2009, the cost of a 30-second ad during the championship game was $1.2 million, a higher rate than that at any other televised sporting event except the Super Bowl.[55] Unlike regular-season college basketball and all of college football, where conferences are chiefly responsible for negotiating television contracts, the NCAA negotiates to sell the right to broadcast this tournament. In 2009, as had been the case for more than 25 years, the tournament was telecast by the CBS television network. Games were played on 10 days spread out over a period of two and a half weeks during March and April. In each TV market, some 27 complete games were broadcast, the exact combination of games in the early rounds being adjusted according to regional interest in the participating teams. In the tournament's first two weeks, those broadcasts were seen in prime time each night by an average of 4.7 million viewers between the ages of 18 and 49. For the last two rounds, the size of the audience grew to 6.6 and 8.3 million, respectively, the last being not too far below the size of the audience for that week's most-watched show, *American Idol* (10.6 million viewers).[56]

As a means of appreciating the commercial value of this famous example of big-time athletic competition, I tabulated all of the advertising that appeared on the 10 days of tournament competition in 2009, as broadcast in

Table 4.1. *TV advertising for the 2009 NCAA men's basketball tournament*

|  | Number | Time (minutes) |
|---|---|---|
| *Commercial break spots* |  |  |
| CBS commercials | 262 | 69.7 |
| NCAA messages | 83 | 38.5 |
| Product commercials | 2,375 | 1,076.0 |
| *Sponsored pseudo-programming* | 29 | 14.5 |
| *Game information with logo* |  |  |
| Statistics box | 140 | 46.7 |
| Scores of other games | 103 | 77.3 |
| *Announcements with logo* |  |  |
| "Brought to you by" | 250 | 20.8 |
| Sponsored features promotion | 45 | 27.5 |
| *Total* | 3,287 | 1,370.0 |

*Note*: For definitions of terms, see text.

*Source*: Analysis of taped broadcasts of the 2009 NCAA men's basketball tournament, broadcast from WRAL, the Raleigh affiliate of CBS.

the Raleigh–Durham, North Carolina, television market. It seems reasonable to assume that the choice of products for which firms spend advertising dollars during the tournament is based on what groups of people make up the anticipated viewing audience. According to survey data and published statements of advertising experts, the demographic profile of viewers of this tournament is thought to be male, young, and college educated.[57] More specifically, marketing experts have concluded that these viewers spend more than average amounts on automobiles, financial services, beer, and fast food.[58]

As was the case with the Fiesta Bowl, conventional commercials, advertisements for consumer products shown during time-outs and halftimes, were only one of several kinds of advertising employed in the broadcasts. As shown in Table 4.1, four kinds of ads were shown. Most common were these conventional commercials, the expertly produced advertisements inserted in commercial breaks. In addition to commercials for consumer products, CBS utilized more than 250 short segments to promote upcoming shows on its network, and the NCAA used slots to promote its programs and policies. What might be called "pseudo-programming" was a second form of advertising. In ads of this variety, clips of past tournaments or highlights from the current tournament were shown, usually right before the resumption of live play, accompanied by a logo and voice references to a product.[59] A third form of advertising consisted of corporate logos affixed to information shown on the screen. In some cases, such as statistics summarizing the game in progress, the information took up most of the screen, but for scores of other tournament games, positioned at the top or bottom of the screen, they were shown as a game was being played. Finally, companies and products were advertised, very briefly, throughout the broadcasts. Most common were "brought to you by" announcements listing several sponsors; each sponsor was allotted five seconds, during which time the corporate logo was prominently displayed. Also included in this count of ads were announcements of upcoming sponsored halftime shows, but not the shows themselves. All together, these various forms of advertising accounted for 1,370 minutes, or 22.8 hours out of the total 65.3 hours of the tournament that were broadcast.

The 17 hours of conventional commercials hawked a host of consumer goods and services.[60] Most prevalent, in number as well as time devoted to them, were new cars and trucks, which accounted for 17% of all the commercial time during the tournament. Ironically, it was General Motors, the auto giant that was at the time on the brink of bankruptcy and massive government assistance, that led the way, with its Chevrolet brand receiving the most advertising time.[61] One indication that advertisers anticipated a viewing audience heavily weighted toward potential buyers of new vehicles is that this 17% share was more than five times the 3.2% share that new vehicle purchases take up in the average household's budget.[62] This ratio, 5.5 to be exact, provides a useful index of the relative emphasis given to advertising for this product. Because average spending on new cars is quite a bit higher among households in higher income brackets than it is for those in lower brackets, this heavy emphasis on new vehicles is wholly consistent with advertisers' expectations of an affluent viewing audience for the tournament.

The second most heavily advertised product was food consumed away from home, primarily that purchased at fast food chains, with McDonald's getting more exposure than any other chain. This category's share was only a little more than twice its share in the average household budget. The emphasis placed on this product group suggests the youth of the expected viewing audience. The next two categories, financial services and computers and other household equipment, are both consistent with the expectation of an affluent viewing audience.

The fifth product category, alcoholic beverages, is one of the most interesting on the list. One reason is that its relative emphasis, indicated by the calculated ratio of 6.2, is the second highest for any product category, receiving more than six times the share of ads as its share of expenditures in the typical household budget. More important, the question of whether to advertise alcoholic beverages at all has been a contentious one because of the harmful effects of such ads on underage drinking and related problems. For these reasons, some have advocated banning alcohol ads in broadcasts of college athletic games. At least one cable network, the Big Ten Network, had done so in its telecasts.[63] For its part, the NCAA in 2009 followed a policy of limiting ads for alcohol products in the tournament to one minute per hour of telecast.[64]

The remaining product categories included familiar products and brands. Note that nonalcoholic beverages, such as Coca-Cola, received the most disproportionate emphasis relative to their importance in the average budget, surely an indication of the heavy representation of young people expected to be part of the viewing audience. It is also noteworthy that Coca-Cola's main competitor, Pepsi-Cola, did not appear in any commercial.

## CONSUMER SURPLUS

Apart from its commercial implications, the extent of demand for college sports has importance for a most intangible concept, happiness. As incongruous as it might seem for the discipline that Thomas Carlyle famously named "the dismal science," economics has been the home of considerable research and writing on the subject of happiness. The 18th-century philosopher-economists, notably John Stuart Mill and Jeremy Bentham, developed the concept of utility and built models of human behavior on the assumption that individuals would seek pleasure and avoid pain. Today's economics texts employ the term "consumer surplus" to represent a consumer's subjective value of consuming a product over and above what he or she paid for it. So it is well within the boundaries of the discipline of economics to highlight the happiness that is surely generated by watching or following college sports. The variety of athletic competition that universities with big-time programs produce and give away delivers happiness, especially to those fans who have formed attachment to their teams. This is an output of universities, spilling freely beyond the campus boundaries, that is rarely acknowledged by those who study higher education, or, indeed, by the universities themselves.

How large a quantity this happiness might amount to is quite unanswerable to any degree of precision, of course, but the available empirical evidence suggests that it might be rather large. We have already seen that attendance at college football games is on the order of 50 million a year, and TV viewership for a single run-of-the-mill regular-season basketball game can exceed 1 million and, for a top bowl game, 10 million. On a local level, anyone who lives in the vicinity of a university with big-time sports has occasion to observe indicators of consumer surplus: sweatshirts, hats, and bumper stickers with college logos are there for all to see.[65]

Using household surveys, marketing firms provide estimates of the number of people who follow big-time college teams, and the number is impressive, to say the least. One leading marketing firm calculates the percentage of adults who, in the past year, have attended, listened to on radio, or watched on TV a football game played by a particular team. In the Atlanta media market, for example, the firm estimated that 29% of all adults had watched or tuned into at least one game played by Georgia Tech, and 42% had done so for the University of Georgia. In the Birmingham market 49% had viewed or listened to at least one Auburn game, and an astounding 74% had done so for an Alabama game. The estimated fan base for those last two teams was smaller in the Mobile–Pensacola market, but still impressive, with corresponding shares for the two teams of 34% and 46%, respectively. Although the South may be noteworthy for its high level of attention, widespread interest in college football is not confined to that region. The same marketing firm estimated shares of adults following other college teams. For example, Arizona State games were witnessed by 29% of the Phoenix market, Pitt by 41% of the Pittsburgh market, and Syracuse by 53% of the Syracuse market.[66]

A survey conducted in Lexington, Kentucky, found that similarly widespread attention can apply to college basketball. In that local area, known for its devotion to college basketball, 40% of respondents reported that they normally attended at least one Kentucky basketball game each season and 56% said that they normally watched at least 11 games on television a season. Only 7.4% said they watched no games. Other indications of the degree to which people in that area were caught up with University of Kentucky basketball were the percentage of respondents who during the season read about Kentucky basketball in the newspaper at least a few days a week (72%) and who regularly discussed Kentucky basketball with others (also 72%).[67] Perhaps the most striking indicator of fan devotion was the 33% of respondents who agreed that the following statement best described their own level of interest in Kentucky basketball: "I live and die with the Wildcats. I'm happy if they win and sad if they lose."[68] To repeat, one out of three adults gave this answer. Economists have tried to place a numerical estimate on fan devotion. Using an approach called contingent valuation, they have resorted to asking consumers directly, usually focusing on consumers' willingness to pay to have a sports team or a new stadium. Although purely hypothetical, these estimates suggest that many people place real value on the presence of a team to cheer for.[69]

Here we come to a consequence of big-time college athletics, a spillover effect only partly exploited by universities and commercial enterprises. It arises from cultural and historical factors far beyond the control of university leaders. Its particular intensity in some parts of the country may be explained simply by the absence of many forms of entertainment, cultural or otherwise, commonly found in large metropolitan areas.[70] In fact, the reasons why this demand arose in the first place, fascinating as they might be, are largely irrelevant for understanding the effects of big-time college sports. What is important is the sheer breadth and intensity of this demand, the corresponding commercial value that the demand makes possible, and the intangible value of the product to the consumers themselves. It seems manifestly clear that the commercial value created by this demand *is* fully appreciated, and exploited, by broadcast media, the firms that want to advertise their own products, and the universities that provide the teams. No college sporting event better epitomizes these market relationships than the annual NCAA men's basketball championship. The widespread interest in this event shows itself in both altered work schedules across the country and the millions of dollars expended for advertising purchases.

What is in it for consumers of big-time college sports? What is left for the fans, once they have purchased their tickets and paid their cable TV bills? The answer is, consumer surplus – the value of the enjoyment that they derive from all of their attention, cheering, and devotion that is over and above the money they actually spent. There is every reason to believe that this is a substantial amount. As evidence, consider the fallout from a standoff between cable providers in the Midwest and the newly created Big Ten Network, which in 2007 became the exclusive network showing Big Ten football games. Because of the price the network proposed to charge for the rights to carry its programming, cable providers such as Time Warner initially refused to include the network in their basic cable plans, thus leaving most cable customers without a way to watch their favorite Big Ten games on TV other than by going to a local sports bar. The *Columbus Dispatch* reported widespread complaints from fans, documented by the results of a poll it ran on the question with more than 5,000 votes tallied. Feeling the wrath of angry fans, the network and the cable providers eventually reached a compromise that allowed the network's telecasts to be included in basic cable packages in the eight-state region during football and basketball seasons.[71]

The lesson from this episode is that fans want to see their teams play. They care, and they care deeply. Beyond the money that they pay, beyond the money that broadcasters collect from advertisers and universities from broadcasters, there remains a potent residual of demand by fans – the consumers. Although it cannot be measured easily, if at all, this consumer surplus is a real benefit of the entertainment that universities provide, despite their reluctance to admit they are in the entertainment business at all. This consumer surplus reveals itself in the sticker on the car bumper, the emblem on the T-shirt, and the obvious pride that fans take in talking about their favorite college team. This is a benefit of big-time college sports that is rarely acknowledged in so many words in the serious debates that take place about college athletics. Particularly in the case of public universities, this would seem to be a legitimate part of the benefit a state university provides to its citizens. Surely this is a consequence of big-time college sports that is worth acknowledging, and taking seriously.

# FIVE

# Commercial Enterprise

The controversy that swirled in Ann Arbor, Michigan, during the spring of 2006 evoked themes reminiscent of student protests a generation before. Critics charged that the university's egalitarian tradition was being threatened by a proposed facility designed to serve the "privileged few." The proposal in question was a $226 million plan to renovate 80-year-old Michigan Stadium, the third-largest sports stadium in the world. The renovation would add the equivalent of two five-story buildings containing 82 enclosed luxury boxes overlooking the existing stands on both sides of the stadium. The university's athletic department argued that the new boxes would generate funds to cover other necessary renovations to the stadium, but opponents denounced it as a step toward commercialization and "a sad corruption of our university's defining traditions."[1] At its April meeting that year, the Michigan Board of Regents approved the plan, thus joining the majority of universities in the Big Ten that had already added such premium boxes to their stadiums.

The debate over these luxury boxes and the decision to go forward with the project are emblematic of the central financial tension surrounding big-time college sports. For better or worse, a big-time sports program is to a large extent an ordinary commercial firm, competing against other firms in a market that is subject to a regulatory environment unique to that market. It will be easiest, and not too big an exaggeration, therefore, to begin by thinking of a big-time university athletic department simply as a business that happens to operate inside the larger university, in much the same way a university medical center does. In his book on intercollegiate athletics, former University of Michigan president James Duderstadt divides the major functions of that university – he calls it "the U of M, Inc." – into seven departments, one of which he calls "Entertainment, Michigan Wolverines."[2] This particular department produces and sells several widely valued products, the two main ones being college football and basketball games.

As the preceding chapter makes clear, the popularity of college football and basketball opens up many potentially lucrative commercial opportunities. For historical reasons unique to the United States, the collegiate versions of these two "revenue sports" have remained intensely popular, for at least a century, even as the professional versions have grown to maturity beside them, making each of the sports a potential source of commercial income for the university. But converting this potential into a self-sustaining athletic program turns out to be much harder than one might suppose. Most big-time college sports operations lose money. According to financial reports produced by the NCAA, only 25 of the 119 universities competing in the Football Bowl Subdivision turned a profit in 2008.[3] Michigan was one of those. In 2009 its athletic department, relying heavily on ticket sales from Michigan Stadium, took in revenues of $95 million and spent just $79 million.[4] Even Michigan, with its 108,000-seat stadium and rich football tradition, is not immune to worry about its bottom line. Following losing football seasons in 2008 and 2009 and in the midst of an NCAA investigation, many of those luxury boxes remained unclaimed, even as construction on them neared completion.[5]

Although the universities with these enterprises want to have winning teams, they are reluctant to subsidize athletics. This reluctance was on full display, for example, when the Berkeley faculty senate voted in 2009 to demand an end to subsidies there.[6] The only way a university can reconcile its demand for winning teams with financial self-sufficiency is to allow the athletic enterprise to seek out and exploit commercial opportunities to generate revenue – thus luxury boxes. And pressed by the imperatives to be both successful and self-sufficient, athletic departments often end up pushing the envelope in ways that can threaten academic values.

This chapter describes the business of running a big-time college sports program. It begins by looking at the makeup of the athletic department's budget and some of the items that distinguish it from the budgets of other departments in the university, on the one side, and commercial entertainment businesses, on the other. Although the items athletic departments spend money on are more or less the same everywhere, the sources of income differ markedly up and down the competitive food chain. The chapter then examines the "business model" – the logic underlying how the athletic department generates its income. Three axioms govern the business of big-time college sports. One of them, governing recruiting, explains why recruiting has been a recurring source of abuse and embarrassment.

## THE ATHLETIC BUDGET

Every university has a unique process for coming up with an operating budget for the following year, but all of these processes have one ritual in common: each dean and vice president must trek to the central administration building to present his or her budget proposal for approval. This budget spells out the school's or department's proposed expenditures and any projected revenues. Some administrative units in universities (called auxiliaries), such as campus stores, dining halls, and parking services, are expected to be financially self-sustaining, by charging fees that more or less cover their costs.[7] But most units are not – not even professional schools like business or law that generate significant revenue through tuition. Where projected income does fall short of spending, university subsidies from general funds must cover the difference.

One of these budget presentations is made by the director of athletics. A great deal no doubt could be learned about the economics of big-time athletics by sitting in on one of these budget meetings. Failing that, it is helpful to imagine what one of these athletic budgets might look like and what kinds of conversations accompany its presentation. Surely the most noticeable feature of any athletic department's budget is its size, or its size relative to that of the university's overall budget. Take, for example, the University of Michigan, which has one of the biggest and historically most successful college athletic programs in the country. In 2008 its athletic department had revenues of $95.2 million, against expenses of just $79.2 million, making it one of the handful of big-time programs to show a profit. By way of comparison, this revenue was more than a quarter of the size of the appropriation the university received from the state of Michigan that year, or some 7% of the size of the university's total general fund revenues (which excluded auxiliaries and the university's giant medical center). The total for expenditures was roughly equal to the general fund budget for the medical school or to the sum of the budgets for the university's library and law school put together.[8] Another striking aspect of the athletic budget is the high degree of dependence on paying customers to generate revenue. In this respect, it is much more like a business than any other part of the university, except perhaps medical centers. This similarity to a commercial business has allowed the academic side of universities, which have been reluctant to use their funds to pay for athletics, to adopt "breaking even" as a reasonable benchmark. As noted earlier, however, most big-time athletic departments do not meet this standard, as conventionally defined. For those programs, a subsidy is required to balance the basic budget equation:

Expenditures = generated revenues + subsidy

## Components of Income and Expense

Like those for the other administrative units, the budgets of athletic departments contain detailed breakdowns of revenues and expenses. Unfortunately for students of university economics, universities guard their athletic budgets closely. It is only by virtue of federal reporting requirements related to gender equity under Title IX and the efforts of news organizations making requests under states' open-records laws that any recent financial information on athletic budgets is available at all.[9] Table 5.1 gives a percentage breakdown for the major items of revenue and expense, based on 98 of the state-supported FBS programs in fiscal year 2008.[10]

Unlike the University of Michigan's sports program, most big-time athletic programs do not make a profit, and the distribution in Table 5.1 makes clear just how far short most are from breaking even. Subsidies, including mandatory student fees, make up 18% of all revenues for the average big-time program. Of the 82% of revenues that are generated by the athletic enterprise, the most important is ticket sales. The bulk of these sales derive from the two big revenue sports, football and men's basketball. Despite the growing importance of television, the greatest source of revenue for big-time college athletics remains the loud and colorful spectacle of the live contest. As significant as this is, it is not as large as it once was, because of the growing importance of televised college games. Whereas athletic departments were almost wholly reliant on ticket sales before the advent of TV, their share fell to something like two-thirds by the mid-1970s and then continued to fall as the TV coverage of big-time college contests steadily expanded.[11]

In generating revenue from ticket sales, no sport rivals football. This dominance derives from football's larger crowds, reflected by the large size of football stadiums. Whereas average attendance at Division I basketball games in 2008–2009 was less than 5,200, average attendance at FBS football games was 46,000. Larger stadiums can accommodate larger crowds, but supply does not necessarily create its own demand, as Stanford concluded when it renovated its venerable stadium in 2006. The university decided to reduce the seating capacity, reasoning that the new stadium's smaller size would produce more sellouts and a boisterous crowd, conditions Stanford

Table 5.1. *The pieces of the athletic department budget, 2008*

|  | Percentage of total |
|---|---|
| *Revenues* | |
| Ticket sales | 25 |
| Contributions | 22 |
| NCAA and conference distributions | 15 |
| Subsidies | 18 |
| Other | 20 |
| Total | 100 |
| *Operating expenses* | |
| Athletic scholarships | 14 |
| Salaries and benefits | 33 |
| Facilities | 17 |
| Travel and games | 12 |
| Other expenses | 24 |
| Total | 100 |

*Note*: Subsidies include direct institutional support, indirect support, student fees, and government support.

*Source*: *USA Today* Web site, financial data for 98 state universities, 2007–2008 fiscal year.

believed would draw more fans and improve the quality of football players it could recruit.[12] In any case, the larger crowds in football make that sport the primary source of revenue for big-time college athletics. In 2008–2009 there were 6.5 times the number of basketball games as football games played in the most competitive divisions, but those basketball games all together drew only three-quarters of the number of spectators the football games did.[13] Among the NCAA's FBS universities, median revenue from football was three times that generated by men's basketball.[14] Despite the large size and expense of its teams and coaching staff, football remains the sport with the greatest potential to make money, although it is certainly possible to operate a big-time program without football, as the examples of Georgetown and Gonzaga illustrate.

It may be surprising to learn that the second-biggest source of revenue generated by athletic departments is contributions. Contributions from individuals, corporations, and foundations made up 22% of all athletic department income for those big-time programs. This source of income, along with the various forms of subsidy, most clearly distinguishes the income statement of big-time college programs from those of a professional sports franchise. In receiving these contributions, universities benefit from the generous tax advantages that the federal tax code gives to charitable and educational organizations. Universities with big-time sports programs, public and private alike, have created tax-exempt athletic booster organizations designed to receive contributions and certify their eligibility for tax deductibility. Federal tax law allows the bulk of gifts to organizations like Stanford's Buck-Cardinal Club, Florida's Gator Boosters, and Ohio State's Buckeye Club to be tax deductible, and their own income is exempt from taxation. Supporters with the wherewithal to make large gifts are typically solicited by development officers working entirely for the athletic enterprise, with the hope of generating gifts large enough to endow scholarships or name buildings. Occasionally, these efforts produce gifts of spectacular proportions, the largest to date being the $165 million that Boone Pickens gave to the athletic department of Oklahoma State in 2006.[15]

But the bread and butter of the athletic development office is not the gargantuan capital gift from the super-rich tycoon. It is the annual contribution from the hundreds of merely affluent boosters. And the ingredient that really drives this source of revenue is the privilege that often comes only to those who contribute enough: the right to buy tickets. Where tickets to football or basketball games are hard to come by, this is a valuable privilege to have, and it means that the contribution becomes little more than a price surcharge. What better way to ration excess demand when faced with a waiting list to buy tickets? Following a successful season under a newly hired football coach, Alabama had a reported waiting list of 10,000 to buy season tickets.[16] At Duke, where demand for basketball tickets has vastly exceeded the 9,000 seats in its old arena, new applicants for season tickets in 2009 had to agree to make an annual contribution of $7,000 for the right to buy two season tickets, making the total cost of a pair of season tickets range from $8,100 to $9,400.[17] Returning season ticket holders had to make a gift of $6,000. At neighboring North Carolina, the required annual contribution to get two seats in a much larger arena was $5,000. Bigger contributions were necessary to ensure the right to buy tickets to the ever-popular conference tournament.

For football powers like Ohio State and Texas, similar premiums were required to purchase season tickets in choice locations. In 2010 the cost at Ohio State was $1,500 for the right to buy two football tickets, rising to $6,600 for two tickets between the 35-yard lines.[18] The University of Texas demanded a minimum contribution of $3,000 for the right to buy one of the 400 seats on the club level in its football stadium and a minimum of $50,000 for one of the luxury suites.[19] Sometimes such contributions become part of a funding plan for a particular capital project, as in the case of seat licenses that became a condition for buying season tickets in choice locations in

Stanford's renovated stadium.[20] That the required contribution levels are determined by supply and demand is not hard to infer. They are highest where fans are numerous, teams are successful, and stadiums are not big enough to accommodate everybody who wants tickets. The required level can even vary from year to year at the same university. To get season tickets to Georgia football games, the minimum contribution to the Bulldog Club, which had been $1,991 before an 11–2 season in 2007, rose to an unprecedented $10,651 after it, only to decline to $4,205 and $1,550 in the next two years, in the wake of a recession and less stellar seasons.[21]

But contribution cutoffs turn out to be too blunt an instrument to allocate seats. It is just as true in a football stadium or basketball arena as it is at the Metropolitan Opera's grand theater in Lincoln Center: not all seats are created equal. Quite naturally, there is more demand for seats at the 50-yard line or midcourt than in the end zone or behind the basket. Because the many gradations in desirability between the best and worst seats make it difficult to establish a price list, it is necessary to provide for finer gradations in allocating good seats to worthy patrons. Many athletic departments have resorted to elaborate point systems to do this job. These systems typically favor big donors and those who have given for a long time. Typically, those priority point systems can be explained in a page on the booster club's Web site, such as the one maintained by Alabama.[22] But they can become quite detailed, as in the case of the system used by the Tiger Athletic Foundation at LSU to determine the priority for assigning seats in the 92,000-seat Tiger Stadium, a stadium that is perennially filled to capacity. Running 43 paragraphs and 3,961 words, the rules spell out in lawyerly detail how points can be earned, transferred, and inherited. Donors earn them through current contributions (one point per $1,000 to one of several athletic funds, two points per $1,000 to athletic endowments, and a quarter of a point per $1,000 to alumni and academic funds), booster club membership (one point), past varsity letters won, and years of past donations at various levels (e.g., seven points for each year with $5,000 or more in donations). The rules cover such questions as whether points can be combined through business mergers or marriage, the disposition of points at death or divorce, and the application to contracts for suites or stadium club use.[23] The attention to such details speaks volumes about the value placed on prime seats at the LSU football stadium.[24] In 2008 the LSU athletic department raised $23 million in contributions, some 27% of its total athletic department income that year, and 45% of the amount contributed by all individuals to the university in 2007.[25]

By making contributions a condition for buying tickets, universities are able to ration excess demand in just the way economics textbooks say the market would do if left to its own devices – by raising the price to reign in that excess demand. In this way, contributions in effect become an extension of ticket sales as an item of revenue. One statistical analysis has shown that contributions to athletic departments are highest for programs with winning records in basketball and bowl appearances in football, lending support to the view that contributions are often little more than surcharges for tickets.[26] The point is illustrated as well by the opposite case. Where demand is weak and tickets are plentiful, such as at Northwestern, the possibility of charging seat premiums simply isn't a feasible option.[27]

Good seats are not the only highly valued commodity that athletic departments can use to generate contributions. In fact, these athletic departments, through their own tax-exempt booster organizations, offer veritable menus of desirable premiums to potential donors. For a sense of what aspects of the big-time college sports experience are valued by boosters with money, there is no better guide than the Web sites of the various athletic booster organizations. These sites describe, usually in tabular form, exactly what items donors can obtain by making annual contributions of specified amounts. The site for Stanford's Buck-Cardinal Club, for example, specified which of 17 different benefits were available to those who gave at each of nine levels. Depending on the level of giving, benefits could include email updates, an invitation to a pre-game gathering at a hospitality tent or an autograph session with athletes, the chance to buy "priority seats," preferred parking, invitations to exclusive events with the athletic director and head coaches, and acknowledgment on the Stanford Athletics Wall of Honor.[28]

To appreciate the sorts of things that have been found to be valued by boosters of various levels of affluence, besides access to tickets, consider the categories of items listed on the Web sites of big-time booster associations.

*Special access to the team.* For boosters with the greatest financial resources, athletic departments offer forms of access comparable to those accorded to partners and major shareholders in the business world. For $50,000, a Stanford booster and a guest could travel with the football team to a selected away game. At Syracuse, a contribution of $25,000 would purchase the same thing. For $50,000, donors to athletics at Connecticut could attend a team practice.

*Invitations to banquets and receptions.* Less exclusive access to coaches and players could be purchased at many universities, usually with more modest contributions. Annual giving of at least $2,000 gave

Texas boosters access to one of two hospitality clubs at home football games or Texas A&M boosters an invitation to the 12th Man Buffet. A gift of $3,000 gave the Pittsburgh booster an invitation to an "exclusive athletic department dinner." For $5,000 Stanford's Buck-Cardinal Club members were invited to receptions before selective basketball games. And Georgia boosters could obtain a seat at the football team's fall kickoff dinner by giving $25,000 or more.

*Recognition.* This might simply be a listing of the booster's name in the game program, just as it might appear in a theater bill or symphony program. But it could be much more. At Arkansas, a contribution of $5,000 got a donor's picture in the football game day program. Donations could even buy a booster's name on the video scoreboard: this ran $25,000 at Connecticut but was a bargain at only a tenth that amount at the University of Louisiana at Lafayette.

*Good parking.* Mundane as it might seem by comparison with the other inducements, the natural complement to season tickets is convenient parking. This is a form of consumption that is as conspicuous as it is functional, because a favored parking place is noticed and envied by hundreds of spectators who walk past it as they make their way to the stadium on the day of a game. As with other benefits, the price depends on the particular conditions that determine local supply and demand. Getting a good parking spot for games could require dona-tion reaching into the thousands of dollars.

These examples demonstrate how athletic departments have recognized and exploited demand for an aspect of their product among an upper crust of consumers. The aspect they have scooped off the top for these affluent fans is special access and recognition. This group of moneyed boosters values the sense of participation that comes with membership, especially that which is available only to a relatively small number of supporters. Donors are offered the chance to be with coaches, players, and other boosters at receptions and banquets. For the few who can afford very large gifts, some universities offer the next best thing to suiting up – the opportunity to travel with the team to an away game or attend a practice session. As the Web site for the Colorado State booster club proclaims, "These benefits put Ram Club members so close to the action it feels like you are actually in the game!"[29] In this way, universities have found a way to raise a lot of additional revenue from a tiny slice of the vast army of fans. At the simplest level, and the most crass, it is reasonable to view contributions generated in this way as surcharges that moneyed customers can pay for aspects of the fan experience available only to a select few. Fortunately for the fund-raisers, these boosters get a price break in buying privileges of this sort, because most of what is spent, like other contributions to the university, is tax deductible.

The third major source of self-generated income for a typical big-time athletic department is the distributions it receives from its athletic conference and the NCAA.[30] These distributions come mostly from three sources of revenue: TV contracts negotiated by conferences, the NCAA men's basketball tournament, and postseason football bowls. In basketball, the NCAA operates postseason championships and distributes most of the profits from them to conferences, the amounts depending on how many tournament games the teams from each conference have played in recent years. The real moneymaker, of course, is the Division I men's tournament. The better your conference is in basketball, the more your university receives. In football, postseason play is considerably less orchestrated – some would say chaotic – with an entire food chain of bowls paying for the right to have teams play in their games. Beginning in 1992, the largest conferences and the most well established of these bowls struck a series of deals (called, most recently, the Bowl Championship Series) specifying which conferences were to supply teams for which bowls, teams with the best records being assigned to the richest bowls.[31] In light of its unsettled nature and the controversy surrounding it (President Obama weighing in on the side of holding a playoff system), this system may well continue to change. But the upshot for the financial statement is parallel to that in basketball: members of strong football conferences receive more than members of weak ones.

Once these revenues are in the conference coffers, a distinctly communistic influence emerges. Each conference has its own rules for how such revenues will be distributed among its members, rules that have emerged from hard bargaining and compromise over time. Although many of their details are not in the public record, their similarities and some of their differences are known. Formulas used to compute these distributions are complex, ever changing, and partially secret. In the Southeastern Conference (SEC), for example, it worked in the following way for bowl games. From the payment made by the bowl (in the case of the Bowl Championship in 2010, this was at least $15.5 million), the participating team received a flat amount determined by the conference, some or all of which could be used to cover the costs of travel and lodging. The remaining portion was split into 13 equal shares, one for each of the 12 member universities and 1 for the conference office.[32] Other conferences share all TV revenue equally. The Pac-10, however, in apparent deference to its members playing in the lucrative Los Angeles TV market, allowed for the distribution of only about half of a team's TV earnings. The Big 12's formula heavily favors teams that appear on TV the most, giving a sizable advantage to its top teams, notably Texas.[33] Such formulas amount to radically redistributive share-the-wealth plans. Whereas each university will typically keep all the additional revenue it gets from selling more tickets, it typically faces a Scandinavian-like high marginal tax rate on the income it earns by playing in a postseason bowl or tournament, depending on the sharing formula used by its conference. From the university's point of view, being a member of a powerful conference is a valuable thing, since the established conferences have almost exclusive access to the lucrative agreements with postseason bowls. The weaklings in these strong conferences benefit from the share-the-wealth redistribution formulas, although being in a strong conference does make it harder to win conference games, and losses in turn tend to hurt ticket sales and make alumni unhappy. For the stronger members, the tax paid to support the also-rans is made up for by the prospect of winning more games as well as the access to postseason football games that membership in a BCS conference brings with it.

The remaining 20% of all revenues raised by the public university FBS programs in 2008 consisted of a variety of items, including royalties and advertising, media rights (TV, radio, and Internet), game-day concessions, and endowment and investment earnings. Royalties and advertising include a form of corporate sponsorship that has become notorious in recent years – the shoe contract. Best exemplified by Nike, Inc., shoe and apparel makers regularly enter into agreements with universities or with individual coaches. In return for the clothing and equipment supplied to teams and coaching staffs, universities agree to use that brand exclusively and prohibit players from covering up the brand logo, for example, with training tape. As a result, the Nike swoosh has become a more common ornament on the jerseys of football and basketball players than the American flag. This revenue category also includes income earned from advertising, such as the brand logos appearing on scoreboards, and income from contracts negotiated directly by athletic departments with local or regional broadcasters, which is separate from universities' share of TV contracts that have been negotiated by their conferences or the NCAA.

What emerges from this look at the revenue side of the athletic budget is a commercial enterprise with three features that distinguish it from the run-of-the-mill business enterprise. One of these is the remarkably heavy reliance on donations. Although largely tax deductible, these donations look less like conventional charitable gifts than price premiums charged for desirable seats. The second unusual element is the income received through revenue sharing within athletic conferences and the NCAA, which lends a collectivist flavor to the economics of big-time college sports. The third distinctive feature is the subsidy, or allocated revenue, which accounted for 18% of the income at public university big-time football programs. Two-thirds of these subsidies come in the form of a simple budget transfer within the university, with the remainder being student fees.[34] Students sometimes complain that these fees amount to a burdensome tax and, indeed, have been known to vote to reduce or eliminate them, when possible.[35] From the perspective of the athletic department, student fees not only bring in revenue but also carry the obligation to set aside seats for students. This is a moneymaker only when those seats cannot be sold at a better price to paying customers. But where sellouts are common, student fees and their attendant obligations are not the good deal that they are at those universities where empty seats abound.

On the expenditure side of the athletic department's budget, the most remarkable feature is the strikingly bimodal distribution of paychecks made to those who do the department's work. At the low end of the pay distribution are the athletes themselves, who receive no payment for their services, of course, other than tuition, fees, and room and board. The prohibition against paying college athletes does not take away from the fact that these individuals are essential to the entertainment that athletic departments provide. At the other end of the pay distribution are the head coaches in football and basketball. Based on the 2008 figures, salaries and benefits accounted for 35% of total budgets. Coaches' salaries and benefits accounted for roughly half of the payroll cost.[36]

The size of coaches' salaries has been a lightning rod for criticism for more than a century, but the magnitudes have ballooned in recent decades. In the late 1920s, writers expressed outrage that head coaches were being paid more than professors.[37] The issue was important enough to be covered in the Carnegie Foundation's massive study published in 1929. That report showed that on average football coaches at large institutions earned more than the highest-paid full professor on campus. But data on salaries are sparse, making comparisons over time difficult at best. Thanks to a study that *USA Today* undertook in 1986, however, it was possible to chart increases in pay for a large sample of public universities, which, unlike private universities, are in most states obliged to reveal such public records. I used data on coaches' salaries and other compensation for 44 public universities belonging to one of the five most established conferences to construct estimates of total compensation, and I did the same using comparable data for 2009–2010. I also collected comparable information on the

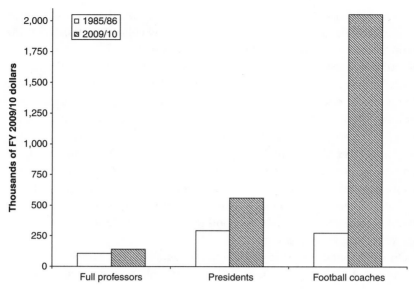

Figure 5.1. Average compensation of full professors, presidents, and football coaches, 1985–1986 and 2009–2010, constant 2009–2010 dollars, 44 public universities.

Universities are those for which data on both presidents and coaches were available for both years. "President" refers to the chief executive officer of the campus, whatever the title. See also Table 5A.2. All figures expressed in thousands of 2009–2010 dollars. *Sources*: Author's calculations, based on data from *Academe*, March–April 1986 and 2009 editions; *USA Today*; and *Chronicle of Higher Education*.

compensation for presidents (or the equivalent chief operating officers) and full professors for these same institutions.[38]

Over this 24-year period, as shown in Figure 5.1, the average full professor's salary, adjusted for inflation, increased by 32%. College presidents did much better, seeing their compensation rise over this period by 90%. But football coaches left both of these groups of university employees in the dust: their compensation increased by an astounding *seven and a half times*.[39] By 2009–2010 the average football coach in these universities made three and a half times what the average president did. Leading the surge in coaches' pay were universities with dominant teams. In 2008 Alabama became the first university to pay its football coach $4 million a year, and Texas was the first to top the $5 million mark in the following year.[40] Basketball coaches also did well but lagged behind football coaches in the rate of increase.[41]

Generous pay for celebrity performers is by no means unique to big-time college athletics. The 1980s and 1990s saw the incomes of highly compensated workers rise faster than those in the bottom four-fifths of the income distribution. And at the very top, incomes increased at breakneck speed. The compensation of the median CEO in very large corporations, for example, rose at an average real rate of 9.6% per year.[42] The comparable rate for these big-time football coaches at public universities was almost as spectacular, at 8.4%. One feature that distinguishes the pay of head coaches from that of corporate executives is the extent to which coaches' pay is rent that arises in large part because of the artificially low payments to athletes. Although the latter is fixed by NCAA rule, the former is not.[43]

## Profit or Loss?

A financial fact widely cited by critics and the NCAA alike is how few big-time programs break even or make a profit. This tendency to lose money is a common cause of chagrin among observers of the college sports scene. Critics see such losses as financial drains on academic programs, while supporters of college athletics have used them to rally support for tapping new sources of income or cutting costs.[44] The authors of one report concluded that traditional revenue sources like ticket sales were "chronically inadequate" to cover costs.[45] It should not be surprising that observers fix upon this bottom-line statistic, because athletic department budgets are so similar to the profit-and-loss statement of ordinary businesses and because universities want to limit the subsidies they provide.

But this seemingly precise financial statistic is not as reliable an indicator as it might appear to be. To begin with, the break-even line it embodies can differ from one university to the next, based entirely on arbitrary administrative decisions. It is a common but quite arbitrary practice to combine into a single administrative unit the two great revenue sports with the dozen or two money-losing sports. Perhaps a university decides to include physical education as well, making it all the more difficult for that administrative unit to stay in the black. Equally arbitrary are decisions about how to account for some types of financial aid. A university may decide, for example, to cover the extra cost of athletes' out-of-state tuition outside the athletic budget or to cover some athletes with need-based or merit scholarships, which are not charged to the athletic department, instead of athletic scholarships, which are. In addition, the usual calculation of budgetary gain or loss is subject to a handful of other seemingly capricious accounting practices that can easily differ from one university to the next. For example, most calculations of profit or loss for athletics leave out items that ideally would be considered in any complete accounting of financial profit or loss. One of these items is overhead costs, those covering centrally provided services that are not charged to individual units, like the cost of operating the university's central administration. Other costs, such as maintenance for athletic facilities that are used for general recreation as well as intercollegiate teams, might be paid for entirely by the athletic department, thus overstating the department's "true" expenses. Items ideally belonging on the revenue side may also be omitted when a university totes up the department's profit or loss – items like additional parking revenues or book store receipts that are generated on game days, or athletics-driven sales of university-branded merchandise.[46] Another reason that net profit is a flawed metric is that athletics may have other effects with financial repercussions for the university that are nowhere accounted for in the conventional profit-and-loss statement. Athletics may affect admissions, with large potential financial implications, or it may affect donations to university programs outside of athletics. These possibilities are discussed in the next chapter.

A last weakness of the conventional profit-and-loss statement is that, like university accounting more generally, it reveals little about the cost or value of the buildings and other structures under the domain of athletics. As we will see, capital projects have become a large item of spending for big-time athletic programs in recent years. And paying to build such new facilities is only part of the cost of these projects. To it must be added the inevitable depreciation that occurs to structures over time, which can be offset only by replacement or by repairs and renovations that are part of a capital budget, if there is one. To get a handle on the magnitude of capital costs in college athletics, one economic study produced an estimate of total capital costs by estimating the value of buildings and land and then applying conventional rates of interest and depreciation to this total value. Using this approach, the authors estimated that, for athletics at FBS universities, annual capital costs were nearly as large as operating expenses. When these estimated capital costs were included, they calculated that the cost of big-time athletic programs amounted to 4.5% of total university costs. Even these calculations may not fully account for the costs of financing athletic facilities with bonds or other borrowing if a result is to increase the interest rate the university will pay for other debt finance.[47]

## Haves and Have-Nots

Not every football stadium in the world of big-time college athletics is part of such a bountiful financial operation as the one at the University of Michigan. Other stadiums may feature comparable enthusiasm, pageantry, and cultural significance, but for the vast majority of major college athletic programs, the financial picture is decidedly less rosy than it is at Michigan. Consider, for example, another big-time sports university that added luxury suites as part of a stadium renovation, Mississippi State. Although a series of renovations added to its capacity, its Davis Wade Stadium held just 55,000 spectators, only about half as many as Michigan's, and Mississippi State's revenues were less than 40% as much.[48] Located in the small and remote town of Starkville, this land grant university has historically played a secondary role in athletic recruiting to the state's flagship, Ole Miss. But in 2009 it hired a new head coach who vowed to capitalize on the university's history of racial inclusivity to recruit a bigger share of the state's top prospects. To pay for the new coach and other expenses of running a big-time football program in the competitive SEC, Mississippi State did what many of the struggling big-time programs are forced to do. They relied on mandatory fees levied on their students and a direct subsidy from the university.[49]

As is true with every other form of commercial endeavor, some participants in big-time college athletics are more successful than others in their pursuit of success. In most industries, the most successful firms are also usually the largest, producing a disproportionate share of total output, but this is not true in either college or professional sports, because each "firm" is limited to one team, and the number of games as well as players is strictly limited. So it is with intercollegiate athletics, where the only real differences in scale of operation are in the size of stadiums and perhaps number of sports. Instead of scale of operation, the way success is manifested in this industry, besides win–loss records, is chiefly in the richness of the budget, the salaries of coaches, and the relative importance of the major sources of income. The variation in budget size is made clear from the list of the largest 100 programs in Table 1.1, showing that the programs at the top end spend more than five times what those at the bottom do. Such disparities are no doubt a source of grievance to those universities that see themselves as have-nots, adding fuel to accusations that the BCS is designed to deny all but a select few athletic programs the fruits of the commercial success of college football.

The differences up and down this college athletic pecking order show up on several dimensions. To illustrate some of those differences, I present some averages for what could be thought of as four generic "types" of big-time programs, each containing five universities. These are displayed in Table 5.2. The first two groups of institutions come from the five most well established conferences (Atlantic Coast, Southeastern, Big Ten, Big 12, and

Pacific 10). These conferences are home to most of the best-known big-time college athletics universities. To represent the most successful of them, I selected from each of these conferences the public university that had the highest total revenues in 2008. This group includes five name-brand, perennial powers in college football and basketball – Florida State, Texas, Ohio State, California, and Florida. I use them as examples of universities with one type of big-time program, the "major power." From the same conferences I also selected the public institutions with the smallest revenues and call them "also-rans."

These two groups of institutions from major conferences represent an illuminating contrast. In terms of pedigree, they are very comparable. The median institution in each group has been playing football for more than a century, and the teams are part of some of the country's most storied rivalries – among them, Ohio State–Michigan, Florida–Georgia, Texas–Oklahoma, and Cal–Stanford.[50] Beyond their historical connectedness, though, the differences between the groups are large. Measured in terms of success in the two major revenue sports, the major powers generally win much more often than their conference siblings, as illustrated by an average winning percentage of 75% in football and men's basketball in 2008–2009, compared with just 44% for the also-rans.[51] The major powers also drew much bigger crowds. Attendance at football games in the top group was almost twice what it was among the also-rans, and total revenues in the top group were more than twice as large. They also paid their head football coaches much more. Whether cause or effect, head football coaches at the major powers were paid some three times what those at the lesser programs earned.

As much as these two sets of programs differed from each other, the contrasts in big-time college athletic programs are more dramatic once one looks beyond the established conferences. To fill out this comparison, I selected two more groups of public universities from the top and bottom of five other conferences, here dubbed "lesser" conferences (although the Big East enjoys the status, along with the five more established conferences and Notre Dame, of being a member of the Bowl Championship group of conferences). These programs were the highest and lowest revenue producers, respectively, in the Big East, Conference USA, Mid-America, Mountain West, and Western Athletic. The top programs in these conferences are well known, but their fame is more limited and their histories more abbreviated than those in the most well established conferences. The incomes of even the best earners in these lesser conferences averaged less than those of the poorest performers in the major conferences. Their football attendance was also smaller. And for those at the bottom of the revenue ranking, average income was less than half of what it was among the major conference also-rans. The low revenues among the lesser conference institutions cannot be blamed on losing games, for the institutions in both of the minor conference clusters had winning records.

Beneath the very visible differences among these four groups of big-time sports universities are significant contrasts in their budgets. The bottom section of the table, based on the 2007–2008 figures collected by *USA Today*, shows that these groups of institutions had strikingly different mixes of income sources. To highlight these differences, I divided income into the same five categories identified in Table 5.1. For each category there is a marked variation across these four types of programs in their degree of reliance. For both the major conference types, ticket sales represented more than a quarter of total revenues, but this share was considerably smaller among those in lesser conferences. In absolute terms, the size of ticket sales for the lesser conference also-rans was just 40% of the sales for the top earners in their own conferences. This difference cannot be explained by smaller football stadiums, but rather by lower ticket prices, smaller crowds, or both. The average revenue from ticket sales differed dramatically across the spectrum, with the major powers averaging 10 times the amount of income of the lesser also-rans.[52]

Dependence on the next three sources listed differed markedly, with each group relying especially on one of them. For the major powers, it was contributions. For this group, contributions exceeded ticket sales in importance for the bottom line, accounting for 30% of total revenues. For the major also-rans, the key revenue source was NCAA and conference distributions. This group's 28% share illustrates the advantage of being the object of redistributive largess in an affluent conference. For both groups of programs in the lesser conferences, the key source of revenue was institutional subsidies. Whereas the members of major conferences relied on subsidies for small fractions of their budgets (4% and 11%, respectively), the lesser powers depended on subsidies for 35% of their total revenues and the lesser also-rans depended on them for a remarkable 43%.

The plight of one lesser also-ran was laid bare in the report issued by a task force at the University of Cincinnati in 2010. Despite a subsidy amounting to a third of its revenue, the athletic department still ran deficits and its teams had only limited success against Big East opponents. The task force explained this lackluster performance by citing the university's small football stadium (32,500 capacity), its paucity of "premium amenities" such as luxury boxes, unfavorable university accounting practices, and a "historical

Table 5.2. *Revenue profiles for four types of big-time college sports programs*

| | "Major Powers" | "Major Also-Rans" | "Lesser Powers" | "Lesser Also-Rans" |
|---|---|---|---|---|
| | Florida State | N.C. State | Connecticut | Cincinnati |
| | Texas | Iowa State | Memphis | Southern Mississippi |
| | Ohio State | Illinois | Miami (Ohio) | Bowling Green |
| | California | Washington State | San Diego State | Colorado State |
| | Florida | Mississippi State | Hawaii–Manoa | Louisiana Tech |
| Average | | | | |
| Football attendance, 2008 | 86,600 | 48,000 | 29,000 | 23,400 |
| Win–loss record, football and basketball, 2008–2009 | 0.748 | 0.443 | 0.540 | 0.538 |
| Revenues (2008–2009, thousands) | $102,880 | $44,549 | $36,331 | $21,241 |
| Football coach pay (2009, thousands) | $3,182 | $1,091 | $898 | $701 |
| Distribution of revenues, 2007–2008 (%) | | | | |
| Ticket sales | 28 | 27 | 18 | 12 |
| Contributions | 30 | 17 | 16 | 14 |
| NCAA and conference distributions | 12 | 28 | 11 | 12 |
| Subsidy | 4 | 11 | 35 | 43 |
| Other sources | 26 | 16 | 19 | 18 |
| Total | 100 | 100 | 100 | 100 |

*Note:* "Powers" are defined as public universities with the highest revenues in 2007–2008. "Also-rans" are defined as those with the lowest revenues in that year. "Major" conferences are defined as the ACC, SEC, Big Ten, Big 12, and Pac-10. "Lesser" conferences are defined as the Big East, Conference USA, Mid-America, Mountain West, and Western Athletic. Percentages are weighted by total revenue. They may not add to 100 due to rounding.

*Sources:* 2007–2008 athletics revenue, U.S. Department of Education, Equity in Athletics Data Analysis Cutting Tool Web site, http://ope.ed.gov/athletics/; NCAA, *2004–08 Revenues and Expenses*, Division I; football records, James Howell, http://www.jhowell.net/cf/scores/byname.htm, 12/28/09; basketball records, ESPN.com, ESPN http://sports.espn.go.com/ncb/teams,12/28/09; football coaches' pay, *USA Today*, http://www.usatoday.com/sports/college/football/2009-coaches-contracts-database.htm?loc=interstitialskip, 12/28/09; 2008 football attendance, http://web1.ncaa.org/web_files/stats/football_records/Attendance/2008.pdf, 122809.

lack of interest in UC sports." In order to become competitive, its athletic department said it would need an additional $11 million a year in revenue, or an increase of some 30%. Among other remedies, the task force recommended student fees earmarked for athletics.[53]

As this example and the figures in Table 5.2 illustrate, the economics of running a big-time college sports program differs markedly up and down the food chain. In particular, the sources of income for athletic departments look quite different, depending on the success of their teams and their membership in a major conference. As is often remarked, membership in a BCS conference brings with it considerable financial advantage. These are the modern-day haves in big-time college sports. All the have-nots can do at this point is argue the equity case for a system of postseason playoffs that would entitle them to a bigger share of the income earned in big-time college football.

## THE BUSINESS MODEL

To understand the logic behind a university's financial decisions regarding its big-time athletic program, it is necessary to know not only its objectives as an institution, but also how it understands the workings of the enterprise itself, that is, how various possible expenditures can bring about certain outcomes. Called variously a "logic model" or "production function," this understanding about how outcomes are actually achieved lies within the special realm of athletics directors and coaches, not presidents and provosts. It is precisely because this knowledge is specialized that experts on athletics are needed to run the athletic enterprise. Having received instructions from university leaders regarding what its ultimate objective should be, the athletics director can then apply this specialized knowledge to formulate what is commonly called a business model. This will be the guide for putting together the athletic department's budget.

Let us consider the two parts of this business model – the objective and the means by which this objective can be attained. A central argument of this book is that universities with big-time athletic programs are ruled by ultimate decision makers – trustees, regents, or boards of governors – who want to have competitive, if not winning, teams. This assertion finds support not only in casual observation, but also in the provisions that universities include in contracts they make with head coaches. As an illustration, the University of Alabama's contract with head football coach Nick Saban in 2010 called for bonuses of $125,000 for winning the SEC championship game, $200,000 for taking his team to a BCS bowl, and another $200,000 for winning the national title. Likewise, assistant football coaches, the athletics director, and others in the department received bonuses based on the team's success on the field.[54] Economist Burton Weisbrod and his colleagues made a systematic analysis of the contracts of 11 football coaches at universities with big-time programs. They focused on performance-based monetary bonuses not only for winning (such as games or championships), but also for academic performance (such as graduation rate for team members). They discovered that the bonuses for winning were considerably larger than those for academic performance: the average maximum attainable bonus based on winning for this group was 12 times the size of that for academically based incentives.[55] A perusal of coaches' contracts will show that universities value other objectives besides winning. The contract for Alabama head coach Saban just cited also gave him $25,000 for being named SEC Coach of the Year and would also award him $50,000 if his team's graduation rate was in the top half of the SEC.[56] In addition, the football coach at the University of Washington was guaranteed a bonus of $20,000 if donations to the athletic department increased by 10%, and the coach at Maryland was promised a bonus if he and his team did not violate the established code of conduct.[57] While winning games was not the only criterion for bonuses, there seems to be little doubt that universities with big-time athletic programs place a great deal of weight on winning.

Turning to the second part of the business model, exactly how does the athletics director turn a budget into winning games? The textbook answer, applicable to any business, is that he puts money into the items that will yield the most bang for the buck. But what are those items?[58] In answering this question, every athletics director must confront three governing truths about the business of college athletics.

## The Centrality of Recruiting

The first of these – one might call it the First Law of Athletic Success – is that recruiting talented players is the unalterable requisite for winning. Many of the ingredients of a winning athletic program are surely as shrouded in mystery as are the keys to success in business or warfare, but it is safe to assume that success depends in large part on the quality of the coaches and the athletes they recruit. Coaches win games and championships by performing at least three important functions: recruiting, instructing, and motivating players. Not surprisingly, teams with very good players tend to win, and there is every reason to believe that coaches can influence the number of such players on their teams. But no amount of coaching, no degree of opulence in facilities can make up for a lack of good high school recruits. This reality makes it imperative to hire coaches who can recruit the best players. Other factors may be helpful in the recruiting of good players, like heavy media coverage, big crowds, and a tradition of winning records, but nothing seems to matter more than having coaches who are good recruiters. And since both the number of scholarship athletes a coach can recruit and the means of recruiting them are strictly limited by the NCAA, each additional star player a coach can recruit is an unambiguous advantage, since that player effectively replaces a lower-quality one who would otherwise have received a scholarship.[59]

Although no one has quantified the process by which good players are made, economists have sought to calculate their monetary value once they put on their uniforms, by calculating the additional revenue a university can expect (the "marginal revenue product") for each additional star player it adds to its roster. For this statistical calculation, a star player is defined as one who is later drafted by a professional team. The best available research on this subject suggests that adding one more such draft-quality player generates additional annual revenue on the order of $500,000 in football and $1.5 million in basketball.[60] Since the extent of recruiting, the size of rosters, and the cost per player are all strictly limited by NCAA rules, a coach who can increase the number of such players – regardless of whether this is due to his ability to recruit talented players or to improve the recruits he gets – is worth real money to a university. So too are any other expenditures that will secure good players. When combined with the imperative to win, this first truth goes a long way in explaining why coaches, and boosters, put so much emphasis on recruiting and why it has been so hard over the years to prevent recruiting violations. More on this later.

## The Revenue Potential in the Revenue Sports

The second governing truth about this business is the revenue potential that arises from the enduring popularity enjoyed by the two main versions – college football and basketball. As the preceding chapter spells out, this general popularity expresses itself in strong brand loyalty toward a host of identifiably differentiated products, one for every university with a history of big-time competition. Each of these universities has a brand name, complete with its own nicknames, mascot, fight song, and distinctive color combination. These aspects of institutional identity are so important that universities have been willing to go to court to protect them. Not only does the University of Michigan have a history of intercollegiate competition dating back to 1881, one that features marquee rivalries with other prominent universities like Notre Dame and Ohio State, it also owns the rights to a famous fight song and a distinctive design on its football helmets.[61] All of these features are part of a brand name that has undeniable commercial value. Although few if any brands in collegiate athletics are more valuable than Michigan's, virtually all of them have some value, in large part because of the existing fan base. Any university that made the decision to drop big-time sports would, in effect, be walking away from an asset with genuine commercial value.

By virtue of the commercial value of the product they make, big-time college athletic departments are the most thoroughgoing commercial entity in American universities. Like professional teams and other for-profit firms in the entertainment industry, they rely on sales revenue, they use television and other commercial media, and they sign contracts having little connection to any traditional academic purposes. Medical centers certainly have their commercial aspects, and are larger than athletic departments, but their commercial dealings are intermixed with noncommercial objectives tightly aligned to traditional aims of universities – research, teaching, and community service. Despite the palpable commercial value of college athletics, however, it bears repeating that the primary objective of athletic departments is not to make money for its own sake. Rather, it is to produce winning teams, for which money is virtually an ironclad necessity. The real importance of this commercial value is therefore its power to generate income that can, in turn, be used to win games. As the escalation in salaries for head coaches illustrates, athletic departments consistently decide to pay whatever the market price dictates for coaches who can recruit star athletes and produce winning records.

## Zero-Sum Competition

The third governing truth of the college athletic business is sometimes as hard to accept as it is obvious: for every winning team, there must be a losing team. Athletic competition is necessarily zero-sum competition. For any given athletic department charged with the task of producing winning teams, therefore, this fact rules out complacence as a promising mode of operation. Add to the zero-sum truism the fact that competition on the athletic field is as close as anything we know of to a true meritocracy. Whereas reputation or connections may help an applicant gain admission or a faculty member obtain a research grant, these things matter very little once a game begins. This is not to say, of course, that reputation is unimportant to financial success, for reputation is the essence of brand names. But the zero-sum character of athletic wins and losses will be an essential contributor to a growing athletic arms race, as discussed later.

## RECRUITING AND THE DARK SIDE

A legendary college basketball coach, who earns several million dollars a year and is a household name to college sports fans across America, invites to his house an 18-year-old high school recruit for a family dinner of steak and lobster. Ranked second-best high school prospect in the nation by one widely cited recruiting Web site, this recruit also meets with the dean of the university's business school and stays in a four-star hotel adjacent to campus. He received similarly warm welcomes on his official visits to five other universities, meeting with the university's president at one and having dinner at the homes of the head basketball coaches at most of them. These details could be gleaned from the young man's widely cited blog, where he chronicled his impressions of all his visits. The culmination of this recruitment occurred on a November afternoon in the gymnasium of his high school in Ames, Iowa, where a press conference had been set up in front of 3,000 people and was viewed by a live national television audience on ESPN. With the drama of an Academy Awards presentation, the recruit announced that he had decided to attend the University of North Carolina, the reigning NCAA men's basketball champion. The press conference concluded with a live TV hookup to the gymnasium where the North Carolina team and coach had stopped practice to gather around the camera to greet their newest recruit.[62]

A second coach earning millions of dollars invites several recruits to his house for breakfast, including another 18-year-old athlete highly recruited for his skills as a defensive back in football. A third coach of one of the premier basketball programs in the country is reported to have told another recruit, described in a gushing *New York Times* article as having "legs that double as trampolines," that he would fire all of his assistants if the young man did not sign with his team. These two coaches, at Alabama and Kansas, respectively, were successful in their entreaties. One recruit announced his decision before a packed high school gymnasium in Gadsden, Alabama. The other, winner of a dunking contest sponsored by McDonald's, announced his widely covered decision during a media time-out of a nationally televised game.[63]

Only the most promising high school stars receive this kind of attention. In his book about the attention given to a running back from Philadelphia, Mississippi, in 1981, *The Courtship of Marcus Dupree*, Willie Morris described the torrent of phone calls to the recruit's home, forcing his family to buy an answering machine. In his book *The Blind Side*, Michael Lewis tells a similar story of the frenzied pursuit of a star high school tackle, marked by constant visits by college recruiters and culminating in plane rides to faraway universities and house calls by famous college coaches. Another book describes how a renowned basketball coach called the home of one prized high school player virtually every day, applying an approach known in recruiting circles as "baby-sitting."[64]

Even for those recruits not pursued by dozens of institutions, there is attention aplenty. Most of the heavy lifting of recruiting is carried out by assistant coaches and recruiting specialists. The intensity of this effort is well illustrated by the travels of the recruiting coordinator for Oklahoma State University, who kept a record of his recruiting visits during the recruiting season preceding the 1975 signing date. Often working 16-hour days, he attended games and practices, called on local sportswriters, and met with coaches, athletes, parents, and alumni. Over a six-month period, he made 93 visits to 49 towns and cities in 10 states, ranging from Kansas to Minnesota to Kentucky.[65]

The motivation for universities to pursue this kind of elaborate courtship can be explained using a simple model from principles of economics. Call it the supply and demand for top-quality high school football and basketball players. Athletic departments have a strong demand for these young men because they are essential to winning, by the First Law of Athletic Success. As we have seen, the value to an athletic program of landing a draft-quality recruit in football has been estimated to be upwards of $500,000 a year, and the value of a draft-quality recruit in basketball is more than $1.5 million.[66] This strong demand comes up against a supply of such potential star players, however, that is more or less fixed.

In freely functioning markets, price is expected to rise to a level at which the demand can be satisfied by the supply. But in the market for star high school athletes, an artificial ceiling has been placed on the price, preventing it from ascending to a level that would bring supply and demand into alignment. This price ceiling has been created by the requirement that college players be amateurs, embodied in the NCAA's rule that recruited athletes receive no more monetary compensation than the cost of a full scholarship. Payments to athletes are prohibited – during recruiting, at the time of signing, or afterward. Every good economics student knows the likely effects of a price ceiling that is set below the market-clearing price. One is that the excess demand will somehow get rationed, perhaps by an arbitrary method like first-come-first-served, or by unsavory means such as under-the-table payments. Any buyer fortunate enough to purchase this item will be effectively receiving a valuable bonus, sometimes called "rent." In this case, the rent is the difference between a player's worth to a university and the modest cost of a scholarship.[67] This sizable rent creates strong incentives for famous coaches not only to humble themselves at the feet of high school stars, but also to seek every possible advantage within the rules to sign those star players.

This rent also creates the incentive to push the envelope at every edge, even cross over the edge and cheat.[68] Indeed, economics textbooks warn that any cartel agreement is constantly at risk because of the incentive it gives members to cheat. As amply demonstrated by more than a century of American intercollegiate football, many college athletic programs have succumbed to the temptation to cross the lines of propriety and rule. As early as 1893, the president of a college in Iowa lamented the violation of the amateur principle in college football: "The hot competition in these games stimulates certain unfortunate practices, such as the admission of professionals into college as nominal students."[69] By the 1920s, violations of recruiting rules, documented by the 1929 Carnegie Foundation report, were common. In those days colleges were prohibited from making initial contact with high school players. Coaches routinely got around this prohibition by arranging to bump into athletes or have alumni get in touch with them and urge them to initiate contact.[70]

Cheating in recruiting reached what seemed to be its logical extreme in the SEC during the 1980s. Players at Texas Christian reported in 1985 that they had been receiving regular cash payments to play.[71] But no other institution rivaled Southern Methodist, where signing bonuses and monthly cash payments became standard operating procedure. In 1984 a player who had been recruited by SMU reported receiving cash and a job for his father, supplied by a booster. In 1986 an SMU player admitted he had been paid $25,000 plus $750 a month to play at the university. Other players were discovered to have received monthly payments, a system maintained with the cooperation of boosters and coaches.[72] For this sustained record of cheating, plus the university's initial resistance to change, the NCAA in 1987 exacted its most severe penalty, a one-year "death penalty" during which football competition at SMU was completely suspended. It is notable that these violations were not simply the work of one or two rogue coaches or alumni boosters, but were carried out with the knowledge of the top university leadership, including the chair of the university's board of governors, himself a once and future governor, reelected shortly before the extent of the scandal and his involvement became known.[73] Years after Morris's book chronicled his recruiting, Marcus Dupree revealed that he was offered $250,000 to play for one team.[74]

It is, of course, impossible to know how widespread such cheating was or is. At the same time the NCAA was investigating SMU, the Lexington *Herald-Leader* won a Pulitzer Prize for a series exposing cash payments to basketball players at Kentucky, and the executive director of the NCAA estimated that 30% of big-time athletic programs were breaking the rules.[75] The best study on the extent of recruiting violations, published in 1991, surveyed professional football players about their experiences as college players. Although the survey's low response rate and exclusive attention to college players make its results an uncertain reflection of the experience of all college players, its results are striking and the large number of former players who did respond (more than 1,000) commands notice. Asked whether they had ever taken illegal payments for signing or playing for a college team, 35% of the respondents who had played for a Division I-A university replied that they had. Although this rate differed across conferences, the inescapable message is that cheating was, in the experience of these former players, remarkably prevalent.[76] The survey also showed that cheating was more frequently reported by recent cohorts and, not surprisingly, by players who had been the most sought after.[77] And there is every indication that cheating continues to occur in the recruiting of high school athletes, as NCAA investigations at Connecticut and Southern California attest.[78]

The mischief that can result from the strong incentives to capture star players plays itself out not in such explicit payments but in the gray area around the edges of allowed behavior. For example, one activity that has raised eyebrows is the use by universities of "recruiting hostesses," student volunteers, predominantly female, who provide hospitality and tours to visiting recruits. Despite new restrictions handed down by the NCAA, parents of recruits have noted that groups such as the University of Tennessee's Orange Pride engage in "a lot of eye contact and touching" during these visits.[79]

Another gray area is the recruitment of athletes through "third parties," usually coaches or trainers other than an athlete's high school coach. In basketball, teams organized through summer leagues and the nonprofit Amateur Athletic Union (AAU) feature top high school players. Coaches of these teams have access to top high school players that is not available to college recruiters. In recent years college basketball recruiting has occasionally involved hiring the coach of one of these teams as a speaker or even as an assistant coach, presumably with the hope of recruiting one of the players on his team. After hiring a coach for one AAU team in Washington, D.C., for a salary higher than the university president's, Kansas State successfully recruited several star players from that AAU team. In other cases in which a coach is not hired, athletics boosters from a university have been known to make (tax-deductible) contributions to support an AAU team having on its roster a desirable recruit. In another case, one university scheduled a game against such an AAU team, paying for the privilege.[80] As even critics of these practices admit, they are not violations of current NCAA recruiting rules. But they do demonstrate some consequences of the powerful incentives that are created by the combination of the First Law of Athletic Success and the prohibition against paying college athletes.

## ZERO-SUM COMPETITION AND THE SPENDING ARMS RACE

In contrast to the many enterprises whose output can be measured in absolute terms of tons, hours, or units, success in athletic competition is almost always measured in relative terms, in comparison with competitors. Economists who study winner-take-all tournaments explain that, when winning is the only objective, it becomes perversely logical to marshal all available resources in an effort to emerge victorious. In one apocryphal story, a client asks his lawyer how much his case will cost him; the lawyer replies, "How much do you have?" The same logic drives arms races, both literal and figurative.[81] From the standpoint of society, the resources devoted to gaining the upper hand in this kind of positional competition are wasted resources, since their use yields no gain for society at large. Such arms races are an example of a well-known case from game theory, the prisoner's dilemma – a class of social interactions in which the players, seeking their own best outcomes, produce a bad collective outcome.

A similar tendency has been observed more generally in higher education, where the aim of universities is often simply "to be the best." Economist Howard Bowen put forward the following axiom to explain the perennially high rate of cost escalation in higher education: universities raise all the money they can, and they spend all that they have.[82] So as university athletic departments vie to recruit among the limited number of potential star players – whether with coaches or handsome facilities – spending more and more resources to sign them up them makes sense if the funds are available. This is the logic of the athletics arms race.

One development that is often pointed to as evidence of an arms race is the boom in capital construction for athletics. Universities with big-time athletic programs have in recent years undertaken capital projects such as stadium improvements and the construction of new arenas, athletic dormitories and special advising centers for athletes, and practice facilities in what some see as an "athletics arms race."[83] Between 1990 and 2005 more than half of the Division I-A universities opened new football stadiums or had major renovations done to existing stadiums.[84] Examples include the football stadium renovation at Michigan ($226 million) and others at universities such as Texas ($176 million), Oklahoma State ($260 million), and Stanford ($90 million). The last of these was a complete makeover. Instead of adding to seating capacity, it involved building an entirely new 50,000-seat stadium inside an aged bowl designed originally to seat 85,000. One argument for renovating Stanford's football stadium, for example, was the notion that the new stadium's smaller size would produce more sellouts and a boisterous crowd, conditions Stanford believed would improve the quality of football players it could recruit.[85]

Two of these renovations included widening stadium seats to accommodate the modern fan's larger girth, and all four of them featured new premium seating areas, including 47 luxury boxes and an enclosed bar at Texas.[86] Nowhere did capital improvements for athletics assume more importance than at Oklahoma State, the recipient of the record-breaking $165 million gift in 2006. It laid out an ambitious plan to clear 100 acres adjacent to its football stadium using eminent domain to build an "athletic village," complete with indoor and outdoor football practice fields, a new baseball stadium, an equestrian center, and practice facilities for soccer and track.[87] A survey of athletic department fund-raising in 2006 revealed that 28 public universities had raised an average of $82 million in capital campaigns for athletics over the previous five years and 7 private universities had raised an average of $87 million.[88]

More evidence that the arms race metaphor applies to spending on big-time athletics is provided by the rapid escalation in pay for head coaches. As noted earlier, head football coaches' compensation at 44 public universities increased in real terms more than sevenfold between 1986 and 2009, compared with the one-third increase enjoyed by full professors at the same universities. Whether or not the spending in big-time athletics can technically be defined in these terms – as a self-perpetuating and collectively wasteful exercise – it does appear to be the case that spending on athletics has been increasing more rapidly than spending on universities in general. Over the period from 1989 to 2003, total spending for the universities in Division I-A grew at an inflation-adjusted annual rate of 2.7%. Over the same period, spending on athletics at these universities increased 4.5% a year.[89] A similar comparison covering 97 public universities in the FBS between 2005 and 2008 reveals an even bigger disparity in rates of increase. For these universities, while academic spending per student increased at an average rate of 3.0% a year, athletics spending per athlete increased an astounding 7.5% a year, a rate that would double spending in a decade.[90] This certainly *looks* like an arms race in spending on athletics.

## THE BUSINESS OF WINNING

Athletics is a basic part of the operation of many American universities, but it is unlike the traditional academic functions in several important ways, one of which is financial. It is by far the most thoroughly commercial of the major activities that these universities engage in. Because its routine operation involves producing a form of entertainment that possesses proven commercial appeal, the athletic department has the capacity to generate sizable revenues. Ticket sales represent a significant share of this potential income, but income is also regularly generated from charitable contributions, much of which is really a kind of premium that affluent fans pay to obtain good seats at games or other perks. These two sources of income are of paramount importance to the established big-time programs, but they are to a surprising extent unimportant at universities with lesser names. For programs below the top rungs of the pecking order, institutional subsidies take on real significance.

Winning is the athletic department's primary aim, for this is what university leaders desire above all for their athletic programs. To be sure, this objective must be pursued within bounds, those set by rules, budgetary realities, and the institution's own weighing of the benefits of athletic success compared with the potential costs associated with unsavory sports headlines. But the emphasis on winning, the reality that there must be as many losers as winners, and the tremendous economic rents that can be achieved by recruiting top-notch players combine to create powerful incentives for coaches and athletic departments to use every conceivable opportunity to sign those players. These forces also push programs to exploit the popular demand for college competition to raise the income required to run a winning program. To a large extent, the fundamentals of this business model have remained unchanged for many decades, but developments in the marketplace have raised the stakes in the past 30 years, resulting in an arms race of rapidly escalating expenditures. This acceleration in spending has served to accentuate pressures that have been present all along: the urge to commercialize and the imperative to recruit star athletes.

# SIX

# Institution Builder

Following months of speculation and debate about the issue and the release of a 100-page feasibility report prepared by a blue ribbon committee, the chancellor of the University of North Carolina at Charlotte announced that he was supporting a proposal to add football to the university's athletic program. He said that his decision was based not on the hope for increases in either enrollment or donations, but rather on the institution's "long-term strategic institutional goals." Quoting the adage "You are judged by the company you keep," he urged the adoption of football because the universities with which UNC Charlotte wished to be associated were members of the Football Bowl Subdivision. Football, he said, would bolster the university's reputation and strengthen "the 'ownership' of the Charlotte community of this institution over the long term, thereby creating secondary benefits for our university in terms of political and financial support, research partnerships, employment and internship opportunities for our students."[1] The committee's feasibility report, while noting the modest potential for ticket sales and some opportunities for corporate sponsorships, placed particular emphasis on the potential for football to improve the community's perception of the university, increase school pride among students and alumni, and "become a significant element in the branding of the University."[2] Two months later, the university's board of trustees approved the plan, pending the sale of 5,000 seat licenses for the as yet unbuilt stadium. Although the university failed to reach this goal, the proponents won the day. A little more than a year later, the statewide UNC board of governors approved the plan to field a team and build a $45 million stadium, to be financed by tax-subsidized state bonds. The plan called for student fees at the Charlotte campus to become the highest in the UNC system, covering more than half of the football program's total cost.[3]

The chancellor's hope might not be a pipe dream. There are in fact precedents to support the idea that big-time college athletics might help to elevate UNC Charlotte to the top echelon of public universities. One case in point is the University of Connecticut, which rose to national prominence on the coattails of its championship men's and women's basketball teams. A leader in that state's senate attributed the legislature's decision in 1995 to allocate $1 billion over 10 years for campus renovation and construction to this prominence: "It was athletics that got people to think again about UConn in a big way." For UConn's president, athletics served as an all-around institution builder because it helped to recruit students, reach out to alumni, solicit donations, and "sell our program to the state legislature."[4] Another case thought to illustrate the power of big-time athletics to assist a university's ascent is the University of South Florida, an urban university whose national recognition lagged far behind its enrollment of 45,000. In a rapid rise in athletic prominence, it began playing football in 1997, gained Division I-A status in 2001, and joined the Big East conference in 2005. Playing to large crowds in a stadium already used by Tampa's professional football team and successfully pursuing corporate sponsorships and a television contract with ESPNR, the university was able to increase its revenues for athletics by 60% in three years. A pledge by boosters to backstop any deficits helped to overcome initial faculty opposition, although the university's provost complained that athletics did end up taking some resources away from academic programs.[5]

The hope for such payoffs from sports prominence remains a frequently voiced justification for getting into or staying in the big-time sports business. A Harvard doctoral dissertation reported that administrators at three private universities expressed that view in interviews. They believed sports enhanced their universities' prestige by generating national news coverage, attracting prospective students, building school spirit, and giving their alumni "bragging rights in offices and bars" across the country.[6] A committee at Berkeley expressed its belief that "Intercollegiate Athletics adds to campus 'spirit' and cohesion" and "serves as a unique and irreplaceable point of contact with the University's alumni and friends."[7] And a task force at the University of Cincinnati argued that its intercollegiate sports program improves the university's image, maintains connections to alumni, stimulates donations, attracts new students, "builds pride," and "enhances the college experience." Administrators also cite diversity among the reasons for having big-time sports. Not only do revenue sports bring nonwhite athletes to campus, these sports are believed to attract male students in general as applicants.[8] After his team's improbable run in the national basketball championship ended on a last-second shot in the final game, the president of Butler University wrote an op-ed for the *Chronicle of Higher Education* proclaiming that his small institution had gained immeasurably despite the loss. He cited the explosive sales of Butler T-shirts, the boost in pride among alumni, the final game's large TV viewing audience (134 million), and the favorable tone of news stories about his team and institution.[9]

The benefits of recognition apply to large and small universities alike. Recalling how often he spotted Michigan jerseys when he traveled in the state, former University of Michigan president Harold Shapiro wrote, "This identification through sports was perhaps the only way for the University to remain part of the daily imagination of alumni as well as a wide spectrum of citizens of the state of Michigan."[10] Indeed, the hope for recognition appears to be a primary impetus for the steady stream of universities entering the fray of big-time football competition. In addition to UNC Charlotte, the list of new and prospective entrants include Old Dominion, South Alabama, the University of Texas at San Antonio, and Georgia State.[11] The last of these universities found itself the subject of a whimsical story on National Public Radio about its new fight song, written in preparation for the university's inaugural football season to replace the former song. The story raised the question of whether it was appropriate for the university to invest in football during a recession. In response, one Georgia State professor wrote in to say that he, too, had been skeptical about the decision, but the potential benefits of fielding a team were perfectly illustrated by the very fact that the university was getting national exposure for its fight song rather than its research.[12]

For many public universities, big-time sports inevitably requires taxpayer support, and that means political support as well. As noted in the preceding chapter, 18% of the average public university's athletic revenues come in the form of subsidies – student fees or allocations from government or the university. Of the 99 public universities whose detailed financial records were publicly available for 2008, 44 depended on such subsidies for more than a third of their income.[13] Yet even these subsidies leave many institutions wanting more in order to be competitive in intercollegiate competition. The task force report at the University of Cincinnati, which noted the athletic department's call for a 30% budget increase, revealed that the department had run up accumulated budget deficits amounting to $24 million.[14] The economic realities of running a successful program, especially one lacking the traditions and popularity of a Texas or Ohio State, surely test a university's commitment to using big-time sports as a means of institutional advancement.

This chapter examines how universities attempt to use spectator sports for the purpose of building support for itself in the world beyond the campus walls. Because of the widespread popularity of college sports and the intense loyalties that it can evoke, the chance to see a game becomes a valuable commodity, one that university leaders can exchange for other things of importance. There is every reason to believe that university leaders recognize this value when considering ways to advance their institutions, given their reliance on the generous inclinations of donors and government officials. College teams and their games can also become a form of mass advertising, one that institutions can use to advance their "brand." The chapter's first section deals with how universities use athletics to build outside support – in particular, support from state government officials. The second section adds donors as another target group and describes how several American universities use their home football games to curry favor with potential angels. The third section examines one potential payoff of the free advertising that a prominent sports program offers, an increase in applications. The fourth section compares the recent academic performance of universities with and without big-time sports, and the last section summarizes the two ways in which these programs work to generate support.

## COURTING THE POWERFUL

One argument used by proponents such as the UNC Charlotte chancellor for investing in big-time athletics is that it offers the opportunity to make and solidify valuable connections to the community and the state. As logical as this argument might sound, it has never received much serious attention from researchers. Surprisingly, political scientists have never, to my knowledge, subjected this belief to empirical test. Yet in light of how dependent state universities are on the good opinion of their state legislators, it is a connection that seems to make sense. In 2007 state universities received a quarter of their total revenue from state governments.[15] Even generously endowed public institutions like the University of Michigan and the University of Virginia, which receive less than a tenth of their annual revenue through state appropriations, need to be attentive to the state power structure.[16] In most states, the power of state government over universities is on display every time a state budget is voted on and a new figure is announced for average faculty salary increases. And this influence goes beyond appropriations. Usually by way of state boards of higher education, state governments determine all manner of policies that govern public universities, from creating degree programs to approving new capital spending projects.

This dependence provides more than enough reason for leaders of state universities to curry favor with those in charge of state government. Legislators are important because they vote on appropriations bills. Governors are important, to various degrees, because they usually determine who will sit on state higher-education boards and may have further powers, such as the legislative veto. Athletic departments may have their own reasons for maintaining good relations with the state capitol, since they often receive support in the form of student fees, institutional support, and direct state appropriations. For the most successful big-time athletic programs, these forms of support accounted for a small fraction of athletic revenues, but for universities in lesser conferences it made up for more than a quarter of the total.[17] Local government is important as well for all universities, private as well as public. Cities and counties have an importance all their own, at once mundane and vital, since the university sits in their domain when it comes to such vulnerable issues as public services, construction, and inspection.

Given the rather obvious value to universities of keeping on good terms with public officials, what role might big-time athletics play? To ask this question is almost to answer it. It seems an obvious tactic to use college sports to influence the politically powerful, but only if those targets of attention have an interest in the entertainment product itself. Luckily for the universities, this is the case. By all appearances, there are few legally permitted perquisites more attractive to state legislators than the chance to attend a football game of one of a state's major college teams. For one thing, many state legislators are alumni of their state flagship universities. Wherever they were educated, however, many legislators and other government officials just seem to value this perk, a supposition supported by the time-honored practice of universities to offer tickets to such VIPs and the enthusiasm with which those officials take up the offer. Consider, for example, these practices, as they stood in 2009:

- Penn State offered to members of the state legislature free seats in a special section of the press box for all of its home football games, giving out some 500 free passes a year.[18]
- By tradition, the home team in the annual Auburn–Alabama football game offered two free tickets to every member of the Alabama legislature, and the state's governor traditionally received two dozen tickets to every Auburn and Alabama home game. In 2007 Auburn and Alabama together gave more than $100,000 worth of tickets to state and federal officials.[19]

- Ohio State gave many public officials, including every state legislator, the opportunity to purchase, at face value, up to four season tickets for football. In 2008 officials purchased 773 of these, which they could legally pay for using campaign funds.[20]
- Universities in Texas, including the University of Texas, Texas A&M, and Texas Tech, gave free and discounted tickets to state officials. In 2006 the University of Texas alone gave out 1,962 tickets, almost half of those for free.[21]
- Louisiana legislators were allowed to buy up to six tickets each for the 2008 Sugar Bowl, paying a face value that was less than a fifth of their market value.[22]
- By virtue of the football tickets it distributed, the University of Georgia was the biggest lobbyist in the state's university system in 2007.[23]
- Legislators in other states, including Utah and Colorado, received free tickets to selected games.[24]

If these examples illustrate the potential effectiveness of distributing tickets to lawmakers, so does the trend for states to regulate, restrict, or prohibit the practice. The practice of giving out free tickets became swept up in state-level campaign finance and lobbying reform efforts. As a result, tickets are increasingly being sold – though sometimes at prices below actual market value – rather than given away, and officials are often required to report such gifts in annual conflict-of-interest reports.[25] Among the states to restrict the practice were Arkansas, North Carolina, Florida, Oklahoma, Tennessee, Texas, and Wisconsin. For example, in Tennessee, legislators were restricted to a single state-subsidized football ticket per year. Legislation in Oklahoma set a $100 limit on gifts to lawmakers, thus cutting to 30% what had been a 90% subsidy on season football tickets for the University of Oklahoma. Still, of all gifts that lobbyists in the state reported giving to legislators in a recent reporting period, more than half were for tickets to football games at Oklahoma or Oklahoma State.[26] Rather than extinguishing legislators' demand for tickets to games, therefore, such legislation may simply serve to document more effectively the enduring demand for this commodity.

Whether such perks actually have the effect of softening the hearts of legislators, county commissioners, and other local officials toward the university is another question, however, and one that is not easily answered. The closest any research has come to answering it, to my knowledge, is a study that asked a related question, whether being in Division I-A is associated with a higher level of state appropriations. Brad Humphreys analyzed the state appropriations to 570 state institutions between 1975 and 1996, using a statistical model that determined whether it made a difference if an institution was in Division I-A. This approach essentially focuses on the experience of universities whose status *changed* during this period. He found that being in this most competitive NCAA division did indeed make a difference: it was associated with appropriations that were some $6 million higher (in 2009 dollars) than those of otherwise similar institutions that were not in Division I-A, or about 8% of the average appropriation level. At the same time, there was no statistical support for believing that bowl appearances or high national ranking mattered. The result for Division I-A membership is independent of any effects that membership might have on enrollment, since enrollment is one of the factors controlled for in the estimation.[27] Although this work cannot prove that being in this most competitive athletic division caused appropriations to be higher, it is certainly consistent with this interpretation. But it says nothing about the exact mechanism through which a big-time program influences the appropriation level.

What makes it possible to believe that college sports might be useful politically is that more than a few state officials really do seem to care about it. This reveals itself most clearly in the way that state political figures have dealt with issues related to athletic schedules and conference membership for universities in their states. As far back as 1947, the Alabama House of Representatives passed a resolution calling on Auburn and Alabama to end what had been a 40-year suspension of their annual football game. Evidently, it worked, for the two universities agreed to resume the series the following year.[28] A common cause célèbre for state politicians to enter the realm of intercollegiate schedules is the up-and-coming state university that seeks the chance to play against an established flagship university. For these flagships, there is usually little to be gained, and a good deal to be lost, by playing against smaller or less prestigious in-state institutions. Such was the case in Kentucky, where the University of Kentucky, a legendary basketball power, had shown little interest in playing against upstart Louisville. The two public universities had not played a regular-season game since 1922. But two years after Louisville won the national basketball championship in 1980, one of the team's supporters in the legislature introduced a bill that would have required the two universities to play against each other. Similar motivations inspired a bill introduced in the North Carolina legislature in 1995 to require the state's flagship universities, North Carolina and NC State, to schedule games against the smaller newcomer, East Carolina University. Although neither of these bills became law, the upstarts in each case eventually got what they wanted, regularly scheduled games against their more established rivals.[29]

In 2005 the governor of West Virginia intervened in a similar standoff by urging the state's two major public universities to schedule an annual football game. West Virginia University, a member of the Big East conference, probably making a similar little-to-be-gained calculation, had been reluctant to play the smaller and less prestigious Marshall University. In fact, it had played Marshall only once in the previous 82 years. For its part, Marshall wanted a scheduled game, but felt it would be demeaning for it to accept a "home and home" arrangement whereby all or most games would be played at West Virginia's stadium. The governor eventually succeeded in brokering a compromise, saying, "It will be the best time you ever had in West Virginia – legally."[30]

Even more than scheduling, the question of conference membership has received the close attention of state officials. Not only is institutional prestige on the line, but the financial stakes can be huge, since under the current bowl alliance system, members of the strongest conferences stand to earn a great deal from conference championships, bowl games, and other televised competition. One colorful case of the politics of conference alignment occurred in 1994, at a time when Texas and Texas A&M were both considering leaving the financially weakened Southwest Conference. Such a move would have dealt a blow to both the reputations and finances of the remaining conference members, in particular the two biggest ones, Baylor and Texas Tech. This unpleasant scenario was averted thanks to a meeting in February 1994 between powerful legislators – among them prominent alumni of Baylor and Texas Tech – and the chancellors of Texas and Texas A&M. Participants in the meeting later reported that Texas A&M agreed not to move to the Southeastern Conference in return for promised support for its proposed new basketball arena. Following the meeting, all four of these Texas universities moved over to what would become, by their addition, the Big 12 Conference.[31]

Another example of the politics of conference alignment came to light in 2003, when the Atlantic Coast Conference (ACC) was considering adding new members. With one eye on the financial payoff of expanding its conference into new media markets and the other on ensuring future participation in the Bowl Championship Series, conference members considered several institutions as potential new members. Among them were Virginia Tech and Syracuse. The governor of Virginia publicly urged the conference to add Virginia Tech and reportedly warned existing member Virginia not to veto its sister university.[32] An invitation to Virginia Tech soon followed.

Taking the opposite tack, the governor of New York publicly opposed ACC membership for Syracuse, because of the likely harm it would do to the Big East (Syracuse's conference), the league's annual conference basketball tournament in Madison Square Garden, and its other Big East members, including another New York institution, St. John's.[33]

Why do politicians care about schedules and conference alignments? If athletics is as peripheral to the core mission of universities as university mission statements imply, why would public officials take such an interest in these seemingly minor aspects of universities? One possible explanation is simply that athletic competition is an activity of universities that most people actually understand, and it is one where success can be readily evaluated by the average person. Certainly comparisons of universities' research and teaching can't easily be done. Not only do the intricacies of university research leave most laypersons scratching their heads, there is no easy way to compare the quality of research across institutions. Nor has anyone, layperson or scholar, come up with a way to measure or compare the effectiveness of teaching, despite the attention the *U.S. News* rankings have garnered. In stark contrast, athletics provides easily understood, head-to-head comparisons that yield clear results in real time. Although the outcomes of athletic contests are sometimes open to Monday morning reinterpretation, their validity is rarely questioned. Lawmakers and citizens alike might then just focus on athletics simply because that is something they can understand. And with reasoning similar to the logic of looking for your keys under the lamppost – because that's where the light is best – some have argued that legislators, lacking any better measures, use the outcomes on athletic fields to *infer* the quality of the larger institution.[34]

This reasoning also suggests why schedules and conference membership may have particular salience. If outcomes have informational content, so does the status of a university's acknowledged peers. Scheduling an opponent is akin to having him over for dinner, and inviting a university to be in your conference is like asking him to join your club. These actions signify a certain level of mutual respect, of institutional parity, and they give significance to the UNC Charlotte chancellor's reference to "the company you keep." Conference stereotypes may well rub off on individual members.[35] Thus it was the instinct to help a state's less prestigious university by improving the company it kept that inspired one governor to urge his state's flagship university to put the state's second-largest institution on its football schedule, and another to warn its venerable flagship to stand up for its humbler land-grant sibling as it sought to join a better conference.

But there is another possible reason for government officials' obvious interest in college sports. Rather than springing from a tendency to link athletic success to institutional quality, it may simply be that political figures enjoy watching games. Their interest may begin and end with the game and its outcome.[36] If a governor or legislator can be enticed into the president's box at the stadium, all the better. Once inside the box, he or she becomes fair game, along with potential donors, in the university's ongoing campaign to build outside support.

## LAYING GROUNDWORK FOR "THE ASK"

Besides political influence, another great reservoir of potential outside support a university might hope to tap through athletics is charitable donations. Once the concern chiefly of private universities, charitable donations have become an increasingly important source of funding for state universities as well.[37] One issue is whether success in athletics stimulates those contributions, as well as contributions to other parts of the university. We have already seen that contributions account for as much as 30% of the revenues for some big-time athletic departments. So it would not be too surprising if contributions to athletics were boosted by athletic success, since winning teams tend to create ticket scarcity and thus the opportunity for athletic departments to use contributions to ration the demand for tickets. Less clear is whether athletic success can create a halo effect over the university as a whole or just siphons off donative dollars that would otherwise have gone to the library or the university's general fund. Certainly there are academic leaders who, like the UNC Charlotte chancellor, claim that a big-time sports program will indeed stimulate overall giving, in part by keeping alumni "engaged with the university."[38]

A smattering of research studies have sought to find a statistical link between athletic success and donations. Although their verdict is not unanimous, the bulk of evidence suggests that donations from alumni do increase after a university's football team goes to a postseason bowl or its basketball team appears in the NCAA tournament.[39] There is, however, little evidence that winning records alone have an effect, in part because universities whose teams win consistently may also be distinctive in other ways. Nor are there definitive findings about the separate effects of postseason appearances on contributions to the academic portion of universities, only the following suggestive result. One of the studies showing that donations increased in years after postseason appearances found that this correlation applied to restricted donations – which include giving to the athletic department – but not for unrestricted giving to the university.[40] It seems likely that athletics reaps the bulk of spikes in giving associated with postseason play. Interestingly, the percentage of donations to universities designated for athletics has been increasing in recent years: between 1998 and 2003 it increased from 15% to 26% for alumni giving and from 12% to 19% for gifts from nonalumni.[41] One of the statistical studies provides fodder for considering athletics a means of achieving institutional goals. Its estimates suggest that a bowl appearance results in about the same increase in donations as a five-point increase in the average SAT score of its entering freshmen. But better than the ephemeral boost of a single bowl win is the effect of "athletic tradition" that comes from being a name brand in big-time athletics.[42] Best of all is athletic tradition *plus* the high SATs.

Not only are these statistical findings highly tentative, they do not address the practical question that university leaders must care about: can charitable giving be increased just by *having* a big-time sports program? It turns out that answering this kind of either–or question statistically is next to impossible, because it comes down to comparing the experiences of universities that are different in more ways than just whether they engage in big-time sports. Consider Emory versus Vanderbilt or UC San Diego versus UCLA. Despite this stumbling block to finding a statistical assessment of the effectiveness of big-time sports in boosting donations, I believe new light can be shed on this question by examining a heretofore unexplored source of data. This evidence is relevant to the question of whether universities act *as if they believe* that their commercial sports programs are effective. As I spell out later, the evidence I have collected strongly suggests that universities with big-time sports programs use them strategically to bolster outside support, particularly support in the form of donations.

The evidence I offer is lists of VIP guests who accept invitations to sit in presidents' boxes at home football games.[43] An inspection of these lists shows consistent patterns in the way universities use the scarce supply of seats in their presidential boxes. These patterns, I believe, suggest what kinds of outside support universities hope to generate in this way. Citing state open-records laws as support, I requested information from eight universities on the names of all those who sat in the president's box at home football games during the 2008 season, and I requested from another eight a list of all those who received complimentary tickets during that season. Although my letters cited the relevant state law requiring the disclosure of public records, at reasonable cost and in a timely manner, some of the universities nonetheless refused to comply with my request fully or at all, a response that would be interesting to study on its own.[44] Using the information from those universities that did send the requested information, I sought to classify the people who accepted these VIP invitations, for the purpose of inferring what might have been the intent of the universities in inviting them. With that aim in mind, I offer descriptions of the guest lists for three universities, followed by a summary for several more.

## University of Washington

The University of Washington plays its football games in 72,500-seat Husky Stadium, which offers stunning views of nearby Lake Washington and two mountain ranges in the distance. During the 2008 football season, which ended in a disastrous 0–12 record, its team played seven home games, featuring such opponents as Oklahoma, Notre Dame, and UCLA. In the fall of 2008 the university might have been especially keen on having both government officials and potential donors as guests at football games. That fall, the university launched an effort to persuade the state to put up $150 million for half of the projected cost of renovating the stadium, whose nearly 90-year-old foundation needed shoring up plus additional earthquake protection. A 14-page color brochure produced to make the case for the funding plan emphasized the public benefits derived from the stadium. In words and pictures, it described the stadium's use in more than 50 community events each year and pointed out that public funds had previously been allocated for two stadiums in Seattle used by professional teams. The brochure proclaimed, "By bringing the community to Husky Stadium, the UW gives back to the people of Washington, reinforces its public mission, and strengthens its ties to its neighborhood, its region, and its State." As it turned out, these efforts to convince the legislature to approve public funding would not succeed over the following two years, but its efforts to raise private donations would prove fruitful.[45]

Records received as a result of my open-records request indicated a total of 481 guest passes to the president's box for the season, not including entries for family members and companions accompanying them. Eliminating records for multiple games showed that 385 of these primary guests attended at least one game during the season. The guests, whom I will describe in some detail later, mostly without their names, fall into three broad groups: employees and students currently at the university, government officials, and members of the Seattle-area business community. Perhaps the most striking feature of this guest list is the heavy representation from the last group. Although the University of Washington is a public university, it was business, not government, that was the dominant professional identity of these guests. Some representation from the first group, however, was necessary to lend authenticity to the gathering. If universities use their president's box to provide potential donors and supporters a chance to gain a favorable impression of more than its football team, which I believe to be the case, there needs to be, sprinkled into the mix, real, live faculty members and students, as well as administrators, to make the experience authentic.

These representatives of the current university – faculty, administrators, other staff, and students – accounted for slightly more than a third of the season's guests, with faculty members being the least numerous. The students who were invited to the box were obviously not picked at random. Among them were student body presidents at all three of the university's campuses, a raft of other student government leaders, members of the homecoming court, and a collection of stellar athletes, among them a star pitcher for the university's softball team, a former pole vaulter turned medical student, and several students who had been gold and silver medal winners at the 2008 Olympics. Invited university administrators included the provost, chancellors and vice-chancellors from two branch campuses, deans, and other officials. In a class by themselves were members of the university's official governing body, the regents, since they really combined the university, government, and business realms. Six of the nine regents attended at least one game, including a Boeing vice president; William Gates, Sr., co-chair of the Gates Foundation; and two Seattle-area professionals working in commercial real estate.[46]

Other guests represented government at the state, local, and federal levels. From state government were 10 members each of the Washington Senate and House of Representatives, the attorney general, the chief justice of the Supreme Court, a higher-education budget analyst, and the governor's chief of staff, legislative director, communications director, and higher-education policy adviser. From local governments in the Seattle area came council members from various jurisdictions, two school superintendants, a mayor, and the King County executive. From the federal level came three members of the U.S. House of Representatives plus several staffers for one of Washington's U.S. senators. One guest of particular importance was Dan Evans, former university president, governor, and U.S. senator, a moderate Republican for whom the university's school of public affairs was named and, thanks to his extraordinary statewide popularity, generously funded through private donations.

Far surpassing the representation by government officials, past and present, was a phalanx of guests from the business and professional world, heavily drawn from the Seattle area. A number of the area's biggest corporations were represented, including Microsoft, Weyerhaeuser, T-Mobile, Wells Fargo Bank, and Boeing. More impressive was the large number of CEOs, founders, and principal partners of lesser-known firms, both large and small. There were producers of helicopters, yachts, electronic equipment, airplane components, industrial lubricants, wine, and tequila. Other industries represented were utility companies providing telephone, gas, and electricity, construction, insurance, commercial real estate development and management, business support services, and financial consulting. Multiple guests also came from biopharmaceuticals, communications, and information technology applications of various sorts. The line of work represented by the largest number of guests was venture capital, much of it IT-related. Several of the business people among the guests also served on visiting committees for schools in the university or on alumni association boards.

Rounding out Washington's guest list was a handful of representatives of the nonprofit sector, such as the CEO of the Seattle Chamber of Commerce, who could arguably be better thought of as a representative of business, and the president of the state's public broadcasting network. But there were no operating officers of charities, and there were no representatives of organized religion.

## University of Georgia

Near the diagonally opposite end of the country's big-time football domain is Athens, Georgia, where the University of Georgia competes as a member of the Southeastern Conference. In this university town, situated 70 miles from the cultural and entertainment competition of the nearest major metropolitan area, devotion to college football easily exceeds what can be discerned in metropolitan Seattle. Among the dozen members of the SEC, Georgia ranks among the most famous names, owing to its perennial success in football. Its regular-season 10–3 win–loss record in 2008 was its 12th successive winning season. Its 80-year-old, 92,000-seat Sanford Stadium occupies a valley on the hilly campus, and its playing field is lined on both sides by a distinctive hedge of privet. Like many other stadiums in big-time college football, this one has been retrofitted in recent years to include luxury boxes, called SkySuites, and outfitted with televisions, wet bars, and private restrooms.[47] Although most of these are leased to individuals or companies, at least one of them is set aside for the exclusive use of the president, and others are used by other administrators for hosting special guests at games.[48]

The list of guests to the president's suite for the six home games during the 2008 season included 258 unique guests, not counting family members or friends, about a hundred less than at Washington's seven home games. It may be recalled from Chapter 3 that Georgia plays its annual game against the University of Florida 350 miles away, in Jacksonville. As was the case with Washington, Georgia's president included on his guest list faculty members, administrators, and current students. Faculty members were drawn from across the university's array of 16 schools and included several recent winners of awards for teaching and research. Among the administrators invited were several vice presidents, the university's legal counsel, and deans of more than two-thirds of the university's 16 schools. Student guests included the president of the student body, the editor of the student newspaper, the head of the student judicial board, the presidents of student associations representing graduate students, fraternities, and sororities, leaders of orientation programs for new students, and members of a student organization who act as hosts at special events.

Among the invited government officials, none had greater direct power over the university than the state's board of regents, the governing authority for all the state's universities, including the two premier research universities, Georgia and Georgia Tech. Of the 19 reigning regents at the time, just 7 accepted invitations to attend any game during the season, though it seems likely that other members attended games in seats outside the president's suite. The 7 regents who did join the president's group at least once included two lawyers, two bankers, a real estate manager, and two executives of manufacturing firms.

In addition to these regents, state government was represented by 29 state legislators, split almost evenly between the state house and senate. Included in this delegation were the majority leader of the senate and the majority whips from both chambers. In addition to these legislators were a handful of guests from the state's executive branch, but these few were consequential. They included the lieutenant governor, the attorney general, heads of the state departments of agriculture and labor, and the governor's chief of staff. Also present were a few federal officials, among them three members of the U.S. House, both of the state's U.S. senators, and one justice of the Supreme Court, Georgia native Clarence Thomas. Just three of the guests were local government officials – the city mayor, the county manager, and the chair of a neighboring county commission.

More numerous than in the case of Washington were appointed members of various university advisory boards and boards of visitors. These boards, often created by universities to cultivate future donors, were in evidence at all the universities studied here except one. To this group I added officers and board members in the alumni association, whose importance to the university may be similar to that of advisory board members. Although not always linked explicitly to fund-raising, it is common for boards of visitors and advisers to combine access and honorific recognition with the expectation of future help with fund-raising and personal contributions.[49] At Georgia, the most important group of this kind, the Arch Foundation, was quite explicit in its expectation that members would not only advise and assist in fund-raising but also make personal gifts. The Arch Foundation was a newly created nonprofit organization set up for the express purpose of taking in tax-deductible contributions and establishing endowments to support the university's academic mission.[50] The dozen and a half Arch Foundation trustees who attended at least one home football game in the president's suite consisted primarily of current and retired executives in banking, finance, and other lines of business, two lawyers, and a retired chief justice of the state supreme court, all of whose brief biographies suggest they had the wherewithal to become significant donors if they were not already. Most were also alumni of the university.

Many more guests, as was the case with Washington, made their livelihoods in the business and professional world. Industries represented by at least a pair of owners, presidents, or CEOs included hotels and real estate, manufacturing, wholesale trade, hospitals, construction, utilities and banking, finance, and insurance. Reflecting differences between the economies of Seattle and Georgia, none of the business guests worked in IT, pharmaceuticals, or air transportation. But despite the importance of agriculture in Georgia, none of the VIP guests there were farmers either. Finally, the Georgia guest list also included a few members each of three professions, only one of which was represented at Washington: lawyers, physicians, and ministers.

## Texas A&M

Removed from both its state capital and the nearest metropolis by some 90 miles each, on a campus once the exclusive province of an all-male corps of military cadets and in a state where the passion for college football rivals that of the SEC, Texas A&M presents a third case of the strategic use of the president's guest box or, rather, boxes. To an extent far surpassing any other university examined in this chapter, Texas A&M is a system of universities. In addition to its main campus at College Station, its system comprises a medical center and 10 other universities across the state. Thus it was necessary to collect information on guests in two boxes – one for the president, who leads the flagship campus, and one for the regents, who rule the state system. This also required two formal requests to two separate offices. Combining the two lists revealed 307 unique guests with only one person, a U.S. congressman, included on both guest lists. All 16 state legislators whose names appeared were in the regents' box. The only government official to appear on the president's guest list was Governor Rick Perry, a Texas A&M graduate.

The other point of distinction for Texas A&M was the large number of guests who were members of some university-sponsored advisory council. The list of such boards suggests that Texas A&M has taken to heart the approach of cementing loyalties through appointment to formal advisory groups. Guests in the president's box included members of the president's board of visitors, the board of visitors for the Galveston campus, the board of the university foundation, the alumni board of directors, the library board, the board of directors of the university's Private Enterprise Research Center, development councils for liberal arts and the college of veterinary medicine, advisory councils for engineering, architecture, education, science, and the real estate center, the Texas A&M Mothers' Club, the Texas A&M Hispanic Network, and the Vision 2020 advisory council, a committee charged with advising the university's president and provost about the university's strategic planning initiative. In the regents' box were 16 members of the Chancellor's Century Council, a group that included almost 200 contributing members in 2009.[51] On the guest list provided by the regents' office, all 16 names of Century Council members were redacted.

The list of industries represented by other guests from the private sector bears the unmistakable marks of the Texas economy, its concentrations of wealth, and the university's land grant tradition. Most numerous by far were representatives of the oil and gas industry, including the giant companies ExxonMobil and British Petroleum. Construction, real estate, and law were next, each contributing at least five guests during the season. Other industries and professions with at least two representatives were agriculture, engineering, banking, marketing, medicine, and veterinary medicine. Texas A&M was one of two universities whose records I obtained that provided almost no names of students included in VIP guest lists, citing the federal law protecting student records. To make it easier to compare the composition of all the guest lists, therefore, I excluded students from the distributions discussed later. With this exclusion, Texas A&M had a bigger share of guests who were advisory board members (18%) than Washington (5%) or Georgia (10%). As for other business and professional people, Washington had the largest share, about one-third.

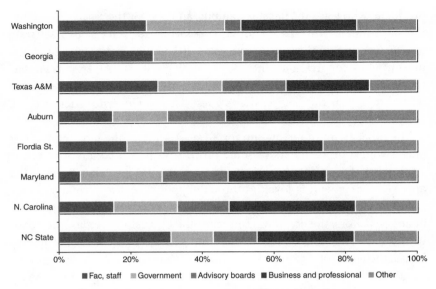

Figure 6.1. Guests in presidential boxes, 2008 football season.

## The Uses of the President's Box

I examined similar lists from other universities that complied with my data requests. Their makeup is summarized in the bar chart shown in Figure 6.1. Leaving out students, I divided guests into five categories: (1) current university employees, who were primarily faculty members and senior administrators; (2) government officials, including members of state boards that governed the university; (3) members of university-created advisory boards and alumni officers; (4) other members of the business and professional private sector; and (5) other guests. This last group included representatives of other universities and nonprofit organizations, members of the military, and guests identified only as donors or alumni. Family members accompanying primary guests were not included in the tabulations, although the ability to get invitations for family and friends must surely be part of the value of this perk.

Although the distributions do differ across the eight universities, perhaps their most striking feature is their similarity. Each guest list contained a healthy share of administrators, and all included faculty members who held no administrative rank.[52] The second common trait was the strong representation from business and the professions. Unusually numerous among those from business were presidents and CEOs. The universities differed in the degree to which these guests from the private sector also held titles bestowed by the institutions meant to signify their participation and influence on university affairs, such as being named to a board of advisers for an academic unit. Judging by the share of guests so designated, this practice was embraced most enthusiastically by Texas A&M and Maryland, but all of the universities included guests with the apparent financial wherewithal to be donors, whether or not they were named as members of advisory groups. Interestingly, I found no clear connection between universities' dependence on donations and their tendency to invite advisory board members or other business and professional guests.[53]

The universities differed most in the reported presence of faculty and staff members. At the low end was Maryland, whose 13 faculty and staff members made up only 6% of its guests. At the other end, 31% of the guests at NC State games were faculty and staff members. Also of note was Auburn, which had the largest number of state legislators, reflecting a tradition in the state of giving out free tickets for games involving the two flagship universities.[54]

What do these lists tell us about how these universities use their big-time sports programs and, by inference, what they hope to accomplish? In my view, they suggest that football games are a means of cultivating personal relationships, which is the time-honored approach of fund-raisers at universities that depend on charitable giving. An administrator at Georgia commented, "If you've ever been in the president's box at a football game, there is not a lot of football-watching going on. There is a lot of conversation, a lot of questions and answers, and a lot of work going on, with people being informed about what's going on at the university."[55] A president interviewed in the Knight Commission's survey of chief executives said, "All five of our top donors have an interest in athletics. They are very pro intercollegiate athletics. That is another way we communicate with them. As we invite them and they come to athletic events, it gives us another opportunity to talk about other important things that need funding at the university."[56]

According to one university fund-raiser I spoke to, a football game is not the occasion for "the ask," the actual request for a donation. But one president interviewed in the Knight Commission's survey offered a contrary view, stating, "I've done most of my fundraising in the football sky box."[57] In any case, the gathering of VIPs in the president's box or during a football game does offer an informal occasion where university officials can begin making the indirect but seldom hidden case for future donative support. To be sure, these public universities pay attention to state government as well, because it is an important source of funding, especially for capital projects, and a prime regulator of state universities.

Essential to the success of this strategy is each university's ability to attract movers and shakers, primarily from their state and surrounding community, who have supported or might support the university financially. It would appear that two ingredients help to induce these individuals to see a game from the president's box. One is the chance it provides all the invitees to meet and socialize with one another – to be part of an exclusive club composed of people at the top of their respective professions. Thus the president's box offers an alternative to the country club or nonprofit board as a venue to commune with other leaders. The second ingredient is surely the spectacle – the tens of thousands of fans, the noise they make, and the game itself. Even beyond the confines of the president's box, big-time sports gives the university a valuable perk that it can bestow on supporters and would-be supporters: the opportunity to purchase good tickets, usually at face value. When such tickets are hard to get, this can be a valuable commodity indeed. Thus big-time sports provides university leaders the chance to dole out valuable perks, as well as the opportunity to mix with scores of business leaders, potential donors, and government officials. Who can blame the chancellor of UNC Charlotte for wanting this for his university?

## ADVERTISING AND THE FLUTIE EFFECT

On the last play of a 1984 nationally televised game, a Boston College quarterback named Doug Flutie threw a long and desperate pass into a crowded end zone. One of his receivers managed to catch the ball, resulting in a celebrated victory over the University of Miami. The subsequent 12% spike in applications to the smallish Jesuit institution in the Boston suburb of Chestnut Hill became the stuff of legend in the world of college admissions. Similar stories are told about college basketball teams that pull off big upsets in the annual NCAA tournament extravaganza, such as the reported 30% increase in calls to Northern Iowa's admissions office following an improbable last-second shot that enabled its team to beat the tournament favorite in 2010.[58] The belief that athletic success can produce an increase in applications has come to be called, in honor of the quarterback who threw that 1984 pass, the "Flutie effect."[59] Although it does not show up on the athletic department's income statement, an effect like this could obviously have a profound financial impact on a university, given the budgetary importance of tuition revenues. Indeed, advocates who want to start new intercollegiate athletic programs at their universities often claim that the heightened visibility of athletics will reap indirect financial dividends. For example, Georgia State hoped to attract more residential students by creating a football program (initially at the Football Championship Subdivision level, one step down from the FBS), thereby allowing itself to be perceived as a "real" university. Likewise, the push for football at UNC Charlotte was spurred in part by its hope to become more competitive for the state's aspiring college undergraduates.[60]

The notion that athletic success boosts applications goes back much further than 1984. In fact, this belief was widespread enough that Harvard president Charles Eliot devoted several pages of his 1900–1901 annual report to a surprisingly detailed statistical analysis of it, using data on admissions trends and athletic success for Yale and Harvard between 1891 and 1900. He concluded "that there is no relation between athletic victory or defeat for Harvard, and the increase or decrease of preliminary candidates in the following year."[61]

Why might success in athletics lead to an increase in applications for admission, anyway? One obvious explanation could be that applicants simply enjoy following college sports and therefore wish to attend a university with successful teams. Although this may be true for some high school students, it seems not to be the case for most college applicants. A survey of college-bound high school seniors found that most were not that aware of the athletic programs of colleges where they were applying and most said the quality of the intercollegiate teams at prospective institutions was not important in their college choice.[62] A more likely explanation for the effect of athletic success on applications, if it exists, is that sports success, by virtue of the publicity and media coverage it elicits, acts in the way a billboard does; that is, it draws attention to the institution. It is "low-cost advertising."[63]

The empirical connection between athletic success and admissions has received considerable attention from social scientists in the years since the famous 1984 game. At least a half-dozen studies used econometric tools to analyze the connection, with most finding a positive but small effect of athletic success on both the number and average SAT level of applicants.[64] For the most part, however, these studies could not exclude the possibility that what appeared to be a positive association between athletic success and admissions might instead be due to other, unmeasured attributes of the same universities. If, for example, flagship public universities feature above-average academic programs as well as successful athletic programs, these analyses might incorrectly attribute application jumps to athletics.

The most convincing evidence on this question appears in a recent study by a pair of economist brothers who overcame the difficulty of omitted variables by analyzing trends over time for a large number of universities with big-time football or basketball programs. In this way, the authors were able to assess the effect of athletic success on each university's trend in applications, as proxied by reports of SAT scores sent by students to prospective colleges.[65] They found strong statistical evidence of a Flutie effect: athletic success in both football and basketball leads to an increase in applications. The boost is by no means permanent, however. In football the effect occurs mainly in the current year and in basketball mainly in the following year. The bigger the success, the bigger the bump. For example, finishing the football season ranked in the top 20 produces an estimated 2.5% boost in applications, but winning the national championship produces a 7–8% jump. Similar increases result from making it to the round of 16 in the NCAA basketball championship and winning the tournament altogether. Significantly, these increases include the applications (scores sent) of students with high as well as low SAT scores. How such victory-fueled applications are converted into actual matriculants is interesting. In the case of football, an increase in applications is followed by a more than proportionate increase in enrollment, but the boost in applications from basketball has no discernible effect on enrollment. The explanation might be that public universities dominate college football, and they are often able or are obligated to accommodate increases in demand for class slots, whereas universities that win in basketball are more often private or more selective and choose instead to respond to increased demand by being more selective.

The demographics of this effect are noteworthy. The authors have found that the high school seniors most subject to it are males, African Americans, out-of-state students, and those who played sports in high school. The apparent receptiveness of men lines up with survey evidence that males are more knowledgeable about and interested in sports, and it has been used to justify at least one university's interest in developing a big-time athletics program.[66]

On the basis of the best available research, therefore, it can be said that a Flutie effect is indeed at work in American higher education. Very successful seasons in either of the big-time sports result in application spikes. But the effect is fleeting. While this research shows the effects of changes in athletic fortunes, it cannot tell us what the long-term effect is of having athletic name recognition, of having a rich tradition of athletic success. This analysis specifically excludes the possibility of measuring that by looking only at each institution's trend in applications. The authors argue that two of their findings suggest that it is the attention that sports success generates that explains the Flutie effect, not applicants' desire to follow sports: the greater effect among out-of-state applicants and the tendency for the effect on all applications to diminish rapidly.

## OVERALL ACADEMIC QUALITY

How effective is big-time sports as a means of institution building? Even if a big-time program does help bring in donations, support, and applications, the costs of running the program might overwhelm those advantages. Indeed, one reason for the current hand-wringing over budgetary subsidies, the escalating salaries of coaches, and the increasing cost of building athletic facilities is the fear that big-time athletics causes university resources to be diverted from academic uses to athletics. Certainly the debate at Berkeley over subsidies to athletics was fueled by this worry. One way to determine whether this fear is justified is to compare the academic fortunes of universities with and without big-time programs. If the appetite of athletic departments is being fed in part by taking away from academic budgets, we could expect to see universities with big-time programs falling behind peer institutions that are free of the burden of paying for big-time sports. But if the main effect of prominence in athletics is to enable universities to attract resources and strong applicants, we would expect instead to see universities with these programs prospering and advancing in academic rankings. There are few questions more important in our assessment of big-time college sports than this one.

Alas, this question is not easily answered, mainly because there are no agreed-upon measures of academic quality (a fact, as has been previously noted, that stands in distinct contrast to the ease of drawing comparisons in athletics!). Rather than surrender entirely, it seems worthwhile to resort to a set of familiar, if denigrated, measures. I refer to the sorts of statistics regularly utilized by *U.S. News and World Report* to produce rankings that are as anxiously anticipated as they are universally dismissed by those who lead American universities. Even if these statistics do not fully capture the quality or effectiveness of what goes on at universities, I believe at least some observers would judge them to be loosely correlated with those more important aspects for which there are no measures. Any reader who believes that the kinds of measures used in the *U.S. News* rankings are worse than no measures at all should, therefore, skip the remainder of this section.

To see whether American universities with big-time sports programs have been falling behind, holding their own, or moving ahead in comparison with their peers that do not have such programs, I examined changes in a half-dozen proxy indicators of quality over a 15-year period. I looked at data for 101 universities for which *U.S. News* collected and published information in both 1995 and 2010 in connection with their rankings. For these universities, the magazine provided detailed information in both years for six measures: the percentage of freshmen who were ranked in the top 10% of their high schools, the percentage of applicants who were accepted for admission, the percentage of freshmen who returned for their sophomore year, the percentage of alumni who made contributions, test scores of applicants accepted for admission, and the subjective ratings that the magazine collected in surveys sent to university administrators.[67] For each of these six measures, I ranked the 101 universities for both 1995 and 2010, and I calculated for them a combined rank for each year based on all six measures, using a weighting scheme based on the method *U.S. News* employed in 2010.[68] I grouped the universities by their NCAA classification – FBS, other Division I, and all others – and then calculated the average change in rank for each of the three groups. Each group featured differences in quality and selectivity, ranging from excellent to outstanding. There were 51 universities in the FBS group, and the average SAT scores of their students ranged from 1090 to 1445. There were another 29 universities in Division I, including all eight members of the Ivy League; their students' average SAT scores ranged from 1045 to 1490. Of the 21 universities with no teams in the most competitive division, average SAT scores went from 1135 to 1515.

Calculations showed that there was virtually no change in relative rankings based on these measures over this 15-year period. For the overall weighted ranking, no group's average rank changed by much more than one position. The FBS universities slipped a little in top 10% students and acceptance rates, but they gained in freshman retention. Taken together, there was almost no movement to speak of. One possibly confounding influence in making this comparison is the large share of these highly rated FBS universities that are state universities. If the country's best public universities have fallen behind their private counterparts, as some indications suggest, our comparison might be reflecting this trend. To remove this possible complicating factor, I did a similar comparison using only the 51 private universities in both *U.S. News* reports. Among this group of highly rated private universities, those in the FBS actually fared better than those with less competitive athletics, paced by sizable improvements in the rankings of Miami, Southern California, Pittsburgh, and Brigham Young. On average, the private FBS universities advanced an average of 4.6 spots over the 15-year period, compared with an average of 2.8 places for the other private universities. Whatever the underlying causes, these calculations suggest that the expense and other costs associated with big-time sports programs are evidently not so serious as to cause the universities that sponsor them to fall in rankings based on these kinds of proxy measures of academic quality.[69]

## TWO AVENUES OF INFLUENCE

In contrast to the state-funded universities of Europe, American universities grew up during the 19th and early 20th centuries as part of a decentralized system of institutions that resembled a market or a collection of regional markets. During the same period, big-time sports became attached to American universities. Whether or not the competition for resources was the reason American universities incorporated commercial sports, the sports enterprise before long became one way to seek support, both financial and political.[70] And whether or not it can be scientifically proved, many university leaders say they believe athletics is effective in doing just that. Donations have been the form of support of primary interest to private universities, although public institutions increasingly rely on them as well.

In the state universities, fostered by the Morrill Acts of 1862 and 1890 and dominant outside the Northeast, support from the state legislature was crucial but by no means ensured. The reality that these state universities have always had to fight against is the spillover of ideas and talent that flows out from every flagship state research university. Because the research and graduates it produces cannot easily be kept within state boundaries, taxpayers in states like California and Wisconsin end up paying a substantial portion of the cost of producing benefits that will be enjoyed across the country and beyond. Illustrating a basic lesson of economics, the spillover of these benefits tends to cause states to underinvest in research universities. Although a state might gain something from the prestige of having a world-class university, it is unlikely that state residents will ever reap all the benefits generated by their tax support.[71] Legislators no doubt sense this and may, quite justifiably, question the payoff from research and graduate education at their states' flagships.

Enter big-time sports and the platform it promises to provide for showing off the university to state officials. To the extent that the overtures of presidents' boxes have been successful, it is plausible that big-time athletic operations have protected state-funded universities by mollifying or distracting legislators who might otherwise have been inclined to cut research programs whose benefits spill out beyond state borders.[72] If so, such world-class state universities as Berkeley, Michigan, and North Carolina owe part of their reputations to the protective armor created by legislators' devotion to their athletic teams.

Big-time athletics offers universities two avenues for building outside support. The first one, stripped of its colorful context, boils down to lobbying. When universities give state legislators free tickets or VIP treatment, the lobbying component is clear enough for the practice to have increasingly fallen under the purview of state ethics laws. Whatever explains the interest that legislators and other officials clearly do have in college athletics, there is no denying that it is there, as illustrated by their willingness to accept free passes to see games. The interest is there as well among county commissioners and local business leaders. It is certainly there among alumni. Inviting such people to the president's box for a home football game gives the university a chance to foster and strengthen valuable bonds. One can easily appreciate why state-supported universities might find irresistible the logic behind inviting them into the president's box. Among the available means of lobbying and institutional advancement, athletics could easily be the most cost effective because it provides an efficient means of access to the politically and economically powerful.

A second avenue of influence through which big-time sports can help build an institution is fame. Any university with a football or basketball team automatically receives regular coverage in the press. A university with successful teams can expect to get even more attention. Thanks to such media coverage, athletics can be a comparatively inexpensive way to build outside support, given the extremely high costs of the alternatives. Although operating a big-time athletic program is not cheap, the cost of achieving greatness in athletics is minor compared with the cost of doing so in important fields of research.

Another reason public recognition might be easier to achieve through athletics than through academics is the essential meritocracy of athletic competition, which is made possible by the objective metric it uses to compare any two teams – the score. Past glory means little when the teams take the field (although scheduling and conference membership may make getting on the field a challenge for some institutions). If athletic success attracts attention, an ambitious university that can achieve athletic success, like the University of Connecticut or the University of South Florida, will have found a cost-effective shortcut on the road to academic renown.

It is not only public universities that come to believe that their institutional aims might be furthered by prominence in athletics. In fact, two of America's most highly ranked private research universities used football as a central pillar in their strategies for achieving academic prominence. Those two universities, Chicago and Duke, began their rapid ascents with large philanthropic gifts – Chicago from John D. Rockefeller and Duke from James B. Duke. Both of these fledgling institutions sought to raid the faculties of established universities by offering high salaries, but both also succeeded in gaining almost overnight prominence by hiring promising or accomplished football coaches. Chicago hired for its coach in 1892 former Yale star Amos Alonzo Stagg, who actually played as well as coached during his team's first two seasons. Following a victory over Michigan in that second season, a Chicago student newspaper proclaimed that success of this sort was "what we most need – a reputation."[73] Stagg soon built Chicago into a football powerhouse, winning the Big Ten championship five times before World War I.[74] In 1931 Duke hired Wallace Wade, another famous coach who had led Alabama to three national championships. Wade proceeded to take Duke to two Rose Bowls. The fortunes of both of these football programs faded in succeeding decades, with Chicago dropping football altogether in 1939. Nevertheless, both universities used big-time football, and the instantaneous fame it brought, to advance their institutional goals. Former University of California president Clark Kerr playfully remarked on the strategic use of big-time athletics to raise a university's standing:

It is often through new academic specialties and through athletics that universities seeking to rise in the academic hierarchy can most quickly and easily attract national attention.... The mark of a university "on the make" is a mad scramble for football stars and professorial luminaries. The former do little studying and the latter little teaching, and so they form a neat combination of muscle and intellect.[75]

At the national level, politics and big-time athletics come together every time a championship team is honored at the White House. Before these ceremonies became a standard ritual, national politics and big-time sports had occasional meetings, as when Grover Cleveland halted the Army–Navy series, Theodore Roosevelt summoned the Yale, Harvard, and Princeton coaches to the White House to urge a change in rules, Richard Nixon visited the locker room after the national championship football game, or Barack Obama urged a national playoff in college football. But the political issues of greatest import for universities have to do with the forces at work inside universities and those at the state and local levels outside them. As outlined in Chapter 2, the position of athletics inside the university is bolstered by a group of supporters, often organized under the banner of a formally constituted booster organization. Whether or not they are guests in the president's box, most of them will surely be somewhere in the stadium, occupying good seats. But in its pursuit of big-time athletics, the university looks beyond simply sustaining the athletic enterprise. It seeks not only to satisfy the demand from its stakeholders for competitive teams, but also to use athletics for its broader institutional goals.

# SEVEN

# Beacon for Campus Culture

The trouble in College Park, Maryland, started shortly before midnight on March 31, minutes after the semifinals of the 2001 NCAA men's basketball tournament. The University of Maryland's team had just lost to archrival Duke in a close game marked by several controversial calls by referees. In addition to the students who had viewed the game on large-screen televisions set up in the basketball arena on campus, hundreds of students and other fans had watched it in one of the several sports bars located in a two-block commercial strip along Route 1, near the southeast tip of the Maryland campus. The Cornerstone, for example, had room for 400 patrons, who could watch the game on one of its 35 screens. The Santa Fe Café could seat another 450. One bar on the strip, Bentley's, had even erected a heated tent with TVs in its parking lot in order to make room for fans to see the game. Although many fans went home right after the game ended, dozens poured out of the Route 1 bars and headed east, in the direction of Fraternity Row, where post-game celebrations, complete with bonfires and firecrackers, had taken place the week before. On this night, however, the crowds congregated in many locations, including street corners closer to Route 1. Before the night was out, some 60 fires would be set at various locations in College Park. The biggest of all the gatherings surrounded a bonfire at the corner of Knox and Dickinson, just two blocks east of Route 1. This was the location where events took an ugly turn.

Local officials were ready for unruly post-game behavior, or so they thought. They had planned for and been successful in dealing with the celebrations following the Maryland team's win the preceding week. On this night, 100 Prince George's County firefighters and 60 county police were stationed near Fraternity Row and other spots around campus. But the bonfire at Knox and Dickinson soon had flames leaping 20 feet into the air, as mattresses, chairs, sofas, fence posts, and a television set were thrown on it. Flames soon engulfed a utility pole carrying fiber-optic cables, and the fire eventually did enough damage to cut off cable TV service to 30,000 local customers. A crowd of some 1,000 chanted, "Go Terps!" while one student showed off by running through the fire. The crowd, now a mob, tore down lamp posts and fences and made away with furniture and gasoline from private residences. When firefighters arrived to put out the fire, rioters pelted them with stones, sticks, and bottles. They mounted a fire truck and rocked it back and forth, driving the firefighters away. Not until the firemen returned under police escort 45 minutes later was the fire brought under control.

The events that occurred in College Park in 2001 were by no means unique. Another student riot occurred the following night in West Lafayette, Indiana, after Purdue lost in the finals of the women's national tournament. Police there used tear gas after students started fires, broke store windows, and overturned cars. Within a 10-day period that spring, outbreaks of student violence occurred as well on or near the campuses of Penn State, Michigan State, and the University of Arizona following losses by their teams in the men's tournament.

These basketball riots of 2001 are just one extreme manifestation of behavior among undergraduates that has over the decades come to be accepted, if reluctantly, as part of the "collegiate experience." From pranks and panty raids to beer pong and fraternity parties, the stereotypical activities of undergraduate life – sometimes harmless, sometimes alcohol related, but always "nonacademic" – make up an important component of what college education is for many undergraduate students. This is college life in the entertainment part of the university, the one that is distinct from the libraries and research labs where American research universities earn their high global standing. This is the part of the university where academic pursuits are only a distant drumbeat. This is the part of the university that has room for the perspective offered by one fraternity man who took part in the 2001 melee at Maryland: "At the time, it seemed like a very logical idea.... I looked out and saw a blazing inferno. I felt like we should go out and burn things. I was having a good time; I admit it."[1]

Although trustees and administrators are unlikely to boast about partying, pranks, and drinking games at their universities, these activities are undeniably a part of the total collegiate package. As rankings like the Princeton Review's "Top Party Schools" suggest, these aspects are a more prominent part of the collegiate package at some universities than at others. The same may be said for commercial sports, which is an integral part of the educational experience at some universities but not at others. Through their degree requirements and the rigor of the courses they offer, universities explicitly advertise their expectations regarding the amount and kind of work students should do. But in the organizations and facilities they provide for students on campus, they also send unmistakable signals about what activities ought to be part of a college education.[2] So it is with the university's sports program, which may affect the educational functions of a university by diverting time and attention from academic pursuits. A big-time sports program simply has too big a footprint on a university campus not to influence the educational experience of its students. To be sure, these enterprises were already in place when most sitting presidents entered office, but the option to discontinue them always exists, at least in principle. For better or worse, therefore, they become part of a university's educational program.

How does the presence of big-time sports on a campus affect the lives of students? Some obvious things about universities with big-time sports distinguish them from other institutions – their large stadiums, unison cheers, painted faces, ubiquitous logos, and extensive media coverage. But these campuses, and the daily lives of students, may differ in less visible ways that are much more significant. How does the presence of a commercial sports enterprise influence the habits, traditions, and daily activities of undergraduates – how much they study, the topics and intensity of their bull sessions, and what they do in their spare time? This chapter looks at big-time sports as part of that educational program. It begins by considering reasons for believing that commercial sports might have any effect, positive or negative. Then it examines in detail what can be learned about how big-time sports relates to the types of students who enroll and about their activities once they arrive on campus. Finally, the chapter asks whether students are happier at institutions with big-time sports than at those without them.

## WHAT DOES COMMERCIAL SPORTS HAVE TO DO WITH EDUCATION?

The educational imprint of big-time intercollegiate athletics has been debated for at least a century. Advocates have touted its community-building power, while critics have seen it as a distraction from the important business of learning. The strongest educational argument in favor of spectator sports on a campus is its power to enfold students within a community that shares a common identity, by building what social scientists call "social capital." A well-recognized downside to life in a large community of individuals such as a university is anomie, the disconnectedness of individuals from the larger society. As Durkheim (1893) argued, such a condition has a number of undesirable outcomes, but one of the most common is a feeling of alienation that is destructive to both emotional and intellectual development. If a university wants the optimal educational experience for its students, it must counteract the tendency for anomie to develop. It is thought that one way of doing so is to bolster community through regular interaction and emphasis on common values.[3] In a survey conducted by the Carnegie Foundation for the Advancement of Teaching in 1989, 96% of university presidents agreed that administrators should do more "to strengthen common purposes and shared experiences."[4] The report emphasized the importance of "rites, ceremonies, and celebrations" because they "unite the campus and give students a sense of belonging to something worthwhile and enduring."[5]

One obvious candidate for strengthening bonds of community on a campus is spectator sports. Since its earliest days, big-time sports in American universities has been seen as a potential conduit for cultivating a sense of community. One report from the 1920s described the effects of rooting for the college football team:

It creates a strong sense of common interest. The sight of the filled stands evokes and intensifies the consciousness of human community, and the sense of the emotional solidarity of each stand, strengthened as each stand participates vicariously in the action of the runner, or passer or tackler, is in itself a stirring thing. This sense of common interest, continuing throughout the season, tends to develop a common bond of loyalty. It affords for the entire football season a clean and interesting topic of conversation and thought.[6]

These quaint sentiments are still echoed today by university leaders. Writing in the *Chronicle of Higher Education*, for example, one provost affirmed, "Sports teams can foster a deep sense of community and social solidarity, even when those teams lose more often than they win."[7] In truth, many American universities do display a community spirit not found, for example, in most European universities.[8] Could it be that this difference is attributable, at least in part, to another aspect of American universities that differs from those in Europe – the presence of university-sponsored sports teams?

On the negative side, critics over the years have seen more in intercollegiate college sports that is detrimental than constructive to the educational mission. Rather than fostering athletic participation, the argument goes, big-time sports programs encourage passive watching, frivolous activity, and harmful behavior.[9] As far back as 1893, Harvard president Charles Eliot criticized competition in football and baseball for its commercial orientation, the excessive time it took from studies, and, in the case of football, the high rate of injury.[10] In 1909, Princeton President Woodrow Wilson warned against the growing attention paid to student activities, including athletics, fraternities, and performing arts clubs, at the expense of "the work of the college, the work of its classrooms and laboratories."[11] An academic study of undergraduate life written in the 1920s by a professor at the University of Michigan professor stated frankly that undergraduates possessed little devotion to intellectual pursuits, a situation made worse by the attention paid to intercollegiate athletics: "Though a certain amount of time is sure to be wasted in idle gossip, the discussion of athletics overleaps all bounds and constitutes a positive distraction from study."[12] This view of collegiate life found cinematic expression in the 1925 movie *The Freshman*. Dressed in beanie and letter sweater, comedic star Harold Lloyd is seen joining throngs of other fans at "a football stadium connected to its own college."

Decidedly unstudious students still populate the campuses of American universities, of course, but their stereotype by no means describes all college students. Scholars who study undergraduate culture emphasize that students are not all the same. To make the point they sometimes divide students into contrasting types. One scholar, for example, distinguishes the "college man" from more serious "rebels" and studious and polite "outsiders."[13] Whereas the "college man" is hostile to faculty authority and academic pursuits, those in the latter groups are academically more serious, being much less likely to join fraternities or engage in stereotypical partying behavior. The term used by another scholar for fraternity partiers is "players," for those whose family resources allow them to pursue those stereotypical collegiate behaviors. Again, in the author's typology, such students make up only one of several student types.[14] Thus heterogeneity is the hallmark of the undergraduate student body. No generalization will apply to all students and few will apply to a majority of them. Even universities at the top of party school lists enroll many sober and studious students who spend out-of-class time in the library or engaged in part-time employment instead of at fraternity or sorority houses and sports bars.

If big-time sports does influence the quality of education a university offers, it could do so via one of two mechanisms, which social scientists call a *selection effect* and a *treatment effect*. The selection effect is the influence such a program has on the kind of students who want to attend the university, and the treatment effect is that of the sports program on those students once they have enrolled. If big-time sports programs disproportionately attract a certain type of student – "players," for example – the quality of life for other students will inevitably be affected, by virtue of the strong peer effects that occur in college.[15] Suppose the presence of spectator sports on campus causes such students to displace some of the more intellectually inclined potential applicants. It follows that the atmosphere of the campus will be transformed, if only marginally, beginning on the first day of freshman year, due to the altered composition of the student body. This is the selection effect. The treatment effect covers any direct effects on campus life once those students have enrolled – most obviously shown by the way students use their time, but also more subtly by the way they develop intellectually, socially, and morally and how they come to view themselves and the world. Both types of effects are clearly germane to weighing the costs and benefits of big-time college athletics, but they are probably among the least well understood among all the possible influences worth considering.

The aim of this chapter is to examine these two sets of influences by comparing measurable aspects of students and student life between groups of universities: those that have commercial sports programs and those that do not. Is there evidence that otherwise similar institutions featuring big-time sports attract different kinds of students? Do students attending such institutions have qualitatively different kinds of experiences in college? It will be possible to answer both of these questions in the sense of *correlation*, but it will be impossible to establish *causation*. The reason is that determining causation requires more demanding statistical support than is feasible in this case, given the available data. Only if students could somehow be randomly assigned to different kinds of universities, or if events conspired to approximate such an otherwise inconceivable assignment (thus producing a "natural experiment"), could a researcher determine causal effects to the satisfaction of scientific standards.[16] Indeed, a vast research literature has uncovered remarkably few definitive causal effects of the college experience itself. Studies of how the college experience affects such things as students' intellectual development, personal growth, attitudes, and occupational choice have uncovered virtually no influences that differ systematically across institutions or types of institutions.[17] This lack of demonstrated effect could mean that it really makes no difference where a student goes to college, or it could signify that the statistical requirements needed to prove such effects are simply too stringent to satisfy. In either case, it should come as no surprise that definitively determining the causal effects of a big-time sports program (something not previously explored in this literature, by the way) is presently out of the question. Therefore, I take on the more modest aim of looking for any systematic differences between universities with and without big-time sports programs in the types of students who enroll and the kinds of experience they have once they have enrolled.

Yet even the modest objective of identifying correlation faces one potentially serious challenge. It is that the universities so classified will invariably differ in more ways than just the presence of a commercial sports program, thus clouding the interpretation of any observed differences. Among public universities, the best-known big-time sports programs are more typically found at established flagship universities than at commuter universities or comprehensive universities. One finds these programs at the University of Oregon and the University of Michigan, for example, not Portland State or Wayne State. Since flagship universities often contain a state's most established academic programs, enroll some of its most talented and affluent students, and differ in other ways from other public universities, simply attributing differences in campus life to the presence of big-time sports could be misleading.[18] Such differences in campus life might simply be the result of differences in student attributes. Among private universities, similar but possibly more subtle differences exist. Consider Stanford and Syracuse, two private universities that have big-time sports programs, versus Cal Tech and New York University, two that do not. Although the undergraduate students attending the first pair may be much more similar in social or economic background to those attending the second than is true for the two pairs of public universities just cited, these two groups of private university students undoubtedly differ in other ways. Thus a simple comparison of the students or other aspects of campus life will not necessarily yield information on any independent differences due to the existence of a competitive sports program.

To address this challenge, I did two things in the statistical analyses that I discuss in this chapter. First, I tried to select for each comparison universities that are as similar to each other as possible, except for the presence or absence of a big-time athletics program. Second, in the analysis of student attitudes, behavior, and happiness, I controlled statistically for a number of important differences among students, such as gender, race, family income, and parents' education.

## SELECTION: WHAT KINDS OF STUDENTS ENROLL IN UNIVERSITIES WITH BIG-TIME SPORTS?

The application and admissions processes, taken together, comprise a giant sorting of young people into colleges of different kinds, a sorting that surely influences the quality of student experiences on college campuses. To see how students who enroll in universities with big-time sports programs differ from those going to other universities, I used data from a survey of freshmen and compared those who enrolled in universities with and without these programs. The survey, conducted by the Higher Education Research Institute at UCLA, asks first-time freshmen questions about their family background, activities and academic performance in high school, attitudes on a range of social and political issues, expectations about college, and personal goals. I obtained data for the survey administered in the fall of 2004.

Essential to this analysis is the ability to compare students according to the presence of big-time sports at the institution where they have enrolled. Each student's university was designated according to its level of athletic competition. Universities in the NCAA's Division I-A (subsequently renamed the Football Bowl Subdivision) were deemed to have big-time sports programs. These were compared with universities not in Division I. The first of these groups contains institutions with teams playing at the most competitive level in both football and basketball. Most of them widely known, universities in this group whose freshmen were covered in this survey included the University of Southern California, Vanderbilt, the University of Maryland, and the University of Michigan. The second group consisted of universities that field intercollegiate teams in the NCAA's Division III or have no intercollegiate teams at all. Some of the universities in this group were Emory, New York University, University of California San Diego, and Wayne State. Excluded from the comparison were universities in the middle – those in Division I but not in the FBS.[19] In addition to this two-way classification based on level of athletic competition, universities were separated into private or public, a distinction of tremendous importance in light of the well-documented public–private differences that exist in such aspects as tuition, admissions selectivity, and family income of students. Combining this public–private split with the two levels of athletics commitment yielded four groups of universities. Finally, to make the comparison group of universities as similar as possible, the sample was restricted to institutions with total enrollments of at least 10,000, and historically black institutions were excluded. A total of 83 of the institutions participating in the 2004 UCLA Freshman Survey satisfied these restrictions.[20]

Although this comparison was designed to focus on universities that are as similar as possible – aside from the level of the intercollegiate competition in which they engage – the freshmen attending these four groups of universities did differ in some discernible ways.[21] These differences tell us a good deal about the world of big-time college sports. Not surprisingly, private universities in the sample on average had more affluent students than did public ones. But within each sector, universities with big-time sports programs enrolled more affluent students than those without big-time ath-letics. To illustrate, the average family income of freshmen attending big-time private universities was more than 25%, higher than that of freshmen at non-big-time private universities. For freshmen at public universities, the difference was 30%. Similar differences showed up in the share of freshmen whose fathers were college graduates. Among freshmen at private univer-sities, the proportion with college-educated fathers was 77% at universities with big-time sports, compared with 65% at universities without. For fresh-men at public universities, the share with college-educated fathers exceeded the share in non-big-time sports universities: 61% vs. 43%. Corresponding differences can also be seen in the percentage of freshmen who attended nonreligious private schools. Not only does attendance at a private univer-sity predict affluence, therefore, so does going to a university with a big-time sports program.

Besides enrolling more affluent students, universities with big-time sports programs tend to be residential universities, not commuter schools. Freshmen were asked whether they were planning to live at home. Virtually no freshmen at the private big-time sports universities planned to do so; for them college was to be a residential experience. By contrast, about 11% of those enrolling in the non-big-time sports private universities planned to live at home. An even larger gap showed up for freshmen attend-ing public universities. While only about 6% of those attending the mainly flagship, big-time sports universities planned to live at home, more than a quarter of those at the other public universities planned to do so. The prevalence of commuting students is perhaps one of the most important differences between big-time sports universities and those without such emphasis, especially in the public sector. Along with the residential expe-rience, the big-time sports institutions offered another element of the tra-ditional collegiate experience: fraternities and sororities. Where big-time sports are available, more freshmen plan to join a fraternity or sorority. In private universities, the big-time sports difference was 48% compared with 26% who planned to join. At the public universities, the gap was 39% versus 31%.

I was interested in finding out whether students who choose univer-sities with big-time sports are distinctive in other ways. Their affluence and planned living arrangements aside, do they differ from other college freshmen in their backgrounds, attitudes, or aims? These are questions the UCLA Freshman Survey is well suited to address, because it contains many detailed questions about students' backgrounds and beliefs. To eliminate the influence of differences in family background and other personal traits across types of institutions, I used a statistically estimated model to predict differences in measures between universities that would apply to students with exactly the same characteristics.[22] Once these student characteristics were controlled for in this way, there remained a few noteworthy differences by type of institution. For example, within both the private and public sectors, those attending the big-time sports universities were more likely to have frequently attended religious services or done volunteer work, and they were less likely ever to have smoked cigarettes.[23]

One factor that might explain some of these differences is region. As shown in Chapter 3, big-time sports universities tend to be geographically concentrated in the South and Midwest, where religion and politics tend toward the conservative. To illustrate the concentration, I calculated the percentage of state vote for Bush in 2004 weighted by the public university enrollments in each state. The percentage for Bush weighted by the number of freshmen in public universities with big-time sports was 54%, compared with just 48% for those public universities without big-time sports. Of course, not all students are drawn from within state, but there is a possibility that the differences across institutional types reflect, at least in part, regional differences in attitudes. To control for this geographical correspondence, I made additional estimates for public universities that controlled for whether the state where the student was attending college was a Red State in 2004. Adding this control virtually erased the nearly 4 percentage point difference in frequent attendance at religious services. It made little difference, however, for volunteering and smoking. Holding constant personal characteristics and the state's 2004 presidential vote, freshmen enrolled at public universities with big-time sports were more likely to have done volunteer work frequently (27% to 25%) and less likely ever to have smoked cigarettes (17% vs. 19%), but these differences are not very big.

A question of great interest and potential importance is whether students attending the two types of universities differed in their ultimate educational and life objectives. When demographic, social, and economic characteristics were controlled for, several small differences did appear. For two life objectives, there were consistent differences between big-time sports universities. Those enrolling at the big-time sports campuses were less likely to aspire to write original works and more likely to hope for business success. Although relatively small, the percentage differences were statistically significant between freshmen enrolling at the two types of institutions. No consistent differences were seen in students' desire to be financially well off or to develop a meaningful philosophy of life.[24]

The UCLA Freshman Survey asked students a long list of questions to probe attitudes about social and political issues of the day. With respect to political orientation, the results were remarkably consistent. Although some differences were evident between students attending public and private universities, the most consistent pattern that emerged was within sectors: those attending big-time sports universities were more conservative than those attending universities placing less emphasis on sports. Most striking was the self-assessment of political orientation: among freshmen going to private universities, the percentage who described themselves as far right or conservative in the big-time sports universities was 25% compared with just 17% at the universities with low sports emphasis. Among students at public universities the corresponding percentages were 25% and 21%.[25] When the Red State regional variable was included in the comparison for public universities, this 4-point gap grew smaller but did not disappear: the share of freshmen at public universities who described themselves as conservative or far right was 24% in universities with big-time sports but just 22.4% where the sports emphasis was minimal. The biggest gap among public university freshmen was in the percentage who opposed more taxes for the wealthy, with those at big-time sports universities expressing opposition by a gap of 3 percentage points, again controlling for the effect of being in a Red State.[26]

## HOW STUDENTS USE THEIR TIME

We turn now to the lives of students once they arrive on campus. Are the behaviors of students at universities with big-time athletics programs any different from those at other universities? Since one of the strongest criticisms of big-time college athletics has been that it diverts attention from studies, it is most pertinent to ask if students spend their time in different ways in universities with different emphases on athletics.

Time spent on academic pursuits, such as attending class and doing homework, is a measure of "input" rather than an ultimate objective of college education. Because there are no agreed-upon measures of educational output at the college level, however, those who study academic quality must be content with measures like this. A recent study of trends in time use by American college students provides reason for concern. Using results from successive national surveys, this study documents a steady decline in the average amount of time undergraduates in the United States spend in class and doing homework, falling from about 40 hours a week in the 1960s to about 25 hours in the 1990s.[27] One explanation the study's authors offer for this decline is that an increasingly research oriented faculty and their students have entered into an implicit contract along these lines: "We the faculty will give you less to do (and give you better grades in the bargain) if you will make modest demands on our time."[28] Whatever the explanation, a decline in academic work done by American undergraduates is not a fact to be dismissed lightly, given the country's receding position in international comparisons of educational attainment and the rise in the percentage of U.S. Ph.D.s that are awarded to students born abroad. Could the prevalence of big-time sports in American universities be a factor in these troubling developments?

To analyze students' time use, I examined data from a survey of students at eight highly selective private universities. Of these eight, four operated big-time FBS athletic programs. None of the other four were in Division I, meaning none were in the Ivy League.[29] As already explained, if these two groups of selective universities systematically differ in more ways than just the presence or absence of a prominent athletic program, any observed differences will necessarily be an ambiguous marker for the investigation at hand. It is pertinent to this inquiry, therefore, to note that these two groups of universities are much more similar to each other than they are different. As compared with the four without prominent sports programs, the four big-time sports universities in this group were slightly larger (11,300 vs. 9,900 full-time equivalent graduate and undergraduate students), had a slightly higher share of students who were undergraduates (54% vs. 51%), had somewhat lower average tuition ($31,800 vs. $33,700 in 2006–2007), took a greater share of its students from out of state (27% vs. 19%), and had comparable average SAT scores.[30] All but one of the eight universities offered students the option of joining fraternities and sororities. Probably the most salient difference between the two groups of universities lay in the share of undergraduates who majored in one of the natural sciences. Among undergraduates graduating in 2006, 17% of those at the big-time sports universities majored in math or a natural science, whereas 28% of those at the comparison universities did.[31]

Data on students in the eight selective universities were obtained for a survey of enrolled students conducted in 2007, which resulted in usable data for 15,979 students from the eight universities.[32] In addition to time use, other information was available for each student, such as gender, race, year in school, age, family income, parents' education, SAT or ACT scores, and living arrangements. Each student record was coded as being from one of the big-time sports universities or not, but the identity of each student's university was not provided.

The eight-university survey asked students to estimate their weekly allocation of time to a variety of academic, extracurricular, and personal activities. Data were collected on 25 activities, a subset of all those covered in the original survey. The 25 activities were combined to make nine groups of activities: (1) attending class or lab; (2) other academic work outside of class (including homework, thesis, internship, or research); (3) extracurricular activities (student government, newspaper, literary magazine, fraternity or sorority, cheerleading, mascot or marching band, musical performance, theatrical performance, religious organization, volunteering, political organization, minority group organization, or other organized group); (4) socializing, talking to friends, or visiting others; (5) athletics and exercise (varsity sports, intramural teams, pickup games, and working out); (6) using a computer for nonacademic purpose such as Facebook or video games; (7) relaxing alone; (8) reading for pleasure; and (9) watching television. Not included in the tabulations are time spent eating, working, and sleeping.[33] Because responses to the questions addressed in this student survey might well differ systematically across students, say, by gender or family income, the analysis employed a statistical model similar to that used for the freshman survey to control for the possible influences of such characteristics.[34]

How did these students spend their time? Because these eight universities were selective, the amount of time students spent on schoolwork tended to be quite high by national standards. Whereas the representative student at these institutions spent roughly 14.5–15 hours a week in class, the median for all college students in the country in 2004 was only about 12.5.[35] The students in our sample of private selective universities also spent more time studying outside of class than the average college student.[36]

But there were also differences in time spent on academics within these two sets of selective universities. Students at the four universities with big-time sports spent considerably less time in class (and lab) than students in the comparison universities: 14.5 hours a week compared with 15.7 at the comparison institutions. They also spent less time doing schoolwork (and internships) outside of class: 20.0 hours a week compared with 21.3 hours. The differences were on the order of an hour and 20 minutes less each week for each of these two activities. One possible explanation for the difference in time spent in class and lab is the smaller role of science courses (and accompanying labs) in the curricula at the big-time sports universities, as suggested by the 11-point difference in the percentage of students majoring in math or natural sciences. But there is no similar "mechanical" explanation for the gap in academic work outside of class. Students at these highly selective big-time sports universities simply spent less time studying and doing research than their counterparts at the other four selective universities.

What did they do with this extra time? Because the remaining categories do not account for all other possible activities, the amounts of time accounted for by the two groups of students do not produce the same total. So we cannot be sure. But the results do suggest at least a partial answer. Students at the big-time sports campuses spent more time engaged in extracurricular activities, devoting about an hour and a half per week more than students at the comparison universities.[37] This gap is driven by differences in several activities, including musical and theatrical performance, volunteering, and religious organizations. Among the remaining six categories, statistically significant differences in time show up in three of them. Time spent in unorganized socializing and visiting did not differ, but students at the big-time sports universities spent more time than their counterparts in the comparison universities getting exercise and participating in team sports (although they spent less time participating in a varsity sport, a point to which I will return).[38] The last four activities (nonacademic computer use, relaxing alone, reading for pleasure, and watching TV) are not as social, and students at big-time universities tended to devote less time to them. In summary, whereas students at the big-time universities spent less time on traditional academic pursuits such as attending class or doing homework and research, they spent more time engaged in organized extracurricular activities.

I had access to a second survey of students, covering freshmen at public universities with enrollments of 10,000 or more.[39] Although I used this survey for questions on overall satisfaction, as explained later, I decided not to use responses to questions about the time spent preparing for class. In contrast to the findings for selective private universities, the freshmen in this sample spent more time preparing for class if they attended a university with a big-time sports program. I believe this finding says less about the effect of big-time sports than it does about the differences in academic rigor between the public universities in this second sample. By and large, the students in the public universities with big-time sports in the sample had higher test scores than those in the non–Division I institutions, suggesting that the former universities might have more demanding course work.[40] For this reason, I believe the higher reported number of hours spent by freshmen at FBS institutions reflects more rigorous courses, not sports. There is no way to prove this conclusion, however.

## DRINKING ALCOHOL

There can be little doubt that alcohol was a factor in the 2001 student riot in College Park, Maryland. But Maryland is not known for an extraordinary amount of drinking among its students, having made the Princeton Review's annual list of 20 top party schools only once between 2007 and 2009.[41] Alcohol consumption has in fact been an acknowledged part of American undergraduate life for many decades, and it remains a serious threat to the health and safety of young drinkers, in part because it is associated with risky behavior. National surveys show that more than 40% of college students, at least once in the preceding two weeks, have consumed five or more alcoholic drinks in a row.[42] Not only is excessive drinking commonplace in American undergraduate life, it appears to intensify around the "tailgates" and other rituals associated with college sporting events, as much as university officials wish to deny it.[43] A question worth asking here, then, is whether binge drinking is more common in universities with big-time sports programs than in other institutions.

A better but harder question is whether big-time athletics can be blamed for any share of the alcohol problems of college students, or rather if athletics is merely an innocent bystander, providing the occasion but not the impetus for drinking. There can be no doubt that athletic events are frequently an occasion for excessive drinking. The name applied to the annual Georgia–Florida football game in Jacksonville – the world's largest outdoor cocktail party – may be meant to be humorous, but on two successive years the game was occasioned by alcohol-related deaths of students at the University of Florida.[44] A study of student drinking at the University of Texas showed that students' consumption of alcohol was unusually high on days of football games, whether or not the team played at home. More than 60% of freshmen and sophomore reported drinking on these football game days, compared with 45% on the typical Saturday. The amount consumed by these drinkers was also higher on game days.[45] A study at another university found that on weekends with football games there were a disproportionate number of rule violations in dormitories, and nearly half of these involved alcohol.[46] After the University of Colorado banned alcohol from its football stadium in 1996, there was a dramatic decline in arrests, assaults, and ejections from the stadium.[47] Much drinking on the days of home football games takes place during traditional pre-game tailgating, a ritualized variant of the more general phenomenon of "pre-gaming," drinking before a social occasion where alcohol is not served.[48] One study focusing on this tradition at another university showed that three-quarters of the students attending tailgating events drank alcohol, consuming an average of 3.8 drinks.[49]

That such drinking might actually influence the educational experience of students, and not simply reflect the preexisting proclivities of students who chose to attend particular universities, is suggested by a study of the effect on students at a selective Midwestern university of having a roommate who drinks. Students who had been (randomly) assigned a roommate who drank alcohol were found to have lower grade point averages as a result.[50]

Although available data do not permit us to determine causal links, it is possible to compare the drinking behavior of students at universities with and without big-time athletics. Any observed differences might be the result of the selection effect or a treatment effect. To illustrate, of the 101 national universities for which *U.S. News* published data in both 1995 and 2010, those with big-time sports programs were more likely to be named in the annual Princeton Review list than were other academically strong institutions. Of the 51 top universities with big-time sports, 16 (or 31%) made it onto the Princeton Review's list at least once between 2008 and 2010, but only 2 (4%) of the remaining 50 did.[51] A more scientific comparison can be made using the survey of the eight private selective universities previously discussed. Students were asked about binge drinking, referred to in the survey as having five or more alcoholic drinks on one occasion. The students at these selective institutions showed rates of binge drinking comparable to those of American college students as a whole. Taking all eight universities together, about 46% of the males and 34% of the females said they had, during the past two weeks, consumed five or more alcoholic drinks on one occasion. Comparable national figures from a 2004 survey of college students found corresponding figures of 44% and 31%, respectively.[52] The question of interest in the present study is whether the rates of binge drinking among students at the four universities with big-time sports programs were higher than those of students at the other four institutions. They were. Combining men and women, students at the universities with big-time athletics were more likely to have engaged in at least one session of binge drinking in the past two weeks (41% vs. 36% for the comparison group of universities), and they were more likely to have had four or more sessions in that period (7% vs. 5%).[53]

## PARTISAN FAN EFFECT

The student riot at College Park, Maryland, mentioned at the beginning of this chapter represents an extreme example of what appears to be a much more general campus phenomenon associated with big-time sports. A big game captures the attention of many students, staff members, and faculty members on campus, in addition to its hold on fans who may follow the team from a distance. Not only during the game itself, but in the hours and perhaps days before the game, these followers – both on and off the campus – adjust their plans to prepare for the game and to watch or listen to it. Much of this activity is done in the company of others who are like-minded.

Although this kind of fan behavior – what might be called the partisan fan effect – is commonplace, I know of no research that has tried to measure its extent. Here I offer one attempt to do just that. I used the measure of research activity described in Chapter 3, the number of articles viewed per day on a Web-based digital archive, to see if any statistical relationship could be observed to sporting events. Specifically, I looked to see if this measure of work was related to the fortunes of a university's basketball team. Partisan fans tend to follow their own team's games much more religiously than they do those of any other, and so the attention they pay to the NCAA tournament will naturally depend on whether their team is playing in the tournament. If their team is in the tournament, these partisans can be expected to pay more attention to the tournament as long as their team remains in contention. To explore this effect, I linked the work done at university libraries to the participation and fortunes of the university's team.

Many supporters of sports teams become zealots when their team plays a game. They usually remain glued to the television and are often gripped by anxiety over the game's outcome. Using the JSTOR daily usage data, it is possible to see whether a tournament has a differential influence on research activity, depending on whether your team wins or loses. But common sense suggests that those who follow successful teams will come to anticipate success and learn to budget their time and plan ahead, so as to leave time to watch tournament games. Parallel but opposite expectations must apply as well to those who think their team will lose. Because of the likelihood of such adaptive behavior, one can achieve a true test of a partisan fan only by observing fans' responses to *unexpected* outcomes. Fan behavior in these cases is akin to a natural experiment, because the outcome of any game is more or less random.

To approximate this random experiment, I looked at JSTOR usage for universities whose teams were involved in tournament games in which the favored team lost ("upsets") or games for which there had been no clear favorite beforehand, defined as games for which the Las Vegas betting spreads were two points or less.[54] I also paid attention to the work done by all library patrons at universities that were in the tournament. The resulting statistical estimates indicate that library patrons at universities whose teams were in the tournament viewed about 6% fewer articles per day as long as their team remained in the tournament. In addition, those whose teams won upsets or close games viewed substantially fewer articles on the day immediately following the victories, some 19% fewer, compared with patrons of all other libraries. There was no discernible effect on work after that first day. For those whose teams lost unexpectedly, there was no effect on work over and above the 6% decline applying to all fans whose teams dropped out of the tournament.[55] As shown by JSTOR usage during the NCAA tournament, therefore, the partisan fan effect produces an unusual form of "winner's curse," consisting of less work while your team remains alive and a lot less work on the day after an unexpected win.

## OPPORTUNITIES TO PLAY NONREVENUE SPORTS

One of the possible educational benefits of a big-time sports program is the generation of income that could be used to finance nonrevenue teams. It is a common perception that big-time sports programs use much of the revenue generated by their football and men's basketball teams to pay for fielding teams in all the other sports. This notion of cross-subsidization is supported by the common practice in university budgeting of combining the revenues and costs associated with all of their intercollegiate teams into a single athletic department budget. One justification for having income-generating teams, then, is the opportunities for participation they give to students in nonrevenue sports. Not only is providing these opportunities seen as a desirable enhancement of undergraduate education, some of it is mandated by the gender equity requirements of Title IX.

One possible direct educational benefit of a big-time sports program, therefore, is the capacity, through this cross-subsidy, to increase the number of students who can play on intercollegiate teams. That is, universities that generate more income from athletics can have more athletes on intercollegiate teams.[56] To see if universities utilize their athletic income in this way, I examined data from the reports that universities submit annually to the Department of Education as a part of its enforcement of Title IX. Since I was interested in the opportunities to play nonrevenue sports, I collected information on the number of nonrevenue athletes as well as the total income of the athletic department. To account for differences in size, I divided both of these measures by the total number of

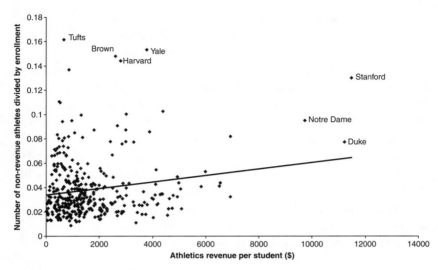

Figure 7.1. Nonrevenue athletes per student versus athletic revenue per student, 2009.

undergraduate students, and I looked only at universities with an under-graduate enrollment of at least 5,000.

The relationship between revenues and opportunities to participate in nonrevenue sports is shown in the scatter diagram in Figure 7.1. Although the points suggest a positive slope, as shown by the fitted line, the statisti-cal relationship is weak, having a correlation of just +0.18. In other words, although generating more revenue per student does give an institution the capacity to increase the number of students who play nonrevenue sports, universities use very little of this money for that purpose. The more impor-tant differences across universities in the percentage of students who play on intercollegiate teams lie elsewhere – they evidently depend on the priority that universities give this kind of participation. A striking aspect of the scat-ter diagram is that all of the outliers – the points at the top and to the far right – are private universities. The points at the top, representing institu-tions with the highest rates of participation in nonrevenue sports, belong to Tufts, Yale, Brown, and Harvard – universities that provided many playing opportunities without having the revenue generated by a big-time football program. The two outliers at the far right, Stanford and Duke, both generated enormous revenues per student, and both, Stanford especially, used some of them to fund more nonrevenue teams. Whatever causes a university to invest in intercollegiate participation, therefore, the size of the athletic budget is not a major part of it. It is suggestive that most of the institutions with high rates of nonrevenue sports participation are private – 13 of the top 15 are. To take one in-state example, the University of Maryland had 603 athletes who played sports other than football and men's basketball, and its athletic revenues were $60 million. Johns Hopkins had more nonrevenue athletes, 695, with revenues of $8 million. This exercise provides little evidence, therefore, that universities use income from their big-time sports programs to give more students a chance to complete in intercollegiate athletics.

## ARE STUDENTS HAPPIER?

We come now to what might be considered the ultimate intangible payoff for students from a big-time athletics program: the sense of community that is supposed to arise from rooting for the same team. Does this "common bond of loyalty" make the undergraduate experience a happier, more rewarding one? This section utilizes the same kinds of analysis discussed previously in this chapter to compare students' responses to three kinds of questions. The first set asked about students' psychological well-being, the second asked about the sense of community on campus, and the third asked for overall evaluations of the educational experience.

Using two subjective markers of well-being, I found no evidence that students on the big-time sports campuses were happier than others. The first subjective question was "How often, if ever, have you have felt out of place or that you just didn't fit in on your campus." By a difference of 16% to 15%, students at the big-time sports campuses were more likely to answer "very often." A stronger indication that a gap exists in overall happiness is that 55% of students at the universities with big-time sports also reported that they often or very often felt "overwhelmed by all [they] had to do," compared with 50% at the other universities.[57] These indications of being overwhelmed seem ironically at odds with the smaller reported time these students spent in class and doing homework in these same sports-oriented universities.[58]

To get at a summary measure of student happiness, I relied on two questions concerning students' overall evaluations of their college experience. As in the happiness surveys used widely in the social science literature in recent years, these questions can be taken to be a summary of students' satisfaction with their college experience. If big-time sports enhances the sense of community on a campus or otherwise adds enjoyment to a student's experience, questions such as these ought to reflect that fact, other things being equal.[59] For these two questions, I was able to compare responses from two surveys, the survey covering eight private selective institutions and the NSSE survey covering freshmen at large public universities.

For the question "How would you evaluate your entire educational experience at this institution?" the results differed between the two surveys. Among the students at the selective universities, those at big-time sports institutions were less likely to answer "excellent." Forty-seven percent of those at the big-time sports universities thought their overall experience was excellent, compared with 48% of those at the non-sports universities. But among the freshmen at public universities, it went the other way, with 32% of those at the FBS universities saying "excellent," compared with just 27% at the other universities.

For the other overall evaluation question, the big-time sports universities came out on top in both samples. In answer to the so-called endorsement question ("If you could start over again, would you go to the same institution you are now attending?"), those enrolled at the big-time sports universities were more likely to say they "definitely" would. The edge was just three percentage points in the selective universities study but eight points among the freshmen at public universities.

In sum, the comparisons of overall evaluations are contradictory and the differences rather small. To be sure, at least two forces could be expected to make responses to questions of this sort to be similar. First, as emphasized in the first part of this chapter, where students end up going to college is the result of a great deal of self-selection. For all the similarities among the eight universities, it is still the case that a student who decides to go to the University of Chicago has signed up for a different college experience than one who decides to go to Northwestern, although the weather will be about the same. Second, we might expect there to be a certain degree of self-justification regarding one's own decisions.

## BIG-TIME SPORTS AND THE CAMPUS SCENE

Because big-time sports is a fixture at some universities but nonexistent at others, attempting to measure its "effect" on the student experience is an impossible task. One might as easily seek to determine the effect of cold weather or gothic architecture. The reason it is impossible is that the students who choose to attend big-time sports universities are probably different in various ways from those who choose a college with no big-time teams. Compared with those who do not, students who choose an institution with commercial sports programs tend to be more affluent, more likely to live on campus, and more likely to join a fraternity or sorority. Holding constant many of their personal characteristics, they are slightly more conservative. That these students study less, drink more, and are more likely to be part of post-game demonstrations should not be especially surprising, for they are a self-selected group. At the same time, it seems entirely plausible that the opportunities for recreation provided on a campus will have an independent influence on the choices students make. By making these opportunities available, a university signals to its students what forms of recreation it deems worthwhile. The universities with big-time sports offer a uniquely American form of commercial entertainment, complete with large crowds and heavy media coverage. These universities do not, however, use the revenues earned from this enterprise to fund additional teams in nonrevenue sports. What big-time sports universities offer is the chance to be a spectator at commercial-grade entertainment events.

My objective in this chapter was modest – to determine whether there are any differences in the behavior or expressed feelings of students in universities with and without big-time sports. Differences between students at these two types of institutions are calculated using regressions that control statistically for some student characteristics, including gender, race/ethnicity, citizenship, and family income. These calculations show that students attending universities with big-time sports programs spent less time in class and studying, spent more time in extracurricular activities, felt out of place and overwhelmed more often, and engaged more often in heavy drinking than did those who attended universities without such programs. Measures of overall satisfaction with their college experiences showed no consistent differences between students in the two groups of institutions.

As I have stressed, these differences need not reflect any influence exerted by the institutions. They may be entirely the result of the selection process entailed in applying to, being accepted by, and enrolling in colleges. The only decidedly causal effect of big-time sports established here is the partisan fan effect, observed in the influence on work patterns of the fortunes of a university's unexpected wins in the annual NCAA basketball tournament. This said, the observed differences between universities with and without big-time sports provide a starting point for discussing the actual effects of big-time sports programs on the quality of student intellectual and social life. Where differences exist, the question can be asked, What portion, if any, is attributable to these programs? Perhaps the measures for which no difference is found provide more interesting fodder for further discussion. If having college teams to root for strengthens community and enhances social integration, why do the measures of overall satisfaction not show this more clearly?

# PART THREE

# RECKONING

# EIGHT

# Ends and Means

Binghamton University is one of the academic jewels of public higher education in the state of New York, boasting the highest SAT scores among the system's major university centers and the second highest among the dozen and a half four-year institutions in the vast SUNY system.[1] In the late 1990s the university decided to begin a process that would elevate its basketball program from the Division III level, which allows no athletic scholarships and attracts minimal attention, to the most competitive level, Division I. The other three SUNY universities, Albany, Buffalo, and Stony Brook, were already playing basketball at the Division I level, and Buffalo had an FBS football team. A required interim step, moving to Division II, was recommended by the university's faculty senate and approved by the university administration in 1996, although the faculty senate's executive committee had originally opposed the move.

When it came time to make the final decision to move to Division I in 1999, the faculty senate demurred, citing concerns about the potential financial and academic effects of such a move. Under no obligation to follow the faculty's recommendation, however, the president announced shortly thereafter that Binghamton would indeed make the move to Division I, beginning in the fall of 2001. In the next four years, the university replaced its head basketball coach, built a new arena with seating for 5,500, and became competitive in its conference, the America East Conference. In March 2009, at the conclusion of the home game at which its basketball team won the conference title and secured a bid to the NCAA tournament, students ran onto the court in jubilation.

But this story of basketball success soon became a cautionary tale of ends and means, of compromises made in the academic realm for the purpose of succeeding in the athletic one. Although the coach was successful in recruiting talented players and the team was successful in winning games, the team was criticized for unbecoming behavior, such as a post-game tussle between opposing coaches and on-court behavior by players that included using foul language and taunting spectators. Following the arrest for drug dealing of one player on the 2009 team just months after the season ended, the dismissal of six players for infractions including theft and drug possession, and a barrage of bad publicity, the SUNY board of trustees hired a renowned law firm to write a report detailing what went wrong.

The report offers a detailed look at the underbelly of a university making compromises. It detailed how the admissions process had become one arena for compromise. Admissions officers, the director of admissions, and the vice-provost for enrollment management were encouraged by their administrative superior, the provost, to give special consideration to basketball recruits, and the provost in turn was encouraged by the university's president. In a memo to the provost, the director of admissions wrote, "We are well aware of the need to make additional allowances in the revenue sports and we have done so." In 2008 the admissions office was asked to approve four basketball recruits as transfers from other institutions. Not only did administrators in admissions receive encouragement from higher up in the administrative chain of command to act favorably on these applications, they were also lobbied by other administrators, who in turn were lobbied by athletics officials and by the faculty member who was the designated faculty athletics representative. The dean of the college where most basketball players took courses weighed in as well, expressing confidence that the mentoring and tutoring services available would ensure that the students would succeed academically.

In the end, the basketball coach was effectively given license to admit any applicant who met the NCAA's minimum requirements. All four of these recruits were eventually admitted. Among the transfer students that Binghamton admitted during its rise to basketball prominence was one whose transcript included 16 credits in physical education and another with 12 credits, despite the university's existing cap of two transfer credits. Among the courses given transfer credit was Theories of Softball. Another arena of compromise was a relaxation of academic standards for coursework undertaken by some athletes. Players were allowed to drop classes after the prescribed date, enrolling instead in independent study courses. One sympathetic professor offered a one-week independent study course in the summer for four basketball recruits. To oversee the academic progress in the college where most players took their courses, the university appointed an administrator from the provost's office with no previous experience in advising.[2]

The compromises that came to light in Binghamton's meteoric rise and abrupt decline in big-time basketball seem stark in retrospect, but in qualitative terms many of them are commonplace for universities with big-time athletic programs. In fact, no university would have a chance of fielding competitive teams in the top divisions of football or basketball without making some compromises in the academic realm. This chapter returns to the theme introduced in Chapter 2: how the aims of universities line up with their actual behavior. Because I am an economist, it should not be surprising that I think here in terms of costs and benefits. Not all of these costs and benefits are readily measured, certainly not in monetary terms, but that limitation does not nullify the value of laying out an accounting. I begin with the part of the story most often told – about the costs that universities accrue when the values they espouse do not mesh with the values embodied in their athletic programs. I then turn to the benefits for the university of participating in big-time athletics. Some of these are of the "instrumental" variety – they support the university's academic mission of research, teaching, and service. But I will argue that there are other important benefits arising from big-time college athletics that are rarely acknowledged by universities, perhaps because those benefits spill out beyond the confines of the campus.

## COMPETING VALUES

Of the several constants related to big-time college athletics over the past century, one of the most striking is the tenor of criticisms leveled at it. The themes that critics have invoked have changed so little that quotations from the 1920s have an eerily contemporary sound to them. One of these themes is that the practice of big-time athletics conflicts with the aims and values of universities. This charge is not leveled against *participation* in athletics, for there has always existed a broad consensus that playing a sport can be a valuable part of a well-rounded education.[3] Instead, the alleged conflicts with the university's academic mission arise with respect to the operation of college spectator sports. To illustrate the tenor of this criticism, consider these five statements, all from the 1920s, linking academic values to big-time athletics:

It has now degenerated into a series of gigantic public spectacles, absorbing the interest of the average student, who, for one-third of the school year, marches, shouts, sings, rallies and roots, but never takes part in the contest itself, any more than he would at a horse race.[4]

Without question the greatest harm flowing from the place which athletes hold in student life is the erroneous viewpoint obtained by undergraduate students. When freshmen arrive at a university they find athletics the chief topic of conversation and football and baseball stars the idols of the campus.[5]

College athletics, under the spur of commercialism, has become a monstrous cancer, which is rapidly eating out the moral and intellectual life of our educational institutions.[6]

[T]he admission to the university of students who are financed because of their athletic prowess and because of their ability to round out winning athletics teams, cannot do otherwise than result in disaster to our educational program and to its standards of scholarship.[7]

The compromises that have to be made to keep such students in the college and to pass them through to a degree give an air of insincerity to the whole university-college regime.[8]

The same arguments can be seen in today's debates over big-time college sports. As any perusal of contemporary current debates about college athletics will attest, the theme of conflicting values continues to inspire concerns about the role of commercial sports in universities. These themes demand attention in any comprehensive assessment of costs and benefits. These conflicts appear in two forms: flagrant and subtle. I begin with the first of these, the clear violations of formal rules and laws, and then turn to those costs that are less obvious and are often accepted as costs of doing business. These are challenges to the fundamental principles of lawfulness, academic merit, intrinsic motivation, free expression, and honesty.

## Lawfulness

The value conflicts that get the most headlines are the ones that are the most blatant. These include violations of the various NCAA rules that regulate recruiting and eligibility, of university rules against plagiarism and other forms of academic dishonesty, and of criminal laws. A few examples will suffice to illustrate the range. One of the most infamous was the point-shaving scandal that rocked the world of college sports in 1951 and 1952. Players from City College of New York and six other universities were found to have accepted money from bookmakers to influence the outcomes of games. In sentencing several bookmakers involved in the scandal, the New York State judge in the case wrote, "Commercialism and over-emphasis in intercollegiate football and basketball are rampant throughout the country." According to the judge, these forces had fostered gambling, bribery, and illegal recruiting, with the result that athletes, coaches, and alumni were corrupted and university integrity was undermined.[9] A decade later, another point-shaving episode ended the Dixie Classic, an annual holiday basketball tournament played in Raleigh, North Carolina.[10] In recent years, a scheme at the University of Kansas allowed several employees to amass more than $1 million selling purloined basketball and football tickets.[11]

Other scandals have involved lawbreaking on a less spectacular scale, such as the arrest of Binghamton basketball players for such crimes as the sale and possession of crack cocaine, the arrest of the head basketball coach at the University of Mississippi for punching a cab driver and using racial insults, or the alleged extortion of the basketball coach at the University of Louisville in a case involving extramarital sex.[12] Less lurid but embarrassing nonetheless was a series of altercations between football and basketball players at the University of Kansas, featuring a highly publicized nightclub brawl and Facebook postings containing racial slurs.[13]

More common are violations of the detailed NCAA rules regulating the lengths to which universities may go in their efforts to entice high school students to play for them. These highly detailed rules, more than 4,000 of them, are set forth in NCAA manuals and elucidated further in an online database containing thousands of interpretations.[14] Universities often report on minor or inadvertent violations, such as calling a recruit too often or making a visit to a recruit's school outside the prescribed period for visits. But in some notorious cases, coaching staffs or boosters affiliated with universities have blatantly exceeded the limits on enticements, in some cases paying recruited athletes after they had enrolled. One of the most flagrant examples, mentioned in Chapter 5, was SMU. With the knowledge of its board of governors, it paid cash to players in the 1980s, some upon signing and some as regular monthly payments. As a result, the NCAA handed down its "death penalty," which required the university to cancel football for one entire season.[15]

Although the SMU case stands out because the violations were so brazen, athletic departments at prominent universities continue to make unwanted headlines, thanks to violations of NCAA rules. One infamous case was the University of Michigan's "Fab Five" basketball class recruits in the early 1990s, whose skill propelled Michigan into the national finals in two successive years. Several of the group were later discovered to have taken money from a booster who was also connected to illegal gambling.[16] Southern California had its 2004 national football championship later nullified because the team's star player had received numerous "improper benefits," including a rent-free apartment for his family.[17] At Florida State University, more than 60 athletes were found to have cheated on online courses, but the university protested the NCAA's decision to nullify 14 previous victories by its football team because that penalty could mean its long-standing coach might not retire with a record number of career victories.[18] And athletes at Kansas and the University of New Mexico were given unauthorized help on correspondence courses.[19] The 2009 national runner-up finish for the University of Memphis basketball team in the preceding year was invalidated because one of its star players had used fraudulent SAT results to gain admission.[20]

## Academic Merit

Just as the admissions process represents the first step in the college experience for students, admissions standards are the first accommodation that American universities make to big-time sports. Before going any further, however, the point bears stating that admissions criteria outside of athletics are not entirely pristine. Members of some underrepresented racial and ethnic groups and residents of underrepresented states are often given special consideration in admissions decisions, as are children of alumni, especially at private universities. Less commonly, children of faculty members, donors or would-be donors, or celebrities have been known to encounter lower hurdles for admission.[21] There is, of course, abundant evidence that universities apply different admissions standards to athletes as well and that this gap is widest for athletes who play revenue sports in big-time sports programs. A survey of 21 public universities with big-time athletic programs, covering data from various years between 1999 and 2007, found that athletes, especially football players, were much more likely than the average freshman to have been admitted as "special admits," that is, were admitted through some exception to the institutions' usual admissions requirements. Whereas an average of 4% of all freshmen at those universities were classified as special admits, the average percentage of all freshmen athletes accepted under such exceptions was 26%, and the corresponding percentage of football players was 49%.[22] In another survey of 52 universities, average SAT scores compiled in 2008 showed an average of 943 for football players, compared with 1154 for all students, leaving a gap of 211 points. For a group of 48 universities with data on basketball, the averages were 1152 for all students versus 930 for basketball players, leaving a gap of 223.[23]

Although the NCAA has paid special attention to disparities in graduation rates between athletes and other students, no one who operates a big-time college sports program pretends that the academic standards applied to athletes in the revenue sports are the same as those for other students.[24] The lowered admissions standards for recruits in the revenue sports find official justification in the following statement, one of five "operating principles" to which each NCAA institution must attest for its Division I programs: "The institution shall admit only student-athletes who have reasonable expectations of obtaining academic degrees."[25] Coaches at some universities appear to hold considerable sway in influencing admissions decisions, as suggested by the jawboning of the South Carolina football coach, who publicly criticized the university's decision to turn down two prospects, or by the provision written into the contract of the football coach for Florida International giving him authority to admit any athlete cleared by the NCAA to play.[26]

Compromises in admissions for big-time sports recruits extend all the way up the ladder of academic prestige, as the unfortunate case of Binghamton illustrates. A doctoral dissertation based on numerous interviews detailed admissions procedures at Stanford, Northwestern, and Duke. It showed that recruits for the revenue sports routinely received special treatment in the admissions process and many benefited from lower standards. At Duke, for example, recruits classified as a "reach" were held to the "reasonable expectations" principle stated earlier: the coach was required to convince admissions officers that the recruit could "handle the curriculum." But for the occasional "stretch" recruit – one who promised to be a "program changer" – Duke might offer admission without that assurance, although the coach would be required to give up one of his allocated admissions slots in each of two successive years.[27]

Once they are admitted, athletes are required to maintain good academic standing in order to be eligible to play in games.[28] Not surprisingly, this can be a daunting challenge. Not only do many players in the revenue sports enter college with weak academic backgrounds relative to their fellow students, their duties as team members can require substantial time commitments. Although the NCAA sets a cap of 20 hours a week for team members, college athletes report that they actually spend more than twice that amount.[29] To meet the challenge of maintaining academic good standing, many athletes – often on the advice of academic advisers devoted exclusively to athletes – search out courses and academic programs that will present a minimum of challenge. As a result of such strategic course selection, certain departments or programs at many universities often become the academic home to a disproportionate share of athletes. At Virginia Tech, for example, 19% of football players were majoring in residential property management, while only 0.4% of all students were. At NC State, a third of the football players were sports management majors, compared with only 0.8% of all students.[30] At Michigan, the major of choice had been sports management until that major was revamped. This caused a migration of football players into the general studies major.[31] Where it occurs, such "clustering" of athletes into certain majors or programs suggests – but by no means proves – that the rigor of the academic programs of many athletes, compared with that of other students at their universities, is diluted. Certainly the circumstances surrounding a few reports strongly suggest that academic standards for some athletes are very low indeed. One prominent case was Auburn, where 18 members of the undefeated 2004 football team took a total of 97 hours of courses from a single sociology professor who required no attendance and little work.[32] Taken to its logical extreme, watering down academic rigor for athletes can reach the ridiculous, as in the case of the physical education course taught by an assistant basketball coach at the University of Georgia, with a multiple-choice test featuring such questions as "How many points does a three-point field goal account for in a Basketball Game?"[33] To be perfectly fair, such courses are no doubt rare. Nor are low expectations to be found exclusively in sports-related courses.

Despite the strategic course taking that these patterns imply and the extra advising and tutoring services that universities routinely provide for athletes in the revenue sports, athletes in these sports nevertheless lag behind their fellow students in their persistence to graduation. To illustrate the gap between athletes in the two revenue sports and all students, I calculated graduation rates for the 58 universities with big-time athletic programs that we examined previously.[34] For all students entering these universities between 1998 and 2001, the average graduation rate was 72%. But the comparable rate for basketball players was only 42%, and for football it was 56%.[35] Within this group of universities, the only ones that stood apart in terms of graduation rates in revenue sports were those ranked in the top 35 by *U.S. News.* Those had rates of 50% for basketball and 68% for football. And within that group, the three highest-ranked universities – Stanford, Duke, and Northwestern – stand further apart still, having average graduation rates in the two sports of 60% and 84%, respectively. But the gaps in graduation rates were large for all of these selective institutions, providing another example of the academic double standard that is routinely applied to big-time college athletes.

This double standard is merely the most obvious academic accommodation that big-time sports universities make in order to succeed in competition. As we saw in Chapter 7, universities with big-time programs also tend to have a bigger fraternity and sorority presence as well as more drinking. It could be simply that universities with big-time sports more generally offer campus environments friendlier to entertainment. Certainly, some of the decisions made by these universities signal, at least at the margin, accommodation of entertainment at the expense of academics. Besides the everyday accommodations – in the timing of tests and meetings, for example – recent years provide at least three telling examples. Two, from the fall of 2009, were mentioned in earlier chapters – the cancellation of work at the University of North Carolina on a weekday afternoon in anticipation of the traffic for an evening football game and Alabama's cancellation of three days of classes to allow students and staff members to attend the national championship football game in California. A third is a midday rally in April 2010 at Duke to welcome the returning champion basketball team, violating, through an apparent oversight, an agreement hammered out by the faculty senate only a few years before.[36]

## Intrinsic Motivation

A third value traditionally associated with universities is more debatable than the first two. It is the idea that education should be pursued for its own sake, not for its monetary payoff. In his biting assessment of higher education, *The Higher Learning in America: A Memorandum on the Conduct of Universities by Business Men*, Thorstein Veblen warned against the "vocationalism" that arose from the practical pursuit of pecuniary gain, arguing instead that universities should be "devoted to a disinterested pursuit of knowledge."[37] Two decades later, University of Chicago president Robert Hutchins likewise opposed professional schools, holding that the aim of universities should be "the pursuit of truth for its own sake."[38] These voices did not win the day, of course, for some of the best American universities now proudly boast about their professional schools, the very manifestation of commercial pragmatism that Veblen and Hutchins opposed. Commercialization is evident in many corners of the contemporary university, from the McDonald's in the cafeteria to the office charged with patenting discoveries made in university laboratories. But this trend is vigorously opposed by some observers, such as former Harvard president Derek Bok, in his book *Universities in the Marketplace*.[39]

But nowhere else in the university is commercialization so advanced as in big-time sports. As far back as 1929, the Carnegie Commission was calling commercialization the chief cause of problems in college athletics: "More than any other force, it has tended to distort the values of college life and to increase its emphasis upon the material and the monetary."[40] If there was ever a conflict built into an organized activity, the tension inside college athletics between the amateur ideal and the opportunities to make money was one. As originally conceived and practiced by Oxford and Cambridge, and then by Harvard, Yale, and their ilk in America, college athletics was intended to embrace games played by gentlemen and to exclude those played by professionals. Although the strict amateur ideal came to be compromised – in the eventual legitimization and acceptance of athletic scholarships in the 1950s – the NCAA's ban on further compensation to college athletes has remained for the higher-education establishment a non-negotiable core principle.

Yet the forces of commercialization – more precisely, the temptation to take financial advantage of the popular devotion to college sports – so vehemently decried in the 1920s, did not subside. Rather, they grew in intensity and flowered in variety. Advertisements were always part of game-day programs, but increasingly they found their way into stadiums and arenas, and onto their scoreboards. Exclusive contracts to sell soda and snacks have been a mainstay at college football and basketball games for decades, but corporate sponsorships took on new and more penetrating forms beginning in the late 1970s, as apparel companies entered into contracts with coaches and universities to supply shoes and uniforms for athletes. Most prominent among these companies was Nike, which by the 1980s was paying some basketball coaches as much as their universities were. A decade later, most of these apparel contracts were made with universities instead of individual coaches, although universities sometimes made payments to coaches based on them.[41] One visible reminder of these contracts is the nearly ubiquitous Nike "swoosh" symbol that appears on the uniforms of big-time college football and basketball players.[42]

Apparel is the vehicle for another form of commercialization: the licensing of a host of products by universities and the NCAA. Famous university "brands," including mascots as well as names and nicknames, represent a growing source of revenue for universities. To appreciate the possibilities in licensing, one need go no further than the NCAA's Web site. Not only does it provide the rules that producers must follow to obtain licenses to sell products with a university's name on them, it also allows the fan an easy way to shop from a university's numerous branded offerings. For example, the link provided to the University of Kansas showed prices and pictures for 589 different items available for purchase. These items included not only banners, decals, T-shirts, sweatshirts, and hats, many bearing the likeness of the red and blue Kansas Jayhawk mascot, but also backpacks, bottle openers, coasters, calculators, Christmas tree ornaments, pet collars, plastic cups, piggy banks, picture frames, playing cards, key chains, license plate frames, lounge pants, toddler socks, tire covers, steering wheel covers, shoulder bags, and Santa hats.[43] University officials report that the university typically earns about $1 million a year through licensing agreements for apparel with its logo and name, but going to the Final Four has meant an increase of 20% or more.[44] Other universities do even better. In 2010 Kansas ranked 19th among the universities handled by the largest licensing company. The leaders that year were Texas, Florida, Alabama, LSU, Georgia, Michigan, and the University of North Carolina. In 2006 Texas earned more than $8 million from this kind of licensing.[45]

But no avenue for the commercialization of college sports compares in revenue potential to television. Initial fears that televising college football games might diminish attendance proved to be unfounded. As spelled out in Chapter 3, TV coverage of football mushroomed after the Supreme Court ended the NCAA's monopoly in 1984.[46] Powered by the rapid growth of cable TV, college football and basketball both became commonplace entries in the country's television listings. Thanks to the strong demand for televised college games, the broadcast rights for these games became a very lucrative asset. To illustrate the stupendous amounts involved, the Southeastern Conference had TV contracts with ESPN and CBS that would bring in more than $3 billion over 15 years, an average of $17 million per year for each member university.[47] The NCAA signed another multiyear contract with CBS and Turner that would bring in an average of $770 million a year.[48] The decision by the Big Ten to start its own network was yet another illustration of the burgeoning commercial opportunities to exploit the demand for big-time college sports.

As technology advances, so do the opportunities to exploit this demand. A case in point is the development of video games based on college football and basketball. These games feature particular college teams, such as the current Oklahoma football team or the 1995 UCLA basketball team, complete with accurately rendered uniforms and school colors. Although players' names are not always used in the versions of the games available for purchase, actual players' numbers and likenesses are easily recognizable. The NCAA initially objected to these games but eventually decided to approve them, for a licensing fee. Past players raised legal objections, however, on the grounds that their likenesses were being sanctioned and sold by the NCAA without their permission, even after those players ceased being students.[49]

Where is the value conflict? It is certainly not in generating revenue in the commercial marketplace, for otherwise universities would be damned along with most institutions of contemporary society.[50] Rather, the potential for value conflict arises from the actions that universities take to earn that revenue. For example, if universities value the time that students have to study, as they say they do, their decision to allow teams to play numerous scheduled games, many of them during the week and at distant locations, often for the purpose of accommodating the wishes of TV broadcasters, then commercialization does have a cost. If educators believe that first-year college students are ill prepared for the time demands of varsity competition, but universities, through the NCAA, sanction the eligibility of freshmen to play on varsity teams, as they did in 1972, there is again a conflict in aims.[51]

One visible arena for value conflict is university policies toward alcoholic beverages. No university can be ignorant of the problems associated with underage and binge drinking.[52] Even in the absence of commercial athletics, institutions must weigh the health and safety consequences of student drinking against the customer-sensitive instinct to make their campuses attractive to young people. Big-time athletics adds another piece to this dilemma. Because of the sizable revenue that broadcasters can earn by selling advertising for alcoholic beverages, most TV contracts involving big-time sports also allow for such products to be advertised. To be sure, there are limitations, most of them self-imposed. For example, the Big Ten Network does not allow ads for alcoholic beverages. Similarly, the NCAA limits alcoholic beverage advertising during its men's basketball championship to 1 minute for every 60 minutes of broadcast time.[53] Nevertheless, there is evidence that a portion of the remaining alcohol advertising reaches underage viewers and that this exposure increases both the likelihood that adolescents will begin drinking early and the amount they will drink once they begin, a conclusion that can only be strengthened in light of the NCAA's reported strategy of building its fan base among teenagers.[54] Allowing beer ads has also been criticized for "linking beer and drinking as integral parts of college life."[55]

The instinct of universities to capitalize on the commercial potential of their big-time sports programs does not come from a drive to make money for its own sake. It merely reflects the logical result of two desires: to win games, which costs money, and to minimize the budgetary burden of the athletic enterprise. Raising more money increases the prospects of achieving what university stakeholders want – a prominent and successful athletic program – without undue burden on academic programs. In fact, a similar aim may explain universities' pursuit of commercial opportunities in other areas. Universities often invite businesses to sell products on campus, to partner with units in moneymaking schemes, and to make gifts that may have commercial benefits for the corporation that gives them. In these cases, one can argue that universities are justified in entering into such an arrangement if they judge that the benefits to the academic mission outweigh the costs.[56] In the case of athletics, however, there is little if any educational benefit to be weighed in the balance. This distinction places the commercialization of athletics in its own category, and it brings its own potential for creating mischief.

## Free Expression

"The mutual confidence on which all else depends can be maintained only by an open mind and a brave reliance upon free discussion." So said federal judge and judicial philosopher Learned Hand to the New York State Board of Regents during the height of McCarthyism.[57] Although Hand surely meant it to apply beyond the college campuses of New York, this statement crisply summarizes a bedrock value underlying the modern university – tolerance and encouragement of free thought and debate, regardless of popular opinion. Although sometimes honored only in the breach, this principle meets its most stringent test when scholars express views that offend the moral, religious, or political sensibilities of the community. When applied to the campus classroom, the principle of freedom of expression also finds imperfect acceptance. Backed by the power implicit in the grade book, many college instructors no doubt impose a certain tyranny of thought upon their students. Nor do universities endorse absolute freedom of expression even in principle, as suggested by restraints on "hate speech." Despite these exceptions, it must be acknowledged that American universities, and the wider international community of scholars, represent an example of unparalleled tolerance of divergent and unpopular opinion and expression. And it is probably not a coincidence that the university's organizational structure – the fragmented and decentralized amalgamation of schools and departments described in Chapter 2 – fosters this freedom.

Against these traditions of decentralization and freedom of expression, big-time college athletics stands in rather stark contrast. Organizationally, it prefers hierarchy to autonomy. Spiritually, it prefers discipline to improvisation, although some of the latter can be useful once the former is mastered. These differences can be seen best in the organizational unit upon which everything else in college athletics depends – the team, including its players and coaches. In the blunt words of one big-time football coach, "Football is not a democracy. There's nothing to debate."[58] One published study of a big-time college basketball team, based on five years of close observation, revealed the absolute power that coaches had over their players. "In their subordinate positions, players at the University were dependent on the coach for almost all their daily needs and responsibilities. Their food, lodging, sense of well-being, and future careers were controlled by him. With little recourse against his superior power, they had to accede to his rules or withdraw from the program."[59] Coaches took charge of their players' daily schedules, down to the timing of classes, team meetings, and meals. In a manner similar to the indoctrination often seen in fraternities, military units, and religious cults, the coaching staff began by humbling the players, many of whom had been stars in high school, so that they might come to accept their new roles on this team. By combining strict discipline with paternal acceptance, the coach was able to create in his players feelings of intense loyalty.[60] "Benevolent dictator" was the term he applied to himself.[61]

Different coaches take different approaches to achieve this discipline and loyalty, of course. One famed Michigan football coach was said to hit his players with a yardstick if they did not line up with the correct space between them. Another Big Ten coach, who later met his downfall after punching a player during a game, would occasionally attempt to motivate his players during practice by hitting himself in the head or throwing down his glasses and stepping on them.[62] Other coaches relied on the combination of inspirational speeches and punishing physical ordeals, sometimes led by seemingly sadistic assistant coaches.[63] An Arizona State football coach explained such tactics this way: "The objective is to keep pressure on these kids so they do things automatically. It's not fun."[64] At Indiana, the faculty senate in 1987 passed a resolution directed at its basketball coach, Bobby Knight: "Athletes shall not be subjected to physically or verbally abusive, intimidating, coercive, humiliating, or degrading behavior." In response, the football coach opined, "It's totally ridiculous. I don't buy that bit about someone telling us how to run our program. We don't tell them [the faculty] how to run theirs."[65] Although many coaches, including many successful ones, do not resort to bullying, former Michigan president James Duderstadt concludes that athletic departments operate under "management values and cultures that depart quite significantly from those of the academic core of the university."[66]

This emphasis on team discipline ran head-on into the academic tradition of free expression during the turbulent years of the 1960s. If student unrest was difficult for university administrators, protests by athletes were intolerable to coaches who demanded absolute obedience. Players at universities across the country joined their fellow students in causes such as civil rights and opposition to the war in Vietnam. A black football player at Oregon State was suspended from the team because he refused to shave off his moustache, violating the coach's ban on facial hair. At Wyoming, black players were suspended when they wanted to wear armbands in their game against Brigham Young, in symbolic opposition to Mormon doctrines on race. In the wake of other protests, black players at Iowa, Washington, and Indiana were suspended by their coaches.[67] In the spirit of the time, white athletes, too, questioned traditional power relationships. Said the captain of Berkeley's football team in 1969, "So the coach is all-dominant, all-powerful. I've never seen one player call a coach a bleephead like they call us all the time.... The most degrading thing is being treated like a child."[68] Addressing the national convention of athletic directors in 1968, the president of the University of Connecticut warned, "Without wanting to be an alarmist, let me say that I think that if the current undergraduate mood persists, intercollegiate athletics are going to be a target of criticism, disruption and protest."[69]

In response to these challenges to the authority of coaches, the NCAA in 1969 passed the "manifest disobedience" rule, which allowed a university to revoke the athletic scholarship of any athlete who violated "established athletic department policies."[70] In 1973 the NCAA strengthened the hand of coaches yet again simply by reducing the number of years covered by athletic scholarships from four to one, thereby eliminating the need for coaches to establish grounds for "manifest disobedience" or to make room for new recruits by taking measures to make life intolerable for underperforming upperclassmen.[71]

Although the days of student protests may now be a dim memory, the issue of free expression in the world of big-time college athletics remains. One manifestation, seemingly a benign one, is the control that universities exert – through their athletic departments – over the local broadcasts of their football and basketball games. It is standard procedure for a university, or its coach, to contract with a local radio station for the exclusive right to broadcast the university's games. These contracts invariably include compensation for the head coach. Explicitly or implicitly, the game announcers are subject to approval by the athletic department. As a consequence, such broadcasts are decidedly unobjective, a fact so common as to be unremarkable. If the same degree of restraint on expression – even unwritten – were placed on a single member of the faculty, there would be howls of protest. At the same time, it is common for universities to publish alumni magazines that specialize in stories that are favorable to the institution. The tension between objectivity and "puffery," therefore, seems to be a more general conflict for the modern corporate university.

A related free speech issue is the attitude taken by coaches toward reporters and student newspapers. Like other celebrities, college coaches have been known to criticize what they see as negative coverage.[72] In the case of student sports reporters, such criticism from a popular coach might well be intimidating. When a sports writer for the Duke student newspaper wrote a column criticizing the play of one of the team's star players, the coach sarcastically derided the suggestion in a news conference.[73] Compared with what one might imagine to be the idealized reaction of a professor to an unpopular or unconventional view expressed in class or on the editorial page, such derision is arresting. Although they rarely preach the virtues of improvisation or nonconformity, coaches do sometimes go on the record to affirm other principles fully consistent with values espoused by universities. That same Duke coach has written books stressing such principles as hard work, adaptability, dependability, poise, selflessness, and collective responsibility.[74]

Another related issue is openness. The *Columbus Dispatch* reported that athletic departments were not forthcoming when the newspaper requested several pieces of information: airplane flight manifests for football travel, lists of people getting free tickets, players' summer employment documentation, and reports of NCAA violations. Some universities charged for making copies, some incorrectly applied the Family Educational Rights and Privacy Act to protect alumni, and a few refused to release any documents at all.[75] I ran into some of this with several institutions during my research for Chapter 6, including the University of Oregon, which has earned a reputation for resisting open-records requests.[76] In response to my request for a list of those who had received complimentary tickets to home football games in 2008, the university sent notice that it would require payment in advance of its estimated cost of securing the information, $791.87.

Finally, there is the NCAA rule promulgated in 2010 forbidding "words, numbers, or symbols" on a player's body or "tape." The target of this rule was writing that began to appear on eye-black, the tape that athletes sometimes wear under their eyes to reduce sun glare. Some college football players had taken to writing on these pieces of tape, often the name of their college and sometimes abbreviated messages of identification or support. One player wore tape with the numbers of his hometown phone area code on it. Another wrote Bible verses, and his appearance in the 2009 national championship game caused a reported 90 million Google hits for that game's passage, John 3:16.[77] Although most messages were innocuous, the potential for controversial ones was highlighted when one Ohio State player used the tape on his face to express support for a professional player who had served time for organizing dog fights.[78] As it had shown during the student unrest of the Vietnam era, organized college athletics demonstrated once again that it had no taste for opening the door to individual expression by players. To be sure, dealing with controversial eye-black messages would have been complicated, but the resulting imbalance in permissible writing upon the uniforms and persons of college players is deeply ironic. While players on many teams are required to display a Nike swoosh or some other trademark, based on lucrative contracts made with their universities or coaches, they are forbidden to wear tape under their eyes reading "619" or "Psalms 23:1."

### Honesty

Written in large letters on a gate near the Foggy Bottom Metro station at the center of the university that bears his name are words from George Washington: "Seek truth and pursue it steadily." Surely no principle has a better claim as a foundational value of universities than this one. So it is fitting that our survey of competing values should not end without a reference to this fundamental one. Rather than comparing the values implied by activities in the athletic sphere and the academic one, the question here is directed at the university as a whole: Is big-time sports an occasion for departing from an otherwise honored principle?

Consider first the record of American universities independent of their association with athletics. By and large, it would be hard to find institutions more consistently devoted to truth than these. Certainly honesty is central to their honor codes and admonitions against plagiarism. The pursuit of truth is also at the heart of three key components of the research enterprise in American universities: peer review, tolerance of unpopular viewpoints, and competition for financial support. These are imperfectly applied, to be sure, but they have been instrumental in creating a system of higher education that has no peer in the world.[79] Perhaps allegiance to the truth is not as complete in the classroom, where the prejudices of professors can have a chilling effect on free expression, as noted earlier. And truthfulness may suffer shading when universities put on their corporate hats. One perhaps benign example is the tendency of admissions departments to overstate the degree of racial diversity on their campuses. A study of published view books sent to prospective applicants documented that three-quarters of the universities surveyed appeared to overrepresent black students in the campus photos included in these promotional publications.[80] One might dismiss this inaccuracy, of course, in the same way one might excuse photos showing sunny days and happy students, as a simple case of accentuating the positive.

Turning to their truthfulness regarding big-time sports, we have already noted the reluctance of universities to include references to sports in their published mission statements. Some of my colleagues have argued that these statements are written to satisfy certain stakeholders or accrediting agencies – as an exercise in public relations rather than literal description. Like the "puffery" often found in commercial advertising, the argument goes, these statements are not meant to be taken literally, so at worst they amount to little more than harmless exaggeration. A more serious challenge to the principle of honesty is what historian Ronald Smith sees as the fundamental contradiction at the heart of big-time college athletics that has existed for more than a century. In order to be successful, Smith argues, universities have had to run essentially professional operations, but their rhetoric says otherwise. "To call collegiate sport amateur was in fact playacting, the ancient Greek definition of the term hypocrisy."[81] Through the NCAA, universities enforce restrictions they say are designed to protect the amateur status of athletes, but the practical effect is often to enrich networks, coaches, and universities. As economist Roger Noll has argued, the position that the NCAA (and therefore its member universities) takes toward commercialization in big-time athletics can engender cynicism. The organization's pursuit of commercial gain, alongside earnest avowals to protect college athletes from corrupting commercial entanglements, invites the charge of "doublespeak."[82]

## THE UNIVERSITY'S BENEFIT–COST CALCULUS

We have now reviewed the categories of benefit and cost that a university would need to consider if it wished to conduct a formal evaluation of its commercial sports enterprise. Let us do a quick review of them. Chief among the benefits are exposure and the good things that come with it. As is readily documented by newspapers and TV coverage, most American universities with big-time sports programs attract much more attention through their athletic teams than through all of their other activities put together. Occasionally this coverage highlights unsavory items, but usually it focuses on the time-honored themes of sports competition: the rivalries, the routs, and the hopes for future success.

This exposure can serve the university's academic mission in four ways: It may induce more potential students to apply for admission, allowing the university to be more selective in choosing whom to admit; it may stimulate more charitable donations; it may distract alumni from noticing how different the values and opinions of the faculty are from their own; and especially in the case of public universities, it may cause state governments to act more favorably toward them. There is empirical evidence to support all four of these possibilities, but the evidence is strong for only the first – the effect on applications. As discussed in Chapter 6, the accumulation of econometric analyses suggests that success in football and basketball, by capturing the attention of potential students, expands an institution's pool of applicants, including the pool of those with high test scores. These statistical findings share a weakness, however. They are based on comparisons only among institutions that have big-time athletic programs, between those with more successful programs and those with less successful ones. For very good statistical reasons, these studies cannot determine the effect of adopting big-time sports in the first place, chiefly because the universities with and without big-time sports usually differ in other important ways as well. Because these studies are based on comparisons only among universities that have chosen big-time sports, they probably understate the true magnitude of the benefits of sports-induced prominence.

Another frequently touted benefit of big-time sports is the favorable effect on campus spirit, especially on the sense of connection and community felt by undergraduates. Indeed, the kinds of preferences that cause applications to rise when a university's team wins a championship would also imply that students are happier when their team is winning and that they are happier to have a team to follow than not to have one. As suggested by the attention paid to "enrollment management" by provosts and presidents alike, as well as by the severe revenue implications that accompany any significant shortfall in matriculations, American universities are deeply invested in having happy students. Indeed, the customer orientation that universities exhibit in their provision of amenities, dining options, and opportunities for amusement sometimes makes them look more like summer camps with classes than the European universities from which they evolved. Providing students with commercial-quality spectator sports can thus be seen as just one component of this larger customer orientation.

But the evidence presented in Chapter 7 is not a ringing endorsement of the capacity of big-time sports to make undergraduates happier. What evidence there is, and it is quite imperfect, suggests that students at universities with big-time sports are no happier or more satisfied with their collegiate experience than students at similar institutions without spectator sports. Still, this nonfinding should be qualified. It is based on responses by students who have shown that they are different from each other in the first place, by their choice to attend universities that differ in this very detail. Ideally, one would like to know what the effect would be for those students of suddenly adding or removing a big-time sports program at their university. But this is a question that cannot be answered without studies that are much better designed.

On the cost side of the ledger are two big items: budget dollars and compromised values. As shown in Chapter 5, most big-time sports programs run budget deficits. A substantial share of the income collected by the average athletic department in the Football Bowl Subdivision comes from subsidies in the form of student fees or budgetary allocations from general institutional funds. As straightforward as these subsidies might appear to be, they are a function not only of the decision to make the expenditures necessary to operate a commercial sports program but also of the decision to pay for nonrevenue sports teams in the same budget. Whether a university increases the total budgetary burden of athletics by going big-time is not really obvious.

The other major cost, however, is not in much doubt, though its importance surely varies across universities with big-time programs. Even the universities with the most scrupulous athletic programs make compromises that are dictated by their desire to be competitive in athletics. These universities with the "cleanest" programs need to compromise their admissions standards for many revenue athletes and accept that many of these athletes will get by with the aid of strategic course selection and extra help. These universities will also have to justify or otherwise live with policies that compromise study time, allow alcohol advertising, take advantage of the commercial value of undercompensated athletes, and restrict free speech. How serious these compromises are is, of course, a matter of debate, but they all emanate from a collective desire among universities to operate their commercial sports enterprises. Note that these conflicts are not the result of misdeeds: they will exist if every single member of the athletic program obeys every single rule and applicable law. Unfortunately, some universities have athletic departments that are not so scrupulous, hiring coaches with histories of rule breaking and recruiting athletes prone to mischief. The fact that big-time college sports programs differ in this regard is surely no accident. Logic suggests that it can be explained by the fact that the benefit–cost calculation is not the same for all universities.

Indeed, the best evidence we have about the benefits and costs of big-time college athletics lies in the decisions made by the institutions themselves. It seems eminently sensible to postulate that universities do not undertake an activity, year after year, unless they judge the benefits of that activity to outweigh its costs. Now confront this postulate with three key facts about big-time athletics in American universities:

1. Excellent American universities include those with commercial sports programs and those without, and neither group of universities has clearly advanced ahead of the other.
2. Once a university adopts such a program, it almost never drops it.
3. There continues to be a small but steady stream of universities that seek to enter the big-time sports ranks.

Despite the cost and the value conflicts inherent in big-time college athletics, many American universities continue to participate, year after year. These facts suggest that the benefits of participation derived by these universities exceed the costs of doing so. This conclusion is bolstered by the continuing interest among universities seeking more exposure, such as the University of South Florida and the University of North Carolina at Charlotte. At the same time, having a big-time sports program is not a requirement for success as a university, as the numerous examples of those without it surely attest. Everything we observe suggests that universities are fully aware of the compromises that are an unavoidable part of running a successful program. What is less certain is the degree to which their decision rests on the desire by stakeholders for athletic success for its own sake. It seems very unlikely, however, that it could be justified solely by the benefits commercial sports brings to the academic program.

One proviso should be added. I argue that the decision of a university to get in or stay in the big-time sports business implies that the program's benefits exceed the costs, as viewed by that institution. This does not necessarily mean that these individual decisions, taken together, are in society's collective best interest. We have seen that sports competition has the nature of a prisoner's dilemma, and one well-known implication of the prisoner's dilemma is that the decisions made by the individual actors are, for society at large, foolish. It is this logic that argues for collective restraint, in the manner of arms control agreements, to hold back wasteful spending and other collectively unwise behavior, a point to which I return in the final chapter.

## BEYOND THE CAMPUS

Beyond the benefits to the academic program and the psychic returns enjoyed by stakeholders, there is another category of benefits that is virtually never mentioned – not by scholars, critics, or policy pundits, and certainly not in mission statements. These are benefits that are so general that they spill out far beyond the university's campus. Because they are free floating, these benefits are unlikely to help a university's bottom line or advance its mission. They are also intangible, amorphous, and ultimately immeasurable. But they are important nonetheless, and they deserve consideration in any serious assessment of the role of commercial college sports in America. These spillover benefits are of two types. The first is the enjoyment that fans and spectators experience, and the second is the civic value that derives from good examples.

## Enjoyment

Like people the world over, Americans follow spectator sports. For reasons that surely lie deep in culture, history, and psyche, college sports has become one of the items in the uniquely American diet of spectator sports. As Chapter 4 spells out, the interest for some people approaches mania or religious devotion. Many Americans develop a lifelong loyalty to the teams of one particular college or university, often early in life and often independently of enrollment in that institution. The tangible markers of the interest in college sports are easily observed: attendance at games, television viewership, all manner of apparel items emblazoned with logos and team mascots, and the ubiquitous bumper sticker. For psychologists and anthropologists, these markers may have deep significance. For economists, they are simply features of consumer demand. Some observers have suggested that the real reason so many Americans get invested in college sports is the absence of other worthwhile activities in the towns and hamlets where football and basketball reign supreme. Be that as it may, and whether or not one approves of how much attention Americans pay to college sports, the attention is there, and it is the universities that make it possible.

Unlike most items of consumption, college sports is seldom enjoyed alone. Its consumption almost always involves a community dimension. It gives fans a sense of pride and belonging. The author of one of the many books describing the popularity of college sports writes, "People who otherwise would not speak to you exchange high fives as you stand as one on a fall afternoon and scream in unison with blood-curdling fury. A feeling comes over you in these moments that is impossible to explain."[83] The communal aspect of college sports is most tangible for those attending a game:

When 106,000 people stand and scream as Tennessee splits the T and comes rushing onto the field, I guarantee that, even if you hate the University of Tennessee with complete and utter passion, your jaw will drop and your heart rate will begin to race. Then, wait until the entire crowd rises to its feet and screams on the opening possession of the visiting team. Your ears will ring and the sheer spectacle of over one hundred thousand people clad in orange will overwhelm your senses.[84]

Former Yale president and major league baseball commissioner A. Bartlett Giamatti wrote with equal reverence about the crowd at a game, and his words apply as well to the fans who follow games by radio, television, and the sports page:

Very soon the crowd is no crowd at all but a community, a small town of people sharing neither work nor pain nor deprivation nor anger but the common experience of being released to enjoy the moment, even those moments of intense disappointment or defeat, moments made better, after all, precisely because our fan is part of a large family of those similarly affected, part of a city of grievers. When people win together, the joy is more intense than when any of us wins alone, because part of any true pleasure is sharing that pleasure, just as part of the alleviation of pain is sharing the burden of pain.[85]

Whether the team wins or loses, the acts of following, cheering, and hoping add up to something like happiness. Here the economic concept of consumer surplus joins the pragmatic world of consumer behavior with the philosophical study of happiness. As noted in Chapter 4, the notion of consumer surplus springs from the recognition that anyone who makes a purchase, such as tickets to a game, derives pleasure that is at least as valuable in his or her mind as the cost of making the purchase. Usually, the benefit to the buyer is more than equal to this cost, and this extra benefit is called consumer surplus. In theory, consumer surplus has a value that can be measured in monetary terms. On the basis of this reasoning, economists seeking to place a dollar value on demand – for items ranging from municipal stadiums to endangered animals – have estimated it using an approach called contingent valuation. Luckily, it is not necessary to make such calculations in order to make this point: the huge sums devoted to ticket sales, cable TV subscriptions, and the allocation of time capture only a portion of the enjoyment that fans and other consumers derive from watching and following big-time college sports. Spending on big-time sports collected by universities alone was well over $3 billion in 2008.[86] In other words, in light of the tremendous demand for big-time college sports that is revealed through attendance and spending, we can be very sure that even more value exists out there that does not show up in dollar value of spending.

"So what?" some might ask. The reason this is important is the same reason the ever-present always risks being overlooked. For all its flaws – and these are real – big-time college sports produces a great deal of enjoyment.

In a word, it produces happiness. This happiness is a large, though amorphous, benefit that Americans receive from universities. So what if it *is* crazy to care about the outcome of, to quote Howell Raines, an "infinitely repeatable recreational game"?[87] It makes no more sense to affix a flag or decal bearing the likeness of a made-up mascot than it does to yell oneself hoarse on a fall afternoon along with 80,000 other people. Nor does it make sense for a fan to cheer for one group of players he does not know and against another group of players he does not know, merely because of the colors of their uniforms. But for all its nuttiness, fan devotion translates into happiness. Even when their team loses, as Giamatti reminds us, there is solace and community bonding that comes when people experience something together.

What this means is that many American universities, by way of their entertainment function, produce a thing of value that is enjoyed by a population potentially much more numerous than its living alumni, not to mention its current student body. For state universities, this benefit in fact has the nature of a public service. Acknowledging the potential costs associated with the kinds of value conflicts discussed earlier in the chapter, what can be wrong with a state university providing to a large portion of its residents, through its football or basketball team, another reason to be proud of their state? To be sure, such feelings of pride are often accompanied by chants, booing, and derisive remarks directed toward opposing teams (with the unkindest jibes reserved for nearby rivals). Rival teams and fans can become, in anthropological terms, the dehumanized "other" who can be demonized in good conscience. As columnist David Brooks has written, though, these rivalries are mostly harmless, certainly less damaging than other types of social divisions, such as those based on ethnicity or religion.[88]

Thought about in this way, the intangible feelings of pride, solidarity, and pleasure that are for most Americans an entirely unremarkable by-product of big-time college sports is a consequence that has real social significance. By virtue of its power, universities extend their reach beyond their accustomed domain of abstract ideas into the popular culture. That this entertainment function is virtually ignored by scholars of higher education and in university mission statements should, perhaps, not be terribly surprising. The explanation for pretending commercial athletics is insignificant may be nothing more than embarrassment. After all, the cultural world of big-time college sports is the world of popular television, not PBS, and the academic leaders who make speeches and devise mission statements seem acutely uncomfortable in it. At least in their official pronouncements, therefore, they choose to ignore the actual importance of big-time athletics and the fact that they are, in part, in the entertainment business.

## Civics Lessons

The second spillover benefit produced by big-time college sports is equally amorphous. It is the salutary effect of a good example. As a natural by-product of the way they go about their core business, college teams have the potential to embody highly valued civic virtues and thereby become teachers by example. These are examples that emanate from watching, not participating. Many would agree that participating in sports competition teaches many valuable life virtues, such as discipline, teamwork, courage, responsibility, and resilience.[89] But on top of the qualities enhanced by being an athlete, there are two lessons for the community or nation as a whole that big-time college sports can teach by way of example. These lessons could comfortably take their place in any high school civics course.

The first of these lessons, embodied in college sports as well as sports competition more generally, is the principle of meritocracy. Our laws and our civic belief system maintain that the rewards from competition should be distributed on the basis of merit, not family name, ethnic origin, religious beliefs, or economic status. Among the arenas for competition in contemporary society, sports may be the closest thing to a pure meritocracy. To be sure, few sports or leagues have perfect equality across teams in resources or player ability. In college football and basketball, certainly there are wide resource gaps between some institutions. But once the teams arrive on the field or court, there are no free passes for past performance or reputation. In a large number of games the chance for an upset is real, however small. David does occasionally defeat Goliath, as perennial football powers Oklahoma and Michigan would acknowledge when they think back to their games in 2007 against Boise State and Appalachian State.[90]

The meritocratic principle extends to individual players as well. Sociologists David Riesman and Reuel Denney made this point 60 years ago by linking the social status of immigrants and their descendants to the football success of upstart institutions such as Notre Dame. In its formative years, college football was a game played by privileged gentlemen and was dominated by elite institutions like Harvard and Yale. But by World War I the locus of power had moved west and in the process begat an "ethnic shift." At Notre Dame, second-generation Americans with names like Rockne, Dorais, and Bergman devised new techniques and strategies (including the spiral pass in 1915) that succeeded in upending the football preeminence of the blue-blooded institutions of the East.[91] If the sons and grandsons of immigrants could compete with those of established families on the football field, was this not possible as well in politics and business?

A second civics lesson extends from this one. Not only could the example of college sports exemplify the value of individual merit, it might also demonstrate the possibility and even the *desirability* of equality and cooperation across identifiable groups in society, in particular across racial lines. No bigger issue has faced the United States during the reign of big-time college sports than the blot of racial segregation and discrimination. It is my belief that the examples presented by college teams to their spectators and viewers has, on the whole, amounted to a positive lesson in civics, one whose message has been that racial tolerance is possible and interracial cooperation can lead to success in social undertakings. This is not to argue that universities or college coaches were necessarily more virtuous than other institutions and leaders, or less so. The civil rights era was marked by breakthroughs when decision makers came to realize that it might be in their own best interest to go against traditions of discrimination. In much the same way, strides in college athletics often had self-interest behind them. And once a university made the decision to desegregate its teams, for example, the change was known immediately and known widely. Once those changes happened, they became a powerful signal, owing to the intense popularity of college sports.

The best example is the reaction of football fans in the South to desegregation. The *Brown v. Board of Education* decision of 1954 set the stage for an epic confrontation between two great forces in the region, the South's devotion to college football and its cultural commitment to Jim Crow segregation. The depth and ferocity of the South's opposition to racial integration were apparent in hundreds of ways, including the Southern Manifesto and "massive resistance" to school integration. But alongside this commitment to segregation stood the love of football – more exactly, the love of Alabama football, the love of Texas football, and so forth. At first, the confrontation between these two great forces did not involve the actual integration of teams. Rather, it was simply a matter of fans not wanting the political struggles over integration to interfere unduly with the natural order of things as they understood them. One component of this natural order was football. So, as noted in Chapter 3, white students at Georgia Tech rose up just two years after *Brown* to protest against a governor who wanted their team to boycott a bowl game against a racially integrated team from the North.[92] But the integration of rosters was not long in coming, once it became clear that football dominance could not be sustained without it. One football game has come to symbolize this epiphany. In September 1970, Southern California traveled to Birmingham to play against the legendary Alabama coach Paul "Bear" Bryant. Led by two African American stars, USC handily defeated the all-white Alabama team, giving Alabama fans a taste of what the future would look like if it continued to embrace Jim Crow. That game, according to a later resolution in the U.S. Senate, was "widely seen as sweeping away the last remnants of the racial divide in college football."[93] Texas, the last university to win a national title with an all-white team, in 1969, played its first black player in 1970, as did Auburn. Alabama integrated the following year.[94] By 1972, with the addition of Georgia, LSU, and Ole Miss, every team in the Southeastern Conference had integrated.[95]

The realization that future success would require integrated teams was not confined to the South, or to football. The victory by an all-black Texas Western team against all-white Kentucky in the championship game of the 1966 NCAA basketball tournament was a signal event, commemorated by Hollywood in the 2006 movie *Glory Road*. College teams in both sports, in all regions of the country, saw increases in the number of black players. This increase is reflected in the percentage of consensus all-American college football and basketball players who were black. In football, there were no black players on the list in 1940 and 1950, and the percentage was only 9% in 1960. It then rose to 23% in 1970, and exceeded two-thirds in 1980, 1990, and 2000. In basketball, the increase happened earlier and went further, rising from zero in 1940 to 25% in 1950, 30% in 1960, 60% in 1970, and 100% in 1990.[96]

As the racial diversity of American universities increased in the post-*Brown* era, especially in the South, basketball teams were far ahead. These increases can be illustrated by tracing the racial composition of the undergraduate enrollment and the men's basketball team at four universities in North Carolina: Duke, North Carolina, NC State, and Wake Forest. The median percentage of blacks among undergraduates at those universities increased from 2% in 1970 to 5% in 1978 to 9% in 1995. For their basketball teams, the comparable medians were 14%, 43%, and 60%, respectively.[97] This disproportionate representation of black players in football and basketball, combined with the underrepresentation of men among black students, made black male athletes remarkably visible among undergraduates at universities with big-time sports programs. For the universities in the five big conferences plus Notre Dame in the 2005–2006 academic year, black male athletes accounted for 14% of all black male students. At universities with small enrollments or low percentages of black students, this share could become strikingly large. At Wake Forest, Oregon State, Oregon, Nebraska,

Colorado, Arkansas, Northwestern, and Iowa, more than 25% of all black males enrolled were athletes.[98]

More important than percentages was the recurring visual enactment of equal treatment and cooperation provided by the players and coaches who made up these racially diverse teams. Beginning in the 1970s, fans old enough to have grown up using separate water fountains and attending segregated public schools witnessed college basketball seasons featuring scores of coaching decisions made with no apparent regard for the race of the players. Fans who watched a racially mixed team through a season were also treated to dozens of gestures between players of different races that clearly signified that team identity, at least temporarily, trumped racial identity. When they occurred between teammates of different races, the shouted words of encouragement and the ritualistic gestures of solidarity – handshakes, high fives, and fist bumps – heralded a new social order for a region and a nation in need of this civics lesson. To be sure, there is a less rosy interpretation of the racial patterns in big-time college sports. Some observers see racial exploitation in the fact that the heaviest concentrations of black players are in the revenue sports of football and basketball, which subsidize the predominantly white nonrevenue sports, or in the success of "nonthreatening" black athletes.[99] Although the exploitation indictment cannot be dismissed entirely, I believe that the social benefits that emanate from highly visible interracial cooperation on college teams vastly outweigh any such harm.

### RECKONING

Through the prism of athletics, it is possible to learn something important about the actual nature of a sizable group of American universities. What we discover is not altogether flattering, but neither is it a scene devoid of promise. A close examination of big-time college athletics reveals that entertainment is a time-honored and rather permanent part of the real mission of those universities. Responding to stakeholders' desire to be successful in athletics, universities end up compromising certain principles for the sake of other objectives, and entertainment becomes a regular function of those universities.

Although we are not accustomed to thinking about our universities in this way, this reality is not an altogether bad thing. By virtue of their entertainment function, universities with big-time sports programs produce widespread benefits for which they rarely take credit and which have rarely been taken seriously. One type of benefit, which economists term consumer surplus, is the sheer enjoyment experienced by individuals over and above what they actually pay to see games. And to the extent that college sports call upon and deepen feelings of affiliation and pride, this unique product may also be helpful in building what sociologists call social capital. Because of its pervasiveness, intercollegiate athletic competition by public universities may therefore be one of the most important outputs of state government. A question worth asking is whether this beneficial effect could be produced if the revenue sports were carried out with smaller budgets and therefore less commercial fanfare. Although less commercialized versions of college football and basketball could produce consumer surplus, such toned-down versions would be less frequently televised and consequently would create a smaller amount of consumer surplus.

Not only is it a source of enjoyment and state pride, college sports can be a benevolent teacher of socially important values. For example, athletic competition affirms the belief that success in life should be based on individual merit rather than family connection or ethnic identity. In sports we find one of the most meritocratic of endeavors. Intercollegiate athletics has also been a leading wedge for racial equality and cooperation. By virtue of the number of African Americans recruited to the football and basketball teams at predominantly white universities, the racial diversity of student bodies is enhanced and examples of interracial cooperation are provided for fans.

But conflicts in values are also a by-product of taking on entertainment as a core university function. The uneasy coexistence between the academic and athletic enterprises creates a tension between rival sets of values. For example, the athletic enterprises rely on hierarchical organizations featuring top-down control, teamwork, and unquestioned obedience, whereas the academic enterprises espouse independence, free expression, and creativity. It is also typical for universities with big-time programs to be disingenuous regarding their corporate aims. Deceit, or at least polite deception, is therefore part of the entertainment–academic partnership. For example, both parties engage in the fiction, embodied in the term "student-athlete," that athletes in the revenue sports are ordinary students, subject to the same standards as other students. The NCAA's invention and use of this hyphenated term can be seen as part of its larger policy of grouping these athletes together with students who play nonrevenue sports. Pursued ostensibly to protect the notion that they are all amateurs, this policy has the additional benefit of blurring the difference in commercial value of college athletes between revenue and nonrevenue sports. Another example of misdirection is mission statements of universities with big-time programs, which seldom contain any reference to intercollegiate athletics.

It would be healthy for American higher education to come to terms with its deep commitment to entertainment in the form of big-time sports. To pretend that this activity is a sideline no more significant than dining halls or art museums, or that athletes in the revenue sports are held to the same academic standards as other students, is to engage in a form of double-talk that would be unacceptable in most of the classrooms of those same universities. It would be more in keeping with the intellectual traditions of the academy to acknowledge the rather unshakable hold that commercial sports has over the universities that engage in it. Besides clearing the air of this kind of polite deception, such an acknowledgment would allow for an open discussion about the potentially important spillover benefits generated by big-time college sports, as well as its more obvious costs. Accepting the potent devotion to college sports also makes it easier to understand why the presidents and trustees of such universities have been unable to accomplish meaningful reform.

NINE

# Prospects for Reform

"What is to be done about college athletics?" This question rings today with as much urgency as it did in the 1920s, when critics like Upton Sinclair lamented the excesses and abuses of college sports. Modern-day muckrakers have continued this tradition, using terms like *conspiracy, show business, sham,* and *hypocrisy* in their denunciations of the commercialized college sports enterprise, together with adjectives like *ugly, dishonest, corrupt,* and *villainous.*[1] The striking constancy of the themes used by such critics ably illustrates the famous dictum from Ecclesiastes, that there is nothing new under the sun.

Not only has the criticism of college athletics persisted, so have the calls for reform. Although a few of the most vehement critics would gladly throw out the whole enterprise of big-time college sports, the more common appeal has been for rule changes that would clean up perceived problems. As we have seen, one of the early objectives of reformers was accomplished soon after the NCAA was formed in 1906 – rules of play that made the game of football less dangerous for athletes. With that one exception, however, the problems have proved stubbornly resistant to correction.

This concluding chapter takes up the question of reform. It does so by discussing, in turn, the three logical questions that must be addressed whenever reform in any field is contemplated. Like the physician's treatment of a patient, reform of institutions involves three parts, whether or not they are explicitly acknowledged: collecting data, diagnosing the problems, and prescribing a course of treatment. In the first of these, the physician listens to the patient's complaints and gathers facts about symptoms, such as pulse, blood pressure, temperature, and heart rate. In the analogy to policy reform, this means paying attention to critics and describing the conditions that seem to indicate a problem. The second step, identifying the causes of those problems, can be only as good as the

existing knowledge about causes and effects. The third step is coming up
with a treatment plan, if there is one to be had. This simple outline provides a useful approach to understanding the perennial debate about what
should be done about college sports.

## WHAT NEEDS REFORMING?

As will be clear to anyone who keeps up with the subject, big-time college
athletics has an ugly side, one that has been a perennial source of embarrassment for otherwise upstanding American universities. Along with
the revenues and recognition that athletic departments generate, all too
often they produce headlines worthy of the tabloid press and news stories
peppered with sordid, shocking, or demeaning details. All this must be
granted because it is a documented part of big-time athletics, and has been
for more than a century. Equally familiar to those who follow the subject
are the complaints raised by critics. Despite their familiarity, these complaints are often mixed with proposals for reform and, as a consequence,
are not always stated explicitly. In these criticisms, six recurrent themes
are evident.

### Unsustainable Economics

More a worry than a complaint is concern about the sustainability of the
status quo, the business model that has sustained big-time college athletics.
At a time of recession-induced budgetary stringencies, universities and
their athletic departments have looked with alarm at escalating coaches'
salaries and burgeoning demands for new facilities. It is no accident that
the term "arms race" has entered the lexicon of those who write or worry
about the economics of college sports. One fact that both motivates and
symbolizes this anxiety is the prevalence of budget deficits among the 120
or so Football Bowl Subdivision athletic departments. As documented
by the NCAA's own reports, only a fifth of these programs made a profit
in 2008.[2] From the university budget officer's perspective, the economic
downturn, the cost of new capital projects, and the market-driven escalation in coaches' salaries make for scary budgetary projections. And the
option of turning to one of the traditional budgetary backstops – subsidies
from student fees or general university funds – appears to face increasing resistance, as illustrated by the complaints about athletic deficits at
Berkeley and Ohio University. To be sure, not everyone who operates or
oversees a big-time athletic program shares this worry equally. Like the

next complaint on the list, this is an anxiety that weighs most heavily on those who operate programs outside the most well established conferences, those that do not reap tremendous benefits from big crowds, lucrative TV contracts, and affluent donors.

## Unfairness to the Have-Nots

A debate sure to break out near the end of every college football season concerns the Bowl Championship Series and proposals for a playoff system for big-time football. Even President Obama weighed in on the subject. Critics believe that the current system favors the rich and established programs at the expense of the have-nots, especially teams that win all their games but are denied a shot at the national championship because they play in minor conferences. Because universities in the Southeastern Conference, Big Ten, and other established conferences enjoy favored treatment in the BCS setup, they collect a disproportionate share of the television-generated financial payoffs of postseason football competition. In addition, these universities take in more revenue by virtue of TV deals negotiated by their conferences. The financial comparisons presented in Chapter 5 show the extent of the disparities that result, which force the have-nots to operate on a comparative shoestring. Forced to work with smaller budgets, these programs tend to lose out in the bidding for top coaches, making it that much harder for them to win.

## Exploitation of Revenue Athletes

A third theme in the criticisms of big-time sports is that the athletes themselves are treated unfairly, by virtue of the NCAA rule prohibiting them from getting any compensation besides their athletic scholarships. Although their economic value to universities can be quite substantial, especially in the case of star players, the NCAA's prohibition against paying athletes means that this financial return goes instead to coaches, athletic departments, and universities. One need not be a Marxist to appreciate the unfairness of the arrangement. Michael Lewis characterizes the business of college football this way: "Everyone associated with it is getting rich except the people whose labor creates the value."[3] There is a racial angle to this inequity as well, which arises from the nonwhite and lower-income profile of athletes in the revenue sports as compared with the athletes who play on other teams. To the extent that money earned from football and basketball goes to subsidize all the other college sports, the effect of limiting compensation is that black and economically disadvantaged athletes end up subsidizing white and affluent ones.[4]

## Abuse of Nonprofit Status

Fourth on the list of complaints against big-time college athletics, although it is the least commonly articulated, is notable for the prominence of its spokespeople. This is the argument that universities are receiving unwarranted financial bonuses by virtue of their tax-exempt status, in the form of tax exemptions and tax-subsidized contributions. In 2006 Representative Bill Thomas, chair of the House Ways and Means Committee, wrote a widely publicized letter to the president of the NCAA, posing a long list of pointed questions. Several of these asked bluntly how big-time college sports programs served the educational purposes that legally justify their universities' tax-exempt status. The letter's tone is illustrated by this question: "How does playing major college football or men's basketball in a highly commercialized, profit-seeking, entertainment environment further the educational purpose of your member institutions?"[5] This line of criticism dovetailed with attacks by Senator Charles Grassley on the high salaries of coaches and other university employees.[6] Few lawmakers have joined those advancing this line of criticism, however, probably because of the perception that current policies toward big-time college sports enjoy widespread political support.[7]

## Crime and Rule Violations

The last two categories of worrisome symptoms are the most commonly invoked by critics of big-time college sports. Because they are discussed in some detail in Chapter 8, I note them here only briefly. Of these, the one that receives by far the most attention in the national media is the violation of laws or NCAA rules. Not surprisingly, the most notorious abuses associated with big-time sports fall into this category. News reports of these violations can receive wide coverage and spark vigorous debate. Infamous examples include the basketball point-shaving scandal of the early 1950s and the blatant violations at SMU during the 1980s. Such examples of illegal or otherwise egregious rule violations are, of course, damaging – not only to the integrity of sports competition, but to the integrity of the universities involved. Episodes like these also draw attention to practices that are permitted but questionable. For example, one writer linked the illegal ticket scheme uncovered at the University of Kansas in 2010 to the ethically suspect resale of complimentary tickets and the involvement in basketball recruiting of teams in the Amateur Athletic Union.[8]

## Sacrificed Educational Principles

The last category of problems, also discussed at length in Chapter 8, encompasses the various indicators suggesting that universities are sacrificing academic standards in order to accommodate the needs of revenue sports teams. The Knight Commission charged, for example, "Big-time athletics departments seem to operate with little interest in scholastic matters."[9] No set of problems is more frequently invoked than this one. Joining the chorus of critics in 2010 was U.S. Secretary of Education Arne Duncan, who denounced low graduation rates and reaffirmed the value of participating in athletics.[10] Other heavily reported indicators included low admissions standards and the concentration of athletes in certain majors.[11]

## DIAGNOSING THE PROBLEM

Those who have complained about big-time athletics over the 90 or so years of episodic debate have typically proceeded directly from indictment to proposed solutions, skipping entirely the intervening step of considering the *causes* of those perceived problems. Implicit in some of these calls for reform have been theories of how things came to be as they were, but seldom have these theories been stated plainly. There have been a few exceptions, however, including four published reports devoted to the problems of big-time college sports. The first of these reports was the famous and exhaustive Carnegie Commission study released in 1929, *American College Athletics*. The others were reports put together by or for special commissions of higher-education groups for the expressed aim of reforming big-time college athletics. Spaced at roughly two-decade intervals, these reports were issued in 1953, 1974, and 1991. The first two were sponsored by the American Council on Education (ACE), and the last was supported by the Knight Foundation.

Boiled down to their essentials, these reports give remarkably consistent explanations for the perceived ills of big-time college sports. They cite two underlying causes: powerful forces of commercialism and institutional weakness of universities. The 1929 Carnegie report pointed to the temptations created by "the monetary and material returns from sport." In particular, certain newspapers gained from sensationalizing college competition.[12] For their part, universities were seen as timid in their response to these outside forces, offering only "pseudo-faculty control" and an insincere devotion to intellectual pursuits.[13]

Fully consistent with this explanation was a report issued 24 years later by a committee empaneled by the ACE, chaired by Michigan State president John A. Hannah. It stated:

> The present situation has been brought about by external pressures and internal weaknesses evident during a considerable period. The rewards in money and publicity held out to winning teams, particularly in football and basketball, and the desire of alumni, civic bodies, and other groups to see the institutions in which they are interested reap such rewards, have had a powerful influence on many colleges and universities. The influence has been magnified when control of athletic policy has been permitted to slip from the hands of the faculty and central administration.[14]

Two decades after that, another report commissioned by the ACE once again pointed to commercialization, but also to the "unhealthy pressure for victory" that alumni and local citizens placed on athletic departments.[15]

The most recent blue-ribbon group to take on the problems of big-time sports, the Knight Commission on Intercollegiate Athletics, reiterated the earlier reports' stress on commercial forces and institutional weakness. It wrote of the inability of "fragile" universities to resist powerful outside forces. In the face of rapid commercialization and rampant abuses in recruiting, "faculty members, presidents and other administrators, unable to control the enterprise, stand by as it undermines the institution's goals."[16] In its follow-up 2001 report, the commission charged universities with "complicity and capitulation," saying that they had "allowed commercial interests – television, shoe companies, corporate sponsors of all sorts – to dictate the terms under which college sports operate."[17]

Despite the consistency with which they have been cited over the years, these two considerations – commercial forces and weak institutions – do not add up to a fully convincing theory. A better explanation begins by recognizing the incentives that confront university leaders. To think of the commercialism of big-time athletics as an outside influence doing battle with the university is to misconstrue the genesis of that commercialism. In fact, for the universities with big-time sports programs, commercial entertainment has been and continues to be basic to what they do. For reasons uniquely American, college football and basketball are so wildly popular that they are ready sources of commercial income just sitting there, waiting to be tapped. Few universities turn away from these potential sources of income, choosing instead to tap them and apply the revenue in the effort to field successful teams. And successful teams are precisely what their stakeholders want. They want successful teams in part because they believe that athletic success will bolster their institutions' academic mission and in part because they value athletic success for its own sake. For such universities, the decision to engage in commercial sports is perfectly rational, a conclusion that is supported by two observations highlighted in Chapter 8. First, once a university embarks on big-time sports, it rarely quits. Second, there continue to be universities outside the circle of big-time sports that want to join its ranks. Evidently, the collateral damage resulting from efforts to have winning teams, such as relaxed academic standards for athletes, is a price these universities are quite willing to pay.

Influences outside the academy have had an effect on this situation, to be sure, and one principal result has been to increase the temptation for outsiders to adopt big-time sports. First among these outside influences is the great exogenous force of college sports – television. Its invention, adoption, and proliferation have led to a dramatic transformation in the scale of big-time college sports, even while the form and challenges of the enterprise have hardly changed at all. Aided by a favorable Supreme Court ruling and the subsequent development of cable TV, television has allowed the audience for a big-time game to balloon from the tens of thousands to the millions.[18] Meanwhile, the rise of cable led to viral growth in the number of college games available for viewing. This growing exposure, in turn, steadily strengthened the commercial potential of the enterprise. A second outside force that bolstered the commercial value of college sports was the country's growing affluence. As incomes grew, so did the demand for entertainment. All boats did not rise at the same rate, however. Beginning in the mid-1970s, the incomes of top earners began to rise at unusually rapid rates. This development helped to boost the pay for coaches, celebrities, and CEOs. But as it raised the cost of running athletic departments, it also enhanced their ability to raise money in the form of tax-deductible charitable giving.

Just as the incentives facing university leaders made it logical to pursue commercial opportunities as a part of running their athletic enterprises, logic also made it desirable for universities to work together. Their cooperative efforts, embodied in the various athletic conferences and, more important, in the NCAA, have had two main effects. One is to legislate and enforce rules that rationalize the terms of engagement. From specifying the width of playing fields to restricting the size of teams and the number of recruiting visits, many if not most NCAA rules enhance the quality of the competition by setting limits on that competition. The NCAA's other function comes as a by-product of protecting the amateur status of players. Whether or not it intends to do so, the NCAA acts as a classical cartel, with the result that athletes have little opportunity to share in the income their efforts help to generate. The success of this cartel provides a good explanation for complaints that athletes are treated unfairly. The explanation for another complaint, about the unfair treatment of have-not universities, lies in the operation of other alliances of universities, including the conferences and the BCS. These alliances have the effect of protecting the interests of the universities with the most well established athletic programs.

What may look like a financial bonanza to the larger group of universities may not seem so profitable to any given institution, even one lucky enough to have inherited a famous name and membership in an established conference. As we have seen, making a profit in big-time college sports is a feat achieved by only a select few. Part of the explanation could, of course, lie in inefficiencies in operation. But the more likely reason arises from the winner-take-all character of the competition. Because the competition is for rank alone, some competitors must inevitably fail. In his efforts to secure a leg up on the competition, the athletic director can always find a useful way to spend more money. Although the cost of one of his inputs, the players, is controlled, the cost of others is not – head coaches and their assistants being well-publicized examples. For their part, coaches face incentives of their own. These incentives accentuate the importance of winning, causing some coaches to yield to the temptation to break rules.

## PRESCRIPTIONS FOR REFORM

We now return to the decades-old question that began this chapter. To begin with, many Americans would surely say that things are fine as they are. Attendance and viewership are strong and growing, as is the public attention given to the annual media extravaganza of "March Madness." Indeed, an unmistakable subtext beneath the breathless coverage of college games on ESPN, Fox, the major networks, and the sports segment of local newscasts, not to mention *Sports Illustrated*, *USA Today*, and other newspapers, is one of appreciation and adoration of college sports as they now exist. Although the media have reason to hype sports for their own purposes, one has to believe that many Americans are genuinely satisfied with the status quo.[19] Yet criticism lingers, keeping alive the urge for reform. Indeed, the production and discussion of proposals to reform college athletics have constituted a reliable American cottage industry. Today's calls for reform come from groups outside the NCAA establishment, including the Knight Commission and the Coalition on Intercollegiate Athletics. They also come in periodic commentaries and proposals from individuals writing in the national press, including the industry standard, the *Chronicle of Higher Education*.

The proposals for reform range in scope from modest to revolutionary. The smallest, and presumably the politically most palatable, are proposals to tinker with the existing structure of rules without resorting to fundamental change in the existing order. Some of these proposed modifications are designed to operate in the spirit of an arms control treaty, to reduce costs through mandatory limitations such as smaller football rosters or shorter playing seasons.[20] Another idea along these lines is somehow to limit the pay for coaches.[21] Other proposed adjustments to the current regulatory structure have called for toughening the minimum criteria for college admission or the sanctions based on the NCAA's calculated Academic Progress Rate, designed to punish programs with low graduation rates.[22]

In the same spirit of what might be termed, perhaps unfairly, modest reforms are more general appeals to universities to take steps to remedy problems, as exemplified by the Knight Commission. In a forceful appeal for moral backbone, the panel called for trustees, presidents, faculty, athletic directors, and alumni to join together to stand up for academic principles in the face of commercial temptations. In its 2001 report, the group suggested some specific changes that universities should push for through the NCAA. Among the suggested reforms were prohibiting company logos on uniforms, exerting control over when games are played, shortening playing seasons, reducing the number of scholarships, and eliminating the one-year scholarship rule.[23]

At the other extreme from marginal changes of this sort are two radical ideas, so radical, in fact, that they have seldom received serious attention. One idea, ironically in sync with both the libertarian sensibilities of free-market economics and leftist sympathies for the oppressed, is the idea of scrapping the NCAA's prohibition against paying players, those "serfs of the turf." Universities could be allowed, for example, to set aside a certain amount to pay highly prized athletes in the form of signing bonuses or season-ending awards. Another idea, whimsically put forward by former Michigan president James Duderstadt, would be to allow each university to spin off its commercial sports operation as a separate entity. This new entity, which could be organized as a firm owned by shareholders or a cooperative owned by fans, would pay the university for the right to use the trademarked name, mascot, and colors. It would pay players (who might or might not be university students) whatever the market required.[24]

Not only would paying players eliminate the need for much of the NCAA's enforcement apparatus, it would also address the glaring inequity in the compensation paid to those who generate the revenues of big-time college sports. It is rightly asserted by proponents of this idea that the NCAA's defense of the prohibition does not always ring true. Despite the organization's protestations that the rule is intended merely to protect the amateur status of the "student-athletes" under its care, this prohibition on pay undeniably benefits the NCAA and its member institutions. That said, a decision to pay college players could spell economic disaster for big-time college sports. Not only would it add another cost to athletic departments' budgets (and, incidentally, require coaches to share some of the revenues), it could do serious damage to whatever mystique has enabled the college version of football and basketball to compete for the attention of fans with the professional versions, in spite of what is agreed to be something of lower quality. In the words of Derek Bok, once college players are paid, "the magic disappears."[25]

Whereas this proposal would require top-down legislation applying to all universities, a second, equally radical idea could be brought about at any moment by the university willing to do so. It is the idea of giving up on the commercial model of college athletics entirely, including the separate admissions standards and the athletic scholarships that go with it. Athletes would be treated just like other students, as they are supposed to be now in Division III institutions.[26] If a university wished to go all the way in integrating athletics into its regular operation, coaches could be given full faculty status.[27] Even without this last step, this option would be nothing short of cataclysmic for the institution that exercised it, as illustrated by the hurdles that Robert Hutchins had to overcome to drop big-time football at Chicago. Indeed, the rarity of such a decision is the best evidence of the benefits derived from the big-time model.

Between the extremes of modest and radical are reform proposals that would require the federal government to modify the legal environment governing big-time college sports. One line of attack that reformers might make use of is legal challenges to NCAA rules by way of antitrust law. Historically, federal courts have not applied antitrust laws to challenge NCAA restrictions on paying athletes, for example, because such rules have been seen as necessary to ensure the amateur status of college players. But some recent court decisions have suggested that the traditional defense against antitrust enforcement may be open to challenges.[28] In the same way that federal antitrust laws were used in 1991 to challenge the practice followed by a group of selective universities of coordinating financial aid offers, the government could decide to view NCAA restrictions as the anticompetitive actions of a cartel.[29] This lever could be used to force changes in NCAA rules on the duration and amount of athletic scholarships.

The realm of control where federal enforcement probably has the greatest potential to bring about change, however, is federal taxation. Currently, college athletics receives favorable tax treatment because of the presumption that athletics is an activity related to the functioning of the attached universities, which have long received special tax treatment because they are educational. There have been proposals to require universities to pay tax on the income derived from commercial sports, through the Unrelated Business Income Tax (UBIT), on the grounds that the activity is not related to the tax-exempt purpose. However, the most likely result of applying UBIT to college sports would be that accountants at universities where athletic budgets now show profits would simply find new costs to attribute to the operation of the sports enterprise, leaving little if any net income to tax.[30]

A more promising avenue for the reform of federal tax treatment would be to reconsider the deductibility of contributions made for the support of commercial sports. There already exists one limitation: only 80% of the value of a contribution can be deducted if it enables the donor to get seats. Further limiting deductibility or entirely eliminating it could be justified by the lack of connection between the commercial sports enterprise and the university's expressed educational mission, which is the basis for tax deductibility in the first place. In fact, the near absence of references in university mission statements to commercial spectator sports itself argues for the lack of connection. Leaving aside the political hurdles that would surely stand in the way of ending or limiting the deductibility of contributions for commercial college sports, such a proposal would also face challenges in implementation like those posed by UBIT. If contributions to football practice facilities were to lose their deductibility, it is not hard to imagine how contributions to a university's general fund might result in a similar outcome by encouraging university trustees to use some of their general endowment earnings to pay for a new practice facility for its football team. Such a ploy might be prevented, however, by a tougher restriction on tax deductibility, one that would deny tax deductibility to all contributions made to a university if certain conditions were not met. For example, conditions for obtaining tax deductibility might include setting aside athletic revenue for scholarships, adhering to Title IX requirements, capping coaches' salaries, or making public financial information on athletics.[31]

## DOMESTICATING THE ENTERPRISE

If the history of big-time college sports in America has any lesson to teach, it is that the prospects for fundamental reform are not bright. This is because the universities that operate big-time sports programs do so with open eyes and a healthy regard for their own interests. They are not ignorant of the costs that accompany this activity. They have simply decided that the benefits of doing it outweigh the costs. The degree to which these universities are comfortable with their decisions to participate in commercial sports can be gauged by the number of decades in which the same institutions have engaged in the same kind of competition, made the same kinds of compromises, and done so in the face of the same kinds of criticisms. History would tell us that, if you want significant reform in big-time athletics, it will be necessary to start by reforming universities, taking away the influence of trustees who want to see games, legislators who associate winning records with institutional quality, taxpayers and fans throughout the provinces who adore their teams, and administrators who respond to the incentives in front of them. Fearless leadership by university presidents is not enough. You must begin with a board of trustees that cares more about the quality of academic research and instruction than about the outcomes of the annual game against a rival. But at most universities in America, the stakeholders care about sports and they care about winning. That is why reform efforts over the years have been so consistently unsuccessful in satisfying the objections of critics.

Despite the slim prospects for satisfying the calls for reform, a careful assessment of the state of big-time college athletics need not be a counsel of despair. The analysis in this book suggests at least three avenues for thinking about future directions of reform, or at least accommodation. The first of these is to give consideration to one of the proposed reforms described in this chapter: eliminating the tax deduction for contributions to commercial college sports. The justification for making this change in the tax law would be what economists call a market failure. Although the decisions that universities make regarding big-time athletics do seem to be based on rational assessments of the costs and benefits facing them, those are not identical to the costs and benefits that are relevant to society at large. What causes these to diverge is the zero-sum character of the winner-take-all competition in intercollegiate athletics. Although there is a grim logic that motivates universities to spend more and more to gain an advantage on their athletic competitors, society at large does not get much out of such an arms race. Yet U.S. taxpayers are subsidizing exactly this kind of spending. Since 1917 contributions to universities and other charitable organizations have been tax deductible, a policy that has been justified because such spending produces benefits for society rather than the individual making the gift. It is not easy to make the same argument, however, for contributions to commercial sports programs, whose primary function has little to do with universities' academic mission. The result of current tax treatment, then, is to encourage a class of expenditures that are socially wasteful. A better use of the country's scarce resources could be achieved by ending the tax subsidy for contributions that pay for commercial college sports programs.

A second point suggested by the analysis speaks to the prospect of making improvements if externally imposed reform does not occur. In spite of the competition-induced arms race and the vast regulatory structure enforced by the NCAA, universities remain to a large extent masters of their own fates. This freedom means that a university always has the option of unilateral disarmament. It can always decide on its own, for example, to raise the admissions standards it applies to the athletes it recruits. But such a unilateral decision would inevitably make its intercollegiate teams less competitive, an outcome sure to displease the institution's stakeholders. A very few universities, most famously the University of Chicago, have made that exact decision, despite the opposition that it ignited.

Any university thinking about deemphasizing sports must weigh the costs, in the form of weakened athletic competitiveness, against any benefits, in terms of lower expenditures or strengthened academics. Anything that reduces the anticipated costs will make change more palatable. One way a university could deal with the prospect of having weaker teams would be to join with like-minded institutions and deemphasize sports on a multilateral basis. This is what eight private universities did in 1954 when they formed the Ivy League and agreed not to give athletic scholarships. It is not inconceivable that another group of academically strong universities might join together to form a similar conference. That seems unlikely to occur, however, barring some future event that might cast a stain on all of big-time college sports. The tremendous financial advantages that universities like Stanford, Vanderbilt, Northwestern, and Duke derive as members of established BCS conferences make them unlikely candidates now to form a new Ivy League. Despite the academic compromises that such universities must make to remain respectable competitors in football and basketball, big-time sports has evidently not done them appreciable harm. As indicated by the comparisons presented in Chapter 6, the academic standing of top-rated universities with big-time programs has not declined appreciably in the past 15 years, in comparison with that of similar institutions without them.

A third possible response to the analysis in this book would be more in the nature of accommodation than of reform. This accommodation would begin with a candid recognition of the true importance of big-time college sports. An argument that runs throughout this book is that commercial sports has been and continues to be a central activity of many American universities. The games played by the teams sponsored by them attract widespread attention. The traditions associated with intercollegiate play loom large in the meaning that these universities have for their alumni, their local communities, and many citizens with no connection to them other than being fans of their teams. Among the many activities of these universities, the exploits of their sports teams typically capture more public attention than all of their other activities combined, despite the fact that some of them are among the most renowned research universities in the world. Yet these universities remain reluctant to acknowledge how important sports is in their operation or reputation. Nor do scholars of higher education often see commercial sports as an important function of universities.

The reality of the important role played by big-time sports calls for a new candor. Rather than pretending that big-time football and basketball are nothing more than a couple of student activities, it would be more in keeping with academic traditions to speak honestly about the actual importance of commercial sports in these universities. For administrators and faculty alike, this importance may not be easy to acknowledge. Few of them may be comfortable with the notion that they work for institutions that are major players in the entertainment industry. Certainly many faculty members in research universities with big-time sports programs believe that too much attention is paid to sports and too many compromises are made in order to field competitive teams. It is perhaps because of this unease and opposition that most university mission statements do not state the obvious, acknowledging the sway that sports holds, not only in the lives of students and alumni boosters, but over the academic operation itself. The reality is that each of the universities that have chosen to operate big-time programs contains a largely commercial enterprise, loosely attached to the academic part of the university, whose aim is to produce competitive teams. The imperatives of successful operation in that realm require compromises in the academic one, and those who run the university are willing to bear those costs. But they are often not willing to acknowledge the fact that compromises are being made. This is a reason that pronouncements they and their alliance, the NCAA, make have been described as doublespeak. These facts do not make the universities that run such operations evil, only not as pure as their official pronouncements would suggest.

A new candor would begin with more accurate mission statements. If a mission statement goes into detail about the activities a university undertakes, why not mention intercollegiate athletics? In public pronouncements, university presidents could mention the benefits that the institution derives from having commercial sports, some of the compromises it has made, and why the benefits justify the costs. These statements might also acknowledge the importance of providing sources of wholesome entertainment in attracting applicants and making their collegiate experience enjoyable. They might mention as well the importance of big-time sports in generating donations and political support. But these officials should also be prepared to defend decisions they and their fellow universities have made in order to enhance the commercial success of big-time college sports. They should be willing to have a frank discussion about the justifications of such collective policies as allowing beer to be advertised with televised games, requiring athletes to wear corporate logos but forbidding their display of Bible verses or other individual expressions, or allowing athletic scholarships to be revoked at the discretion of coaches. This candor should also allow universities to take credit for social benefits that are produced by big-time sports, including the enjoyment it brings to ordinary citizens and the example it often provides of successful interracial cooperation.

There is no foreseeable force that is likely to sever the century-old marriage between commercial athletics and American higher education. But a fresh acknowledgment of the marriage's benefits and costs, and a willingness to act on this understanding, should help. By acknowledging the actual importance that this form of commercial entertainment plays in their regular operation, the universities that incorporate it can initiate a more honest and informed discussion of trade-offs, and of potential remedies. Big-time sports is evidently not so damaging as to cause serious harm to universities where it has lived and grown. Among the top-ranked universities in the world are some of the very same institutions with long-standing reputations as powers in football or basketball. But as we enter an era in which the preeminence of American higher education can no longer be taken for granted, it will serve us to have a more candid discussion about the benefits and costs of this athletic enterprise.

# Appendix

Table 1A.1. *Top universities in the world, 2008, according to Shanghai Jiao Tong University ranking*

| World rank | Institution | Country |
|---|---|---|
| 1 | Harvard University | USA |
| 2 | Stanford University | USA |
| 3 | University of California – Berkeley | USA |
| 4 | University of Cambridge | UK |
| 5 | Massachusetts Institute of Technology (MIT) | USA |
| 6 | California Institute of Technology | USA |
| 7 | Columbia University | USA |
| 8 | Princeton University | USA |
| 9 | University of Chicago | USA |
| 10 | University of Oxford | UK |
| 11 | Yale University | USA |
| 12 | Cornell University | USA |
| 13 | University of California – Los Angeles | USA |
| 14 | University of California – San Diego | USA |
| 15 | University of Pennsylvania | USA |
| 16 | University of Washington – Seattle | USA |
| 17 | University of Wisconsin – Madison | USA |
| 18 | University of California – San Francisco | USA |
| 19 | Tokyo University | Japan |
| 20 | Johns Hopkins University | USA |
| 21 | University of Michigan – Ann Arbor | USA |
| 22 | University College London | UK |
| 23 | Kyoto University | Japan |
| 24 | Swiss Federal Institute of Technology – Zurich | Switzerland |
| 24 | University of Toronto | Canada |
| 26 | University of Illinois – Champaign-Urbana | USA |

*(continued)*

Table 1A.1.  *(continued)*

| World rank | Institution | Country |
|---|---|---|
| 27 | Imperial College London | UK |
| 28 | University of Minnesota – Twin Cities | USA |
| 29 | Washington University in St. Louis | USA |
| 30 | Northwestern University | USA |
| 31 | New York University | USA |
| 32 | Duke University | USA |
| 32 | Rockefeller University | USA |
| 34 | University of Colorado – Boulder | USA |
| 35 | University of British Columbia | Canada |
| 36 | University of California – Santa Barbara | USA |
| 37 | University of Maryland – College Park | USA |
| 38 | University of North Carolina – Chapel Hill | USA |
| 39 | University of Texas – Austin | USA |
| 40 | University of Manchester | UK |
| 41 | University of Texas Southwestern Medical Center | USA |
| 42 | Pennsylvania State University | USA |
| 42 | University of Paris 06 | France |
| 42 | Vanderbilt University | USA |
| 45 | University of Copenhagen | Denmark |
| 46 | University of California – Irvine | USA |
| 47 | University of Utrecht | Netherlands |
| 48 | University of California – Davis | USA |
| 49 | University of Paris 11 | France |
| 50 | University of Southern California | USA |

*Source*:  http://www.arwu.org/rank2008/en2008.htm, 8/31/09.

## METHODOLOGY FOR PARTY REGISTRATION
## OF UNIVERSITY STAKEHOLDERS (CHAPTER 2)

We collected voter registration information for 2,190 individuals associated with 30 universities in 9 states from January to June 2009 using LexisNexis software.[1] From a list of universities in 21 states for which voter registrations are available, with total graduate and undergraduate enrollments above 6,000 students, we selected 8 private and 22 public universities from Arkansas, Colorado, Connecticut, Louisiana, Ohio, Massachusetts, New York, North Carolina, and Utah.[2] Within each state, we paired FBS institutions with non-FBS Division I institutions by selecting institutions closest in enrollment size. All enrollment data were taken from the NCES IPEDS navigator Web site.[3] We excluded all military service academies and historically black colleges and universities.

The universities were the following: FBS: Private: MA: Boston College; NC: Duke University; Wake Forest University; NY: Syracuse University; Public: AR: University of Arkansas; CO: Colorado State University; CT: University of Connecticut; LA: University of Louisiana, Lafayette; University of Louisiana, Monroe; Louisiana State University; Louisiana Tech University; OH: Bowling Green State University; University of Toledo; UT: University of Utah; Utah State University. Other Division I: Private: MA: Harvard University; NC: Elon University; Campbell University; NY: St. John's University; Public: AR: University of Arkansas, Little Rock; CO: University of Northern Colorado; CT: Central Connecticut State University; LA: McNeese State University; University of New Orleans; Northwestern State University; Southeastern Louisiana University; OH: Wright State University; Youngstown State University; UT: Utah Valley University; Weber State University.

Up to 20 individuals were selected from each university's (1) business and finance (or equivalent) departments, (2) athletic department, (3) board of trustees, (4) athletic booster organization, and (5) economics department. In cases where more than 20 individuals met the search criteria as outlined later, we selected names randomly. For some university booster organizations, it was possible to create a hierarchical list based on donor levels. When such information was available, individuals in the booster groups were sorted according to the hierarchy first and the random ordering process second, if necessary.

Details on the selection of individuals are available on my Web site appendix.

We used the LexisNexis research software (http://www.lexisnexis.com/lawschool) to determine registrations for all individuals, using last name, first name, middle initial if known, and common variations or nicknames of the first name, if necessary. We confined searches to the state in which the school was located unless (1) there was specific information to indicate that the individuals lived outside of the state or (2) when no matches were found for individuals within the state. To search for individuals outside the state in question, we used the "all available states" feature of the LexisNexis search engine. In most instances, more than one possible match was returned for individuals searched. To determine the correct match, we narrowed the list of returned matches by cross-referencing county information and searching only the counties closest to the institution in question. When this was not enough to determine the correct match, we performed Google and university directory searches to find a middle name or middle initial, date of birth, spouse's name, and other amplifying information to help distinguish

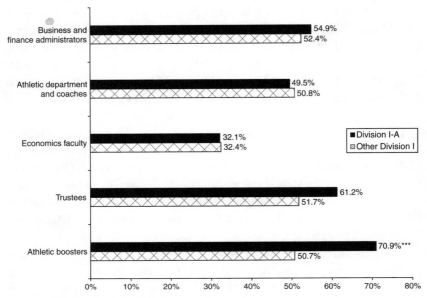

Figure 2A.1. Percent Republican, selected groups of employees and stakeholders, 34 universities. Bars indicate predicted percent Republican among those registered as either Republican or Democrat, holding constant state and enrollment, in probit equations. *** = significant at the 1% level.
*Source*: Publicly available voter registration information.

the correct match. Occasionally, searches returned multiple matches for individuals all having the same political affiliation. In such instances, we attempted to resolve the multiple matches by searching for amplifying information but did use the political affiliation listed when matches could not be resolved.

In many instances, multiple registrations for the same individual were found in the database. A small number of individuals were found to have changed political affiliations. To ensure consistency, we therefore selected only the most recent registration on record. The only exception to this rule was in Arkansas, where an unusually large number of individuals changed from Republican and Democratic affiliations to undeclared status.[4] In Arkansas, we therefore used the last party affiliation for which individuals were registered rather than the most recent affiliation. We additionally used the Web site www.opensecrets.org, which lists campaign contributions for individuals nationwide, to help determine party affiliation for individuals in Arkansas. Due to the small number of returns that this search engine yielded, however, we used this method only to resolve undeclared party affiliations for individuals in Arkansas.

Table 2A.1. *Functions or administrative units mentioned in mission statements, 52 universities with big-time athletic programs*

| | Number of universities that | | Percentage that mention it |
|---|---|---|---|
| | Have that function or unit | Mention it in its mission statement | |
| *Broad functions* | | | |
| Teaching | 52 | 52 | 100.0 |
| Research | 52 | 52 | 100.0 |
| Service | 52 | 51 | 98.1 |
| *Administrative units* | | | |
| School of education | 47 | 8 | 17.0 |
| Extension service | 26 | 8 | 30.8 |
| Medical school | 32 | 8 | 25.0 |
| Architecture school | 34 | 6 | 17.6 |
| Business school | 52 | 9 | 17.3 |
| Law school | 39 | 6 | 15.4 |
| Veterinary school | 19 | 3 | 15.8 |
| Engineering school | 48 | 7 | 14.6 |
| Pharmacy school | 26 | 3 | 11.5 |
| Social work school | 32 | 4 | 12.5 |
| Journalism school | 33 | 4 | 12.1 |
| Nursing school | 35 | 4 | 11.4 |
| Athletics | 52 | 5 | 9.6 |

*Source*: Mission statements posted on the Internet, May 2008.

## JSTOR SAMPLE AND ANALYSIS OF WORK PATTERNS IN RESEARCH LIBRARIES (CHAPTER 3)

A group of 78 research libraries in the United States belonging to the Association of Research Libraries or the Association of Southeastern Research Libraries gave permission to access JSTOR usage data for their libraries. Daily data on the number of articles viewed through JSTOR at these libraries were compiled by JSTOR for the months of February through April for the years 2006, 2007, and 2008.

I am grateful to these research libraries, to JSTOR for assisting with the collection of these data, and to Deborah Jakubs of the Duke University Library for requesting permission from the research libraries on my behalf to obtain the data from JSTOR. In addition to the following listed libraries, four that did not want to be listed allowed their data to be accessed: Arizona State University, Auburn University, Boston College, Brown University, Brigham Young University, Case Western Reserve University, Clemson

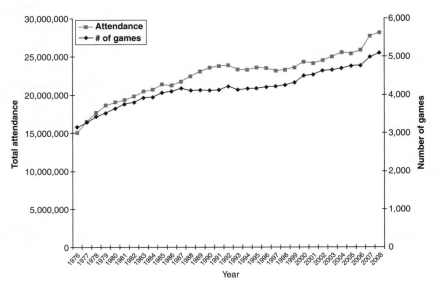

Figure 3A.1.  NCAA Division I men's basketball annual attendance and games.
*Source*: NCAA, *NCAA Attendance Records*, 2009, http://www.docstoc.com/docs/
4844529/2008–2009-NCAA-Mens-Basketball-Attendance-Records, 5/6/10; http://www.
ncaa.org/wps/portal/ncaahome?WCM_GLOBAL_CONTEXT=/wps/wcm/connect/
ncaa/NCAA/Sports+and+Championship/General+Information/Stats/M+Basketball/
Attendance/index2.htmlz, 5/6/10.

University, College of William & Mary, Colorado State University, Columbia
University, Cornell University, Dartmouth College, Duke University, East
Carolina University, Emory University, Florida State University, Georgetown
University, George Washington University, Georgia State University, Harvard
University, Iowa State University, Johns Hopkins University, Library of
Virginia, Massachusetts Institute of Technology, Michigan State University,
New York Public Library, Northwestern University, Ohio State University,
Pennsylvania State University, Princeton University, Purdue University, Rice
University, Rutgers University, Smithsonian Institution Libraries, Southern
Illinois University Carbondale, Stony Brook University, Syracuse University,
Temple University, Texas A&M University, Texas Tech University, University
of Alabama, University of California –Berkeley, University of California –
Davis, University of California – Los Angeles, University of California – San
Diego, University of Central Florida, University of Cincinnati, University
of Colorado at Boulder, University of Delaware, University of Hawaii,
University of Houston, University of Illinois at Chicago, University of Illinois
at Urbana-Champaign, University of Kansas, University of Maryland,
University of Massachusetts, Amherst, University of Michigan, University

Table 3A.1. *Big-time college football then and now: institutions ranked by football power in 1920, athletic spending in 2009*

| University | 2009 Rank | 1920 Rank |
|---|---|---|
| *Top 100 in 1920, still top 100 in 2009* | | |
| University of Texas at Austin | 1 | 18 |
| Ohio State University – Main Campus | 2 | 23 |
| University of Florida | 3 | 50 |
| Louisiana State University | 4 | 22 |
| University of Tennessee | 5 | 30 |
| University of Wisconsin – Madison | 6 | 32 |
| Auburn University | 7 | 10 |
| University of Alabama | 8 | 11 |
| University of Oklahoma | 9 | 26 |
| University of Michigan – Ann Arbor | 11 | 43 |
| University of Georgia | 12 | 8 |
| Pennsylvania State University | 13 | 1 |
| University of South Carolina | 14 | 57 |
| Stanford University | 15 | 83 |
| University of California – Berkeley | 16 | 19 |
| University of Iowa | 19 | 27 |
| University of Minnesota | 20 | 74 |
| University of North Carolina at Chapel Hill | 21 | 47 |
| Texas A & M University | 22 | 4 |
| Oklahoma State University | 23 | 84 |
| University of Kentucky | 25 | 59 |
| University of Kansas | 26 | 41 |
| University of Notre Dame | 27 | 5 |
| University of Virginia | 28 | 42 |
| University of Arkansas | 29 | 66 |
| Boston College | 30 | 89 |
| University of Nebraska – Lincoln | 31 | 21 |
| University of Washington | 33 | 79 |
| University of Oregon | 34 | 55 |
| University of Maryland – College Park | 35 | 54 |
| Purdue University | 37 | 97 |
| Clemson University | 38 | 52 |
| University of Missouri – Columbia | 39 | 16 |
| Indiana University – Bloomington | 40 | 64 |
| Rutgers University – New Brunswick | 43 | 69 |
| University of Illinois at Urbana-Champaign | 44 | 37 |
| West Virginia University | 45 | 25 |
| Syracuse University | 47 | 12 |

*(continued)*

Table 3A.1. *(continued)*

| University | 2009 Rank | 1920 Rank |
|---|---|---|
| Virginia Polytechnic Institute and State University | 49 | 45 |
| Oregon State University | 50 | 76 |
| Northwestern University | 51 | 91 |
| Baylor University | 52 | 53 |
| University of Colorado at Boulder | 53 | 75 |
| Georgia Institute of Technology | 54 | 1 |
| Texas Christian University | 55 | 63 |
| Kansas State University | 56 | 68 |
| University of Pittsburgh | 57 | 5 |
| North Carolina State University | 58 | 33 |
| Iowa State University | 59 | 43 |
| Vanderbilt University | 60 | 9 |
| Wake Forest University | 61 | 96 |
| University of Mississippi | 63 | 58 |
| Mississippi State University | 64 | 51 |
| Washington State University | 65 | 46 |
| Southern Methodist University | 67 | 88 |
| University of Utah | 74 | 85 |
| Rice University | 75 | 38 |
| University of Wyoming | 86 | 91 |
| Colorado State University | 93 | 49 |
| Tulane University of Louisiana | 98 | 35 |

| Dropouts from top 100 (*not in top 100 programs in 2009 by expenditure*) | 1920 Rank |
|---|---|
| Centre College | 3 |
| Harvard University | 5 |
| Washington and Lee University | 13 |
| Dartmouth College | 13 |
| Washington and Jefferson College | 15 |
| Furman University | 17 |
| U.S. Naval Academy (Navy) | 20 |
| Lafayette College | 24 |
| Yale University | 27 |
| Princeton University | 29 |
| Virginia Military Institute | 31 |
| University of Pennsylvania | 33 |
| Lehigh University | 35 |
| Sewanee (University of the South) | 39 |
| University of Chicago | 40 |

| Dropouts from top 100<br>(*not in top 100 programs in 2009 by expenditure*) | 1920<br>Rank |
|---|---|
| Brown University | 48 |
| Utah State University | 56 |
| Colgate University | 59 |
| Mississippi College | 59 |
| Davidson College | 62 |
| Washington University in St. Louis | 64 |
| Cornell University | 67 |
| Drake University | 70 |
| Oglethorpe University | 71 |
| U.S. Military Academy (Army) | 72 |
| Presbyterian College | 73 |
| The Citadel | 77 |
| Colorado College | 78 |
| Erskine College | 80 |
| Georgetown University | 81 |
| Birmingham – Southern College | 82 |
| Spring Hill College | 85 |
| Samford University | 87 |
| University of Tennessee – Chattanooga | 90 |
| Bucknell University | 91 |
| Grinnell College | 94 |
| University of Denver | 94 |
| Wofford College | 97 |
| Newberry College | 97 |
| Mercer University | 97 |

| "New" big-time programs since 1920<br>(*unranked in 1920, top 100 in 2009*) | 2009<br>Rank | Began<br>Football |
|---|---|---|
| University of Southern California | 10 | 1922 |
| Florida State University | 17 | 1954 |
| Duke University | 18 | 1922 |
| University of California – Los Angeles | 24 | 1928 |
| Michigan State University | 32 | 1918 |
| University of Connecticut | 36 | 1979 |
| University of Miami | 41 | 1936 |
| University of Louisville | 42 | 1962 |
| Arizona State University | 46 | 1931 |
| University of Arizona | 48 | 1922 |
| Texas Tech University | 62 | 1932 |
| Brigham Young University | 66 | 1922 |
| University of South Florida | 68 | 2000 |

(*continued*)

Table 3A.1. *(continued)*

| "New" big-time programs since 1920 (*unranked in 1920, top 100 in 2009*) | 2009 Rank | Began Football |
|---|---|---|
| University of Cincinnati | 69 | 1954 |
| San Diego State University | 70 | 1969 |
| University of Memphis | 71 | 1960 |
| University of New Mexico | 72 | 1931 |
| University of Nevada – Las Vegas | 73 | 1978 |
| University of Hawaii at Manoa | 76 | 1991 |
| University of Central Florida | 77 | 1996 |
| University of Houston | 78 | 1949 |
| Georgetown University | 79 | 1902 |
| East Carolina University | 80 | 1965 |
| University of Tulsa | 81 | 1933 |
| Temple University | 82 | 1930 |
| California State University – Fresno | 83 | 1969 |
| New Mexico State University | 84 | 1931 |
| Miami University – Oxford | 85 | 1962 |
| University at Buffalo | 87 | 1962 |
| The University of Texas at El Paso | 88 | 1935 |
| Central Michigan University | 89 | 1975 |
| University of Alabama at Birmingham | 90 | 1996 |
| Eastern Michigan University | 91 | 1975 |
| Ohio University | 92 | 1962 |
| Western Michigan University | 94 | 1962 |
| University of Nevada – Reno | 95 | 1946 |
| Florida International University | 96 | 2004 |
| Western Kentucky University | 97 | 2007 |
| Boise State University | 99 | 1996 |
| Marshall University | 100 | 1962 |

*Note*: Rank for 1920 is based on the mean of power rankings for 1919, 1920, and 1921, or 101 if not ranked in the top 100. Blank indicates not ranked in top 100. Institution names are current, not necessarily the same as those in 1920.

*Source for power rankings*: James Howell, power rankings, http://www.jhowell.net/cf/cfindex.htm, 2/13/10.

of Minnesota, University of Mississippi, University of North Carolina at Chapel Hill, University of North Carolina at Greensboro, University of Notre Dame, University of Pennsylvania, University of Pittsburgh, University of Rochester, University of South Carolina, University of Southern California, University of Texas at Austin, University of Utah, University of Washington, Virginia Commonwealth University, Wake Forest University, Washington State University, and Wayne State University.

Table 3A.2. *Televised basketball games, Chicago market, first Saturday in February, 1983, 1990, and 2009*

| February 5, 1983 | | February 3, 1990 | | February 7, 2009 | |
| --- | --- | --- | --- | --- | --- |
| Game | Network | Game | Network | Game | Network |
| Iowa–Purdue | WGN | NC State–Nevada Las Vegas | WMAQ | Coppin State–South Carolina State | ESPN2 |
| Alabama–Kentucky | WMAO | Loyola Marymount–LSU | WBBM | Bowling Green–Western Michigan | ESPNU |
| Minnesota–Indiana | WMAO | De Paul–UCLA | WMAQ | Cincinnati–Georgetown | WCIU-DT |
| South Carolina–Notre Dame | WGN | Seton Hall–Boston College | WWOR | Notre Dame–Baylor | WBBM |
| | | Xavier–Dillard | BET | Fordham–George Washington | CBS-CS |
| | | Illinois State–Tulsa | Sports Channel | Western Kentucky–Murray State | FCS-Atlantic |
| | | Loyola–Butler | Sports Channel | Colorado–Oklahoma | WLS-DT |
| | | Northwestern–Iowa | Sports Channel | Pittsburgh–De Paul | WWME |
| | | Wyoming–Colorado State | ESPN | Indiana State–Illinois State | ESPNU |
| | | Georgetown– St. John's | WBBM | Texas–Nebraska | ESPN |
| | | | | South Alabama–Western Kentucky | ESPN2 |
| | | | | Oklahoma State–Kansas | WLS |
| | | | | Cleveland State–Loyola | Lakeshore Public |
| | | | | Valparaiso–Detroit | HLN |
| | | | | Indiana–Michigan State | ESPN |
| | | | | Southern Illinois–Missouri State | ESPN2 |
| | | | | Lehigh–American | ESPNU |
| | | | | Kansas State–Texas A&M | WLS |
| | | | | Binghamton–Stony Brook | FCS-Central |
| | | | | St. Francis (PA)–Wagner | FCS-Atlantic |
| | | | | Tulane–Marshall | CBS-CS |

*(continued)*

233

Table 3A.2. (continued)

| February 5, 1983 | | February 3, 1990 | | February 7, 2009 | |
|---|---|---|---|---|---|
| Game | Network | Game | Network | Game | Network |
| | | | | Northwestern–Iowa | Big 10 Network |
| | | | | Michigan–Connecticut | ESPN |
| | | | | Charleston–Davidson | ESPN2 |
| | | | | Morgan State–Winston-Salem State | ESPNU |
| | | | | Georgia–South Carolina | FCS-Atlantic |
| | | | | Youngstown State–University of Illinois Chicago | HLN |
| | | | | Minnesota–Ohio State | Big 10 Network |
| | | | | Baylor–Texas Tech | ESPNU |
| | | | | New Mexico State–Nevada | ESPN2 |
| | | | | Nevada Las Vegas–New Mexico | ESPN2 |
| | | | | Arizona State–Oregon State | FCS-Pacific |
| | | | | Memphis–Gonzaga | ESPN |
| | | | | Air Force–San Diego State | CBS-CS |
| | | | | Washington State–California | FCS-Pacific |
| | | | | Bradley–Drake | Comcast SportsNet |
| | | | | Syracuse–Villanova | ESPN |

Table 4A.1. *Fans by gender and age*

| Age | Fans | |
|---|---|---|
| | Male (%) | Female (%) |
| College football | | |
| 18–34 | 53 | 22 |
| 35–54 | 41 | 25 |
| 55+ | 50 | 29 |
| Professional football | | |
| 18–34 | 64 | 37 |
| 35–54 | 60 | 35 |
| 55+ | 52 | 33 |
| College basketball | | |
| 18–34 | 37 | 18 |
| 35–54 | 30 | 17 |
| 55+ | 36 | 20 |
| Professional basketball | | |
| 18–34 | 36 | 20 |
| 35–54 | 24 | 20 |
| 55+ | 26 | 22 |

*Note:* The figures in the table give the percentage who are fans.
*Source*: Calculations based on AP/Ipsos Public Affairs Poll, October 16–18, 2007, Roper Center, using population weights.

Table 4A.2. *TV commercials for the 2009 NCAA men's basketball tournament, by product category*

| Product category | Brand with most ad time in category | Number | Minutes | % of total minutes | Relative emphasis[a] |
|---|---|---|---|---|---|
| Cars and trucks (new) | Chevrolet | 368 | 186.0 | 17.3 | 5.5 |
| Food away from home | McDonald's | 320 | 134.3 | 12.5 | 2.3 |
| Financial services and other miscellaneous items | E*Trade | 166 | 72.0 | 7.3 | 4.5 |
| Computers and other miscellaneous household equipment | IBM | 120 | 67.8 | 6.3 | 3.7 |
| Alcoholic beverages | Bud Lite | 156 | 61.5 | 5.7 | 6.2 |
| Movies and other fees and admissions | Movie Trailers | 169 | 59.1 | 5.5 | 4.1 |
| Telephone services | AT&T | 109 | 54.5 | 5.1 | 2.3 |
| Nonalcoholic beverages | Coca-Cola | 104 | 52.5 | 4.9 | 7.3 |
| Television, radio, and sound Equipment | DirecTV | 109 | 48.5 | 4.5 | 2.3 |
| Vehicle insurance | State Farm Insurance | 89 | 44.5 | 4.1 | 1.9 |
| Owned dwellings | Lowe's | 80 | 39.5 | 3.7 | 0.3 |
| Drugs | Lipitor | 32 | 27.5 | 2.6 | 2.6 |
| Other entertainment equipment and services | Nike | 58 | 23.8 | 2.2 | 2.0 |
| Life, endowment, annuities, and other personal insurance | The Hartford | 45 | 22.5 | 2.1 | 3.4 |
| Public service announcements | U.S. Army | 56 | 20.8 | 1.9 | |
| Gasoline and motor oil | Exxon-Mobil | 33 | 20.5 | 1.9 | 0.4 |
| Personal care products and Services | Axe Deodorant | 41 | 20.3 | 1.9 | 1.6 |
| Vehicle rental | Enterprise Rent-A-Car | 66 | 16.5 | 1.5 | 1.6 |
| Commercial | UPS | 32 | 16.0 | 1.5 | |
| Public transportation | Southwest Airlines | 57 | 14.3 | 1.3 | 1.2 |
| Retirement, pensions, and social security | TIAA-CREF | 25 | 12.5 | 1.2 | 0.1 |
| Other lodging | Sheraton Hotels | 25 | 12.0 | 1.1 | 0.8 |
| Food at home other than sweets and beverages | Texas Pete Hot Sauce | 23 | 9.8 | 0.9 | 0.1 |

| | | | | | |
|---|---|---|---|---|---|
| Sugar and other sweets | Hershey's | 38 | 9.5 | 0.9 | 3.5 |
| Housekeeping supplies | Scott's Turf Builder | 22 | 7.0 | 1.0 | 0.8 |
| Medical services | UNC Health System | 13 | 6.5 | 0.6 | 0.4 |
| Men's and boys' apparel | S&K Menswear | 13 | 3.3 | 0.3 | 0.3 |
| Vehicle maintenance and repairs | Jiffy Lube | 2 | 1.0 | 0.1 | 0.0 |
| Other household expenses | CPI Security | 2 | 1.0 | 0.1 | 0.1 |
| Furniture | Rooms2Go | 1 | 0.5 | 0.0 | 0.1 |
| Other products and services | Jarrett's Jewelers | 1 | 0.3 | 0.0 | 0.0 |
| Total | | 2,375 | 1,076.0 | 100.0 | – |

*Note:* Since two minutes of advertising during each broadcast hour during the NCAA tournament are sold by the local affiliates, totals given here will differ slightly from those in other markets.

[a] Ratio of the share of total minutes of commercials to the share of household expenditures devoted to that product category. U.S. Bureau of Labor Statistics, *Consumer Expenditure Survey 2007*, table 2.

*Source:* Analysis of taped broadcasts of the 2009 NCAA men's basketball tournament, broadcast from WRAL, the Raleigh affiliate of CBS.

Table 5A.1. *Illustrative benefits for donations to booster organizations*

| Benefit | University | Minimum qualifying donation ($) |
|---|---|---|
| Right to buy tickets | | |
| Season basketball tickets for two | Pittsburgh | 300 |
| Season football tickets for two | Ohio State | 1,500 |
| Season basketball tickets for two | Florida | 2,000 |
| Season basketball tickets for two | North Carolina | 5,000 |
| Season basketball tickets for two[a] | Duke | 6,000 |
| Conference tournament basketball tickets | Wake Forest | 7,000 |
| Conference tournament basketball tickets | Duke | 15,000 |
| Parking | | |
| Premium parking at Heinz Field | Pittsburgh | 750 |
| Football parking | North Carolina | 1,000 |
| Parking pass at Moby Arena | Colorado State | 4,000 |
| Receptions and dinners | | |
| Access to hospitality club at football games | Texas | 2,000 |
| 12th Man Buffet | Texas A&M | 2,000 |
| Exclusive athletic department dinner | Pittsburgh | 3,000 |
| Men's basketball pre-game reception (select games) | Stanford | 5,000 |
| VIP reception with athletic director and head coaches | Syracuse | 10,000 |
| Fall kickoff reception | Georgia | 25,000 |
| Recognition | | |
| Video board recognition during football season | Louisiana – Lafayette | 2,500 |
| Picture in football game day program | Arkansas | 5,000 |
| Video board recognition | Connecticut | 25,000 |
| Other | | |
| Reduced greens fees at university golf course | Michigan | 1,500 |
| Travel to away basketball game and football game | Syracuse | 25,000 |
| Travel with football team to a select away game for two | Stanford | 50,000 |
| Invitation to a practice session | Connecticut | 50,000 |

[a] $7,000 for new donors.

*Source*: Web sites visited in 2010 for these booster organizations: Iron Dukes, Pitt Golden Panthers, UConn Club, Louisiana – Lafayette Ragin' Cajuns Athletic Foundation, Stanford Buck-Cardinal Club, Syracuse Orange Club, Michigan Victors Club, North Carolina Rams Club, Texas Longhorn Foundation, Georgia Bulldog Club, Texas A&M 12th Man Foundation, Florida Gator Boosters, Arkansas Razorback Foundation, Ohio State Buckeye Club, Wake Forest Deacon Club, and Colorado State Ram Club.

Table 5A.2. *Total compensation for faculty, presidents, and football coaches, 44 universities, 1985–1986 and 2009–2010 (thousands of FY 2009–2010 dollars)*

| University | 1985–1986 | | | 2009–2010 | | |
|---|---|---|---|---|---|---|
| | Full professors | Presidents | Football coaches | Full professors | Presidents | Football coaches |
| *ACC* | | | | | | |
| Clemson | 103.8 | 193.0 | 355.1 | 133.0 | 428.4 | 825.1 |
| Florida State | 102.0 | 260.2 | 330.6 | 131.0 | 700.4 | 2,327.6 |
| Maryland | 122.1 | 318.3 | 333.6 | 164.3 | 501.5 | 1,885.3 |
| North Carolina | 117.9 | 253.9 | 197.5 | 173.2 | 436.7 | 1,710.2 |
| NC State | 116.3 | 232.2 | 202.3 | 141.3 | 464.2 | 1,208.2 |
| Virginia | 131.7 | 261.0 | 201.2 | 166.8 | 778.6 | 2,080.5 |
| Virginia Tech | 118.5 | 426.0 | 370.4 | 145.7 | 736.9 | 2,146.2 |
| *SEC* | | | | | | |
| Alabama | 110.3 | 214.4 | 503.6 | 158.2 | 608.1 | 3,908.2 |
| Arkansas | 98.6 | 317.8 | 395.7 | 125.3 | 309.6 | 2,866.2 |
| Auburn | 102.0 | 320.8 | 427.1 | 132.5 | 732.5 | 2,058.2 |
| Florida | 114.5 | 490.1 | 414.9 | 147.6 | 527.1 | 4,008.2 |
| Georgia | 116.7 | 330.0 | 198.8 | 133.0 | 608.8 | 3,104.8 |
| Kentucky | 99.8 | 399.3 | 195.8 | 129.7 | 402.2 | 1,625.7 |
| LSU | 94.4 | 223.8 | 330.0 | 136.7 | 402.6 | 3,759.2 |
| Mississippi State | 91.2 | 219.7 | 213.2 | 108.3 | 458.5 | 1,208.2 |
| Ole Miss | 91.2 | 185.9 | 164.9 | 126.7 | 458.5 | 2,517.2 |
| South Carolina | 103.2 | 193.0 | 83.8 | 138.5 | 538.5 | 2,039.7 |
| Tennessee | 106.6 | 218.7 | 373.9 | 139.1 | 341.2 | 2,008.2 |
| *Big Ten* | | | | | | |
| Illinois | 112.3 | 396.4 | 624.0 | 159.1 | 413.2 | 1,513.2 |
| Indiana | 112.3 | 312.7 | 176.5 | 153.4 | 339.3 | 667.0 |
| Iowa | 105.8 | 266.9 | 318.4 | 158.2 | 596.8 | 3,032.7 |
| Michigan | 124.1 | 277.4 | 258.4 | 175.6 | 789.0 | 2,529.2 |
| Michigan State | 104.4 | 237.0 | 261.4 | 161.8 | 575.7 | 1,819.5 |
| Minnesota | 116.3 | 305.6 | 204.2 | 165.3 | 647.6 | 1,008.2 |
| Ohio State | 120.7 | 417.0 | 207.3 | 107.5 | 1,587.0 | 3,730.2 |
| Wisconsin | 109.7 | 309.2 | 136.1 | 145.4 | 468.2 | 1,489.7 |
| *Big 12* | | | | | | |
| Colorado | 94.6 | 307.2 | 267.1 | 149.5 | 421.0 | 1,008.8 |
| Iowa State | 100.8 | 313.1 | 157.3 | 139.3 | 524.7 | 958.2 |
| Kansas | 96.8 | 239.9 | 167.1 | 143.2 | 371.3 | 2,311.7 |
| Kansas State | 92.2 | 218.7 | 155.3 | 121.2 | 366.4 | 1,858.2 |
| Missouri | 95.0 | 194.1 | 168.2 | 134.5 | 388.0 | 2,533.2 |
| Nebraska | 91.0 | 333.1 | 199.0 | 139.2 | 382.5 | 1,860.2 |

*(continued)*

Table 5A.2. *(continued)*

| University | 1985–1986 | | | 2009–2010 | | |
|---|---|---|---|---|---|---|
| | Full professors | Presidents | Football coaches | Full professors | Presidents | Football coaches |
| Oklahoma | 101.0 | 201.7 | 178.8 | 147.4 | 635.1 | 4,311.2 |
| Oklahoma State | 97.4 | 218.7 | 271.8 | 127.3 | 439.8 | 1,808.2 |
| Texas | 114.1 | 556.9 | 221.9 | 104.9 | 705.8 | 3,068.7 |
| Texas A&M | 105.8 | 334.4 | 534.9 | 142.2 | 555.6 | 1,809.9 |
| *Pac-10* | | | | | | |
| Arizona | 109.9 | 311.1 | 355.0 | 146.8 | 573.7 | 1,273.2 |
| Arizona State | 103.6 | 318.4 | 354.3 | 147.7 | 713.8 | 1,510.8 |
| Cal Berkeley | 143.4 | 376.9 | 193.5 | 192.4 | 470.6 | 2,815.7 |
| Oregon | 96.0 | 201.3 | 235.7 | 137.9 | 640.5 | 1,508.2 |
| Oregon State | 97.6 | 461.7 | 207.7 | 127.4 | 598.2 | 958.2 |
| UCLA | 139.6 | 205.6 | 429.6 | 95.2 | 427.7 | 1,284.2 |
| Washington | 103.0 | 355.7 | 245.4 | 151.0 | 910.9 | 1,841.5 |
| Washington St. | 95.8 | 225.2 | 202.0 | 127.7 | 652.2 | 608.3 |
| Average | 107.4 | 294.4 | 273.3 | 141.6 | 559.7 | 2,054.7 |

*Note*: Presidents' compensation is for most recent year available, in FY 2009–2010 dollars.
Data on compensation (salary plus benefits) were collected for 44 public universities for which information was publicly available. Compensation for full professors was obtained from the March–April issue of *Academe* for 1986 and 2010. The 1985–1986 salary data for presidents and football coaches came from *USA Today* for September 24 and 26, 1986. Presidents' and coaches' pay included base salary from the university plus other forms of income paid through the university or guaranteed by the university that were deemed to be recurring and quantifiable. To estimate medical benefits, the average value of medical benefits for faculty receiving medical benefits, $1,350, was added to the figures for presidents and coaches for 1985–1986. To estimate retirement benefits, the ratio for faculty of retirement benefits to salary in that year, 0.179, was applied to base university salary and added. All figures for 1985–1986 were converted to 2009–2010 dollars using the CPI. For 2009–2010, total compensation for presidents, for the most recent year available, was taken from data made available by the *Chronicle of Higher Education*, http://chronicle.com/stats/990/public.htm, 8/20/10, and they were converted to 2009–2010 dollars. Data for the pay of head football coaches were taken from *USA Today*, http://www.usatoday.com/sports/college/football/2009-coaches-contracts-database.htm. These explicitly did not include medical benefits, but they were assumed to include retirement benefits. Thus they were augmented by the average medical benefit for professors who received this benefit in 2009–2010, $8,198.
*Source*: Author's calculations. See text.

Table 6A.1. *Changes in academic ranking, 1995–2010*

|  | FBS | Other division I | Not division I |
|---|---|---|---|
| 101 universities appearing in both years' surveys | | | |
| Average SAT | −0.6 | 2.1 | 0.1 |
| Acceptance rate | −2.6 | 1.5 | 4.3 |
| Freshmen in high school top 10% | −2.1 | 2.0 | 1.2 |
| Freshman retention rate | 2.2 | −4.4 | 3.8 |
| Peer evaluation | 0.5 | 0.5 | −1.4 |
| Alumni giving rate | 1.4 | 3.0 | −6.0 |
| Six measures, USN method | −0.5 | 1.0 | 1.2 |
| 51 private universities appearing in both years' surveys | | | |
| Average SAT | 6.8 | 1.2 | 2.8 |
| Acceptance rate | 8.6 | 2.2 | 5.7 |
| Freshmen in high school top 10% | 0.9 | 2.6 | 0.9 |
| Freshman retention rate | 4.3 | −0.6 | 7.7 |
| Peer evaluation | −0.6 | 0.5 | 0.5 |
| Alumni giving rate | 7.7 | 2.5 | −9.2 |
| Six measures, USN method | 4.6 | 2.8 | 2.8 |

*Note*: Improved rankings are indicated by positive values.
*Source*: Author's calculations based on data published by *U.S. News and World Report*, 1995 and 2010 rankings.

## UNIVERSITIES IN *U.S. NEWS* SAMPLE (CHAPTER 6)

The 101 national universities for which *U.S. News* published detailed data for both 1995 and 2010 were, by NCAA designation: FBS: Auburn University, Baylor University, Boston College, Brigham Young University, Duke, Florida State University, Georgia Institute of Technology, Indiana University, Iowa State University, Miami University Oxford, Michigan State University, North Carolina State University, Northwestern, Ohio State University, Ohio University, Pennsylvania State University, Purdue University, Rice, Rutgers, Southern Methodist University, Stanford, Syracuse University, Texas A&M, Tulane, University of Arizona, University of California – Berkeley, University of California – Los Angeles, University of Colorado at Boulder, University of Connecticut, University of Denver, University of Florida, University of Georgia, University of Illinois at Urbana-Champaign, University of Iowa, University of Maryland, University of Miami, University of Michigan – Ann Arbor, University of Minnesota, University of Missouri, University of North Carolina, University of Notre Dame, University of Pittsburgh, University

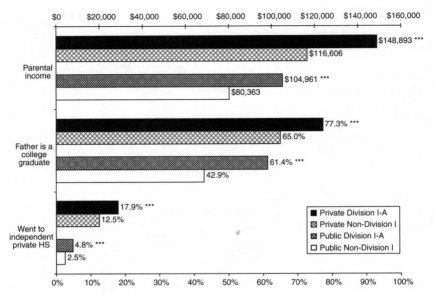

Figure 7A.1. Indicators of social and economic status of incoming freshmen in 2004, 115 public and private universities, by level of athletic competition. Figures show group means. Asterisks indicate FBS and non–Division I difference statistically significant at *10%, **5%, ***1% level.

*Source*: 2004 HERI Survey of Incoming Freshmen.

of Tennessee, University of Texas, University of Virginia, University of Washington, University of Wisconsin, University of Southern California, Vanderbilt, Virginia Tech, Wake Forest University.

Other Division I: American University, Boston University, Brown University, College of William and Mary, Columbia University, Cornell University, Dartmouth College, Fordham University, George Washington University, Georgetown University, Harvard University, Lehigh University, Marquette University, Pepperdine University, Princeton University, St. Louis University, Binghamton University, Stony Brook University, University of California – Davis, University of California – Irvine, University of California – Riverside, University of California – Santa Barbara, University of Delaware, University of Massachusetts, University of New Hampshire, University of Pennsylvania, University of San Diego, University of Vermont, Yale University.

Not Division I: Brandeis University, California Institute of Technology, Carnegie Mellon University, Case Western Reserve University, Clark University, Colorado School of Mines, Emory, Illinois Institute of Technology, Johns Hopkins University, Massachusetts Institute of Technology, New

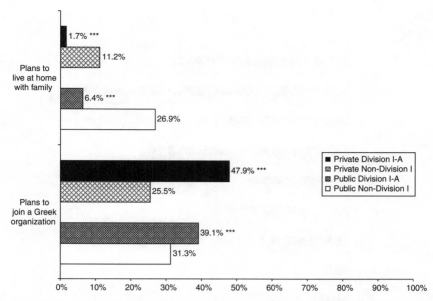

Figure 7A.2. Living arrangements of incoming freshmen in 2004, 115 public and private universities, by level of athletic competition. Figures show group means. Asterisks indicate FBS and non–Division I difference statistically significant at *10%, **5%, ***1% level.
*Source*: 2004 HERI Survey of Incoming Freshmen.

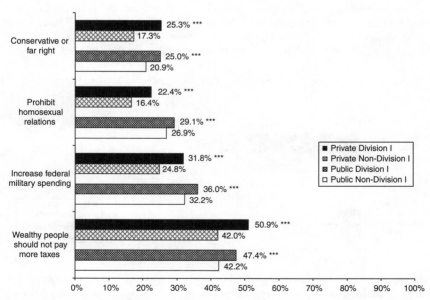

Figure 7A.3. Indicators of political and social attitudes of incoming freshmen in 2004, 115 public and private universities, by level of athletic competition. Figures show predicted values calculated at sample means from probit equations of the type described in Table 7A.1 Asterisks indicate FBS and non–Division I difference statistically significant at *10%, **5%, ***1% level.
*Source*: 2004 HERI Survey of Incoming Freshmen.

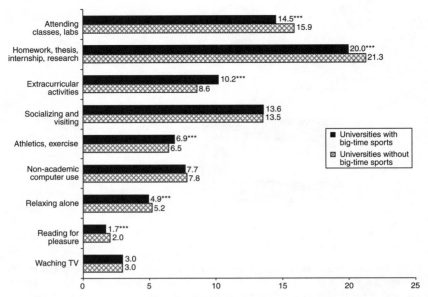

Figure 7A.4. Weekly time use of undergraduates, eight selective universities. The predicted time for each category is calculated from OLS equations, holding constant gender, race/ethnicity, U.S. citizenship, year in school, family income, parents' education, and SAT/ACT scores, and excluding intercollegiate football and basketball players and individuals who did not have a total weekly time from 50 to 140 hours. *** = Statistically significant difference between two types of universities at the 1% level, ** = 5%, * = 10%.

*Source*: Consortium on Financing Higher Education, Enrolled Student Survey, 2007.

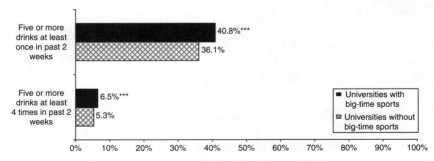

Figure 7A.5. Undergraduate binge drinking, eight selective universities. The predicted share of students for each category is calculated from probit equations, holding constant gender, race/ethnicity, U.S. citizenship, year in school, family income, parents' education, and SAT/ACT scores, and excluding intercollegiate football and basketball players. Binge drinking equations include an under 21 indicator. *** = Statistically significant difference between two types of universities at the 1% level, ** = 5%, * = 10%.

*Source*: Consortium on Financing Higher Education, Enrolled Student Survey, 2007.

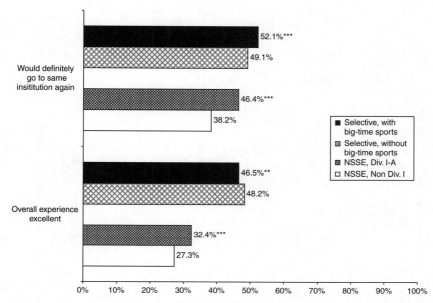

Figure 7A.6. Overall ratings of college experience by undergraduates in eight selective universities and freshmen in public universities with enrollments of more than 10,000. The first set of bars give the predicted percentages of students answering "Excellent" to the question, "How would you evaluate your entire educational experience at this institution?" where the other possible answers were "Good," "Fair," or "Poor." The second set of bars give the predicted percentages of students answering "Definitely Yes" to the question, "If you could start over again, would you go to the same institution you are now attending?" where the other possible answers were "Probably Yes," "Probably No," "Definitely No." *** = Statistically significant difference between two types of universities at the 1% level, ** = 5%, * = 10%.

*Source*: The data are taken from two surveys: Survey of Enrolled Students, 2007, Consortium on Financing Higher Education, covering undergraduate students at eight private, selective universities; and the National Survey of Student Engagement, covering first-year students at 53 public universities with enrollments of more than 10,000 in 2004 and 70 such universities in 2005.

Jersey Institute of Technology, New York University, Rensselear Polytechnic Institute, Stevens Institute of Technology, Tufts, University of California – San Diego, University of California – Santa Cruz, University of Chicago, University of Rochester, Washington University in St. Louis, Worcester Polytechnic Institute.

Table 7A.1. *Characteristics of incoming freshmen in 2004, 115 public and private universities, by level of athletic competition*

| Survey question | Private universities | | Public universities | | Public universities, with Red State control | |
|---|---|---|---|---|---|---|
| | FBS | Non–division I | FBS | Non–division I | FBS | Non–division I |
| 1 *Parental income* | $148,893*** | $116,606 | $104,961*** | $80,363 | $101,348*** | $78,540 |
| Father is a college graduate (%) | 77.3*** | 65.0 | 61.4*** | 42.9 | 61.4*** | 42.9 |
| Went to independent private high school (%) | 17.9*** | 12.5 | 4.8*** | 2.5 | 4.8*** | 2.5 |
| Hours per week spent working at job in high school | 4.91*** | 7.04 | 8.08*** | 9.21 | 8.08*** | 9.21 |
| 2 Lives at home with family (%) | 1.7*** | 11.2 | 6.4*** | 26.9 | 6.7*** | 27.3 |
| Plans to join a Greek organization (%) | 47.9*** | 25.5 | 39.1*** | 31.3 | 39.1*** | 31.3 |
| 3 Attended religious services frequently (%) | 42.9*** | 32.3 | 41.2*** | 37.5 | 39.9 | 39.5 |
| Performed volunteer work frequently (%) | 38.7*** | 31.2 | 27.0*** | 25.0 | 27.3*** | 24.6 |
| Smoked cigarettes ever (%) | 14.3*** | 18.8 | 17.2*** | 18.2 | 17.0*** | 18.7 |
| 4 Being financially well off (%) | 72.0*** | 68.7 | 75.4 | 75.0 | 75.4 | 75.1 |
| Writing original works (%) | 16.7*** | 19.9 | 12.8*** | 14.9 | 13.0*** | 14.5 |
| Success in own business (%) | 43.9*** | 38.3 | 41.9*** | 39.7 | 41.4** | 40.5 |
| Developing a meaningful philosophy of life (%) | 52.0 | 51.8 | 41.5** | 42.4 | 41.9 | 41.8 |
| 5 Conservative or far right (%) | 25.3*** | 17.3 | 25.0*** | 20.9 | 24.0*** | 22.4 |
| Prohibit homosexual relations (%) | 22.4*** | 16.4 | 29.1*** | 26.9 | 27.8*** | 28.9 |
| Increase federal military spending (%) | 31.8*** | 24.8 | 36.0*** | 32.2 | 34.6*** | 34.4 |
| Wealthy people should not pay more taxes (%) | 50.9*** | 42.0 | 47.4*** | 42.2 | 46.6*** | 43.6 |

*Note:* Figures show sample means (1–2), or predicted values calculated as sample means from probit equations with variables for institution's FBS status and students' gender, race, high school grades, family income, parents' education and religion, type of high school attended, and SAT score (3–5). Asterisks indicate FBS and non–Division I difference statistically significant at *10%, **5%, ***1% level.

*Source:* 2004 HERI Survey of Incoming Freshmen.

Table 7A.2. *Estimated media event and partisan fan effects on number of articles viewed on JSTOR*

| Explanatory variable | Dependent variable: logarithm of articles viewed | | | |
|---|---|---|---|---|
| | Model 1 | | Model 2 | |
| | Estimated coefficient | Standard error | Estimated coefficient | Standard error |
| **Days after unexpected win** | | | | |
| First day | −0.264* | (0.070) | −0.210* | (0.073) |
| Second day | −0.098 | (0.067) | −0.042 | (0.069) |
| Third day | −0.053 | (0.075) | −0.036 | (0.076) |
| **Days after unexpected loss** | | | | |
| First day | −0.035 | (0.070) | −0.041 | (0.071) |
| Second day | −0.031 | (0.059) | −0.036 | (0.060) |
| Third day | 0.002 | (0.052) | −0.003 | (0.052) |
| Team still in tournament | | | −0.066* | (0.019) |
| Monday–Wednesday bracket week | −0.065* | (0.013) | −0.067* | (0.013) |
| **Days of tournament** | | | | |
| Round of 64 | −0.058* | (0.016) | −0.051* | (0.016) |
| Round of 32 | 0.010 | (0.020) | 0.013 | (0.020) |
| Round of 16 | −0.027 | (0.014) | −0.026 | (0.014) |
| Round of 8 | 0.009 | (0.018) | 0.010 | (0.018) |
| Round of 4 | −0.033 | (0.045) | (0.045 | (0.045) |
| Championship game | −0.041 | (0.028) | (0.02 | (0.028) |
| Super Bowl Sunday | −0.260* | (0.021) | −0.260* | (0.021) |
| Easter Sunday | −0.133* | (0.031) | −0.133* | (0.031) |
| $R^2$ | 0.22 | | 0.22 | |

*Note*: Estimates based on pooled regressions explaining logarithm of daily articles viewed on JSTOR in 75 university libraries, February–April in 2006, 2007, and 2008 ($n = 20,100$). All variables shown are dichotomous. Also included as explanatory variables are days until the end of the term and dichotomous indicators for day of the week, breaks for spring or between quarters, and days after the end of the spring term. Asterisk indicates significance at 1%.

Table 8A.1. *Graduation rates, 58 universities with big-time athletic programs*

| U.S. news ranking | Number of Universities | Basketball | Football | All students |
|---|---|---|---|---|
| Top 35 | 14 | 50 | 68 | 88 |
| 36–61 | 14 | 42 | 52 | 75 |
| 62–96 | 11 | 37 | 55 | 68 |
| Over 100 | 19 | 40 | 52 | 60 |
| All | 58 | 42 | 56 | 72 |

*Sources*: *U.S. News and World Report*, Best Colleges 2010; NCAA reports on four-year-average graduation rates for athletes and all students covering the cohorts entering in 1998–2001. Rates are federal graduation rates.
http://ncaa.org/wps/ncaa?key=/ncaa/ncaa/academics+and+athletes/education+and+research/academic+reform/grad+rate/2008/2008_d1_school_grad_rate_data.html, 3/15/10.

# Notes

## Preface

1. Rates based on total NCAA football attendance for 1978 to 2008 and basketball for 1976 to 2008, *NCAA Attendance Records*. Resident population of the United States from *Statistical Abstract of the United States 2006*, tables 2 and 3, from 1976 to projected 2008 population.
2. Author's calculations, based on information in Christine Brennan, "Who's No. $1?" *Miami Herald*, May 23, 1982, and *USA Today*, http://www.usatoday.com/sports/college/football/2009-coaches-contracts-database.htm?loc=interstitialskip, 5/20/10.

## Chapter 1

1. Goldin and Katz (1999, p. 38).
2. Rankings of graduate programs at the University of Texas: http://74.125.47.132/search?q=cache:wbJOODktGXAJ:www.utexas.edu/welcome/rankings.html+national+research+council+rankings+texas&cd=9&hl=en&ct=clnk&gl=us, 9/11/09.
3. http://www.utexas.edu/welcome/mission.html, 1/28/08.
4. *Times* of London, http://www.timeshighereducatioin.co.uk/Rankings2009-Top 200.html, 10/8/09.
   Shanghai Jiao Tong University Center for World-Class Universities, 2008, http://www.arwu.org/rank2008/EN2008.htm, 9/11/09.
5. Eric Dexheimer, "The Longhorn Economy," *American-Statesman*, September 30, 2007.
6. http://www.texassports.com/sports/m-footbl/spec-rel/football-tv-radio.html, 9/12/09.
7. http://www.mackbrown-texasfootball.com/sports/m-footbl/spec-rel/fb-all-time-tv.html, 10/2/09.
8. Toma (2003); Angell (1928, p. 119): "Intercollegiate athletics are the feature of our universities best known to the American public."
9. Only a few people objected, for example, when the University of North Carolina sent its employees home early, without pay, on a weekday when an evening

football game threatened to cause a traffic jam. "Major Inconvenience," *Daily Tar Heel*, September 3, 2009.

10. Pritchett (1929, p. vi.)
11. Eliot (1894, p. 19). For a contemporary exposition of the same virtues, see Arne Duncan, Excerpts of remarks to the NCAA, "Building a Better Front Porch for Higher Education," January 14, 2010, https://www.ed.gov/news/speeches/building-better-front-porch-higher-education%E2%80%94excerpts-secretary-arne-duncans-remarks, 6/7/10.
12. Actually, revenue generated by the university's basketball program was only about half that amount. Joe Nocera, "Jim Calhoun Defends His Salary," *New York Times*, February 23, 2009.
13. See, e.g., Lynn Zinser, "A Revived Program and an Altered State at Rutgers," *New York Times*, August 26, 2007.
14. Gary A. Olson, "Should We Ditch Football?" *Chronicle of Higher Education*, May 5, 2010.
15. Eliot (1894, pp. 12–13).
16. Thelin (1994, p. 15).
17. Savage (1929, pp. 306–307); "College Sports Tainted by Bounties, Carnegie Fund Finds in Wide Study," *New York Times*, October 24, 1929; Thelin (1994, pp. 11, 25).
18. Knight Commission on Intercollegiate Athletics (1991, p. 5).
19. Knight Commission on Intercollegiate Athletics (1991, p. 6).
20. Knight Commission on Intercollegiate Athletics (2001, p. 21).
21. Michael Lewis, "Serfs of the Turf," *New York Times*, November 11, 2007; William H. Honan, "If Games Are a Business, Colleges Invite Problems," *New York Times*, August 16, 2000.
22. Sperber (1991, 2001); Yost (2010, p. 195).
23. The eight that have big-time sports are Stanford, UC Berkeley, UCLA, Washington, Wisconsin, Michigan, Illinois, and Minnesota.
24. Top 100 ranking for 1920 was an average of the 1919, 1920, and 1921 power rankings as given by the James Howell Web site, http://www.jhowell.net/cf/scores/byName.htm, 5/10/10. The nine that made the unusual decision to drop big-time sports did so deliberately. Seven pulled out to form their own conference (the Ivy League), in which they would agree to limit recruiting by forbidding athletic scholarships. The other two were Washington University and the University of Chicago.
25. James Howell Web site, http://www.jhowell.net/cf/scores/byName.htm, 5/10/10.
26. There are some notable exceptions to this tendency for athletics to be excluded from studies of universities, however. Other books that seek to integrate athletics into a broader analysis of universities include three written by former university presidents – Duderstadt (2000), Bok (2003), and Shapiro (2005) – as well as Thelin (1994), Toma (2003), Zemsky, Wegner, and Massy (2005), and Weisbrod, Ballou, and Asch (2008). The lack of attention to commercial athletics in scholarly research is discussed at greater length in the next chapter.
27. Letter sent to NCAA president Myles Brand from House Ways and Means Committee Chairman Bill Thomas on October 2, 2006; *USA Today*, posted 10/5/09.

28. In the 2008–2009 season, the average Broadway show grossed $21.9 million. (There were 43 shows, and they grossed a total of $943.3 million.) Andrew Gans, "Broadway Grossed Nearly $1 Billion in 2008–2009," Playbill.com, May 26, 2009, http://www.playbill.com/news/article/129587-Broadway_Grossed_ Nearly_$1_Billion_in_2008–2009, 9/12/09.
29. These conferences include Atlantic Coast (ACC), Southeastern (SEC), Big Ten, Big 12, Pacific Coast (Pac-10), and Big East.
30. See http://espn.go.com/college-football/rankings/_/year/2009, 5/11/10. Basketball is not as dominated by these 100. Basketball rankings are from espn/usatoday, http://sports.espn.go.com/ncb/rankings?seasonYear=2010, 5/11/10.
31. The top universities referred to here are the top 90 American universities as listed by Shanghai Jiao Tong University Center for World-Class Universities, 2008, and the top 101 national universities listed by *U.S. News* in its 2010 ranking. http://www.arwu.org/rank2008/EN2008.htm, 9/11/09; *U.S. News and World* Report 2010 ed., August 2009; http://colleges.usnews.rankingsandreviews.com/best-colleges/national-universities-rankings, 9/4/09. Because universities were ranked by group, it was not possible to identify just the top 100 in either ranking.

## Chapter 2

1. Malia Wollan and Tamar Lewin, "Students Protest Tuition Increases," *New York Times*, November 21, 2009.
2. Doug Lederman, "Bad Time for Sports Overspending," *Inside Higher Ed*, October 30, 2009.
3. Zach E. J. Williams, "Resolution Urges End to Campus Athletic Funding," *Daily Californian*, November 6, 2009, http://www.dailycal.org/article/107387, 1/16/10.
4. Lance Williams, "Amid Fiscal Crisis, UC Berkeley Commits $320 Million to Football," *California WatchBlog*, February 17, 2010; James Zhao, "New Council to Look into Athletics Funding," *Daily Californian*, April 5, 2010.
5. Stan Diel, "University of Alabama Cancels Three Days of Classes Surrounding Championship Game," *Birmingham News*, December 8, 2009.
6. http://www.ua.edu/mission.html, 1/25/08.
7. "Major Inconvenience," *Daily Tar Heel*, September 3, 2009; Office of Sponsored Research, http://74.125.47.132/search?q=cache:fyhToXCtOdMJ:research.unc. edu/osr/information/general_info.php+unc+chapel+hill+number+of+employ ees&cd=5&hl=en&ct=clnk&gl=us, 1/9/10.
8. For example, the president of the University of Oklahoma met with basketball recruit Harrison Barnes during the latter's official campus recruiting visit, according to Barnes's diary posted on Highschoolhoop.com, http://www. highschoolhoop.com/recruiting-news/2009/10/the-harrison-barnes-diary-official-visit-to-oklahoma/, 8/24/10.
9. Knight Commission on Intercollegiate Athletics (2009, p. 30).
10. Bok (2003, p. 125).
11. Duderstadt (2000, p. 11).
12. Shapiro (2005, p. 29).

13. Hutchins (1936, p. 11).
14. Wilson (1909, p. 576).
15. Kerr (1994).
16. The five established conferences in 2010 and their 57 members in 2010 were as follows: Southeastern Conference (SEC): Alabama, Arkansas, Auburn, Florida, Georgia, Kentucky, LSU, Mississippi, Mississippi State, South Carolina, Tennessee, Vanderbilt; Atlantic Coast Conference (ACC): Boston College, Clemson, Duke, Florida State, Georgia Tech, Maryland, Miami, North Carolina, NC State, Virginia, Virginia Tech, Wake Forest; Pacific 10 (Pac-10): Arizona, Arizona State, UC Berkeley, Oregon, Oregon State, Stanford, UCLA, USC, Washington, Washington State; Big Ten: Illinois, Indiana, Iowa, Michigan, Michigan State, Minnesota, Northwestern, Ohio State, Penn State, Purdue, Wisconsin; Big 12: Baylor, Colorado, Iowa State, Kansas, Kansas State, Missouri, Nebraska, Oklahoma, Oklahoma State, Texas, Texas A&M, Texas Tech.
17. UCLA had its own, but UC Berkeley did not, so the latter was not included. Other universities without mission statements were the University of Arkansas, Louisiana State, Florida State, Arizona State, and Stanford.
18. The five universities whose mission statements included references to athletics were the University of Nebraska ("Special units with distinct missions include ... Intercollegiate Athletics"); Ohio State University ("Our intercollegiate athletic programs will routinely rank among the elite few"); University of Southern California ("Our first priority as faculty and staff is the education of our students, from freshmen to postdoctorals, through a broad array of academic, professional, extracurricular and athletic programs of the first rank"); University of Virginia ("To seek the ablest and most promising students, within the Commonwealth and without; and, in keeping with the intentions of Thomas Jefferson, to attend to their total development and well-being; and to provide appropriate intellectual, athletic, and social programs"); and Wake Forest University ("The University recognizes the benefits of intercollegiate athletics conducted with integrity and at the highest level").
19. These results are described in more detail in Appendix Table 2A.1.
20. Altbach (2004, p. 364).
21. Michener (1976, p. 9).
22. Gould (2003); Kirp (2004); Kezar, Chambers, and Burkhardt (2005); Altbach, Berdahl, and Gumport (2005); and Clotfelter (2010).
23. Of the 70 articles published in the journal in 2007 and 2008, none had titles that mentioned athletics. Frey (1987, pp. 50–51) did a similar survey of journals on higher education and made a similar point: "Most treatises on academic administration or college governance make no mention of athletics.... It is as if athletics did not exist, was not a problem, or was so unimportant that it did not deserve mention."
24. Duderstadt (2000), Bok (2003), and Shapiro (2005).
25. Columbia Alumni Magazine, Summer 2001, http://74.125.47.132/search? q=cache:eQwt8cMWGNwJ:www.columbia.edu/cu/alumni/Magazine/ Summer2001/Rabi.html+eisenhower+president+of+columbia+fellow+employ ees&cd=5&hl=en&ct=clnk&gl=us, 1/31/10.

26. Feldstein (1993, pp. 38–39) argues that university administrators not only lack power, but lack the incentive to bring about any changes that would make too many waves or enemies.

27. Private correspondence with Paul Courant, provost from 2002 to 2005. He noted that, as a practical matter, the provost dealt largely with general fund budgets. Because the hospital and most auxiliaries other than athletics depended in part on general fund revenues, the provost could learn about the operations of those units.

28. Peter J. Boyer, "Big Men on Campus," *New Yorker*, September 4, 2006.

29. Interview with president of the University of Florida, J. Bernard Machen, *Chronicle of Higher Education*, August 31, 2009.

30. David Moltz, "Powerless, or Passing the Buck?" *Inside Higher Ed*, October 27, 2009. See also Katie Thomas, "Call to Curb Athletic Spending Strikes Some as Unrealistic," *Chronicle of Higher Education*, October 27, 2009.

31. See Clotfelter (1996); Frey (1994, p. 116), who stresses the university's "diffuse goals."

32. Coleman (1973, p. 369).

33. Savage (1929 p. 78).

34. Frey (1987, p. 53) writes: "Their influence is negligible and few care to take the time and energy to be concerned with a program that is of low priority and tainted ethical quality. About the best any institution can do is to identify the few faculty who seem to be 'local' in their orientation and 'fans' of athletic programs. These persons then serve on the athletic councils; they do not get in the way, and they are there when you need them for an *ex post facto* affirmation of a decision already made."

35. Scott Jaschik, "The Trustee–Faculty Relationship," *Inside Higher Ed*, January 25, 2010.

36. The appointment in question was the naming of a new head football coach in 2005 by the athletic director and former head football coach in 2005. The negotiations concerning the Big Ten Network occurred in 2007. In an open letter to the university chancellor, history professor Jeremi Suri explained his decision to resign by saying, "I am now convinced that the Athletic Board is only promoting the agenda of a small group of stakeholders." Todd Finkelmeyer, "Board Members Say Suri's Wrong about Sports Oversight; Suri Calls UW Athletic Board a Rubber Stamp," *Capital Times*, October 3, 2008; Todd Finkelmeyer, "Athletic Board: Rubber Stamp or Independent Voice? *Capital Times*, October 24, 2009; Steven Underwood, and Donald Down, "UW's Athletic Board is Not a Rubber Stamp," *Capital Times*, November 2, 2008.

37. In fact, few faculty members seem bothered by this lack of clout. According to Weick (1984, p. 278), most faculty are "loners," who resist authority from above and welcome the university's relative inattention to coordination and control."

38. David Moltz, "Seething over Sports Subsidies," *Inside Higher Ed*, May 20, 2010, and "A Sense of the Senate Resolution on the Sustainability of Intercollegiate Athletics," resolution approved by the Ohio University Faculty Senate, May 17, 2010.

39. The coach was Jim Valvano of N.C. State. Malcolm Moran, "Backtalk; Smart Enough to Know Better, Funny Enough Not to Care," *New York Times*, May 2, 1993.

40. Coleman (1973, p. 360).
41. Chu (1989, p. 17).
42. Sinclair (1922, pp. 370–372).
43. Frey (1985, p. 119).
44. A survey described by Boone et al. (1998) showed that more than a third of CEOs surveyed had played an intercollegiate sport, compared with just 2–3% of all undergraduates.
45. Frey (1994, pp. 110, 119).
46. When the SMU coach put out a full page ad thanking 110 people for support, there was no official contribution listed for more than half of them. Trustee and former Texas governor William Clements in 1985 made it clear that he wanted payments to players continued (Byers 1995, pp. 22, 27).
47. Paul Fain, "Booster Offered U. of Washington $200,000 to Fire Coach and Athletics Director," *Chronicle of Higher Education*, January 10, 2008.
48. Doug Lederman, "A Trustee Calls the Plays," *Inside Higher Ed*, October 7, 2009. The chairman of the board of trustees said, "I do appreciate what he's done for us.... But I think the record will show that the Seminole Nation has been more than patient. We have been in a decline not for a year or two or three but I think we're coming up on seven or eight. I think enough is enough." Richard T. Legon, president of the Association of Governing Boards of Colleges and Universities, stated, "If intercollegiate athletics is going to be seen as part of the mainstream element of an institution, then boards, and individual trustees, need to recognize that they have no more role in calling the shots in intercollegiate athletics than they might if they have a problem with a dean."
49. Kathryn Masterson, "Texas Tech Reaches Out to Alumni Who Are Upset About Coach's Firing," *Chronicle of Higher Education*, January 8, 2010. Another display of fan and stakeholder wrath occurred at Indiana University, following President Miles Brand's firing of basketball coach Bobby Knight. Angry fans marched on Brand's house while police in riot gear stood by. A student whose complaint against Knight was the final precipitating factor leading to his firing was the target of students: Demonstrators handed out flyers with the student's picture and the caption "Wanted Dead." James C. McKinley, Jr., "College Basketball; At Indiana, Players Dig in Over Firing of Knight," *New York Times*, September 12, 2000.
50. "Fowler's Exit from N.C. State Linked to E-mails," *Raleigh News and Observer*, June 6, 2010.
51. For a complete list of the institutions used and a description of the method, see the Appendix.
52. For comparisons of the political leanings of faculty members in various departments, see, e.g., Bill Harbaugh, "Political Diversity at UO," Unpublished manuscript, Department of Economics, University of Oregon, http://darkwing. uoregon.edu/~klesh/DS.pdf, 11/24/08, and Klein and Stern, who used surveys of faculty members in six disciplines and found that those who voted Republican as a percentage of those voting Republican or Democratic ranged from 3% for anthropology and sociology to 25% for economics, "How Politically Diverse Are the Social Sciences and Humanities? Survey Evidence from Six Fields,"

Unpublished manuscript, Santa Clara University, http://lsb.scu.edu/~dklein/survey/survey.htm, 11/24/08.

53. The sample of institutions included 15 universities in the FBS and an equal number, matched by state, size, and sector, in some other subdivision of Division I. Of the 2,220 individuals identified, 1,809 could be located on state registration rolls, 1,415 indicated some political affiliation, and 1,300 registered as either Republican or Democrat.

54. As shown in Appendix Table 2A.1, the only difference between FBS and other Division I institutions that was statistically significant was that for boosters.

55. Scott (1971, pp. 187–188).

56. Duderstadt (2000, pp. 87–88).

57. Adler and Adler (1988).

58. This is a 1957 remark, quoted by *Time* and *Playboy*. *UC Berkeley News*, on the death of Clark Kerr, http://74.125.47.132/search?q=cache:ZJ3-orn0iFwJ:berkeley.edu/news/media/releases/2003/12/02_kerr.shtml+clark+kerr+the+uses+of+the+university+athletics&cd=2&hl=en&ct=clnk&gl=us, 1/9/10.

## Chapter 3

1. Street and Smith's Sports Business Daily, "Final Nielsen Ratings for Recent Sports Events," *Sports Media*, February 8, 2008. http://www.sportsbusinessdaily.com/, 2/19/08. *American Idol* was the top-rated show for the week of February 4–10, 2008, garnering 27.9 million viewers ("Prime-Time Nielsen Ratings," *News and Observer*, February 12, 2008, http://www.newsobserver.com/1569/v-print/story/940371.html, 2/19/08. (Note: February 11, 2009 was the Duke–UNC game.) The 1.2 million came from Raycom Sports, personal correspondence. The 2.6 million is also enough to fill Madison Square Garden more than 1,300 times. (Its capacity for basketball is 19,763.)

2. Two types of football were played in its earliest days, one resembling soccer (the so-called kicking game) and one more akin to rugby (the "running game"). The first collegiate game in America featuring the first type was played between Rutgers and Princeton in 1869. The latter was the one that evolved into American football (Riesman and Denney 1951; Smith (1988, pp. 219–220).

3. Smith (1988, third unnumbered page following p. 146).

4. Smith (1988, pp. 148, 169).

5. Smith (1988, p. 127).

6. Eliot (1894, pp. 13–14).

7. Smith (1988, pp. 122, 123). Foster (1915) says that students were still in charge in some universities in 1915.

8. Eliot (1894, p. 20); Smith (1988, pp. 88–91).

9. Smith (1988 p. 93); James Howell football statistics, www.net/cf/scores/Army.htm, 5/23/10.

10. Riesman and Denney (1951, p. 319n) noted that a photo of the bloody face of Swarthmore (player) Bob Maxwell appeared in a newspaper read by President Roosevelt.

11. Smith (1988, pp. 193–205).

12. Kerr (1994, p. 16).

13. See Griffith (1926). Date of stadium construction taken from statistics on attendance in 1949 and 1967 (NCAA Football Guides, 1950, 1968). The exceptions were Penn State and Wisconsin. Michigan stadium capacity at its opening was taken from http://74.125.47.132/search?q=cache:UH1Nn8zFKScJ:www.umich.edu/stadium/history/+university+of+michigan+football+stadium+built&cd=1&hl=en&ct=clnk&gl=us, 4/21/09.
14. http://www.jhowell.net/cf/scores/Illinois.htm, 4/21/09.
15. Edwards et al. (1928, p. 129).
16. For the study, researchers visited campuses and conducted more than 1,000 interviews. Founded with Rockefeller support and heavily influenced by the University of Chicago social services movement, the Institute sponsored numerous community studies in the 1920s, including the classic study of Muncie, Indiana, *Middletown*. See Rita Caccamo De Luca, *Back to Middletown* (Stanford: Stanford University Press, 2002), pp. 38–39.
17. Savage et al. (1929); "College Sports Tainted by Bounties, Carnegie Fund Finds in Wide Study," *New York Times*, October 24, 1929; Thelin (1994, p. 13).
18. Savage et al. (1929, p. viii).
19. Savage et al. (1929, p. 173). The report noted (p. 173) that coaches' salaries were larger at larger institutions: "The larger the sums that are available for athletics, the more will be spent upon athletics. Thus extravagance has grown by what it fed on."
20. Appendix Table 3A.1 lists the 100 institutions with the most successful football programs around 1920 (based on the three-year average of power rankings from 1919 to 1921), together with the universities that were in the top 100 by athletic spending in 2009. Of the top 100 institutions ranked by expenditures in 2009, 60 were also among the 100 programs with the highest power ratings. James Howell, http://www.jhowell.net/cf/cf2009.htm, 2/13/10.
21. In the years between 1929 and 2009, Michigan played Ohio State every year, Michigan State 79 times, Minnesota 78, Illinois 77, and Wisconsin 48. http://football.stassen.com/cgi-bin/records/all-opp.pl?start=1927&end=2007&team=Michigan&sort=g, 4/21/09; www.jhowell.net/cf/scores/Michigan.htm, 5/23/10. Football schedules are available on www.jhowell.net/cf/scores/team.htm.
22. Two large universities dropped big-time football but kept their Division I basketball program: Georgetown after 1950 and the University of Denver after 1960. Georgetown's athletic expenditures in 2009 were large enough to put it in the top 100 programs in 2009 and so is counted among the 60 institutions that remained in the top 100. The University of Denver is included among the 28 colleges and regional universities that dropped out of the top 100, although it may be unjust to include Denver among regional universities.
23. Thelin (1994, pp. 44–43).
24. James Howell, http://www.jhowell.net/cf/scores/Chicago.htm, 2/13/10.
25. In a memorandum to the university trustees in December 1939, Hutchins delivered this eulogy for big-time football at Chicago: "Since we cannot hope to win against our present competition and since we cannot profitably change our competition, only two courses are open to us: to subsidize players or to discontinue intercollegiate football. We cannot subsidize players or encourage

our alumni to do so without departing from our principles and losing our self-respect. We must therefore discontinue the game" (Lester 1995, p. 185).

26. For an accounting covering the top 100 big-time programs in 2009, see Table 1.1.

27. U.S. Bureau of the Census, *Historical Statistics of the United States, Colonial Times to 1970* (Washington, DC: Government Printing Office, 1975), p. 796.

28. Four black players integrated the NFL in 1946, a year before Jackie Robinson did the same for major league baseball. http://nflretirees.blogspot.com/2006/08/senate-commemorates-60th-anniversary.html, 9/21/09.

29. In his appeal to the board of regents, Griffin wrote, "The battle is joined. We cannot make the slightest concession to the enemy in this dark and lamentable hour of struggle." Pete Thamel, "Grier Integrated a Game and Earned the World's Respect," *New York Times*, January 1, 2006.

30. Interview on Ole Miss campus, September 19, 1962, PBS series, *Eyes on the Prize*.

31. See Appendix Table A2.1. For example, the University of Michigan enrolled 12,695 around 1924. See Edwards, Artman, and Fisher (1928, p. 368).

32. In current dollars, the first two amounts were $500 and $500,000, respectively. William Johnson, "TV Makes It All a New Game," *Sports Illustrated*, December 29, 1969, p. 90, http://sports.espn.go.com/espn/wire?section=ncf&id=3710611 http://sports.espn.go.com/espn/wire?section=ncf&id=3710611, 6/20/10.

33. Zimbalist (1999, p. 184). *National Collegiate Athletic Association v. Board of Regents of the University of Oklahoma*, 468 U.S. 85 (1984).

34. Berryman and Hardy (1983, p. 69).

35. "Excerpts from Judge Streit's Comments on College Basketball Fixing Scandal," *New York Times*, November 20, 1951.

36. Rupp had been named Coach of the Year by the Metropolitan Basketball Writers Association in 1950. Alfred E. Clark, "Judge in Fix Case Condemns Kentucky Teams and Coach," *New York Times*, April 30, 1952.

37. See Appendix Figure 3A.1.

38. To illustrate, the number of college basketball games televised in the Chicago TV market on the first Saturday in February increased from 4 in 1983 to 10 in 1990 to 37 in 2009. See Appendix Table 3A.2, based on TV listings in the *Chicago Tribune*. Total attendance at Division I basketball games increased from 15.3 million in 1976 to 27.1 million in 2009, not counting the NCAA tournament. NCAA http://www.ncaa.org/wps/ncaa?ContentID=1093, 10/18/09.

39. Not all Division I institutions follow this principle, but it is basic for all big-time athletics programs. See Thelin (1994, pp. 101–103) and Oriard (2009, p. 129).

40. See, e.g., Chu (1989).

41. U.S. Bureau of the Census, *Historical Statistics of the United States*, p. 383; U.S. Department of Education, *Digest of Education Statistics 2002*, Table 186.

42. Edwards et al. (1928, App.) and *Digest of Education Statistics 2002* (2003, Table 215).

43. These institutions included all eight of the Ivy League (Princeton, Harvard, Yale, Penn, Columbia, Dartmouth, Cornell, and Brown) plus Cal Tech, MIT, Chicago, Washington University, Johns Hopkins, Emory, Carnegie Mellon, and Georgetown. Of these, Georgetown has a Division I, and therefore big-time, basketball program.

44. In 2007 the *Times* ran 33 stories about the infamous Duke lacrosse case, 32 other stories about Duke sports, and 3 non-sports stories about Duke. Since this case was both a sports story and a story about much more than sports, I included these stories in both categories. If these stories had been eliminated from the calculations altogether, the percentage of non-sports stories for the 58 big-time sports universities would have been 8% rather than 13%.

45. One possible drawback of using *Times* coverage as a measure is that that newspaper covers local universities such as Columbia more intensively than it does universities in other regions. However, it is not clear how this affects the sports/non-sports breakdown.

46. Source: Athletic department Web pages for 56 teams in the SEC, ACC, Big Ten, Big 12, and Pac-10, plus Notre Dame. No information could be obtained for Mississippi State.

47. All of these were shown on ESPN. For comparison, a weeknight game between Duke and North Carolina earlier in the same month (February 2, 2008) drew an estimated audience of 2.6 million viewers on ESPN, not counting viewers who saw the same game on a regional network. Street and Smith's Sports Business Daily, "Final Nielsen Ratings for Recent Sports Events," *Sports Media*, February 8, 2008, http://www.sportsbusinessdaily.com/, 2/19/08.

48. See note 1, this chapter.

49. Chuck Stogel, "Era of Explosion Continues for TV Sports," *Sporting News*, April 23, 1990, p. 48 Regular-season football games garner respectable TV audiences. For example, a Saturday night game between California and USC in October 2009 had an estimated viewing audience of 6.5 million. http://tvbythenumbers.com/2009/10/04/tv-ratings-abc-saturday-college-football-trojans-win-again/29448, 2/18/10.

50. Hoover (1926, p. 57).

51. Byers and Hammer (1995, p. 137).

52. For each search, the name of the university and the name of the coach or president were entered into the search box, with variants on the names of universities and individuals allowed for. Each search item consisted of the first and last name in quotation marks plus the name of university, entered in two ways (e.g., "Northwestern" and "Northwestern University"), in quotation marks, with the larger number counted. The individual used was the chief campus official, whose title could be chancellor.

53. Without Georgetown and its nearly 10:1 coach-to-president ratio of hits in basketball, however, presidents among the non-football universities would have easily exceeded basketball coaches in this measure.

54. The term "March Madness" is trademarked by a company owned in part by the NCAA. See Alana Semuels, "March Madness Attracts the Eagle Eyes of Trademark Lawyers," *Los Angeles Times*, March 18, 2009. See also *March Madness Athletic Association v. Netfire, Inc.*, 120 Fed. Appx. 540, 2005 WL 147264 (C.A.5 (Tex.)).

55. "2008 NCAA March Madness on Demand Traffic Figures," News release of CBS Sports, June 9, 2008.

56. http://www.jstor.org/page/info/about/organization/index.jsp, 6/19/09.

57. A list of the libraries that gave permission to use data and also agreed to be acknowledged in print is given in the Appendix (section on Chapter 3).
58. Figures on daily usage for each of the 78 libraries in all three years were standardized according to the library's average volume for the months of February, March, and April of the same year. Thus each day's volume is expressed as the ratio of the articles viewed to the average daily volume for the three-month period.
59. A third advantage is that using these three weekdays avoids the question of whether to include in weekly averages the weekends immediately before and after spring breaks.
60. See Appendix Table 7A.2 for estimates based on regressions covering all days in the 75 university libraries, taking into account other factors associated with research activity, such as day of the week, school breaks, and days until the end of the term. The estimated equations imply a 6.4% reduction in articles viewed after Selection Sunday and a 5.6% drop during the first two days of the tournament.
61. A back-of-the-envelope calculation using enrollment and staffing numbers for the University of North Carolina, together with estimated viewing audiences for its football and basketball games over the course of a year, yielded an estimate for hours spent attending and viewing games that was more than double the total estimated hours spent by students, faculty, and staff doing academic work and extracurricular activities.
62. Attendance excluding the NCAA tournament. NCAA attendance statistics, http://www.ncaa.org/wps/ncaa?ContentID=1093, 10/18/09.

## Chapter 4

1. Michener (1976, p. 219).
2. St. John (2004).
3. For descriptions of fan behavior during college games, see Greer (1983) and Wann, Carlson, and Schrader (1999).
4. Thirer and Rampey (1979, p. 1049). Still, as one pundit has observed, this accepted form of collective dislike is surely preferable to the horrible examples of ethnic discrimination and violence that have marred our recent history. David Brooks, "The Sporting Mind," *New York Times*, February 5, 2010.
5. For a musical analysis of the "air ball" chant, see Heaton (1992).
6. According to Beyer and Hannah (2000, p. 108), the ingredients of athletic rituals are repetition, regularity, emotionality, drama, and symbolism. See also Sweet (2001, p. 102).
7. Wann and Branscombe (1993, p. 3).
8. Gantz and Wenner (1995, table 3, p. 68).
9. Cialdini et al. (1976).
10. Wann and Branscombe (1990); Hirt et al. (1992).
11. For a discussion of the term as applied to higher education, see Hartley and Morphew (2008).
12. The Michigan helmet design was adopted in 1938. Bentley Historical Library, University of Michigan, http://bentley.umich.edu/athdept/football/helmet/mhelmet.htm, 3/25/10.

13. See, e.g., St. John (2004); Blythe (2006).
14. Howell Raines, "Editorial Notebook: The Iron Bowl Cometh; The Impossible Task of Ceasing to Care," *New York Times*, November 19, 1994, writes of "childhood imprints," quoted below. See also Blyth (2006) and Travis (2007) for other examples.
15. Bronnenberg, Dube and Gentzkow (2010) examine buying patterns by migrants, summarizing their findings (p. 1) as follows: "Preferences develop endogenously as a function of consumers' life histories and are highly persistent once formed, with experiences 50 years in the past still exerting a significant effect on current consumption."
16. Robert Weintraub, "I Spit on Your Mascot," *New York Times*, November 2, 2008.
17. Shropshire (2007, p. viii).
18. Blythe (2006, p. 5).
19. Paul Gattis, "Secondary Violations at Auburn? Who Cares?" *Huntsville Times*, posted on blog.al.com, June 2, 2009, http://blog.al.com/chatter/2009/06/secondary_violations_at_auburn.html, 6/20/09.
20. St. John (2004, p. 7).
21. Raines, "Editorial Notebook," November 19, 1994.
22. *Birmingham News*, July 25, 2010.
23. Michener (1976, p. 12).
24. Giamatti (1989, p. 23).
25. Michener (1976, p. 188).
26. By way of comparison, the percentage who reported being fans of professional football was considerably higher, at 47%, whereas the percentage for professional basketball was only 24%. Another 5% for these sports (6% for college football) volunteered that they were "somewhat" of a fan, but these responses are not counted in the percentages cited and shown here. Associated Press/Ipsos Public Affairs Poll, October 16–18, 2007, Roper Center.
27. See Appendix Table A4.1.
28. Harris Interactive, November 12, 2004.
29. CNN / Opinion Research Corporation Poll, December 16–20, 2009, Roper Center, USORCNN2009–019.
30. U.S. Statistical Abstract; Official 2008 NCAA (R) Division I Football Records Book, http://www.jhowell.net/cf/cfindex.htm, ESPN.com.
31. See Associated Press, "Senate Marks 60th Anniversary of NFL's Integration," July 18, 2006, http://sports.espn.go.com/nfl/news/story?id=2523315, 7/30/09.
32. "The Nielsen Company's Guide to the 2009 NCAA Basketball Tournament," March 16, 2009; http://en-us.nielsen.com/main/news/news_releases/2009/march/the_nielsen_companys, 7/30/09.
33. According to the 2007 AP/Ipsos poll, 25% of adults said they were fans of either college football or pro football, but not both, compared with 29% who said they were fans of both. For basketball, 19% said they were fans of either college basketball or pro basketball, but not both, while 15% said they were fans of both.
34. A study of the demand for attendance at college football games by Price and Sen (2003) supports the notion that professional football is a substitute good. They found that attendance in the 1997 season was lower when a professional football team was nearby.

35. Jason Whitlock, "NCAA Caves to TV Pressure by Going Easy on Duke," *Kansas City Star*, March 14, 2010, for example, argues that the departure of star players after one year has pushed the NCAA to highlight "legendary coaches and tradition-rich programs" like Duke in their men's basketball tournament.
36. This term was reportedly coined by Walter Byers, who was for many years executive director of the NCAA (Oriard, 2009, p. 130).
37. Harris Poll, December 9–15, 2008, http://www.harrisinteractive.com/harris_poll/pubs/Harris_Poll_2009_01_27.pdf, 2/20/10.
38. Estimates given by Kahn (2006, tables 1 and 2) in 2009 dollars were as follows: NFL, $3.3 billion; NBA, $2.1 billion, NCAA Division I football and basketball, $1.7 billion, and major league baseball, $1.5 billion.
39. These are Washington University in St. Louis, the University of Chicago, and seven members of the Ivy League. See Chapter 3.
40. For a description of the realignment issues of 2010, see David Moltz, "The Great Conference Confusion," *Inside Higher Ed*, June 9, 2010.
41. Among the economic studies of the NCAA as a cartel are Fleisher, Goff, and Tolleson (1992), Koch (1983), Siegfried and Burba (2004), and Kahn (2006, 2007). For a contrary view that seems based largely on semantic distinctions, see McKenzie and Sullivan (1987). For recent discussions of the market structure of college athletics, see Noll (2009) and Zimbalist (2009).
42. The NCAA's rules pertaining to "electronic media time-outs" specify in great detail how the timing and length of time-outs in basketball games depend on the "electronic-media agreement." http://www.ncaapublications.com/Uploads/PDF/Basketball_Rules_2008–09fb2fc956–7592–4877–993e-dae20a6f90ed.pdf, 6/16/09.
43. William Johnson, "TV Makes It All a New Game," *Sports Illustrated*, December 29, 1969, p. 89.
44. Fleisher et al. (1992, p. 8) state the charge succinctly: "Schools have successfully colluded to restrict growth in student-athlete compensation to levels below the value of the athletes to the schools." Noll (2009, pp. 49–59) offers evidence that the NCAA is a monopsonist: there is a single national market for recruited high school athletes, and virtually all such recruits who receive offers of admission from FBS institutions in football or Division I in basketball choose an offer from one of those institutions rather than any institution outside those most competitive subdivisions.
45. *N.C.A.A. v. Board of Regents of University of Oklahoma*, 468 U.S. 85, 1045 S. Ct. 2948 (1984); Siegfried and Burba (2004, p. 801).
46. Siegfried and Burba (2004, p. 802).
47. For a description of the specifics of the 2010 agreement, see Michael Smith, "The BCS' Big Split," *Sports Business Journal*, January 25, 2010, p. 1.
48. See Noll (2009, pp. 19–21) and Zimbalist (2009) for descriptions of these agreements and Dunnavant (2004, pp. 262) for an argument that these arrangements favor the most successful athletic programs.
49. Media Dynamics, Inc., *TV Dimensions 2007* (2007); covers Winter 2006. Daytime serials not included in drama series.
50. TVB Research Central Ratings Track, "Top 100 Programs for the A35+ Demo," http://www.tvb.org/rcentral/viewertrack/trends/A35-Ranker.asp, 2/20/10.

51. Indices showing the degree, by sport, of overrepresentation of viewers of various educational categories are presented in Schlosberg (1987, pp. 46–47).
52. Its rating was 8.2, which was the estimated percentage of the universe of TV households tuned to it in the average minute. Rick Porter, "TV Ratings: Decent 'Bachelor' Premier, but FOX, Fiesta Bowl Win Monday," ZAP2it, January 5, 2010, http://blog.zap2it.com/frominsidethebox/2010/01/tv-ratings-decent-bachelor-premiere-but-fox-fiesta-bowl-win-monday.html, 2/16/10.
53. Julie Bosman, "March Madness Afflicts Advertisers," *New York Times*, March 16, 2006.
54. "The Nielsen Company's Guide to the 2009 NCAA Basketball Tournament," March 16, 2009, http://en-us.nielsen.com/main/news/news_releases/2009/march/the_nielsen_companys, 7/30/09.
55. Jason Zengerle, "March Payday Madness," *Business Week*, March 25, 2010.
56. "Nielsen Primetime Ratings Report," *Variety*, March 30, April 6, 13, and 20, 2009, http://find.galegroup.com, 7/31/09.
57. Julie Bosman, "March Madness Afflicts Advertisers," *New York Times*, March 16, 2006.
58. "The Nielsen Company's Guide to the 2009 NCAA Basketball Tournament," March 16, 2009, http://en-us.nielsen.com/main/news/news_releases/2009/march/the_nielsen_companys, 7/30/09.
59. The names of these examples of pseudo-programming from the 2009 tournament telecast were "The Vitamin Water Revive to Survive Moment" and "The Pontiac Game-Changing Performance."
60. These commercials are summarized in Appendix Table 4A.2.
61. A further irony was the prominence of two other GM brands, Pontiac and Saturn, which were in the process of disappearing and being sold, respectively.
62. U.S. Bureau of Labor Statistics, *Survey of Consumer Expenditures, 2007*, table 2.
63. Katie Ressmeyer, "Big Ten Network Institutes a Dry Policy on Advertisements," *University Wire*, May 17, 2007.
64. No ads for beverages containing more than 6% alcohol were allowed. Ira Teinowitz, "NCAA Keeps Beer Ads," *Advertising Age*, August 11, 2008.
65. A survey in Auburn, Alabama (population 56,000), revealed that 7% of the houses in town displayed some sign or sticker supporting Auburn (not including stickers on automobiles) (Laband et al. 2008).
66. Estimates by Scarborough Research provided by ISP Marketing. Scarborough Research is a local marketing research firm affiliated with Nielsen and Arbitron. http://www.scarborough.com/about.php, 8/5/10. Estimates were based on "designated market areas, whose total populations were estimated in 2009 to be as follows: Atlanta, 4.9 million; Birmingham, 1.4 million; Mobile–Pensacola, 1.1 million; Phoenix, 3.8 million; Pittsburgh, 2.2 million; and Syracuse, 0.7 million.
67. Johnson and Whitehead (2000, pp. 50–51).
68. Personal correspondence from Bruce Johnson, March 2, 2010. The other possible responses, along with the percent who gave each answer, were as follows: (2) I'm a casual fan. I like the Wildcats, but I don't lose sleep over them. (55%); (3) I don't pay any attention to UK basketball (3%); (4) I am tired of hearing about UK basketball (8%).

69. See, e.g., Johnson, Mondello, and Whitehead (2007, p. 131), who estimated that residents of Duvall County, Florida, were willing to pay, on average, a little more than $8 a year each to keep their professional football team, the Jaguars.

70. James Michener writes of someone he met at a dinner at the University of Nebraska, who explained the popularity of Nebraska football this way: "The State of Nebraska has no opera, no drama, no symphony, no exalted social life and not much intellectual life. In this state if you don't go for football, you're a pariah.' As I pondered this, he added, 'And it's the same throughout the Big Eight. Our football is good because we haven't anything else. And if you look at it honestly, that holds true for Ohio State and Arkansas and Penn State and Texas and Auburn and all the powers. They support football because their towns don't offer anything else'" (Michener 1976, p. 221).

71. Bob Baptist, "Money at the Center of TV Tussle – Fans in Middle as Big Ten Network, Cable Providers Haggle," *Columbus Dispatch*, August 30, 2007; Mya Frazier and Andrew Hampp, "Big Mess in the Big Ten: Why Die-Hard Fans Can't Tune In," *Advertising Age*, September 17, 2007; Paul J. Gough, "Big Ten, Comcast Going Long," *Hollywoodreporter.com*, June 19, 2008.

## Chapter 5

1. Joe Lapointe, "College Football: For the People or the Powerful? Skybox Plan Divides Michigan," *New York Times*, April 9, 2006.

2. Duderstadt (2000, p. 91).

3. NCAA, *2004–08 NCAA Revenues and Expenses of Division I Intercollegiate Athletics Programs Report* (Indianapolis, August 2009), p. 8.

4. U.S. Department of Education, Office of Postsecondary Education, the Equity in Athletics Data Analysis Cutting Tool, http://ope.ed.gov/athletics/, 12/29/09.

5. Joe Lapointe, "Big Problems in the Big House," *New York Times*, November 20, 2009.

6. See Chapter 6.

7. For a definition of auxiliaries, see NACUBO, "Accounting and Reporting for Auxiliary, Auxiliary-Other, and Other Self-Supporting Activities," July 8, 1999. According to this report, intercollegiate athletics is considered an auxiliary "only if essentially self-supporting." http://www.nacubo.org/Business_and_Policy_ Areas/Accounting/Advisory_Reports/Advisory_Report_1999-2_Accounting_ and_Reporting_for_Auxiliary_Auxiliary-Other_and_Other_Self-supporting_ Activities.html, 1/11/10.

8. The appropriation from the state of Michigan in 2007–2008 was $320.2 million. The budgeted expenditures out of the university's general fund for the medical school, university library, and law school were, respectively, $80.4, $43.2, and $37.9 million. All of these units had revenue sources in addition to the general fund, and most of the athletic budget came from sources other than the general fund. University of Michigan Office of Budget and Planning, *FY 2007–2008 Ann Arbor Campus Summary of Budgeted Revenues and Expenditures, 2007/08*, http://sitemaker.umich.edu/obpinfo/um_budget_detail, 11/27/09.

9. The first to obtain such financial data was the *Indianapolis Star*, which procured copies of the detailed reports for the 2004–2005 year that all Division I programs submit to the NCAA. With the exception of private universities and two states without laws obligating public universities to disclose such information (Oklahoma and Pennsylvania), the *Star* obtained reports for all of the public universities. See Mark Alesia, "Colleges Play, Public Pays," *Indianapolis Star*, March 30, 2006. More recently, *USA Today* and ESPN.com have done the same.

10. The NCAA publishes aggregated budget data covering public and private FBS programs. Although they are presumably based on the same reports made by athletic departments to the NCAA, summary measures based on tables in the NCAA report are not consistent with the detailed information that *USA Today* published for the 2007–2008 fiscal year, which it obtained through state open-records laws for public FBS universities in every state except Pennsylvania. The percent distribution of revenues published in the NCAA report for fiscal year 2008 (NCAA, *2004–2008 Revenues and Expenses of Division I Intercollegiate Athletics Programs Report*, Football Bowl Subdivision, pp. 41–43) for public FBS universities was as follows: ticket sales, 20%; contributions, 18%; NCAA and conference distributions, 13%; subsidies ("allocated revenues"), 30%; and other, 18%. The report's corresponding percentages for all FBS institutions were 20%, 18%, 14%, 16%, and 30%, respectively. My attempts to reconcile these differences were unsuccessful.

11. Hanford (1974, p. 104) estimates that two-thirds of athletic department revenues came in the form of gate receipts.

12. Roy S. Johnson, "Ready for Kickoff," *Stanford Magazine*, September–October 2006, http://www.stanfordalumni.org/news/magazine/2006/sepoct/features/stadium.html, 6/28/10.

13. NCAA: basketball: http://www.ncaa.org/wps/ncaa?ContentID=1093, 10/18/09; football: http://www.ncaa.org/wps/ncaa?key=/ncaa/ncaa/sports+and+championship/general+information/stats/football/attendance/index.html, 10/18/09.

14. Median revenues in 2008 were $14.2 million for football and $4.7 million for men's basketball (NCAA, 2009, p. 27).

15. Erin Strout, "Oklahoma State U. Receives a Record $165-Million Donation for Athletics," *Chronicle of Higher Education*, January 11, 2006.

16. Following seasons with win–loss records of 6–7 and 7–6, Alabama reported in 2008 having a waiting list of 10,000 to buy season tickets after the arrival of the new coach. "Saban Shows His Value at Alabama," *New York Times*, October 2, 2008.

17. In 2009–2010 the cost of season tickets ranged from $555 to $1,195 per seat. The $7,000 minimum contribution was up from $5,000 earlier in the decade (DiStanislao 2005, pp. 51, 134; and the Web site for Duke's Iron Dukes organization, http://www.irondukes.net/ViewArticle.dbml?DB_OEM_ID=5100&ATCLID=178240 2/4/10).

18. Web site for the Ohio State Buckeye Club, platinum level, http://webcache.googleusercontent.com/search?q=cache:KswlrZCjMagJ:www.ohiostatebuck-eyes.com/ViewArticle.dbml%3FDB_OEM_ID%3D17300%26ATCLID%3D925254+ohio+state+buckeye+club+tickets+35+yard+line&cd=1&hl=en&ct=clnk&gl=us, 6/26/10.

19. Web site for Buckeye Club, http://www.ohiostatebuckeyes.com/ViewArticle.db
    ml?&SPSID=103576&SPID=10400&DB_OEM_ID=17300&ATCLID=925254,
    6/15/09; Gwynne (2008).

20. Selling these licenses went against previous Stanford policy not to use contribu-
    tions as a price premium for good seats. Roy S. Johnson, "Ready for Kickoff,"
    *Stanford Magazine*, September–October 2006, http://www.stanfordalumni.
    org/news/magazine/2006/sepoct/features/stadium.html, 6/28/10; DiStanislao
    (2005, p.78).

21. Bill King, "Bottom Line on Donations: UGA Season Tickets Still Sold Out,"
    Junkyard Blawg, http://blogs.ajc.com/junkyard-blawg/2010/06/12/bottom-
    line-on-donations-uga-season-tickets-still-sold-out/?cxntfid=blogs_junkyard_
    blawg, 6/14/10.

22. Web site for Alabama boosters, http://www.rolltide.com/boosters/tide-totals.
    html, 6/26/10.

23. The wording is as follows: "[P]riority points shall be credited first, in accor-
    dance with the terms contained in the written contract if different from the
    procedures described herein and, second, in accordance with the procedures
    described herein." Web site for the booster club.

24. The athletic department's Web page proclaims, "'It's Saturday Night in Death
    Valley ... and here come your Fighting Tigers of LSU.' Hearing those words
    from public address announcer Dan Borne as the Tigers enter the stadium
    brings chills to even the casual LSU football fan and sends shivers to those on
    the opposing sideline. Eight nights a year, Tiger Stadium becomes the fifth larg-
    est city in the state of Louisiana as over 92,000 fans pack the cathedral of col-
    lege football to watch the Tigers play." http://www.lsusports.net/ViewArticle.
    dbml?DB_OEM_ID=5200&ATCLID=177159, 4/8/10.

25. Kaplan (2008, data p. 3).

26. Coughlin and Erekson (1984).

27. DiStanislao (2005, p. 109).

28. Web site for Stanford Buck-Cardinal Club, http://grfx.cstv.com/photos/schools/
    stan/genrel/auto_pdf/BCC-Benefits-chart.pdf, 3/25/10.

29. Web site for Colorado State Ram Club, http://csuramclub.colostate.edu/pages/
    club_benefits.asp, 3/16/10.

30. A few universities choose not to affiliate with a conference, Notre Dame being
    the best-known example in football. In such cases, the university dispenses with
    any sharing arrangements but also loses any benefits that might come with con-
    ference membership, such as in television and postseason bowl negotiations.

31. Noll (2009, pp. 19–22) provides a detailed summary of the evolving
    agreements.

32. Tommy Deas, "Bowl Game Payout a Boon for Coaches, University," *Tuscaloosa
    News*, December 23, 2009.

33. The Big Ten, ACC, and the Big East shared TV revenues equally. Bud Withers,
    *Seattle Times*, July 18, 2010.

34. NCAA (2009, p. 41).

35. Students at three California universities voted down increases in student fees
    to support athletics. Jere Longman, "As Costs of Sports Rise, Students Balk at
    Fees," *New York Times*, May 30, 2009.

36. Author's calculations based on 2007–2008 figures for public FBS universities.
37. Griffith (1926, p. 46) expressed shock that head coaches were being paid more than assistant professors. As noted in Chapter 2, the Carnegie Foundation report of 1929 surveyed coach salaries and found that the average football coach earned $86,000 in 2009 dollars (Savage 1929, p. 173).
38. See Appendix Table 5A.2 for details on data and calculations.
39. Between 1985–1986 and 2009–2010 at 44 universities in one of the five major conferences, average compensation expressed in 2009–2010 dollars increased for full professors from $107,400 to $141,600, for presidents from $294,400 to $559,700 and for head football coaches from $273,300 to $2,054,700. See Appendix Table 5A.2.
40. "Saban Shows His Value at Alabama," *New York Times*, October 2, 2008. "U. of Texas Football Coach Passes the $5-Million Mark," *Chronicle of Higher Education*, December 11, 2009.
41. For a smaller sample of 22 universities in the same conferences, average compensation for basketball coaches increased fourfold, from $300,800 in 1985–1986 to $1,218,400 in 2006–2007, all expressed in constant 2006–2007 dollars.
42. Calculations based on total compensation at 101 very large corporations in 1989–1990 and 2000–2005 (Frydman and Saks, 2008, table 3). Over the same period, the median of the three highest-paid officers in those corporations rose at an annual rate of 6.6%.
43. The economic concept of rent and its effects on incentives and compensation in the case of college athletics is discussed later in this chapter.
    One other item deserves mention. "Guarantees," accounting for about 3% of expenses in 2007–2008, are payments promised to visiting teams. It is standard practice for teams in prominent conferences to schedule one or more home games against weaker nonconference opponents, in part to boost their win–loss percentage. Occasionally, this strategy backfires, when a David shocks a Goliath., as with Appalachian State's win over Michigan in the fall of 2007.
44. See, e.g., Murray Sperber, "Stop Hiding the Financial Truth about College Athletics," *Chronicle of Higher Education*, May 23, 2008: "Higher education is in dire financial shape, rattling the tin cup in front of often unsympathetic state legislators, taxpayers, and potential donors. The reality, which the NCAA now acknowledges, is that institutional subsidies for intercollegiate athletics usually come out of funds that could go to academic purposes." Also see Zimbalist (1999).
45. Thelin and Wiseman (1990, p. 2). This report used the results of a 1986 survey of athletic department finances by the American Association of State Colleges and Universities. Concern over the financial viability of big-time college sports is not merely a recent phenomenon. Worried about falling revenues, the major football powers considered in 1931 reducing the number of games played each season as a cost-cutting measure. "Football Viewed as Facing Crisis," *New York Times*, January 3, 1931. See also Savage and McGovern (1931).
46. A task force at the University of Cincinnati suggested changes in several of these accounting conventions as ways of reducing deficits in athletics, including crediting athletics for revenues from parking and licensing, sharing the

maintenance cost of athletic facilities, letting the university pay for out-of-state tuition for athletes, and covering more athletes' financial aid costs with regular scholarships. University of Cincinnati Athletics Task Force, All-University Athletics Task Force Report: DRAFT, unpublished report, January 4, 2010, pp. 7, 9, http://www.uc.edu/news/docs/Athletics_Report_Final.pdf, 7/11/10.

47. Orszag and Orszag (2005, pp. 2, 3, 7). They assumed a 2.5% annual rate of depreciation and a 7.5% opportunity cost of capital.

48. U.S. Department of Education, Office of Postsecondary Education, the Equity in Athletics Data Analysis Cutting Tool, http://ope.ed.gov/athletics/, 12/29/09.

49. In 2007–2008, Mississippi State obtained 13.8% of its total athletic revenues from student fees and 1.6% from direct institutional support. *USA Today* data set. For a description of Mississippi State's recruiting strategy, see Pete Thamel, "Mississippi State's Mullen Learns How Other Half Wins in SEC," *New York Times*, October 23, 2009.

50. Among the five institutions in the major powers group, the median year in which they started playing football was 1904. The medians for the other three groups of institutions shown were 1902, 1969, and 1962.

51. Win–loss records were obtained from esp.com (http://sports.espn.go.com/ncb/teams, 12/13/09) and James Howell (http://www.jhowell.net/cf/scores/byname.htm, 12/13/09). Source for attendance data: http://web1.ncaa.org/web_files/stats/football_records/Attendance/2008.pdf, 12/13/09.

52. For 2007–2008 the average revenue from ticket sales was $2.6 million for the lesser also-rans, compared with $6.6 million for the lesser powers and $26.7 million for the major powers.

53. University of Cincinnati Athletics Task Force, *All-University Athletics Task Force Report: DRAFT*, unpublished report, January 4, 2010, pp. 7, 8.

54. Tommy Deas, "Bowl Game Payout a Boon for Coaches, University," *Tuscaloosa News*, December 23, 2009.

55. Weisbrod et al. (2008).

56. Deas, "Bowl Game Payout," 2009; Saban contract; see *USA Today* information on coach contracts, http://www.usatoday.com/sports/college/football/2009-coaches-contracts-database.htm?loc=interstitialskip, 12/13/09.

57. Provisions in coaches' contracts collected and put on the Web by *USA Today*, 2009.

58. Ideally, any spending that does not serve the ultimate objective should be eliminated from the budget. But former Michigan president James Duderstadt argues that athletic departments do not follow this principle, instead focusing on generating revenue rather than managing costs. Unfortunately, with the available data it is impossible to prove this assertion one way or the other (Duderstadt 2000, p. 145).

59. Noll (2009, p. 90) works out in equations this advantage, which he then incorporates into an expression showing the value of a coach who is skilled in signing up such players.

60. Brown and Jewell (2004). In 2009 their estimates yielded values of $550,000 and $1.6 million for football and basketball, respectively. Amounts expressed in 2008–2009 dollars. January Consumer Price Index values used: 1996: 154.4; 2009: 211.1.

61. Michigan played three games in 1881, against Harvard, Princeton, and Yale, losing all three. http://www.jhowell.net/cf/scores/byname.htm, 1/6/10.
62. The coach was Mike Krzyzewski of Duke, and the player was Harrison Barnes. Rick Brown, "Barnes Announces He'll Play Hoops at North Carolina," *Des Moines Register*, November 14, 2009; Harrison Barnes Diary, http://www.highschoolhoop.com/high-school-stories/2009/10/the-harrison-barnes-diary-official-visit-to-kansas/, 12/30/09; http://rivals.yahoo.com/cal/basketball/recruiting/player-Harrison-Barnes-67225, 12/30/09.
63. Thayer Evans, "In Alabama, a Top Prospect Responds to Tugs from Home," *New York Times*, February 5, 2009. Kevin Armstrong, "Colleges Waiting to Hear Their Name," *New York Times*, April 17, 2010; http://webcache.googleusercontent.com/search?q=cache:4JHtjG5TWZgJ:www.draftexpress.com/profile/Josh-Selby-5682/+josh+selby+announces+media+timeout&cd=2&hl=en&ct=clnk&gl=us, 6/26/10.
64. This was the University of Nevada at Las Vegas coach Jerry Tarkanian (Wolff and Keteyian 1990, p. 12).
65. Rooney (1987, p. 38).
66. Brown and Jewell (2004, p. 159) estimates of "monopsony rents," expressed in 2008–2009 dollars.
67. Lewis (2006, p. 195) writes, "There were a number of colleges – and Ole Miss was one of them – for which the expropriation of the market value of pre-professional football players was something very like a core business."
68. Noll (1991, p. 198) states, "Cheating against the NCAA rules will continue – indeed, increase – because it is the profit-maximizing strategy for nearly all universities and the income-maximizing strategy for coaches." For economic models of cheating on NCAA rules, see Fort and Quirk (1999) and Humphreys and Ruseski (2009).
69. Sears (1992, p. 218). President Charles Eliot of Harvard also warned against using professionals in college football games (Eliot 1894, p. 21).
70. Savage (1929, p. 183).
71. Rooney (1987, pp. 159–160).
72. Byers and Hammer (1995, pp. 24, 27, 31).
73. This was Republican William Clements, who served as Texas governor from 1979 to 1983 and 1987 to 1991. In 1987 he apologized for approving a continuation of payments to players. T. James Munoz, "Clements Apologizes for SMU Role," *Washington Post*, March 11, 1987, p. A3; Byers and Hammer (1995, pp. 24, 31).
74. Tom Weir, "Marcus Dupree Says He Turned Down $250K as a Recruit," *USA Today*, November 12, 2010, http://content.usatoday.com/communities/gameon/post/2010/11/marcus-dupree-says-he-turned-down-250k-as-a-recruit/1, 11/13/10.
75. As reported on the Web site for the Pulitzer Prizes, this was the 1986 prize for investigative reporting, http://webcache.googleusercontent.com/search?q=cache:aUZ_eq_xmf0J:www.pulitzer.org/bycat/Investigative-Reporting+lexington+herald+leader+1986+playing+above+the+rules+marx&cd=3&hl=en&ct=clnk&gl=us, 8/8/10;Wolff and Keteyian (1990, pp. 22–23); Rooney (1987, p. 147).

76. By conference, the average percentages of respondents who reported having taken illegal payments while in college were as follows: SEC, 52%; Big 8, 40%; Big Ten, 39%; Southwest, 35%; Pac-10, 31%; Western Athletic, 27%; and Atlantic Coast, 19%. The rate among those who played for major independents was 36% (Sack 1991, table 2).

77. The percentage of former Division I-A players who reported having taken such payments was 28% for those who had graduated in the 1950s, while it was 36% or more among more recent cohorts (Sack 1991, table 3). Among all former players, 25% of those who had been recruited by fewer than 20 institutions reported taking payments, but the percentage increased for those getting more attention, rising to 46% of those who had been recruited by 50 or more (Sack 1991, table 5, p. 9).

78. Lynn Zinser, "Connecticut Receives Notice of N.C.A.A. Violations," *New York Times*, May 29, 2010; Lynn Zinser, "U.S.C. Sports Receive Harsh Penalties," *New York Times*, June 12, 2010. An agent for NFL players asserted that some college football programs are known to condone cheating. Ray Glier, "With a Player Under Investigation, Saban Criticizes Agents," *New York Times*, July 22, 2010. A case likely to lead to an NCAA investigation involves financial offers made to the father of an Auburn star quarterback. See Pete Thamel, "A Question of Eligibility: Auburn Star's Father Sought Signing Money, Recruiter Says," *New York Times*, November 12, 2010.

79. Jennifer Epstein, "Be Their Guest," *Inside Higher Ed*, December 29, 2009.

80. For descriptions of third-party recruiting, see Wolff and Keteyian (1990); Dana O'Neil, "Gray Scale: Recruiters Struggle with Perfectly Legal Yet Ethically Questionable," ESPN.com, November 19, 2008; Eric Prisbell and Steve Yanda, "A Whole New Ballgame That Williams Won't Play," *Washington Post*, February 13, 2009; William C. Rhoden, "For Coaches, Recruiting Top Players Can Lead to a Dark Side," *New York Times*, March 30, 2009; Thayer Evans and Pete Thamel, "College Recruiting's Thin Gray Line,' *New York Times*, February 9, 2009.

81. For discussions of winner-take-all tournaments, see Frank and Cook (1995) and Frank (2004).

82. See discussion of the hypothesis developed by Howard Bowen in Clotfelter (1996, pp. 34–35).

83. The term was used in the 1980s by Berkeley chancellor Ira Heyman (Thelin and Wiseman 1990, p. 7).

84. Orszag and Orszag (2005, p.5).

85. Roy S. Johnson, "Ready for Kickoff," *Stanford Magazine*, September–October 2006, http://www.stanfordalumni.org/news/magazine/2006/sepoct/features/stadium.html, 6/28/10.

86. S. C. Gwyne, "Come Early. Be Loud. Cash In," *Texas Monthly*, November, 2008.

87. Caroline Preston, "A Gift for Athletics from a Wealthy Oilman Triggers a Furor at Oklahoma State U.," *Chronicle of Higher Education*, February 20, 2006; Erica Hendry, "Plans for Oklahoma State U's Athletic Village Are Still on Hold," *Chronicle of Higher Education*, June 8, 2008; Ben Gose, "Concerns Are Raised

About How Okla. State U. Handled a Big Gift," *Chronicle of Higher Education*, October 30, 2008.

88. Brad Wolverton, "Growth in Sports Gifts May Mean Fewer Academic Donations," *Chronicle of Higher Education*, October 5, 2007.

89. Author's calculations based on data from Daniel L. Fulks, *2002–03 NCAA Revenues and Expenses of Divisions I and II Intercollegiate Athletics Programs Report* (Indianapolis: National Collegiate Athletic Association, February 2005); National Center for Education Statistics, Integrated Postsecondary Education Data System.

90. Knight Commission on Intercollegiate Athletics (2010, p. 4).

## Chapter 6

1. Statement of Chancellor Philip L. Dubois Concerning Initiation of an Intercollegiate Football Program at UNC Charlotte, September 18, 2008.

2. *UNC Charlotte Football Feasibility Committee Report*, February 2008.

3. Student fees were to rise to $320 in 2014. These fees were expected to cover $3.2 million of the $6.2 million projected operating costs plus $2.4 million in debt service. By the time of the state board's approval, 3,200 seat licenses had been sold, raising $5.8 million. The North Carolina legislature approved the sale of bonds in its 2010 legislative session. Mark Johnson and Meghan Cooke, "Board Approves UNCC Football," *Charlotte Observer*, February 13, 2010; "49ers Football in 2013 – It's Official," UNCC Public Relations news release, August 4, 2010, http://www.publicrelations.uncc.edu/campusnews/current/, 8/11/10; Libby Sander, "Charlotte Makes Way for Football," *Chronicle of Higher Education*, August 10, 2010.

4. Mike Allen, "UConn Finds Rich Off-Court Gains in Basketball Power," *New York Times*, March 31, 1999.

5. The provost reported that funds previously used for scholarships, academic advising, and college discretionary accounts were diverted to athletics. *UNC Charlotte Football Feasibility Committee Report*, February 2008, surveys of athletic directors and provosts; University of South Florida Web page, http://74.125.47.132/search?q=cache:MKm0P_-nRnoJ:www.usf.edu/About-USF/points-of-pride.asp+university+of+south+florida+enrollment&cd=2&hl =en&ct=clnk&gl=us, 6/21/09.

6. Shavers (2004, pp. 77, 219).

7. University of California, Report of the Chancellor's Committee on Intercollegiate Athletics, July 6, 2010, http://www.berkeley.edu/news/media/releases/2010/07/ IA-Council-Report.pdf, 8/8/10.

8. University of Cincinnati Athletics Task Force, *All-University Athletics Task Force Report: DRAFT*, unpublished report, January 4, 2010, p. 7. http://www.uc.edu/ news/docs/Athletics_Report_Final.pdf, 7/11/10.

9. Bobby Fong, "How Butler Won the NCAA Tournament," *Chronicle of Higher Education*, April 23, 2010.

10. Shapiro (2005, p. 31).

11. Libby Sander, "At What Price Football?" *Chronicle of Higher Education*, February 14, 2010.

12. Letters to NPR, October 5, 2009, http://www.npr.org/templates/story/story. php?storyId=113513740, 10/12/09.
13. Doug Lederman, "Sports Subsidies Soar," *Inside Higher Ed*, January 19, 2010.
14. University of Cincinnati, All-University Athletics Task Force Report, January 4, 2010.
15. U.S. Department of Education, *Digest of Education Statistics, 2009*, table 352.
16. In fiscal year 2007, state appropriations accounted for 7.8% of core revenues for the University of Michigan and 8.6% for the University of Virginia. http://nces. ed.gov/ipeds/datacenter/Default.aspx, 7/21/09.
17. As shown in Chapter 5, 30% of the revenues of the average FBS athletic department came from state appropriations, institutional allocations, or mandatory student fees.
18. "Freebies Available to Pennsylvania from Movie and Football Tickets to Ski-lift Passes – All Courtesy of Grateful Lobbyists," *Philadelphia Inquirer*, April 16, 2006, http://74.125.47.132/search?q=cache:PGoc5OS6fc4J:nalert.blogspot. com/2006/04/freebies-available-to-pennsylvania.html+legislators+free+footba ll+tickets&cd=12&hl=en&ct=clnk&gl=us, 6/21/09.
19. "State Lawmaker Controls Football Tickets Through Marketing Deal," *Gadsden Times*, January 1, 2008, http://www.gadsdentimes.com/article/20080101/NEWS/ 801010305?Title=State-lawmaker-controls-football-tickets-through-market-ing-deal, 6/21/09.
20. Ohio State took 485 guests to the national championship game in 2008. Among them, 45% went for free. Julie Carr Smyth, "Ohio Lawmakers Spend Thousands on Ohio State Football Tickets," *Kalamazoo Gazette*, August 1, 2008, http:// blog.mlive.com/kzgazette/2008/08/ohio_lawmakers_spend_thousands. html, 6/21/09; Alan Johnson and Lee Leonard, "OSU Tickets Popular Gift for Lawmakers," *Columbus Dispatch (Ohio)*, April 26, 2003.
21. Ralph Haurwitz, "Lawmakers Get UT Ticket Perk," *Austin American-Statesman*, May 29, 2006.
22. Jordan Blum, "State Lawmakers Scoop up Tickets," *Advocate*, December 12, 2007.
23. James Salzer, "Football a Pivotal Player in Lobbying: Dogs No. 1: UGA Leads State Universities in Total Spending on Officials, Most of it in Game Tickets," *Atlanta Journal-Constitution*, January 12, 2008; Jake Parkinson, "U. Utah Ranked as Largest Lobbying Spender in State," *University Wire*, January 17, 2002.
24. Kyle Henley, "Legislators Accept Lots of Freebies / Lobbyists Bestow Free Tickets," Colorado Springs *Gazette*, January 20, 2002, http://findarticles.com/p/ articles/mi_qn4191/is_20020120/ai_n9998206/?tag=content;col1, 6/21/09; "Utah Lawmakers under Fire for Free Football Tickets," ABC4 News, January 15, 2008, http://74.125.47.132/search?q=cache:oZ-pzflWZB0J:www.abc4. com/news/local/story.aspx%3Fcontent_id%3Df148770f-c220–47e6-b93f-6e7 5f8303b5a+legislators+free+football+tickets&cd=21&hl=en&ct=clnk&gl=us, 6/21/09.
25. See, e.g., Rebecca Ferrar, "Law Director Advises Knox Commissioners to Pay for UT Basketball Tickets," KnoxNews.com, November 2, 2007, http://www. knoxnews.com/news/2007/Nov/02/law-director-advises-knox/, 6/21/09; Henley, "Legislators Accept Lots of Freebies; Nolan Clay, "Lobbyists Use Sports Tickets as Gifts," *Daily Oklahoman*, February 5, 2006, http://www.

redorbit.com/news/technology/380212/lobbyists_use_sports_tickets_as_gifts/index.html#, 6/21/09; Hinton 1/26/08; Ed Anderson, "House Weakens Free Ticket Ban," *Times-Picayune*, February 21, 2008, http://74.125.47.132/search?q=cache:wwYP61ktfbUJ:www.nola.com/news/index.ssf/2008/02/house_adds_exceptions_for_free.html+legislators+free+football+tickets&cd=20&hl=en&ct=clnk&gl=us, 6/21/09.

26. Arkansas: Rob Moritz, "Ethics Panel's Football – Passes Ban Peeves Legislators," *Arkansas Democrat-Gazette* (Little Rock), October 8, 1999; North Carolina, Florida: Steve Bousquet, "Donations Welcome, but 'Gifts' Forbidden," *St. Petersburg Times*, January 1, 2006; Oklahoma: Mick Hinton, "Members Approve Passel of New Rules," *Tulsa World*, January 26, 2008; Tennessee: Dorie Turner "No More Comps for UT games," *Chattanooga Times Free Press*, September 24, 2002; Texas: Jennifer Peebles, "Public Can Take Closer Look at Legislators' Finances Via Interactive Map," *Texas Watchdog*, http://74.125.47.132/search?q=cache:oLonkDxKEdEJ:www.texaswatchdog.org/2008/10/legislators-financial-disclosures-get-full-airing/+legislators+free+football+tickets&cd=28&hl=en&ct=clnk&gl=us, 6/21/09;

Wisconsin: "Accept No Lapses in Capitol Ethics: A UW – Madison Lobbyist and 11 Legislators Should Have Known Their Cozy Football Ticket Arrangement Was Wrong," *Wisconsin State Journal* (Madison), December 30, 2005.

27. The model employed was fixed effects (Humphreys 2006).

28. Encyclopedia of Alabama, http://74.125.47.132/search?q=cache:wBCE2doYIkMJ:www.encyclopediaofalabama.org/face/Article.jsp%3Fid%3Dh-1797+Alabama+Auburn+resolution+1947&cd=4&hl=en&ct=clnk&gl=us, 6/24/09.

29. Richard L. Walker, "Kentucky Versus Louisville: A Natural, College Basketball Rivalry That Isn't," *Christian Science* Monitor, March 10, 1982; Wilt Brownin, "ECU to Get Dates with Carolina, State," *News & Record*, June 28, 1995; Murray Evans, "UK, U of L Sign Four-Year Deal to Renew Series," Associated Press, August 11, 2005.

30. Ivan Maisel, "Who Says Politics and Football Don't Mix?" ESPN.com, May 25, 2005, http://sports.espn.go.com, 11/7/08. The sticking point in negotiations had been WVU's insistence on having most games played at home. The compromise involved making the location of one game dependent on the outcome of the preceding one.

31. Among those attending the meeting were Lieutenant Governor Bob Bullock (a graduate of both Texas Tech and Baylor), state senator David Sibley (Baylor), and chair of the Senate Finance Committee John Montford (Texas Tech). Russell Gold, "Bullock Called Final Play of the SWC; Lieutenant Governor Quarterbacked Four Texas Universities' Entry into Big 12," *San Antonio Express-News*, May 25, 1997.

32. Josh Barr, "A Final Hurdle to ACC Expansion; U-Va. Said to Prefer Including Virginia Tech, May Hold up Deal Otherwise," *Washington Post*, May 15, 2003; "Talking It Over: Virginia Governor Asks for Mediation in ACC Expansion," SI.com, June 10, 2003, cnnsi.com; Josh Barr, "ACC Invites Miami, Virginia Tech; Big East's Boston College, Syracuse Are Excluded," *Washington Post*, June 25, 2003.

33. Josh Barr, "ACC Decision Remains on Hold," *Washington Post*, June 11, 2003.
34. Beasley (1974, p. 97).
35. Rooney (1969, p. 475) suggests this.
36. Beasley (1974, p. 99, n. 12).
37. Gifts were 2.4% of revenues for four-year public universities in 2006–2007. U.S. Department of Education, *Digest of Education Statistics, 2007*, tables 352 and 356, http://nces.ed.gov/quicktables/result.asp?SrchKeyword=revenue+of+public+institutions&topic=All&Year=2007, 5/17/10.
38. Gary A. Olson, "Should We Ditch Football?" *Chronicle of Higher Education*, May 5, 2010.
39. See Baade and Sundberg (1996), Rhoads and Gerking (2000), and Humphreys and Mondello (2007). Contrary results were obtained by Turner, Meserve, and Bowen (2001) in a study examining alumni giving over time at several selective Division I-A universities.
40. Humphreys and Mondello (2007, pp. 273–276).
41. Stinson and Howard (2007, p. 249). Another study compared donations at five branches in California's state university system. Two of these had football teams in the most competitive division, and each attracted growing coverage on regional and national television. Compared with the other three, these universities saw increases in donations (Anctil 2003).
42. Rhoads and Gerking (2000, pp. 256–257).
43. I am grateful to the following universities for their cooperation in supplying lists of guests in their president's or chancellor's box during the 2008 football season: the University of Washington, the University of Georgia, Texas A&M University, Auburn University, Florida State University, the University of Maryland, the University of North Carolina, and North Carolina State University.
44. The University of Colorado wrote to say that its lawyers did not interpret the documents requested as subject to the statute. The University of Oregon replied that it would provide the requested information after its estimated $791.87 cost was paid in advance. The University of California Berkeley, denied the request on the grounds that "the public interest served here by protecting the identity of major or potential donors, and thereby increasing the likelihood of acquiring financial support for the University, outweighs any incidental interest served by disclosing who those individual are (Letter from Alan Kolling, Public Records Coordinator, July 31, 2009). The University of Tennessee said that such requests would be honored only if they come from state residents. The University of Nebraska, in response to my request in July 2009, stated that no list of the guests in its chancellor's box for the 2008 season existed. When I asked again during the 2009 football season for the lists covering two home games for that season, I again was told that no list existed. After I wrote to say that readers might find that implausible, I was sent 15 names applying to one game and 19 to the other. The University of South Carolina sent a list, but with no names for the president's box. Its designated official stopped responding to my requests for the missing names. Michigan State, after charging $57.90 for labor, sent seven pages, on which 568 of the 686 names had been redacted with black marker. For an article about universities' responses to requests from a newspaper, see

Jill Riepenhoff and Todd Jones, "Secrecy 101," *Columbus Dispatch*, May 31, 2009,http://www.dispatch.com/live/content/local_news/stories/2009/05/31/copy/secrecy-redirect.html, 10/31/10.

For eight universities, I requested a list of the traveling party to the bowl the team played in following the 2008 football season. No private universities or public universities from Pennsylvania were included in the requests because no law required them to provide such information.

45. *Husky Stadium: Community Resource and Public Asset for Everyone*, brochure produced by the University of Washington State Relations and Intercollegiate Athletics, September 2008; Bob Condotta, "Huskies Haven't Given up on Plans to Renovate Husky Stadium," *Seattle Times*, June 2, 2009.

46. To fill out the commercially oriented profile of this board of regents, the three members who did not attend any games included the founder and chairman of Costco, the owner of a marine transport company, and a financial planning CPA.

47. Stanford Stadium SkySuites are described at the Web site georgiadogs.com, http://webcache.googleusercontent.com/search?q=cache:zA8NY46jVz8J:www.georgiadogs.com/ViewArticle.dbml%3FDB_OEM_ID%3D8800%26ATCLID%3D305393+georgia+sanford+stadium+Sky+Suites&cd=1&hl=en&ct=clnk&gl=us, 6/8/10.

48. Although guests are typically invited to the president's house for lunch and drinks, the president's box does not serve alcohol.

49. This is a time-honored approach to fund-raising. According to the 1929 Carnegie Foundation report on athletics, "The attitude of the college toward its alumni and of the alumni toward their college is at the root materialistic. Between the graduate and the university there has for years existed a tacit bargain: for money and for activity of interest the college in effect offers certain rewards. The alumnus of to-day is thought of principally as a source of funds.... In return he receives prominence, the promise of power, and the self-satisfaction that these and his activities bring. With repetition of these conditions the attitude of the alumnus may end by becoming proprietary. The power which he has received takes the form of governance and trusteeship, whether of the university or of athletics (Savage et al. 1929, p. 191).

50. It took over this role from the University of Georgia Foundation, a private foundation whose independence had proved frustrating to university leaders.

51. Web site for the Texas A&M system, http://www.tamus.edu/offices/chancellor/centurycouncil/membership.html, 8/4/10.

52. Department chairs were counted as faculty members.

53. In 2007 the totals received in donations (in millions) were as follows: Washington, $300; UNC, $247; Texas A&M, $169; NC State, $162; Georgia, $88; Maryland, $86; Auburn, $77; and Florida State, $57 (Kaplan 2008, pp. 1–10).

54. In 2007 an Alabama legislator complained publicly that he had not received his pair of free tickets from Auburn to that year's Alabama game, charging that Auburn was retaliating for past statements of his that were unfavorable to Auburn. Lobbyists could spend no more than $250 per day on entertainment for state legislators, well above the $120 face value of two tickets. "Auburn, Alabama Say Free Football Tickets for Officials is a Tradition," December 1, 2007, ABC 33 40, http://74.125.47.132/search?q=cache:q2Q31qSyvA4J:www.

abc3340.com/news/stories/1207/477153.html+legislators+free+basketball+tic
kets&cd=12&hl=en&ct=clnk&gl=us, 6/21/09.

An unrelated news story reported that the Republican minority leader of the state house, in his private role as representative of a marketing firm, received more than 500 tickets to every Auburn game in 2008 for distribution to advertisers. Presumably, none of these tickets would have been included in those listed for the presidential box. Associated Press, "State Lawmaker Controls Football Tickets through Marketing Deal," *Gadsden Times*, January 1, 2008.

55. James Salzer, "Football a Pivotal Player in Lobbying: Dogs No. 1: UGA Leads State Universities in Total Spending on Officials, Most of It in Game Tickets," *Atlanta Journal-Constitution*, January 12, 2008.

56. Unidentified president surveyed by Knight Commission on Intercollegiate Athletics (2009, p. 45).

57. Knight Commission on Intercollegiate Athletics (2009, p. 46).

58. Dana O'Neil, "Northern Iowa: The Shot and the Effect," ESPN.com, August 4, 2010.

59. See also Brad Wolverton, "George Mason U. Drew Big Spike in Interest Following Final Four Run," *Chronicle of Higher Education*, March 17, 2008. In 2006, after its basketball team went to the Final Four in the NCAA men's championship, freshman applications to George Mason increased 22%.

60. Doug Lederman, "Flocking to Football," *Inside Higher Education*, May 20, 2008; David Scott, "UNCC Football Deflated," *News and Observer*, February 23, 2008.

61. Eliot, *Annual Report for 1900/01* (1902), p. 16.

62. Art and Science Group, StudentPOLL 4 (No. 4, 2001), "Intercollegiate Athletics Have Little Influence on College Choice – Intramural And Recreational Opportunities Matter More", http://www.artsci.com/studentpoll/archivedissues/4_4.pdf, 6/11/09.

63. McCormick and Tinsley (1987, p. 1108).

64. See, e.g., McCormick and Tinsley (1987), Tucker (2005), and Smith (2008).

65. Pope and Pope (2009). Their sample consisted of 332 universities with big-time football or basketball programs observed over the years 1983–2002. The estimating equation included institution and year fixed effects plus a linear time trend for each institution.

66. The minority of surveyed college-bound students for whom athletics was important or who showed knowledge of college sports – by being able to name at least one Division I conference – was preponderantly male. Art and Science Group, StudentPOLL 4 (No. 4, 2001).

67. SAT or ACT scores corresponding to the 25th and 75th percentile of scores of accepted applicants were published. I converted the ACT scores into their SAT equivalents and averaged the two percentile scores. I restricted myself to measures that were published for both years. Although these surveys and their scoring differed between the two years, I converted their results into a form that could be compared, using the same approach used to calculate ranks for each of the measures. For each measure, a standardized score was calculated for each institution in each year, equal to the difference between that institution's value for that measure and the mean of that measure for all 101 institutions in that year, divided by the standard deviation of all values in that year. Then those

standardized scores were ranked. The scores were adjusted where necessary so that an improvement in the measure would lead to a higher rank. For example, an increase in selectivity is indicated by a lower rather than a higher rate.

68. "Rankings: National Universities," *U.S. News and World Report*, September 18, 1995, "America's Best Colleges," *U.S. News and World Report*, www.usnews. com/college, 6/2/2010. To make the combined rankings comparable in the two years, I used the same weights for both years. These are based on the relative weights used by *U.S. News* for its 2010 rankings. They were as follows: academic reputation, 0.385; SAT, 0.115; freshmen in the top 10% of their high school class, 0.092; acceptance rate, 0.023; freshman retention rate, 0.308; alumni giving rate, 0.077. These were applied to standard scores for each measure, and the resulting weighted average was ranked, producing the rank labeled "Six Measures, USN method," in Appendix Table 6A.1. Since the published rankings used different weights for these years and included additional measures used in just one of the years, my calculations do not replicate the published rankings.

69. See Appendix Table 6A.1. The complete sample included 51 universities in the FBS, 29 in other Division I classifications, and 21 not in Division I. The sample of 51 private universities had, respectively, 16, 17, and 18 universities in these three groups. The advance in ranking spots by the four named private universities were Miami, 34; Southern California, 22; Pittsburgh, 20; and Brigham Young, 18.

70. Chu (1989, pp. 27–36) argues that colleges and universities in the United States adopted athletics for the purpose of attracting financial resources.

71. For a study of the spillovers in the form of educated doctoral scientists, see Stephan et al. (2004).

72. Lowi (1974, p. 359) speculates that winning teams probably caused legislators to devote more money to state universities.

73. Lester (1995, pp. 22–25).

74. For a list of conference champions, see http://webcache.googleusercontent.com/ search?q=cache:UkXiug4xKoUJ:www.collegefootballpoll.com/champions_ bigten.html+big+ten+football+championship+history&cd=3&hl=en&ct= clnk&gl=us, 5/24/10.

75. Kerr (1994, p. 90).

## Chapter 7

1. Manuel Roig-Franzia, "A Tough Defeat, Then Mayhem; After NCAA Game, Bonfire Near U-Md. Causes $250,000 Loss," *Washington Post*, April 2, 2001. See also Nurith C. Aizenman, "U-Md. Campus Readies for Big Party; Police, Fire Departments Plan Patrol During Terps' Final Four Game," *Washington Post*, March 29, 2001; John Drake, "Residents Fault PG Police for Not Quelling Riots," *Washington Times*, April 3, 2001; Nurith C. Aizenman and David Nakamura, "Police Blamed in Post-Game Violence; Pr. George's Chief Faults Students," *Washington Post*, April 4, 2001; Nurith C. Aizenman, Town-Gown Relationship Hurt by Postgame Fires," *Washington Post*, April 5, 2001; Brian DeBose, "Second Student Charged in Riot," *Washington Times*, April 7, 2001; Andy Proffett, "Purdue Students Light Fires, Throw Rocks at Police," Associated

Press, April 2, 2001; Tom Davies, "Postgame Troubles Plague Purdue Campus," *South Bend Tribune* (Indiana), April 3, 2001.

2. The term "invisible curriculum" has been used to describe implicit teaching not appearing in the formal curriculum. See, e.g., James M. Lang, "The Invisible Curriculum," *Chronicle of Higher Education*, November 2, 2010.

3. Hurtado (2007).

4. Boyer (1990, p. 65).

5. Boyer (1990, p. 55).

6. Committee G, "Intercollegiate Football," in Edwards et al. (1928, p. 146). A contemporary commentator (Angell (1928, p. 115) agrees but sees this unifying effect as something of a consolation prize: "Since there is no common devotion to learning, intercollegiate athletics supply the only truly unifying force of any strength in our large universities."

7. Gary Olson, "Should We Ditch Football?" *Chronicle of Higher Education*, May 5, 2010. One strand of sociological reasoning holds that sports spectatorship, like religion, has the potential to build social cohesion. By extension, following a common team could engender cohesion within a university community. See Sweet (2001, pp. 110–113). In a study done at the University of Kansas, Branscombe and Wann (1991) showed that students' identification with the basketball team was positively correlated with measures of self-esteem and positive outlook on life and negatively correlated with measures of alienation and depression. Although they argued that these results show that strong identification with a specific sports team can ward off feelings of depression and alienation and foster self-esteem, the study's results indicate only correlation, not a causal effect.

   It is interesting to note, because it is one of the universities used in the present analysis, that the University of Chicago, after going for 30 years without football after President Robert Hutchins abolished it in 1939, reintroduced it at the Division III level in 1969 (University of Chicago Web page, http://athletics.uchicago.edu/football/fb-records-1969.htm). According to Toma (2003, p. 92n) it did so in order to build community on its campus.

8. In an article describing French universities, a *New York Times* reporter wrote of a campus of the University of Paris with 32,000 students that had "no student center, no bookstore, no student-run newspaper, no freshman orientation" and a campus that emptied out every afternoon. "While students are ready to protest against something they dislike, there is little sense of belonging or pride in one's surroundings." Elaine Sciolino, "Higher Learning in France Clings to Its Old Ways," *New York Times*, May 12, 2006.

9. Hoch (1972, p. 132) writes, "Sports watching is still one of the most powerful socializers for the habit of passive consumption around."

10. Eliot (1894, pp. 12–14).

11. Wilson (1909, p. 574).

12. Angell (1928, p. 115).

13. Horowitz (1989).

14. Schneider (2008).

15. See, e.g., Sacerdote (2001).

16. Such natural experiments have been utilized in economic studies to find the causal effects on student learning of remedial programs, studying, and teacher

characteristics. See Bettinger and Long (2005), Stinebrickner and Stinebrickner (2007), and Carrell and West (2008).

17. Pascarella and Terenzini (1991)'s exhaustive review of between-college effects turns up a few small and uncertain effects, including these: the "collegiate" aspects of college (e.g., fraternities, sororities, and dorm life) appear to reduce some aspects of cognitive development (p. 137); artistic interests increased among students at private colleges more than among other students (p. 297); and decreases in dogmatism and growth in psychosocial adjustment and maturity were greatest on campuses with nonconformists and more active student involvement in class activities (p. 606). The authors conclude by noting the general absence of between-college effects: "The body of evidence reviewed casts considerable doubt on the premise that the conventional, if substantial, structural, resource and qualitative differences among schools are translated into correspondingly large differences in average educational effects" (pp. 589–590).

18. One reflection of the presence of established programs and a strong faculty at flagship state universities is the higher average SAT scores for entering students. As an illustration, the 2005 NSSE included two Michigan universities with enrollments of more than 10,000 that were in the FBS (Michigan and Central Michigan) and two that were not in Division I (Grand Valley State and Wayne State). The average SAT for students entering the first pair was 12% higher than the average for the second pair.

19. This excluded group is composed of universities that do not have football teams playing at the most competitive level but have teams playing some other major sport at the top level, usually basketball, such as Marquette, Georgia Southern, and Western Illinois. Because their partial participation in big-time athletics makes them a combination of the two comparison groups analyzed here, they are excluded. If they had been included, they would in most cases, as one might suspect, have yielded results falling between those of the two comparison groups.

20. Counting the excluded middle group (universities in Division I but not Division I-A), the number of private universities in the three groups were as follows: Division I-A, 8; other Division I, 9; not Division I, 15. The corresponding numbers of public universities were 32, 23, and 28.

21. Appendix figures and tables report detailed estimates, along with statistical significance. Figures 7A.1 and 7A.2 and panels 1 and 2 of Table 7A.1 present mean values. Figures 7A.3–7A.6 and panels 3–5 of Table 7A.1 give predicted values for a student whose characteristics equal the sample mean values.

22. Estimated probit models controlled for a student's gender, race, high school grades, family income, parents' education, and religion, type of high school attended, and SAT score.

23. Similar tests revealed no significant differences in time spent partying, watching TV, or reading in high school.

24. Among freshmen attending private universities, those going to places with big-time sports were more likely than others to say they aimed to be financially well off in life, but there was no statistically significant difference on this question among public university students. The percentage saying that they wanted to develop a meaningful philosophy of life differed according to the presence of

big-time sports only for those going to public institutions (those in sport-heavy universities were less likely to say so), but the difference is less than a percentage point. See Appendix Table 7A.1.

25. In this connection, Prisuta's (1979, pp. 97–98, table 1) finding is interesting: high school students who watched sports on TV tended to have conservative political views. In a study of 600 high school students in Michigan, he found that sports viewers were typically male, had higher socioeconomic status than those who did not watch sports on TV, and were involved in sports in other ways. He also found sports watchers to have views that were more authoritarian, nationalistic, and conservative than those who did not watch sports. The association between sports viewing and conservative attitudes is based on a regression controlling for socioeconomic status, gender, and race (Prisuta 1979, table 1, p. 98).

26. See Table 7A.1 for a summary of these findings.

27. Babcock and Marks (forthcoming). For estimates of the amount of time undergraduates spent on academic work at one college in the 1920s, see Angell (1928) and Hutchinson and Connard (1926).

28. Babcock and Marks (forthcoming).

29. All are members of the Consortium on Financing Higher Education, a group that contains the eight Ivy League institutions, another 10 private universities, and 13 liberal arts colleges. This organization periodically conducts surveys of students attending its member institutions, and it allowed me to use information from two of those surveys. It asked that I not name the institutions whose student surveys constitute the data for this section.

30. Unweighted averages of university figures based on Integrated Postsecondary Education Data System (IPEDS) data for the fall of 2006.

31. IPEDS 2005–2006, based on first majors only.

32. The data set obtained was in fact a 95% random sample of all students for whom information was collected originally.

33. The survey's questions on time use asked students to check, for each activity, one of several categories corresponding to the number of hours spent in a typical week, with the categories ranging from "None" and "Less than 2 hours" to "31–40 hours" and "More than 40 hours." A few student respondents evidently did not make a serious effort to answer all these questions, e.g., answering "Less than 2 hours" or "More than 40 hours" for all activities. To eliminate such unreasonable responses, I excluded any respondents whose total for all activities was less than 50 or more than 140 hours a week. This restriction eliminated 12% of the sample from the time use analysis only.

34. Each regression therefore included variables for gender, race/ethnicity, noncitizen status, year in school, family income, parental education, and SAT score. Dichotomous variables were defined for these characteristics, with separate indicators for missing data. Specific variables were formed for students: with family income of $100,000 under $200,000, $200,000 under $300,000, and $300,000 and above; with SAT or equivalent ACT score of 1470 or more; with one or both parents having a college degree. Students indicating two or three racial/ethnic categories were combined with those indicating other race, and those indicating more than three were deemed to be missing the race/ethnicity variable. Mean values of variables are given in Table 7A.1.

To reflect the legal drinking age, equations explaining binge drinking included an indicator for age under 21. Research shows that both drinking and binge drinking increase at a person's 21st birthday (Carpenter and Dobkin 2008, figure 1).

Although information on living arrangements and participation in a varsity athletic team was available, neither was included in these regressions, because both of these reflect choices made by students that themselves could be affected by the existence of a big-time athletic program. The possible mitigating effect of residence is discussed later in the chapter, however.

Equations explaining hours spent in various activities were estimated with ordinary least squares. Those with dichotomous measures as dependent variables were estimated using probit. Varsity football and basketball players were excluded from the analysis. They were eliminated because of the possibility that athletes might differ between big-time and other programs for reasons distinct from the kinds of campus effects being studied here. In fact, their exclusion makes no qualitative difference to the results. In addition, respondents whose answers produced unreasonable totals were excluded from the analysis of time use only.

35. Babcock and Marks (forthcoming, table 2).
36. Time spent on homework by a student with average characteristics, not shown separately in Figure 7A.4, was 15.5 and 17.1 hours per week in the big-time sports and comparison universities, respectively. Babcock and Marks (forthcoming, table 2) estimate the corresponding national median to be about 8.5.
37. This category included participation in student government, campus newspaper or literary magazine, fraternity or sorority, musical groups or theatrical production, religious organizations or services, volunteering, political organizations, minority or ethnic organizations, or other student activities or clubs.
38. Because varsity football and basketball players are not included in the analysis, this gap in time spent on varsity sports arises from all other sports with intercollegiate teams.
39. This data set was a sample taken from a much larger survey of first-year students at large public universities, the NSSE. This annual survey, conducted at colleges and universities that wish to do so focuses on aspects of the undergraduate experience thought to be related to important educational processes. The survey covered first-year students and seniors. I obtained a 20% sample of the first-year student surveys for 53 public universities with enrollments of more than 10,000 in 2004 and 70 such universities in 2005. As with the eight-university survey, I did not have information on a specific student's university. The only institution-specific data items were whether the enrollment was over 20,000, whether it was in one of the 11 states of the South, and whether it operated a big-time athletics program. As with the eight-university sample, this survey provided information on personal characteristics of students, including gender, race, parents' education, and SAT scores. It also included responses regarding students' overall evaluation of their university experience.
40. As already noted, state universities with big-time sports are often the flagship institution in a state. These also tend to have the most established academic programs and the strongest faculty. In the NSSE sample for 2005, e.g., the Division

I-A vs. non–Division I institutions in Washington, Colorado, and Georgia were the University of Washington, Colorado State, Georgia Tech, and the University of Georgia, whereas the non–Division I universities were Central Washington, University of Colorado at Denver, Kennesaw State, and Valdosta State. The average SAT for entering students at the Division I-A institutions exceeded that for the non–Division I institutions in these three states by 22%, 8%, and 23%, respectively (U.S. News, *Ultimate College Guide*, 2009).

41. For lists of the top 20 in these three years, see "Top Party and 'Stone Cold Sober' Schools, According to the Princeton Review," kmov.com, August 20, 2007; "Party School List from Princeton Review Released; University of Florida on Top," *Huffington Post*, July 28, 2008; "List of Top Party Schools by Princeton Review," *Raleigh News and Observer*, July 27, 2009.

42. Five or more drinks corresponds to the common definition of "binge drinking" for men. For women, the standard is four or more drinks.

43. In his description of traditions surrounding college football at the University of Nebraska, Stein (1977, p. 39) reports that ordinary rules are relaxed on football game days: "[T]he consumption of alcohol is seen by many as an appropriate pre-game and post-game ritual." For examples of heavy drinking traditions at other prominent big-time sports campuses, see Toma (2003, p. 85). For studies of the rise in alcohol consumption in connection with college spectator sports, see Borman and Stone (2001), Glassman et al. (2007), and Neal and Fromme (2007). See also Byers and Hammer (1995, pp. 139–140) for an amusing story about the angry reaction of the Ohio State president to an ABC story that showed OSU students drinking before a big football game.

44. Nathan Crabbe, "Machen, Johnson Butt Heads over UF–UGA Game," *Gainesville Sun*, July 22, 2009. See also Jack Stripling, "Beer Pong under Fire at U of Fla.," *Inside Higher Ed*, August 8, 2008.

45. Neal and Fromme (2007, pp. 2685, 2689).

46. Coons, Howard-Hamilton, and Waryold (1995).

47. Borman and Stone (2001).

48. Ben Eisen, "Surviving the Party School Rankings," *Inside Higher Ed*, July 28, 2009.

49. Neighbors et al. (2006).

50. Kremer and Levy (2008).

51. Author's calculations. For a list of the top universities, see the Appendix for Chapter 6.

52. Glassman et al. (2007, p. 255).

53. The basic regressions on which these differences are based do not include indicators for whether the student was a varsity athlete or for type of residence, because both of these are choices made by the student. Results for equations that include these variables are quite similar to those reported here.

54. Steve Makinen of StatFox provided these betting spreads.

55. Results based on a pooled regression, using university-by-year fixed effects explaining the logarithm of articles viewed per day, where the explanatory variables included the number of days until the end of the term plus dichotomous indictors for the three days following an unexpected win, the three days following an unexpected loss, each day between Monday and Saturday, days during

a break, days following the end of a term, days a university's team remained unbeaten in the tournament, days corresponding, respectively, to the tournament rounds of 64, 32, 16, 8, 4, and championship games, Easter Sunday, and Super Bowl Sunday. Declines in work are also associated with the days of the tournament's first round (-5%), Super Bowl Sunday (-23%), and Easter Sunday (-12%). The three libraries with no university were excluded from the sample. The estimated coefficients of the regression equations, along with their clustered standard errors, are shown in Appendix Table 7A.2.

56. An effect in the opposite direction, wherein big-time sports serves to reduce nonrevenue sports, is suggested by a development reported at Berkeley. A grass field previously used by the rugby team was converted to one with artificial turf so that the football team could practice on it, thereby making it unplayable for rugby. Lance Williams, "Amid Fiscal Crisis, UC Berkeley Commits $320 Million to Football," *California WatchBlog*, February 17, 2010.

57. The predicted percentages for "feel out of place often" were 16.4% and 15.0% in the sports-intensive and comparison groups, respectively. For "feel overwhelmed often," they were 55.4% and 50.2%. In both cases, the differences were statistically significant at the 1% level.

58. To address the question of whether big-time sports programs contribute to a sense of community in a university, I turned to a survey of seniors at the same eight private selective universities administered by the Consortium on Financing Higher Education in 2006. Seniors were asked three questions that would appear to provide direct evidence on this point. They were asked how satisfied they were with (1) the sense of community on campus, (2) the sense of community where they lived, presumably dorm, fraternity or sorority house, or private housing, and (3) the social life on campus. At least the first of these questions seems exactly on target. The third question also seems relevant, concerning satisfaction about social life on campus.

The results were decidedly mixed. In what is probably the best question for the purpose – concerning satisfaction with the sense of community on campus – seniors at the four big-time sports campuses indicated they were very satisfied with their university less frequently than did those in the four comparison universities. There were no significant differences on the second question. However, views on social life on campus did favor the sports-intensive campuses. Whereas 27% of seniors at the big-time sports universities said they were very satisfied with social life on campus, only 23% of those at the comparison institutions said they were.

59. See Figure 7A.6.

## Chapter 8

1. U.S. News and World Report, *Ultimate College Guide* (2009).

2. Judith S. Kaye, *Report to the Board of Trustees of the State University of New York*, Skadden, Arps, Slate, Meagher & Flom LLP, February 11, 2010; quotation, p. 48; see also pp. 10–11, 20, 28–36, 46, 49, 55; Pete Thamel, "In Pursuing Sports Glory, Ignoring All the Rules," *New York Times*, February 28, 2010; Pete Thamel, "At Binghamton, Concern That Sports Still a Focus," *New York Times*, February

28, 2010; Julia Hunter and Brandon Thomas, "Former BU Basketball Star DJ Rivera Charged with Using Stolen Debit Card," June 1, 2010, Pressconnects.com, http://www.pressconnects.com/apps/pbcs.dll/article?AID=/201006012125/ NEWS01/6010373, 6/15/10.

3. See, e.g., Harvard President Charles Eliot (Eliot 1894, p. 19), footnote 11 in chapter 1; Wilson (1909); Savage (1929, p. 310); Scott (1971, pp. 30–31); Arne Duncan, excerpts of remarks to the NCAA, "Building a Better Front Porch for Higher Education," January 14, 2010. https://www.ed.gov/news/speeches/ building-better-front-porch-higher-education%E2%80%94excerpts-secretary-arne-duncans-remarks, 6/7/10.

4. Hoover (1926, p. 256).

5. Angell (1928, p. 117).

6. Sinclair (1922, pp. 370–371).

7. Purdue University faculty committee, quoted in Savage (1929, p. 302).

8. Carnegie Foundation president Henry Pritchett in the preface to Savage (1929, p. xxi).

9. "Excerpts from Judge Streit's Comments on College Basketball Fixing Scandal," *New York Times*, November 20, 1951.

10. Beezley (1988). Arguably, point shaving is the form of rule breaking that has the biggest potential to harm the commercial value of college sports. A recent statistical study of point spreads and outcomes of Division I college basketball games over a six-year period found evidence consistent with point shaving, namely, that teams that were strong favorites to win games covered the point spread only 48.4% of the time, rather than the expected 50% (Wolfers 2006).

11. Associated Press, "Kansas Details Ticket Scams," *New York Times*, May 26, 2010.

12. "Mississippi Coach Kennedy Charged with Assault of Cabbie," ESPN. com News, December 18, 2008, http://sports.espn.go.com/espn/print? id=3777703&type=story, 4/17/10; "Pitino Extortion Attempt Investigated," ESPN.com News, April 18, 2009, http://sports.espn.go.com/espn/ print?id=4080340&type=story, 4/17/10.

13. J. Brady McCollough, "Kansas Football, Basketball Players' Hostility Erupt," *Wichita Eagle*, September 24, 2009.

14. There is a separate manual for each division. Bridget Booher, "Playing by the Rules," *Duke Magazine*, March–April 2010.

15. Finley, Finley, and Fountain (2008, pp. 95–97).

16. Pete Thamel, "On the Cusp of Their Reunion, the Fab 5's Impact Is Still Felt," *New York Times*, April 3, 2009.

17. Lynn Zinser, "U.S.C. Sports Receive Harsh Penalties," *New York Times*, June 12, 2010.

18. Doug Lederman, "Fraud and Friction at Florida State," *Inside Higher Ed*, March 9, 2009.

19. Doug Lederman, "NCAA Cracks Down on Kansas," *Inside Higher Ed*, October 13, 2006; Doug Lederman, "Another Case of Academic Fraud Involving Athletes," *Inside Higher Ed*, August 21, 2008.

20. "NCAA Says Ineligible Player Means U. of Memphis Must Forfeit Final Four Run," *Chronicle of Higher Education*, August 20, 2009.

21. See Golden (2006).

22. "Special Admits" at the Nation's Biggest Public Universities," *Indianapolis Star*, http://www.indystar.com/assets/pdf/BG11724397.PDF, 3/24/10.
23. Data based on Doug Lederman, "The Admissions Gap for Big-Time Athletes," *Inside Higher Ed*, December 29, 2008; Mike Knobler, "AJC Investigation: Many Athletes Lag Far Behind on SAT Scores," *Atlanta Journal-Constitution*, December 28, 2008.
24. For a discussion of NCAA policies, including the application of the Academic Progress Rate (APR), see Denhart, Villwock, and Vedder (2009, pp. 9–11).
25. The operating principles are contained in the "NCAA Certification Self-Study," reproduced on the Web site for the University of Texas, http://www.utexas.edu/provost/planning/accred/athletic/ath_integ.html, 3/6/10. The NCAA generally leaves it up to institutions to apply admissions standards to athletes, stating that athletes should be subject to an institution's usual requirements or exceptional standards that have been approved by academic officers, such as the president or designated admissions officer or committee. See NCAA bylaws 14.1.7.1 and 14.1.7.1.1.
26. Associated Press, "Spurrier Blasts South Carolina Admissions for Denying Two Recruits," August 6, 2007; Jodi Upton, "Unique Clause Addresses Admissions," *USA Today*, December 5, 2007.
27. DiStanislao (2005, pp. 72, 99, 125).
28. Under current NCAA regulations, student-athletes maintain eligibility for competition by remaining in good academic standing and completing 40% of the required course work by the end of the second year, 60% by the end of three years, and 80% by the end of four years. In addition, there are minimum grade point average and other requirements. See NCAA bylaw 14 and NCAA Essential Rules Reference Guide, http://www.ncaa.org/wps/wcm/connect/f3f413804e0b5327bbf1fb1ad6fc8b25/Best_Practices_Essential_Rules_Reference_Guide.pdf?MOD=AJPERES&CACHEID=f3f413804e0b5327bbf1fb1ad6fc8b25, 6/15/10.
29. Brad Wolverton, "College Football Players Spend 44.8 Hours a Week on Their Sport, NCAA Survey Finds," *Chronicle of Higher Education*, January 14, 2008. The NCAA cap on hours does not apply to training room, travel, or any "voluntary" athletic activities. According to one source, an old joke among compliance officials is that time in the weight room is often "voluntary," but so is playing time.
30. Douglas Lederman, "Major Issue: Athletes' Studies," *USA Today*, November 19, 2003; Suggs Welch, "Jock Majors," *Chronicle of Higher Education*, January 17, 2003.
31. John Heuser and Jim Carty, "Kinesiology Reserves Slots for University of Michigan Athletes," *Ann Arbor News*, March 17, 2008; Denhart et al. (2009, p. 12).
32. Pete Thamel, "Top Grades and No Class Time for Auburn Players," *New York Times*, July 14, 2006.
33. Lori Johnston, "Ex-Georgia Assistant's Exam Laughable: Can You Pass?" *USA Today*, March 4, 2004.
34. These are members of the five most well established conferences plus Notre Dame. For a list, see Chapter 2, note 16.
35. These are so-called federal graduation rates. The NCAA prefers to use an alternative (the Graduation Success Rate), which takes into account incoming

transfers and excludes from consideration athletes who transfer to other institutions before graduation or who otherwise leave an institution in good academic standing, even if such players do not eventually graduate from college. Comparable calculations are not available for all students, however. I therefore use the federal rate because comparable calculations are available for all students. The resulting comparisons may be unfavorable to athletes, however, if the transfer rate for athletes is higher than that for students in general or if the rate of eventual college completion is higher among athletes than among all students who transfer from one college to another.

36. William C. Rhoden, "A Celebration at Duke, but Not Everyone Cheers," *New York Times*, April 8, 2010.

37. Veblen ([1918], 1957, pp. 43, 85).

38. Hutchins (1936, p. 33).

39. See Bok (2003).

40. Savage (1929, p. 307).

41. See Jason Zengerle, "The Pivot: The Man Who Commercialized College Basketball Reconsiders," *New Republic*, July 9, 2008, and "March Payday Madness," *Business Week*, March 25, 2010.

42. See, e.g., the photographs of two players in the *New York Times* sports page, December 7, 2009. It is worth noting that the NCAA allows such advertising but regulates it. The applicable rule stipulates that the logo "not ... exceed 2 1/4 square inches in area (rectangle, square, parallelogram) including any additional material (e.g., patch) surrounding the normal trademark or logo," and that it not differ from that normally found on that manufacturer's apparel sold commercially (rule 12.5.4.4).

43. The NCAA store Web site, http://www.shopncaasports.com/, linked to pages covering Kansas merchandise: http://www.shopncaasports.com/NCAASports_Kansas_Jayhawks/browse/page/1/results/12/sort/None, 3/27/10.

    The NCAA licensing program was described on the NCAA Web site: http://www.ncaa.org/wps/portal/ncaahome?WCM_GLOBAL_CONTEXT=/ncaa/NCAA/About%20The%20NCAA/Corporate%20Relationships/Licensing/faqs.html#15.WhatistheCollegiateLicensingCompanyCLC, 6/15/10.

44. Michael Hooper, "Businesses Capitalize on Jayhawks' Success; KKU Expects Record Royalty Profits on Merchandise," *Topeka Capital-Journal*, April 15, 2008.

45. Collegiate Licensing Company, http://www.clc.com/clcweb/publishing.nsf/Content/Second+Quarter+Rankings+2009–2010, 6/15/10; "Longhorns Knock Off Tar Heels to Lead Nation in Merchandising Revenue," *USA Today*, August 26, 2006.

46. *National Collegiate Athletic Association v. Board of Regents of the University of Oklahoma*, 468 U.S. 85 (1984).

47. Stewart Mandel, "De Facto TV Network Will Push SEC Even Further Ahead of Competitors," SI.com, July 24, 2009.

48. Steve Wieberg and Michael Hiestand, ""NCAA Reaches 14-Year Deal with CBS/Turner for Men's Basketball Tournament, Which Expands to 68 Teams for Now," *USA Today*, April 22, 2010.

49. Libby Sander, "NCAA Takes Heat over Commercialization of Athletics," *Chronicle of Higher Education*, October 28, 2008; Katie Thomas, "College Stars

See Themselves in Video Games, and Pause to Sue," *New York Times*, July 4, 2009; Dan Weitzel, "O'Bannon Case Could Be a Game Changer," *Yahoo! Sports*, February 8, 2010.

50. Whether that revenue is subject to tax is a separate question, one addressed in the provisions of the Unrelated Business Income Tax (UBIT), which requires nonprofit organizations to pay corporation income tax on income generated by activities not related to its tax-exempt purpose.

51. Oriard (2009, p. 224).

52. Jernigan and Mosher (2005) document the harmful effects of alcohol marketing, including worse educational outcomes, death and disability, higher crime rates, and unprotected sex.

53. Thomas O'Toole and Steve Wieberg, "NCAA Says It Followed Self-limit on Final Four Beer Ads," *USA Today*, April 25, 2008.

54. For evidence on the effect of viewing alcohol ads on underage viewers, see Center on Alcohol Marketing and Youth, *Youth Exposure to Alcohol Advertising on Television, 2001 to 2007*, June 24, 2008. www.comy.org and Anderson et al. (2009). Gotwals, Hedlund, and Hacker (2005, p. 8) report on the NCAA's "youth-recruitment" policy.

55. Welch Suggs, "Group Urges NCAA to Cut Ties to Beer Company; Professors Seek College-Sports Reforms," *Chronicle of Higher Education*, April 15, 2005.

56. See, e.g., David Debolt, "When Ads Enter the Classroom, It's a Deal with El Diablo," *Chronicle of Higher Education*, December 12, 2008.

57. Speech to the Board of Regents, October 24, 1952; *Bartlett's Familiar Quotations* (Boston: Little Brown, 1968, p. 912).

58. Carl DePasqua, University of Pittsburgh (Hoch 1972, p. 193).

59. Adler and Adler (1988, p. 405).

60. Adler and Adler (1988).

61. John Pont, Indiana University (Scott 1971, p. 199).

62. Rosenberg (2009, pp. 11, 19).

63. Shaw (1972).

64. Padwe (1970, p. 68).

65. Sperber (1991, p. 201).

66. Duderstadt (2000, p. 87).

67. Michael Oriard, "College Football's Season of Discontent," *Slate*, September 3, 2009.

68. Padwe (1970, p. 67).

69. Quoted in Hoch (1972, p. 3).

70. "Scorecard," *Sports Illustrated*, January 20, 1969.

71. In his memoir about Texas football, Shaw (1972, p. 122) offers detailed descriptions of drills for poorly performing upperclassmen during spring practice, conducted "for the purpose of running guys off – making them quit." Oriard (2009, pp. 4–5, 137–141) argues that the one-year scholarship rule was adopted as a response to the protests by athletes that began in the late 1960s, with the intent and effect of reducing the power of players to speak out.

72. See, e.g., "Urban Meyer Threatens Orlando Sentinel Reporter Jeremy Fowler," *Orlando Sentinel*, March 25, 2010. One basketball coach who famously disdained critical reporters was Bobby Knight of Indiana University. Robert J. Elisberg,

"Good Knight, What Is ESPN Thinking?" *Huffington Post*, March 4, 2008, http://webcache.googleusercontent.com/search?q=cache:5if-m3bhLbgJ:www. huffingtonpost.com/robert-j-elisberg/good-knight-what-is-espn-_b_89819.ht ml+bobby+knight+reporters&cd=28&hl=en&ct=clnk&gl=us, 7/12/10.

73. The coach was Mike Krzyzewski of Duke. Joe Drews, "It's Time to Bench Singler," *Duke Chronicle*, January 13, 2010; Ken Tysiac, "Krzyzewski Backs Singler," *Raleigh News and Observer* blog, January 14, 2010, http://blogs.news-observer.com/accnow/krzyzewski-backs-singler?storylink=misearch, 4/17/10. The coach said, "There were some suggestions in our student newspaper that we shouldn't start him tonight. The first day back (from holiday break) and we read the student newspaper and he's benching our guy. It's welcome back, I guess. Unbelievable."

74. Krzyzewski and Spatola (2006).

75. Jill Riepenhoff and Todd Jones, "Secrecy 101: College Athletic Departments Use Vague Law to Keep Public Records from Being Seen," *Columbus Dispatch*, May 31, 2009.

76. See Eric Kelderman, "At Oregon, Sports Turmoil Marks Leader's First Year," *Chronicle of Higher Education*, June 13, 2010.

77. Michael D. Rocco, "The Message Is Out on Eye Black in College Football and the NFL," jacksonville.com, April 17, 2010, http://jacksonville.com/print/407728, 4/23/10; Jeremy Fowler, "NCAA Makes Tebow Rule … er, Bans Eye Black," *Orlando Sentinel*, February 12, 2010, http://blogs.orlandosentinel.com/sports_ college_uf/2010/02/ncaa-makes-tebow-rule-er-bans-eye-black.html, 4/23/10.

78. Ohio State quarterback who wore the tribute to Vick, Terrelle Pryor, blamed himself for the NCAA ban on such written messages. Tim May, "Pryor Says He Caused Eye-black Rule Change," *Columbus Dispatch*, April 17, 2010.

79. American universities do not have a monopoly on devotion to the truth, of course, though America's decentralized structure does set it apart. See Clotfelter (2010, pp. 7–9). For a famous case testing the truthfulness of university research, see Justin Gillis, "British Panel Clears Scientists," *New York Times*, July 7, 2010.

80. Going beyond benign, two universities actually doctored photos, inserting pictures of black students in otherwise all-white group pictures. Scott Jaschik, "Viewbook Diversity vs. Real Diversity," *Inside Higher Ed*, July 2, 2008.

81. Smith (1988, pp. 165–171). Summarizing the dilemma facing the college football powers at the turn of the 19th century, Smith writes (p. 171): "If a college had truly amateur sport, it would lose contests and thus prestige. If a college acknowledged outright professional sport, the college would lose respectability as a middle-class or higher class institution. Be amateur and lose athletically to those who were less amateur; be outright professional and lose social esteem.

"The solution to the dilemma, then, was to claim amateurism to the world while in fact accepting professionalism."

82. Noll (1991, p. 209).

83. Travis (2007, p. 3).

84. Travis (2007, p. 363).

85. Giamatti (1989, p. 32).

86. Revenues for the 120 FBS institutions, estimated by prorating totals for 99 public universities, based on revenues for ticket sales, student fees, concessions, and

contributions amount to $3.2 billion for 2008. Author's calculations based on financial data made available by *USA Today*, http://www.usatoday.com/sports/college/ncaa-finances.htm, 8/19/10.

87. Howell Raines, "Editorial Notebook: The Iron Bowl Cometh; The Impossible Task of Ceasing to Care," *New York Times*, November 19, 1994.

88. David Brooks, "The Sporting Mind," *New York Times*, February 5, 2010.

89. These were among the virtues Education Secretary Arne Duncan cited in a speech to the NCAA in 2010, attributing them to former basketball player and U.S. Senator Bill Bradley. Arne Duncan, excerpts of remarks to the NCAA, "Building a Better Front Porch for Higher Education," January 14, 2010, https://www.ed.gov/news/speeches/building-better-front-porch-higher-education%E2%80%94excerpts-secretary-arne-duncans-remarks, 6/7/10.

90. Boise State, a member of the unheralded Mountain West Conference, upset perennial powerhouse Oklahoma in the 2007 Fiesta Bowl, on the strength of several 11th-hour trick plays. The same year, Appalachian State, a member of the less competitive Football Championship Subdivision, traveled to Ann Arbor to upset the highly ranked Michigan team, 34–32.

91. Riesman and Denney (1951, p. 322). Rockne's status as a first-generation American was emphasized and romanticized in the 1940 movie *Knute Rockne: All American*.

92. For a retrospective, see Pete Thamel, "Grier Integrated a Game and Earned the World's Respect," *New York Times*, January 1, 2006.

93. See Blythe Bernhard, "The Game That Changed the World," *Orange County Register*, September 13, 2007. Fullback Sam Cunningham of USC was recognized in 2009 by a Senate resolution, http://info.sen.ca.gov/pub/09–10/bill/sen/sb_0001–0050/scr_11_bill_20090127_introduced.pdf, 9/21/09.

94. Encyclopedia of Alabama, http://encyclopediaofalabama.org/face/Article.jsp?id=h-1668, 5/7/09; Joe Drape, "Colleges; Changing the Face of Texas Football," *New York Times*, December 23, 2005.

95. Michael Oriard, "College Football's Season of Discontent," *Slate*, September 3, 2009.

96. The NCAA compiles lists of consensus all-Americans. For census years, the percentages of consensus all-Americans in football who were black were as follows: 1940 and 1950, 0%; 1960, 9%; 1970, 23%; 1980 and 1990, 70%; and 2000, 68%. For basketball, the percentages were 1940, 0%; 1950, 25%; 1960, 30%; 1970, 60%; 1980, 67%; 1990, 100%; and 2000, 82%. Percentages are based on players for whom a racial identification could be made, which was virtually all such players. http://web1.ncaa.org/web_files/stats/football_records/DI/2009/2009Awards.pdf, 8/10/10; http://web1.ncaa.org/web_files/stats/m_basketball_RB/2009/Award.pdf, 8/10/10.

97. Based on author's calculations (Clotfelter 2004, ch. 6) and data collected from team view books, Duke University Archives.

98. Calculations based on NCAA data included in Doug Lederman, "Diversifying through Football," *Inside Higher Ed*, January 11, 2008.

99. See, e.g., Noll (1991), King and Springwood (2001), and Hawkins (2010). A related criticism focuses on the disproportionately small number of nonwhites hired to coach college teams. See, e.g., Bob Hohler, "Few Minorities Get the Reins in College Football," *Boston Globe*, September 21, 2006. Some of the scholarship on race and college sports evidently requires special training to

unravel. For example, King and Springwood (2001, p. 155) write that their book began "with the understanding that the American university has become deeply vested in a relationship to athletics and that a deeply imbricated constellation of racial spectacles and commodities anchors this relationship."

## Chapter 9

1. Scott (1956, 31), Duderstadt (2000, 92), Sperber (1991, pp. xi, xii); Deford (1989); Yost (2010, 195); Arne Duncan, excerpts of remarks to the NCAA, "Building a Better Front Porch for Higher Education," January 14, 2010, https://www.ed.gov/news/speeches/building-better-front-porch-higher-educa-tion%E2%80%94excerpts-secretary-arne-duncans-remarks, 6/7/10; William C. Rhoden, "Coaches Shouldn't be Immune to Penalties, *New York Times*, November 5, 2010.
2. NCAA, "Behind the Blue Disk: FBS Athletic Revenues and Expenses," http://webcache.googleusercontent.com/search?q=cache:g3Y5IJdiucUJ:www.ncaa.org/wps/portal/ncaahome%3FWCM_GLOBAL_CONTEXT%3D/ncaa/ncaa/media%2Band%2Bevents/press%2Broom/current%2Bissues/behind%2Bblue%2Bdisk/20100114%2Bbehind%2Bthe%2Bblue%2Bdisk%2B-%2Bfbs%2Bathleti c%2Brevenues%2Band%2Bexpenses+ncaa+revenues+media+rights&cd=3&hl =en&ct=clnk&gl=us&client=firefox-a, 5/30/10.
3. Michael Lewis, "Serfs of the Turf," *New York Times*, November 11, 2007.
4. See Noll (1991, p. 198) and Kahn (2007, pp. 212, 214).
5. Letter to Dr. Myles Brand, President of the NCAA, from Rep. Bill Thomas, October 2, 2006.
6. "Senator Grassley and Private-Colleges Group React to Chronicle Report on Pay," *Chronicle of Higher Education*, February 23, 2009. An IRS report released in 2010 examined sources of income and pay practices of universities. It found that coaches were the highest-paid employees at 43% of the large universities surveyed. It also surveyed universities to find out whether they used an approach known as "rebuttable presumption" in setting and justifying the pay of highly compensated employees, since nonprofit organizations are not allowed to pay what is called "excessive compensation." This approach, which requires trustees to survey the pay of comparable employees at other institutions, was not used in more than one-third of the large universities surveyed, although it has the advantage of shifting the burden of proof to the IRS to show that compensation is excessive. See Doug Lederman, "Colleges as Potential Tax Targets," *Inside Higher Ed*, May 10, 2010.
7. Noting the large number of members of Congress who have universities in their districts, one attorney opined, "College sports are one of the last sacred cows." Gilbert M. Gaul and Neill A. Borowski, "Colleges Score with Tax-Free Income from Big-time Sports," *Philadelphia Inquirer*, April 20, 1993. Reflecting the same sentiment, sports commentator Frank Deford said about Rep. Thomas's aggressive letter to the NCAA: "Representative Thomas' barbed inquiry was the first real evidence I had that the Republicans knew they were going to lose the House. Would any politician dare take on the college football and basketball constituency if he knew he was staying in power?" (Actually, Rep. Thomas had announced his retirement. Due to term limitations, he would have had to step down as chair of Ways and Means.)

8. Jason Whitlock, "NCAA Breeds a Culture of Corruption," *Kansas City Star*, May 26, 2010.
9. Knight Commission on Intercollegiate Athletics (2001, p. 14).
10. Arne Duncan, excerpts of remarks to the NCAA, "Building a Better Front Porch for Higher Education," January 14, 2010 https://www.ed.gov/news/speeches/ building-better-front-porch-higher-education%E2%80%94excerpts-secretary-arne-duncans-remarks, 6/7/10.
11. See, e.g., Letter to Dr. Myles Brand, President of the NCAA, from Rep. Bill Thomas, October 2, 2006, and Arne Duncan, excerpts of remarks to the NCAA, "Building a Better Front Porch for Higher Education," January 14, 2010, https://www.ed.gov/news/speeches/building-better-front-porch-higher-education%E2%80%94excerpts-secretary-arne-duncans-remarks, 6/7/10; Arne Duncan, "Building a Better Front Porch for Higher Education," Excerpts from remarks to the NCAA convention, January 14, 2010, U.S. Department of Education Web site, https://www.ed.gov/news/speeches/building-better-front-porch-higher-education%E2%80%94excerpts-secretary-arne-duncans-remarks, 6/7/10.
12. Savage (1929, p. 306; chapter 2).
13. Ibid., pp. 100, ix, and xii.
14. Pritchett (1953, p. 247).
15. Hanford (1974, p. 39).
16. Knight Commission on Intercollegiate Athletics (1991, pp. 4, 6). A recent news article set forth the same theory, saying the NCAA "can't control the vast commercial forces that, for better or worse, shape today's landscape of big-time college sports." Libby Sander, "On Eve of NCAA Meeting, College Sports Wrestles with Vexing Questions," *Chronicle of Higher Education*, January 11, 2010.
17. Knight Commission on Intercollegiate Athletics (2001, pp. 16, 25).
18. Ireland (1974, p. 308) and Hart-Nibbrig and Cottinghorn (1986, ch. 4) discuss the effects of television on college sports, and the latter includes a discussion of cable TV as well.
19. Oriard (2009) argues that the media tend to sensationalize college sports.
20. The Knight Commission on Intercollegiate Atheltics (2010) advocated both of these cost-cutting approaches, as well as a reduction in staff attached to teams. See also David Moltz, "Curbing Athletic Spending," *Inside Higher Ed*, January 14, 2010, and David Moltz, "Trimming Athletic Seasons," *Inside Higher Ed*, January 18, 2010.
21. For a discussion of problems in implementing caps on coaches' salaries, see, e.g., Katie Thomas, "Call to Curb Athletic Spending Strikes Some as Unrealistic," *New York Times*, October 27, 2009.
22. In a speech to the NCAA convention, Secretary of Education Arne Duncan proposed banning teams with low graduation rates from postseason play more quickly than current rules allowed for. Arne Duncan, excerpts of remarks to the NCAA, "Building a Better Front Porch for Higher Education," January 14, 2010. https://www.ed.gov/news/speeches/building-better-front-porch-higher-education%E2%80%94excerpts-secretary-arne-duncans-remarks, 6/7/10.The idea was taken up by the Knight Commission on Intercollegiate Athletics (2010).

See also George Vecsey, "Modest Proposal Says Colleges Should Educate," *New York Times*, January 15, 2010.

23. Knight Commission (2001, pp. 26–28).

24. Noll (1991, p. 209) advocated allowing universities to set aside a budget for paying athletes, arguing that doing so would be a "step in the direction of honesty." Duderstadt's idea takes as its model European professional soccer team FC Barcelona, which has over 100,000 club members who also are shareholders (personal correspondence). Another model might be the Green Bay Packers, which is operated by a community-owned nonprofit organization. See http://webcache.googleusercontent.com/search?q=cache:_PhpnoXJrnkJ:www.scribd.com/doc/492029/How-Barcelona-football-club-was-founded+fc+barcelona+shareholders&cd=2&hl=en&ct=clnk&gl=us, 8/8/10; http://webcache.googleusercontent.com/search?q=cache:_PhpnoXJrnkJ:www.scribd.com/doc/492029/How-Barcelona-football-club-was-founded+fc+barcelona+shareholders&cd=2&hl=en&ct=clnk&gl=usm 8/8/10.

25. Bok (2003, p. 124).

26. Most important, there would be no athletic scholarships. For a summary of rules applying to Division III, see NCAA, *Summary of NCAA Regulations – NCAA Division III, Academic Year 2010*, http://web1.ncaa.org/web_files/AMA/compliance_forms/DIII/DIII%20Summary%20of%20NCAA%20Regulations.pdf, 11/14/10. The Knight Commission's call for "mainstreaming" athletes academically, though not spelled out in detail, could amount to the same thing if taken to its logical extreme (Knight Commission on Intercollegiate Athletics 2001).

27. See Scott (1956, p. 34).

28. The NCAA was successfully challenged by a group of assistant coaches, whose salaries the NCAA had restricted in 1991. Libby Sander, "Justice Department Examines NCAA Scholarship Rules," *Chronicle of Higher Education*, May 6, 2010.

29. For an analysis of that antitrust action, see Carlton, Bamberger, and Epstein (1994).

30. See David Moltz, "Athletics, Antitrust and Amateurism," *Inside Higher Ed*, May 13, 2009.

31. See Colombo (2009) for a discussion of this policy option.

### Appendix

1. Available at http://www.lexisnexis.com/lawschool/login.aspx.

2. Although LexisNexis lists a total 21 states with publicly available voter registration data, several states had data that were incomplete or severely limited. See Appendix I for a complete list of states for which voter registration is available through LexisNexis along with the specific limitations observed.

3. Located at http://nces.ed.gov/collegenavigator.

4. Further research indicated that the most likely explanation for this anomaly was the change from a closed primary system to an open one following the decision of the 8th Circuit Court in 1995 that, when the state requires parties to nominate by primary, the state must pay the costs of those primaries.

# References

Adler, Patricia A., and Peter Adler. 1988. "Intense Loyalty in Organizations: A Case Study of College Athletics," *Administrative Science Quarterly* 33: 401–417.

Altbach, Philip G. 2004. "Review of The Future of the City of Intellect: The Changing American University," *Journal of Higher Education* 75: 364–365.

Altbach, Philip G., Robert O. Berdahl, and Patricia J. Gumport. 2005. *American Higher Education in the Twenty-First Century: Social, Political, and Economic Challenges* (Baltimore: Johns Hopkins University Press).

Anctil, Eric J. 2003. *An Exploratory Analysis of the Relationship Between Higher Education and Television: A Focus on Big-time College Sports*, Ph.D. dissertation, University of Wisconsin.

Anderson, Peter et al. 2009. "Impact of Alcohol Advertising and Media Exposure on Adolescent Alcohol Use: A Systematic Review of Longitudinal Studies," *Alcohol & Alcoholism* 44 (January 14): 229–243.

Angell, Robert Cooley. 1928. *The Campus: A Study of Contemporary Undergraduate Life in the American University* (New York: D. Appleton and Co.).

Baade, Robert A., and Jeffrey O. Sundberg. 1996. "Fourth Down and Gold to Go? Assessing the Link between Athletics and Alumni Giving," *Social Science Quarterly* 77: 789–803.

Babcock, Philip, and Mindy Marks. Forthcoming. "The Falling Time Cost of College: Evidence from Half a Century of Time Use Data," *Review of Economics and Statistics*.

Beasley, Jerry. 1974. "The State Politics of Intercollegiate Athletics," App. C in George H. Hanford, *An Inquiry into the Need for and Feasibility of a National Study of Intercollegiate Athletics* (Washington, DC: American Council on Education).

Beezley, William H. 1988 "The 1961 Scandal at North Carolina State and the End of the Dixie Classic," in Donald Chu, Jeffrey O. Seagrave, and Beverly J. Becker (eds.), *Sport and Higher Education* (Champaign, IL: Human Kinetics), pp. 81–99.

Berryman, Jack, and Stephen H. Hardy. 1983. "The College Sports Scene," in William J. Baker and John M. Carroll (eds.), *Sports in Modern America*. (Saint Louis: River City Publishers), pp. 63–76.

Bettinger, Eric P., and Bridget Terry Long. 2005. "Addressing the Needs of Under-Prepared Students in Higher Education: Does College Remediation Work?" NBER Working Paper no. 11325, May.

Beyer, Janice M., and Hannah, David R. 2000. "The Cultural Significance of Athletics in U.S. Higher Education," *Journal of Sport Management* 14 (2): 105–132.

Blythe, Will. 2006. *To Hate Like This Is to Be Happy Forever: A Thoroughly Obsessive, Intermittently Uplifting, and Occasionally Unbiased Account of the Duke–North Carolina Basketball Rivalry* (New York: Harper Collins).

Bok, Derek. 2003. *Universities in the Marketplace* (Princeton, NJ: Princeton University Press).

Boone, Louis E., David L. Kurtz, and C. Patrick Fleenor. 1988. "CEOs: Early Signs of a Business Career," *Business Horizons* 31 (5): 20–24.

Borman, Carol A., and Michael H. Stone. 2001. "The Effects of Eliminating Alcohol in a College Stadium: The Folsom Field Beer Ban," *Journal of American College Health* 50 (2): 81–88.

Boyer, Ernest L. 1987. *College: The Undergraduate Experience in America* (New York: Harper and Row).

——— 1990. *Campus Life: In Search of Community* (Princeton, NJ: Carnegie Foundation for the Advancement of Teaching).

Branscombe, Nyla R., and Daniel L. Wann. 1991. "The Positive Social and Self-Concept Consequences of Sports Team Identification," *Journal of Sport and Social Issues* 15 (2): 115–127.

Brint, Stephen (ed.). 2002. *The Future of the City of Intellect: The Changing American University* (Stanford, CA: Stanford University Press).

Bronnenberg, Bart J., Jean-Pierre H. Dube, and Matthew Gentzkow. 2010. "The Evolution of Brand Preferences: Evidence from Consumer Migration," NBER Working Paper 16267, August.

Brown, Robert W., and R. Todd Jewell. 2004. "Measuring Marginal Revenue Product in College Athletics: Updated Estimates," in John Fizel and Rodney Fort (eds.), *Economics of College Sports* (Westport, CT: Praeger), pp. 153–162.

Byers, Walter, with Charles Hammer. 1995. *Unsportsmanlike Conduct: Exploiting College Athletes* (Ann Arbor: University of Michigan Press).

Carlton, Dennis W., Gustavo E. Bamberger, and Roy J. Epstein. 1994. "Antitrust and Higher Education," Working Paper 107, Center for the Study of the Economy and the State, University of Chicago, January.

Carpenter, Christopher, and Carlos Dobkin. 2008. "The Drinking Age, Alcohol Consumption, and Crime," Unpublished Paper, Merage School of Business, University of California, January; presented at the NBER Summer Institute, July 24, 2008.

Carrell, Scott E., and James E. West. 2008. "Does Professor Quality Matter? Evidence from Random Assignment of Students to Professors," NBER Working Paper no. 14081, June.

Chu, Donald. 1989. *The Character of American Higher Education and Intercollegiate Sport* (Albany: State University of New York Press).

Cialdini, Robert B, Richard J. Borden, Avril Thorne, Marcus Randall Walker, Stephen Freeman, and Lloyd Reynolds Sloan. 1976. "Basking in Reflected Glory: Three (Football) Field Studies," *Journal of Personality and Social Psychology* 34 (3): 366–375.

Clotfelter, Charles T. 1996. *Buying the Best: Cost Escalation in Elite Higher Education* (Princeton, NJ: Princeton University Press).

2004. *After Brown: The Rise and Retreat of School Desegregation.* (Princeton, NJ: Princeton University Press).

(ed.). 2010. *American Universities in a Global Market* (Chicago: University of Chicago Press).

Coleman, James S. 1973. "The University and Society's New Demands Upon It," in Carl Kaysen (ed.), *Content and Context* (New York: McGraw-Hill), pp. 359–399.

Colombo, John D. 2009. "The NCAA, Tax Exemption and College Athletics," Illinois Public Law Research Paper no. 08–08, February 19.

Coons, C. J., M. Howard-Hamilton, and D. Waryold. 1995. "College Sports and Fan Aggression: Implications for Residence Hall Discipline," *Journal of College Student Development* 36: 587–593.

Coughlin, Cletus C., and O. Homer Erekson. 1984. "An Examination of Contributions to Support Intercollegiate Athletics," *Southern Economic Journal* 51 (1), 180–195.

Deegan, Mary Jo, and Michael Stein. 1989. "The Big Red Dream Machine: Nebraska Football," in M. J. Deegan (ed.), *American Ritual Dreams: Social Rules and Cultural Meanings* (New York: Greenwood Press), pp. 77–88.

Deford, Frank. 1989. Statement at Hearings on the Role of Athletics in College Life before the House Subcommittee on Postsecondary Education of the Committee on Education and Labor, May 18, 1989 (Washington, DC: U.S. Government Printing Office), pp. 22–26.

Denhart, Matthew, Robert Villwock, and Richard Vedder. 2009. *The Academics–Athletics Trade-off*, Center for College Affordability and Productivity, April.

DiStanislao, Mary. 2005. *Competitive Advantages: What Three Prestigious Private Universities Do to Compete in Their Elite Division IA Athletic Conferences*, Ph.D. dissertation, University of Pennsylvania.

Duderstadt, James J. 2000. *Intercollegiate Athletics and the American University: A University President's Perspective.* Ann Arbor: University of Michigan Press.

Dunnavant, Keith. 2004. *The Fifty-Year Seduction: How Television Manipulated College Football, from the Birth of the Modern NCAA to the Creation of the BCS* (New York: St. Martin's Press).

Edwards, R. H., J. M. Artman, and Galen M. Fisher. 1928. *Undergraduates: A Study of Morale in Twenty-three American Colleges and Universities* (Garden City, NY: Doubleday, Doran and Co.).

Eliot, Charles William. 1894. "President's Report for 1892–93," *Annual Reports of the President and Treasurer of Harvard College, 1892–93* (Cambridge, MA: Harvard University), pp. 12–22.

Feldstein, Martin. 1993. "Comment," in Charles T. Clotfelter and Michael Rothschild (eds.), *Studies of Supply and Demand in Higher Education* (Chicago: University of Chicago Press), pp. 37–42.

Finley, P. S., L. L. Finley, and J. J. Fountain. 2008. *Sports Scandals* (Westport, CT: Greenwood Press).

Fleisher, A. A., III, B. L. Goff, and R. D. Tollison. 1992. *The National Collegiate Athletic Association: A Study in Cartel Behavior* (Chicago: University of Chicago Press).

Fort, Rodney, and James Quirk. 1999. "The College Football Industry," in John Fizel, Elizabeth Gustafson, and Lawrence Hadley (eds.), *Sports Economics: Current Research* (Westport, CT: Praeger), pp. 11–26.

Foster, William T. 1915. "An Indictment of Intercollegiate Athletics," *Atlantic Monthly* 116 (November): 577–588.

Frank, Robert H. 2004. "Challenging the Myth: A Review of the Links Among College Athletics Success, Student Quality, and Donations," Paper prepared for the Knight Foundation Commission on Intercollegiate Athletics, May.

Frank, Robert H., and Philip J. Cook. 1995. *The Winner-Take-All Society* (New York: Free Press).

Frey, James H. 1985. "College Athletics: Problems of a Functional Analysis," in C. Roger Rees and Andrew W. Miracle (eds.), *Sport and Social Theory* (Champaign, IL: Human Kinetics), pp. 199–210.

　1987. "Institutional Control of Athletics: An Analysis of the Role Played by Presidents, Faculty, Trustees, Alumni, and the NCAA," *Journal of Sport and Social Issues* 11: 49–59.

　1985. "Boosterism, Scarce Resources, and Institutional Control: The Future of American Intercollegiate Athletics," in Donald Chu, Jeffrey O. Seagrave, and Beverly J. Becker (eds.), *Sport and Higher Education* (Champaign, IL: Human Kinetics), pp. 115–129.

　1994. "Deviance of Organizational Subunits: The Case of College Athletic Departments," *Journal of Sport and Social Issues* 18 (2): 110–122.

Frydman, Carola, and Raven E. Saks. 2008. "Executive Compensation: A New View from a Long-term Perspective, 1936–2005," NBER Working Paper 14145, June.

Gantz, Walter, and Lawrence A. Wenner. 1995. "Fanship and the Television Viewing Experience," *Sociology of Sports Journal* 12 (March): 56–74.

Giamatti, A. Bartlett. 1989. *Take Time for Paradise: Americans and Their Games* (New York: Simon and Schuster).

Glassman, Tavis, Chudley E. Werch, Edessa Jobli, and Hui Bian. 2007. "Alcohol-Related Fan Behavior on College Football Game Day," *Journal of American College Health* 56 (3): 255–261.

Golden, Daniel. 2006. *The Price of Admission: How America's Ruling Class Buys Its Way into Elite Colleges – and Who Gets Left Outside the Gates* (New York: Crown).

Goldin, Claudia, and Lawrence F. Katz. 1999. "The Shaping of Higher Education: The Formative Years in the United States, 1890 to 1940," *Journal of Economic Perspectives* 13 (Winter): 37–62.

Gotwals, Amy E., Jay Hedlund, and George A. Hacker. 2005. *Take a Kid to a Beer: How the NCAA Recruits Kids for the Beer Market* (Washington, DC: Center for Science in the Public Interest).

Gould, Eric. 2003. *The University in a Corporate Culture* (New Haven, CT: Yale University Press).

Greer, Donald L. 1983. "Spectator Booing and the Home Advantage: A Study of Social Influence in the Basketball Arena," *Social Psychology Quarterly* 46 (1983): 252–261.

Griffith, John L. 1926. "The Annual Football Debate," *Athletic Journal*, 7 (1): 44–46.

Gwynne, S. C., 2008. "Come Early. Be Loud. Cash In." *Texas Monthly*, November.

Hanford, George H. 1974. *An Inquiry into the Need for and Feasibility of a National Study of Intercollegiate Athletics* (Washington, DC: American Council on Education).

Hartley, Matthew, and Christopher C. Morphew. 2008. "What's Being Sold and to What End? A Content Analysis of College Viewbooks," *Journal of Higher Education* 79 (November–December): 671–691.

Hart-Nibbrig, Nand, and Clement Cottingham. 1986. *The Political Economy of College Sports* (Lexington, MA: D. C. Heath).

Hawkins, Billy. 2010. *The New Plantation: Black Athletes, College Sports, and Predominantly White NCAA Institutions* (New York: Palgrave Macmillan).

Heaton, Cherrill P. 1992. "Air Ball: Spontaneous Large-Group Precision Chanting," *Popular Music and Society* 16: 81–83.

Hirt, E. R., D. Zillmann, G. A. Erickson, and C. Kennedy. 1992. "Costs and Benefits of Allegiance: Changes in Fans' Self-Ascribed Competencies after Team Victory versus Defeat," *Journal of Personality and Social Psychology* 63: 724–738.

Hoch, Paul. 1972. *Rip Off the Big Game: The Exploitation of Sports by the Power Elite* (Garden City, NY: Doubleday).

Hoover, Glenn E. 1926. "College Football," *New Republic* 46 (April 14): 56, 58.

Horowitz, Helen Lefkowitz. 1989. "The Changing Student Culture: A Retrospective," *Educational Record* 70 (3–4): 24–29.

Humphreys, Brad R. 2006. "The Relationship Between Big-Time College Football and State Appropriations to Higher Education," *International Journal of Sports Finance* 1: 119–128.

Humphreys, Brad R., and Michael Mondello. 2007. "Intercollegiate Athletic Success and Donations at NCAA Division I Institutions," *Journal of Sports Management.* 21: 265–280.

Humphreys, Brad R., and Jane E. Ruseski. 2009. "Monitoring Cartel Behavior and Stability: Evidence from NCAA Football," *Southern Economic Journal* 75 (January): 720–735.

Hurtado, Sylvia. 2007. "The Study of College Impact," in Patricia J. Gumport (ed.), *Sociology of Higher Education* (Baltimore: Johns Hopkins Press), pp. 94–112.

Hutchins, Robert Maynard. 1936. *The Higher Learning in America* (New Haven, CT: Yale University Press).

Hutchinson, Ruth, and Mary Connard. 1926. "What's in a College Week," *School and Society* 24, 768–772.

Ireland, Bernard P. 1974. "New and Changing Circumstances Which Have Influenced the Conduct of Intercollegiate Athletic Programs in the United States Since 1930," App. F in George H. Hanford, *An Inquiry into the Need for and Feasibility of a National Study of Intercollegiate Athletics* (Washington, DC: American Council on Education).

Jernigan, David H., and James F. Mosher. 2005. "Alcohol Marketing and Youth: Public Health Perspectives," *Journal of Public Health Policy* 26: 287–291.

Johnson, Bruce K., and John C. Whitehead, 2000. "Value of Public Goods from Sports Stadiums: The CVM Approach," *Contemporary Economics Policy* 18 (1): 48–58.

Johnson, Bruce K., Michael J. Mondello, and John C. Whitehead. 2007. "The Value of Public Goods Generated by a National Football League Team," *Journal of Sport Management* 21: 123–136.

Kahn, Lawrence M. 2006. "The Economics of College Sports: Cartel Behavior vs. Amateurism," IZA Discussion Paper no. 2186 (June).

2007. "Cartel Behavior and Amateurism in College Sports," *Journal of Economic Perspectives* 21 (Winter): 209–226.

Kaplan, Ann E. 2008. *2007 Voluntary Support of Education* (New York: Council for Aid to Education).

Kerr, Clark. 1994. *The Uses of the University*, 4th ed. (Cambridge, MA: Harvard University Press).

Kezar, Adrianna J., Tony C. Chambers, and John C. Burkhardt. 2005. *Higher Education for the Public Good: Emerging Voices from a National Movement* (San Francisco: Jossey-Bass).

King, C. Richard, and Charles F. Springwood. 2001. *Beyond the Cheers: Race as Spectacle in College Sport* (Albany: State University of New York Press).

Kirp, David L. 2004. *Shakespeare, Einstein, and the Bottom Line: The Marketing of Higher Education* (Cambridge, MA: Harvard University Press).

Knight Commission on Intercollegiate Athletics. 1991. *Keeping Faith with the Student-Athlete: A New Model for Intercollegiate Athletics* (Charlotte, NC: Knight Foundation Commission on Intercollegiate Athletics, March).

Knight Commission on Intercollegiate Athletics. 2001. *A Call to Action: Reconnecting College Sports and Higher Education* (Miami: John S. and James L. Knight Foundation, June).

Knight Commission on Intercollegiate Athletics. 2009. *Quantitative and Qualitative Research with Football Bowl Subdivision University Presidents on the Costs and Financing of Intercollegiate Athletics* (Baltimore: Art and Science Group, October).

Knight Commission on Intercollegiate Athletics. 2010. *Restoring the Balance: Dollars, Values, and the Future of College Sports* (Miami: John S. and James L. Knight Foundation).

Koch, James. 1983. "Intercollegiate Athletics: An Economic Explanation," *Social Science Quarterly* 64: 360–374.

Kremer, Michael, and Dan Levy. 2008. "Peer Effects and Alcohol Use among College Students," *Journal of Economic Perspectives* 22 (Summer): 189–206.

Krzyzewski, Mike, with Jamie K. Spatola. 2006. *Beyond Basketball: Coach K's Keywords for Success* (New York: Warner Books).

Laband, David N., Ram Pandit, Anne M. Laband, and John P. Sophocleus. 2008. "Pigskins and Politics: Linking Expressive Behavior and Voting," *Journal of Sports Economics* 9: 553–560.

Lester, Robin. 1995. *Stagg's University: The Rise, Decline, and Fall of Big-Time Football at Chicago* (Urbana: University of Illinois Press).

Lewis, Michael. 2006. *The Blind Side* (New York: Norton).

Litan, Robert E., Jonathan M. Orszag, and Peter R. Orszag. 2003. *The Empirical Effects of Collegiate Athletics: An Interim Report* (Indianapolis: NCAA, August).

Lowi, Theodore J. 1974. "Campus, Society, and the Place of Amateur Sport: A Research Perspective," App. G in George H. Hanford, *An Inquiry into the Need for and Feasibility of a National Study of Intercollegiate Athletics* (Washington, DC: American Council on Education).

McCormick, R. E. and M. Tinsley. 1987. "Athletics versus Academics? Evidence from SAT Scores," *Journal of Political Economy* 95 (October), 1103–1116.

McKenzie, Richard B., and E. Thomas Sullivan. 1987. "Does the NCAA Exploit College Athletes? An Economics and Legal Reinterpretation." *Antitrust Bulletin* 32 (2): 373–99.

Michener, James. 1976. *Sports in America* (New York: Random House).

NCAA. 2009. *Revenues/Expenditures 2004 through 2008* (Indianapolis: NCAA).

Neal, Dan J., and Kim Fromme. 2007. "Hook 'Em Horns and Heavy Drinking: Alcohol Use and Collegiate Sports," *Addictive Behaviors* 32 (11): 2681–2693.

Neighbors, Clayton, Laura Oster-Aaland, Rochelle L. Bergstrom, and Melissa A. Lewis. 2006. "Event- and Context-Specific Normative Misperceptions and High-Risk

Drinking: 21st Birthday Celebrations and Football Tailgating," *Journal of Studies on Alcohol* 67 (March): 282–289.

Noll, Roger. 1991. "The Economics of Intercollegiate Sports," in Judith Andre and David James (eds.), *Rethinking College Athletics* (Philadelphia: Temple University Press), pp. 197–209.

Noll, Roger G. 2009. "Antitrust Economics of the NCAA Restrictions on Athletic Scholarships," Unpublished Paper, Stanford University, January.

O' Toole, Thomas. 2002. "'Celebratory Riots' Creating Crisis on Campus," *USA Today*, April 9, 2002.

Oriard, Michael. 2009. *Bowled Over: Big-Time College Football from the Sixties to the BCS Era* (Chapel Hill: University of North Carolina Press).

Orszag, Jonathan M., and Peter R. Orszag. 2005. *The Physical Capital Stock Used in Collegiate Athletics*, Report Commissioned by the NCAA, Compass Lexecon, LLC, April. http://www.ncaa.org/wps/wcm/connect/c9b763004e0dac1d9f6aff1ad6fc8b25/physical_capital_stock_used_in_collegiate_athletics.pdf?MOD=AJPERES&CACHEID=c9b763004e0dac1d9f6aff1ad6fc8b25, 11/12/10.

Padwe, Sandy. 1970. "Big-time College Football is on the Skids," *Look*, September 22, pp. 66–69.

Pascarella, Ernest, and Patrick Terenzini. 1991. *How College Affects Students* (San Francisco: Jossey-Bass).

Pope, Devin G., and Jaren C. Pope. 2009, "The Impact of College Sports Success on the Quantity and Quality of Student Applications," *Southern Economic Journal* 75 (January): 750–780.

Price, Donald I., and Kabir C. Sen. 2003. "The Demand for Game Day Attendance in College Football: An Analysis of the 1997 Division I-A Season," *Managerial and Decision Economics* 25: 35–46.

Prisuta, Robert. 1979. "Televised Sport and Political Values," *Journal of Communications* 29 (1979): 94–102.

Pritchett, Henry S. 1929. Preface to Howard J. Savage et al., *American College Athletics*, Bulletin 26 (New York: Carnegie Foundation for the Advancement of Teaching).

    1953. "Report of the Special Committee on Athletic Policy," *Educational Record* 33: 246–255.

Rhoads, Thomas A., and Shelby Gerking. 2000. "Educational Contributions, Academic Quality, and Athletic Success," *Contemporary Economic Policy* 18 (April): 248–258.

Riesman, David, and Reuel Denney. 1951. "Football in America: A Study in Culture Diffusion," *American Quarterly* (4): 309–325.

Rooney, John F. 1969. "'Up from the Mines and Out from the Prairies': Some Geographical Implications of Football in the United States," *Geographical Review* 59: 471–492.

    Jr. 1987. *The Recruiting Game* (Lincoln: University of Nebraska Press).

Rosenberg, Michael. 2009. *War as They Knew It: Woody Hayes, Bo Schembechler, and America in a Time of Unrest* (New York: Grand Central Publishing).

Sacerdote, Bruce. 2001. "Peer Effects with Random Assignment: Results for Dartmouth Roommates," *Quarterly Journal of Economics* 116 (May): 681–704.

Sack, Allen L. 1982. "Cui Bono? Contradictions in College Sports and Athletes' Rights," in James H. Frey (ed.), *The Governance of Intercollegiate Athletics* (Champaign, IL: Leisure Press).

1991. "The Underground Economy of College Football," *Sociology of Sport Journal* 8 (1): 1–15.

Sack, Allen L, and Ellen J. Staurowsky. 1998. *College Athletes for Hire: The Evolution and Legacy of the NCAA's Amateur Myth* (Westport, CT: Praeger).

St. John, Warren. 2004. *Rammer Jammer Yellow Hammer: A Journey into the Heart of Fan Mania* (New York: Crown).

Savage, Howard J., and John T. McGovern. 1931. *Current Developments in American College Sport* (New York: Carnegie Foundation for the Advancement of Teaching).

Savage, Howard J., et al. 1929. *American College Athletics*, Bulletin 26 (New York: Carnegie Foundation for the Advancement of Teaching).

Schlosberg, Jeremy. 1987. "Who Watches Television Sports?" *American Demographics* 9 (February): 44–59.

Schneider, Barbara. 2008. "Challenges of Transitioning into Adulthood," Unpublished Paper, University of Chicago.

Scott, Harry A. 1956. "New Directions in Intercollegiate Athletics," *Teachers College Record* 58 (October).

Scott, Jack. 1971. *The Athletic Revolution* (New York: Free Press).

Sears, Hal. 1992. "The Moral Threat of Intercollegiate Sports," *Journal of Sport History* 19 (3): 211–226.

Shapiro, Harold T. 2005. *A Larger Sense of Purpose: Higher Education and Society* (Princeton, NJ: Princeton University Press).

Shavers, Frances L. 2004. *Who Calls the Plays? The Role of the University President and Other Participants in Division I Athletics-Related Decisions*, Ph.D. dissertation, Harvard University, 2004.

Shaw, Gary. 1972. *Meat on the Hoof: The Hidden World of Texas Football* (New York: St. Martin's).

Shropshire, Mike. 2007. *Runnin' with the Big Dogs: The True, Unvarnished Story of the Texas–Oklahoma Football Wars* (New York: William Morrow).

Shulman, James Lawrence, and William G. Bowen. 2001. *The Game of Life: College Sports and Educational Values* (Princeton, NJ: Princeton University Press).

Siegfried, John J., and Molly Gardner Burba. 2004. "The College Football Association Television Broadcast Cartel," *Antitrust Bulletin* 49 (3): 799–819.

Sinclair, Upton. 1922. *The Goose-Step* (Pasadena, CA: Upton Sinclair).

1926. "Shall We Abolish Intercollegiate Football?" *Forum* 76 (December): 838–843.

Slaughter, Sheila, and Gary Rhoades. 2004. *Academic Capitalism and the New Economy: Markets, State, and Higher Education* (Baltimore: Johns Hopkins Press).

Smith, D. Randall. 2008. "Big-Time College Basketball and the Advertising Effect: Does Success Really Matter?" *Journal of Sports Economics* 9: 387–406.

Smith, R. 1988. *Sports and Freedom: The Rise of Big-Time College Athletics* (New York: Oxford University Press).

Sperber, Murray. 1991. *College Sports, Inc.: The Athletic Department vs. the University* (New York: Henry Holt).

2001. *Beer and Circus: How Big-Time College Sports Is Crippling Undergraduate Education* (New York: Henry Holt).

Stein, Michael. 1977. "Cult and Sport: The Case of Big Red," *Mid-American Review of Sociology* 11 (Winter): 29–42.

Stephan, Paula E., Albert J. Sumell, Grant C. Black, and James D. Adams. 2004. "Doctoral Education and Economic Development: The Flow of New Ph.D.s to Industry," *Economic Development Quarterly* 18 (May): 151–167.

Stinebrickner, Todd R., and Ralph Stinebrickner. 2007. "The Causal Effect of Studying on Academic Performance," NBER Working Paper no. 13341, August.

Stinson, Jeffrey L., and Dennis R. Howard. 2007. "Athletic Success and Private Giving to Athletic and Academic Programs at NCAA Institutions," *Journal of Sport Management* 21 (2): 235–264.

Sweet, Stephen. 2001. *College and Society: An Introduction to the Sociological Imagination* (Boston: Allyn and Bacon).

Thelin, John R. 1994. *Games Colleges Play: Scandal and Reform in Intercollegiate Athletics* (Baltimore: Johns Hopkins Press).

Thelin, John R., and Lawrence Wiseman. 1990. *Fiscal Fitness? The Peculiar Economics of Intercollegiate Athletics* (Washington, DC: U.S. Department of Education, Office of Educational Research and Improvement, Educational Resources Information Center).

Thirer, Joel, and Mark Rampey. 1979. "Effects of Abusive Spectator Behavior," *Perceptual and Motor Skills* 48 (1979): 1047–1053.

Toma, J. Douglas. 2003. *Football U.: Spectator Sports in the Life of the American University* (Ann Arbor: University of Michigan Press).

Travis, Clay. 2007. *Dixieland Delight: A Football Season on the Road* (New York: Harper Entertainment).

Tucker, Irvin B. 2005. "Big-Time Pigskin Success," *Journal of Sports Economics* 6 (May): 222–229.

Tucker, I. B., and L. Amato. 1993. "Does Big-Time Success in Football or Basketball Affect SAT Scores?" *Economics of Education Review* 12 (June), 177–181.

Turner, Sarah E., Lauren A. Meserve, and William G. Bowen. 2001. "Winning and Giving: Football Results and Alumni Giving at Selective Private Colleges and Universities," *Social Science Quarterly* 82 (4): 812–826.

U.S. News and World Report. 2008. *Ultimate College Guide, 2009 Edition* (Naperville, IL: Sourcebooks).

Veblen, Thorstein. 1957 (1918), *The Higher Learning in America: A Memorandum on the Conduct of Universities by Business Men* (New York: Sagamore Press).

Wann, Daniel L., and Nyla R. Branscombe. 1990. "Die-Hard and Fair-Weather Fans: Effects of Identification on BIRGing and CORFing Tendencies," *Journal of Sport and Social Issues* 14 (2): 103–117.

  1993. "Sports Fans: Measuring Degree of Identification with their Team," *International Journal of Sport Psychology* 24: 1–17.

Wann, Daniel L., Jeffrey D. Carlson, and Michael P. Schrader. 1999. "The Impact of Team Identification on the Hostile and Instrumental Verbal Aggression of Sport Spectators," *Journal of Social Behavior and Personality* 14: 279–286.

Wann, Daniel L., Merrill J. Melnick, Gordon W. Russell, and Dale G. Pease. 2001. *Sport Fans: The Psychology and Social Impact of Spectators* (New York: Routledge).

Weick, Karl E. 1984. "Contradiction in a Community of Scholars," in James L. Bess (ed.), *College and University Organizations: Insights from the Behavioral Sciences* (New York: New York University Press).

Weisbrod, Burton A., Jeffrey P. Ballou, and Evelyn D. Asch. 2008. *Mission and Money: Understanding the University* (New York: Cambridge University Press).

Wilson, Woodrow. 1909. "What Is a College For?" *Scribner's* 46 (November): 570–577.

Wolfers, Justin. 2006. "Point Shaving: Corruption in NCAA Basketball," *American Economic Review* 96 (May): 279–283.

Wolff, Alexander, and Armen Keteyian. 1990. *Raw Recruits* (New York: Pocket Books).

Yost, Mark. 2010. *Varsity Green: A Behind the Scenes Look at Culture and Corruption in College Athletics* (Stanford, CA: Stanford University Press).

Zemsky, Robert, Gregory R. Wegner, and William F. Massy. 2005. *Remaking the American University: Market-Smart and Mission-Centered* (New Brunswick, NJ: Rutgers University Press).

Zimbalist, Andrew. 1999. *Unpaid Professionals* (Princeton, NJ: Princeton University Press).

2009. "The BCS, Antitrust and Public Policy," *Antitrust Bulletin*. 54 (Winter): 823–856.

# Index

*Page numbers followed by italicized letters indicate tables (t) or figures (f)*